BEING-IN-CHRIST AND PUTTING DEATH IN ITS PLACE

MILES RICHARDSON

BEING-IN-CHRIST AND PUTTING DEATH IN ITS PLACE

An Anthropologist's Account of Christian Performance in Spanish America and the American South

LOUISIANA STATE UNIVERSITY PRESS
BATON ROUGE

Manufactured in the United States of America
First printing
12 11 10 09 08 07 06 05 04 03
5 4 3 2 1

Designer: Laura Roubique Gleason
Typeface: Janson Text with Castellar MT display
Typesetter: Coghill Composition Co. Inc.
Printer and binder: Thomson-Shore, Inc.

Library of Congress Cataloging-in-Publication Data:

Richardson, Miles, 1932–
Being-in-Christ and putting death in its place : an anthropologist's account of Christian performance in Spanish America and the American South / Miles Richardson.
p. cm.
Includes bibliographical references and index.
ISBN 0-8071-2849-X (cloth : alk. paper)
1. Latin America—Church history. 2. Southern States—Church history. 3. Christianity and culture. 4. Catholic Church—Latin America—History. 5. Baptists—Southern States—History. 6. Latin America—Colonization. I. Title.
BR600.R53 2003
277—dc21 2002156054

The paper in this book meets the guidelines for permanence and durability of the Committee on Production Guidelines for Book Longevity of the Council on Library Resources. ♾

To Miguel, Hank, and Jesús;
and to all I've shortchanged
(an enormous list);
but most of all,
to you

CONTENTS

ILLUSTRATIONS

PLATE

FIGURES

MAPS

TABLES

ACKNOWLEDGMENTS

What you are about to read is truly a life's work: the work of a life as lived, as Miles, ex-redneck, and the work of a life as studied, as Dr. Richardson, anthropologist. These works are not separate lives but intertwine to make me. The life as lived got me into the profession, and the life as studied has tried to make sense of what I saw and heard since that fateful day—April 16, 1953, at Castle Air Force Base in Merced, California, to be precise—when it came to me that I, a high school dropout, should become an anthropologist (Richardson 1975).

In working at living, I have become a husband and a father, achievements beyond compare. My debts to Valerie, my wife, continue to accumulate, especially as we approach our forty-fifth year together, and the returns from Victoria, Penn, and Stanley have far exceeded my earlier, inept investments. From my pre-anthropological days, when I ran around barefooted and without good sense, two friends, George Thomas and Albon Quarles, have stayed the course. I glow with warm nostalgia generated by the generosity of the class of 1950 who, at various reunions—our latest being our fiftieth!—kindly overlooked my absence from graduation. I recognize, finally, after all these years, the love of my sister, Frances.

In my working at being an anthropologist, many have helped me to become worthy of the name. Here are only a few: from graduate-student days, William Haag (d.) and Fred Kniffen (d.) at Louisiana State University and Munro Edmonson (d.), Forrest LaViolette (d.), Arden King (d.), John Fischer (d.), and, however belatedly, Ann Fischer (d.) at Tulane University; from days as a professor, Raymond Lee (d.) at the now–University of Indiana at Pennsylvania and Robert West (d.), William Davidson, Donald Vermeer, Sam

Hilliard, and Jill Brody at Louisiana State University; and from the occasions of our once-a-year renewals at the American Anthropological Association, Marea Teski (d.), Stan Wilk, Gil Kushner, Dan Ingersoll, Bruce Grindal, Patricia Beaver, and Gregory Reck. At the annual meeting of the Association of American Geographers, former students from the Louisiana State University graduate program, some of whom I've known since my first days in the department, greet me warmly, especially at the now-famous LSU-Texas parties. Three geographers in particular have helped shape my thinking about place, Yi-Fu Tuan, Nicholas Entrikin, and James Duncan. Each year I look forward to renewing our acquaintance. Finally and most important, my attempts to learn what we humans, in our differences, are up to began on the streets of Spanish American towns, where people, in chance encounters or in longer exchanges that continue even today, have guided my questioning, and in the South, in Southern Baptist churches where members have welcomed my presence in their midst and whose "professions of faith" have helped clarify my own.

As a teacher for thirty-nine years and counting, I have been blessed with the opportunity to hold forth about the strange story of us humans on this planet. I am grateful to students for stoically enduring my less-than-elegant ramblings. I am particularly appreciative of those graduate students in anthropology and in geography who have, over the years, chosen to work with me. We, together, create.

Three sabbatical leaves have played critical roles in the evolution of this work, and I recognize with gratitude Louisiana State University for granting those leaves and the host institutions for welcoming me to their campuses. The first was Princeton University, where, in 1980, I actually committed thoughts to paper and where James Fernandez gave kind encouragement and has continued to do so through the years; the second was the University of Texas, where, in 1987, I wrote a first chapter and where E. Mott Davis (d.) resumed a mentoring role he began when I was his laboratory assistant in the summer of 1957 and where Joel Sherzer in anthropology and William Doolittle in geography took an immediate and continuing interest in this project; and the third was the University of North Carolina, where, in 1994, I discovered how to present my ethnographic material and comment on it at the same time (i.e., when I found you) and where James Peacock, a fellow southerner, graciously opened doors for me and shared thoughts about being an anthropologist from the South.

Now, in this current sabbatical year comes the news announcing the acceptance of my manuscript, and I have the unanticipated respite to reflect and to polish, and for that I express again my gratitude toward the LSU administration, especially for their confidence in me as a "mature" scholar. I should warn them, however, that six years from now, they may well find before them a request for yet another sabbatical.

The Middleton Library at LSU has, during my stay, added two additional stories, recataloged from Dewey Decimal to the Library of Congress system, computerized its entire holdings, added data bases galore, and did all these things and more in the face of undignified carping and miserly budgetary increases—if not negative increases! The open-stack policy allowed me to browse for likely volumes on the Pleistocene, Spanish America, the American South, and Christianity. This "search procedure," more times than not, put me face-to-face with an unexpected treasure. Thus, I am grateful to all, and particularly to Flores St. Amant.

The talented hand of Mary Lee Eggart has produced the maps, tables, and figures, and I am indebted to her artistry. William Fagan and Charlotte Cavell guided me through the labyrinths of word processing. Matt Samson reviewed Chapter 4 in draft form and improved it with his insightful comments. Scott Smiley proofread the entire manuscript and enriched it with his thoughtful suggestions. He should not be held accountable for my hardheaded refusal to follow his discerning eye.

The biblical references in English are to the Holy Bible, King James Version (Nashville: Thomas Nelson Publishers, 1989), and in Spanish to Sagrada Biblia (Mexico City: Ediciones Paulinas, 1984). The translations of material cited in the original Spanish are mine.

None of what you see here would you read were it not for the decision of the Louisiana State University Press to publish the manuscript. Eternally grateful for that decision, I thank Les Phillabaum, director, who brought the manuscript before the Faculty Press Committee for their approval; Sylvia Frank Rodrigue, executive editor, who quickly obtained a reader, patiently endured my impatient queries, and produced from my rantings and ravings a document from which the Press Committee could derive their evaluation; Maureen Hewitt, associate director, who listened with great understanding to my words as they tumbled over one another in their anxious effort to describe a work so close to my heart; and Christine Cowan, copy editor, who applied her sharp eye and blue pencil to the unenviable task of removing my inelegancies. Gerry Anders at the Press guided the manuscript from text to book, while Charlotte Cavell put the final touch to the galleys. None of the above should be held responsible for the final product, for that belongs exclusively to you and me. I especially appreciate the comments of the anonymous reader who offered a thorough and generous review at a time when doubts, as is their way, began their stealthy invasion.

A most generous fellowship from the International Center for Medical Research and Training, Tulane University and the Universidad del Valle, funded my dissertation research in 1962 and 1963, and an equally supportive Douglas Manship Grant, College of Arts and Sciences, Louisiana State University, returned me thirty years later to recount the changes occurring in Colombia during that interval. A training grant from the International Center for Medical Research and Training, Louisiana State University, allowed me to investigate medical practices among the people of Puntarenas, Costa Rica, in the summer of 1967, and research grants from the Graduate School, Louisiana State University, helped defray expenses during field trips to Costa Rica, Honduras, Guatemala, and Mexico in various summers beginning in 1970 and continuing into the 1990s.

At the bottom of many pages, you will see an array of footnotes. My major professor told me, back at the beginning when I was struggling to make my writing scholarly, "Miles, if it is worth saying, it's worth saying in the text." For most of my writing life, I have faithfully followed his advice. But here, in its culmination, I have abandoned the principle. Some of my best "sayings" are in the footnotes, so I hope you will read them, just as I hope my major professor, looking down from that special place reserved for brilliant and sorely missed mentors, will forgive me.

To bring this manuscript to completion, I established 1999, with excursions into 2000 and even quicker forays into 2001, as the point beyond which I would not consult the expanding fossil record, the fortunes of Spanish American Catholics, the aspirations of Southern Baptists, or the criticism of the theories and theorists cited within. I remain painfully aware of important contributions that I have failed to consider, and I apologize to the authors of those works and ask their pardon.

I thank the following publishers for permission to reprint excerpts from the indicated work: *Passional Culture: Emotion, Religion, and Society in Southern*

Spain by Timothy Mitchell. Copyright © 1990 University of Pennsylvania Press. *Pilgrims of the Andes: Regional Cults in Cusco* by Michael J. Sallnow. Copyright © 1987 Smithsonian Institution Press. "To Christ Crucified" by Miguel de Guevara and translated by Iain Fletcher, from *An Anthology of Spanish Poetry from Garcilaso to García Lorca*, edited by Angel Flores (New York: Anchor Books, 1961). Copyright © 1961 by Angel Flores. with the permission of Barbara Dederick c/o The Permissions Company, P.O. Box 243, High Bridge, NJ 08829, USA. "Poetics in the Field and on the Page" by Miles Richardson, *Qualitative Inquiry* 4 (4):451–62. Copyright © 1998 Sage Publications. *Mexico in Sculpture, 1521–1821* by Elizabeth Wilder Weismann. Copyright © 1950 by the President and Fellows of Harvard College (Harvard University Press). *The Denial of Death* by Ernest Becker. Copyright © 1973 The Free Press, a Division of Simon & Schuster. *Giving Glory to God in Appalachia* by Howard Drogan. Copyright © 1987 University of Tennessee Press. "Devotion" by Margaret Hebblethwaite, *Modern Catholicism: Vatican II and After*, with permission of SPCK, Holy Trinity Church.

I thank the Hal Leonard Corporation for permission to reprint excerpts from the following:

"'Neath a Cold Gray Tomb of Stone." Words and Music by Hank Williams and Mel Forsee. Copyright © 1949 (Renewed 1976) by Acuff-Rose Music, Inc. and Hiriam Music in the U.S.A. All rights for Hiriam Music Administered by Rightsong Music, Inc. All Rights outside the U.S.A. Controlled by Acuff-Rose Music, Inc. All Rights Reserved. Used by Permission.

"Ramblin' Man." Words and Music by Hank Williams. Copyright © 1951 (Renewed 1979) by Acuff-Rose Music, Inc. and Hiriam Music in the U.S.A. All Rights for Hiriam Music Administered by Rightsong Music, Inc. All rights outside the U.S.A. Controlled by Acuff-Rose Music, Inc. All Rights Reserved. Used by Permission.

"Highway of Sorrow." Words and Music by Bill Monroe and Pete Pyle. Copyright © 1951 Unichappell Music Inc. Copyright Renewed. International Copyright secured. All Rights Reserved. Used by Permission.

"Sunday Mornin' Comin' Down." Words and Music by Kris Kristofferson. © 1969 (Renewed 1997) TEMI COMBINE INC. All Rights Controlled by COMBINE MUSIC CORP. and Administered by EMI BLACKWOOD MUSIC INC. All Rights Reserved. International Copyright Secured. Used by Permission.

I also thank the following publishers for permission to adapt illustrations from the indicated work: *Principles of Human Evolution* by Roger Lewin. Copyright © 1998 Blackwell Science LTD; *Space and Place: The Perspective of Experience* by Yi-Fu Tuan. Copyright © University of Minnesota Press; "The African Emergence and Early Asian Dispersal of the Genus *Homo*" by Roy Larick and Russell L. Ciochon, *American Scientist* 84:538–51. Copyright © 1996 *American Scientist*; *Encyclopedia of Southern Baptists* 1:68. Copyright © 1958 Baptist History and Heritage Society; *Human Evolution: An Illustrated Guide* by Peter Andrews and Chris Stringer. Copyright © Natural History Museum, London. I also thank Valerie Frazer for permission to adapt the picture appearing on p. 131 of her *Architecture of Conquest: Building in the Viceroyalty of Peru, 1535–1635*. Cambridge: Cambridge University Press, 1990.

I particularly thank the publishers listed below who considered the material I excerpted from their volumes as being covered by the doctrine of fair use: American Anthropological Association; Mercer University Press; Johns Hopkins University Press; and University of Texas Press.

Finally, I thank Elena Peters-Spencer for her gracious permission to adapt the image of the "bestial Neanderthal" that appeared in her late husband's copyrighted work.

BEING-IN-CHRIST AND PUTTING DEATH IN ITS PLACE

Florence Adams Richardson, the two children, and Mr. Richardson

I have read that the greatest contribution of Protestantism to the conceptual order is in the art of music. . . . And this is what Protestantism dissolves into, *celestial music*! On the other hand, we can say that the loftiest Catholic, or at least Spanish, artistic expression, is in the more material, tangible, and permanent art—since sounds are carried off in the wind—of sculpture and painting, in the Christ of Velázques, in that Christ who never dies but who is forever dying so that he may give us life!

—Miguel de Unamuno, *Del Sentimiento Trágico de la Vida*

I love you, baby, but you gotta understand,
When the Lord made me, he made a Ramblin' Man.

—Hank Williams, "Ramblin' Man"

PROLOGUE

In 1937, give or take a year, probably on a Monday, but in any case, long before I found you, I put on my Red Ryder gloves, stuck my Tom Mix cap gun in my belt, and rode my stick horse down the rickety steps off the back porch and down the trail past the chinaberry tree to the washhouse. President Roosevelt had seen to it that electricity reached our place, but running water, despite the president, still stopped at the city limits, so the washhouse stood next to the well where the washerwoman, a colored lady who sometimes came to help out, was drawing up a fresh bucket. The weekly washing took a lot of water, so she was constantly hauling at the rope that ran through the pulley fixed above the wide mouth of the well shed and down to the water below. Fortunately, the well diggers had shoveled down to a vein of water that flowed continuously, even during the hot, dry East Texas summers when other wells went dry. As the colored lady emptied a fresh bucket into a galvanized tub perched on a wobbly stand, my mother lifted my father's union suit, the long-handle underwear that he wore come winter or summer, from the nearby boiling wash pot. With the steaming mass dripping from a pole in her hand, she went inside the washhouse to run the thick garment through the wringer of the new washing machine the Montgomery Ward's man had brought out last week.

I had a question I wanted to ask her. The question had hold of me, and I couldn't shake it. I'd be riding my coaster wagon like a stagecoach out of Reno with howling Indians so close behind I could breathe their war paint. Figuring I'd fool those Indians the way Buck Jones did, I circled the blackjack oak in the front yard to plunge down the dirt drive toward the road to Dodge City, sometimes called Palestine, Texas. Right at the edge of the road, I leaped from the boot of the stagecoach to land astride the tongue between the horses, and unhooking the wagon by pulling the linchpin on tongue, I managed to turn the horses in the nick of time, while the horseless wagon and the Indians, still howling, went over the cliff. And in the middle of all that fun, the question would get me. It got me worse than the worms I had to drink castor oil for, worse even than the castor oil. It got me so bad I thought I'd rather be a rock. Rocks couldn't get in the Model A and go to the Ritz on Saturday to see Wild Bill Elliot while mamma did the week's shopping, but nothing hurts a rock.

Mamma was good with questions. Frances, my sister, wouldn't know the answer, but because she was five years older, she'd act like she did, and I couldn't tell the acting from the truth, or the truth from the acting. Daddy—Mr. Richardson, mamma called him—wasn't any good with questions or answers. He didn't talk, and when he did, it was to tell me to shut up. He worked seven days a week at the shops the Missouri Pacific Railroad had located in Palestine, and maybe he was too tired for questions or maybe, the thought came to me later, he didn't have a lot of answers. My worst nightmare, however, worse than having an African native from a Tarzan movie under my bed about to stab me with a spear, was a steam locomotive chasing me across the cow pasture that stretched forever between the woods and the house. I woke up screaming from those nightmares. From their bedroom next to mine, mamma called, "Miles, what's the matter?" Because I was too ashamed of being scared, I'd tell her I had indigestion. I didn't know what indigestion was except when I had it, it got me a glass of water, a cool hand, and, if I had it real bad, a kiss.

"Mamma?" I asked at the door of the washhouse.

"Mmm" was all I got. The wringer on the new washing machine was truly a marvel, but getting anything as thick as long-handle underwear through the two rollers required considerable concentration and not a little luck, though one day later on my sister got her whole arm through the rollers with no thought at all.

"Mamma?" I tried again.

"Mmm."

"Mamma," and this time I didn't wait on the "Mmm." "Mamma, I wanta know something."

"Well, what?"

I was making progress, but for my question, I needed more attention than that. "Mamma, I wanta know something."

And maybe it was because she finally got the underwear through the wringer, but mainly I believe it was because she loved me, she smiled,

"Whacha wanta know, honey?"

"Do cowboys ever die?"

"Do cowboys ever die?" she repeated the question, I guess to make sure she heard it right. "Do cowboys ever die?" she said again.

"Do they?"

"What do you wanta know for?" she stalled. But I wasn't getting involved in any side issues.

"Do they?"

"No, sweetheart." And her love flowed through me. "No, cowboys don't die."

"Never ever?" I wanted to be certain.

"No, cowboys don't ever die. They live forever."

I was twelve years old and in the sixth grade before I found out that mamma had lied. That afternoon, I got out of the pickup truck that a neighbor had converted into a bus so he could earn a little extra hauling us country kids to school in town, and they told me. But I didn't believe them; I couldn't. I cried, but the crying was to get them to leave me alone. My daddy cried too, the only time I ever saw him cry, except later on, when he got old, old and shaky, so shaky he had to drink his coffee through a plastic straw.

A week before, two weeks, a month, two months, a year, a year before, for all that time she had told him she wasn't right. One evening, after he had come home from his long day of crawling in and out and under locomotives, she asked him. "Mr. Richardson," she asked him. Could she drive the Model A back to town to see the doctor?

No, he told her. No, because the trip would cost gas. No, because the doctor would tell her the same thing he had told her before. She wasn't sick; she just had female trouble.

So that day, when I was twelve and in the sixth grade, she left him a note pinned to the back screen door. "I'm sorry for being so bothersome," the note said. "But I won't worry you anymore. I've gone to go live with Jesus. You can find me in the well." Always thoughtful, she took off her shoes before she climbed the well shed to drop to the dark water below.

* * *

Jesus was Christ, our Lord and Savior, who so loved us that he died on the cross for our sins. I tried hard to accept Jesus as my Personal Savior. I never tried anything harder. I was a child of the church, the First Baptist Church of Palestine, pronounced not like "nine" but like "teen," as in the Spanish "Pales*tin*a." "Your mother," Aunt Kate told me, "carried you to church on a pillow." In Sunday School, I sang,

Yes, Jesus loves me.
Yes, Jesus loves me.
Yes, Jesus loves me,
The Bible tells me so.

When I was ten, I did what every child of the church did. I walked the aisle and confessed my sins. And several Sundays later, I was baptized. But it didn't work out. After my mother went to live with Jesus, I heard Reverend Summerall preach from Luke, chapter 16, verses 22–24.

> And the rich man burning in hell looked up onto heaven. And in heaven, he saw Lazarus cradled in Father Abraham's bosom. "Father Abraham," the rich man pleaded. "Father Abraham," he cried. "Have mercy. Send Lazarus with water to cool my parching tongue. Ask him to dip his finger in water, well water, cold well water, and let him come down and put his finger on my lips. My burning lips. Father Abraham, have mercy!"
>
> Are you the rich man? Are you going to hell? Are you going to burn forever in hell because you are too proud? Too proud to fall on your knees before God, before God, the Father, and cry, "Forgive me. Forgive me, Father."

Sunday evening, it was Training Union and another sermon. And at any time, it was no smoking, no drinking, no cussing, no dancing, and no mixed bathing, which meant you couldn't go swimming in City Park Pool.

Into adolescence, I couldn't talk to girls. I couldn't talk to anybody, maybe my friend George, who lived up the road a half a mile and whose mother would fix lunch and sometimes even let me stay for supper, but nobody else. Not my sister and not my father and nobody else. Company would come, and I'd head for the barn. Mulely, the Jersey milk cow with no horns; Dolly, the plow horse I rode bareback; Midnight, the cat who drank milk I squirted from Mulely's teats; and Laddie, the dog—they all, each one, lived in the barn.

I could talk to Mulely, Dolly, Midnight, and Laddie, but I couldn't talk to girls, but worse, I couldn't keep my mind off them, not even the preacher's wife. And cowboys died. They died. Which meant they disappeared. Like mamma. I'd rather burn in hell, like the rich man, than disappear. At least if I was burning, I'd still be something, not nothing.

If I was saved? If I was saved, I'd live forever with Jesus.

> Good works won't get you to heaven. Giving money to poor won't get you to heaven. Being nice to people won't get you to heaven. The only way you can get to heaven is to fall down on your knees and beg forgiveness.
>
> "Forgive me, Father, for I have sinned and fallen short of your glory. Forgive me, Father."
>
> Now, while every head is bowed. Now, while every eye is closed. Now, while the choir sings the invitational hymn. Come now and confess. Confess your sins to the Father.

Every Sunday, once in the morning, and again that night, I heard, "Don't wait. Don't wait. Don't wait until it is too late. He's knocking now. Now. Open the door. Open the door and let him into your heart."

Each service, I promised myself, "Next Sunday," and each Sunday, I left church miserable.

"For God so loved the world that he gave his only begotten son that whosoever believeth in him should not perish, but have everlasting life."

A summer Sunday evening, home from church with nothing, a summer evening with the sun's last light gentle in the darkening sky, home from church and with nothing but nothing. I went to the barn to be with the animals, Mulely in her stall, Dolly in the lot, Midnight in the rafters, and Laddie at my side, ready to go wherever it was I wanted to go. I went to the barn with the animals, and I prayed. I prayed. I prayed with all of my heart. I said the words out loud, the very words the preacher said to say. I even went to my knees. I prayed. I said the words. From my knees in the barn with the animals, I said all I could say. And the nothing stayed.

I tried hard to accept Christ as my Personal Savior. I walked the aisle a second time and was rebaptized. I tried hard. I never tried anything harder. I failed, so I became an anthropologist.

In my nothing, I turned to anthropology, and in anthropology, my nothing turned to solitude, and in solitude, I learned to talk.

> There is no truer dialogue than the dialogue you transact with yourself, and this dialogue you can only transact when alone. In solitude, and only in solitude, can you know yourself as another; and when you cannot know yourself as another, you will not succeed knowing in others yourself.
>
> Only in solitude, which breaks apart the thick husk of modesty that separates us from each other and all of us from God, have we no secrets. Only in solitude, do we raise our hearts to the Heart of the Universe. And only in solitude, does the redemptive hymn of supreme confession burst forth from our souls. (Unamuno 1974b, 32–33)

In my solitude, with Miguel de Unamuno, I came to understand that for humanity there is but one toil, one work, one struggle: "Each day I believe less in the social question, in the political question, in the aesthetic question, in the moral question, in the religious question, and in all the other questions that people have asked so as not to confront the true question, which is my question, your question, and their question, and that is, the human question" (1974b, 33–34). And the human question is what to do about death. This book is my answer.

1

THE STRUGGLE OF CULTURE WITH DEATH

"Who is Jesus Christ in Latin America today?" liberation theologian David Batstone asks fellow liberationists as they search for a way to make the tortured Nazarene relevant to the oppressed in today's world (Batstone 1991, 139).[1] Being theologians, even if liberationists, Batstone and his fellow scholars inevitably turn to the text of the New Testament to clarify who Christ is. Being anthropologists, you and I turn to the "text" of the people, to the creative acts that humans perform. In so doing, we change the who to the where. "Who is Jesus Christ?" leads us to search not for who Jesus is but to where people are. For where people are, specifically Christians, Christ is.

Where Christians are, Christ is, but where? Where is Christ? Should we, you and I, address this question to the man seated on a bench in the central plaza of Nueva Esperanza, a small city in Spanish America surrounded by volcanoes and coffee trees, the answer, politely given, would be accompanied by a gesture pointing to the *iglesia* across the street. Were we, in our quest, to ask this question of the man coming down the steps of the county courthouse in Mt. Hope, another small city, but one located in the piney woods region of the American South, the answer, enthusiastically asserted, would be accompanied by a hand clapped over the heart.

In Nueva Esperanza, should we continue our search and enter the *iglesia* through its massive doors, we would find that though the morning weekday mass is over and the priest has left, the *iglesia* is by no means empty. In the

1. Fellow liberationist José Míguez Bonino asks the same question in his introduction to *Faces of Jesus: Latin American Christologies* (1984).

front, near the altar, ancient ladies in black kneel in mourning for the departed. Behind them and in equal solemnity, three teenage girls, fresh in their green and white school uniforms, prepare for the future. Nearby, a man in a business suit crosses himself, picks up his briefcase, and heads for the door and the affairs of the day. At the door, however, he turns to cross himself in a final act of veneration. In front, above the altar, above the ladies in their somber black, above the teenage girls in their fresh green, hangs on the cross in perpetual agony the object of his devotion.

Pursuing our search in Mt. Hope, since we cannot look beneath the man's hand and into his heart, we might rephrase our question from where Christ is to a seemingly related one: Where is Mt. Hope's largest church? Since he himself is a member of the congregation, our guide without hesitation directs us to the First Baptist Church, hardly more than a block from the courthouse. Before we can get away, he grabs our hands, introduces himself, "My name is Womack," and invites us to the service, "The doors of our church are always open." At the church, in fact, we find the front doors locked, it being a weekday, but the secretary at the church's office, located in the adjacent structure and with hours, "Monday through Friday, 8 to 5," lets us through a side door. Inside, the auditorium is empty of both people and statues. In front and below the massive pulpit, a large Bible lies open on the table for the Lord's Supper, and above the pulpit and in back of the choir, with the curtains pulled closed, is the baptistery. Should the curtains be drawn apart, we might well read the message inscribed on the walls: "Why seek ye the living among the dead? Luke 24:5."

Where is Christ? Our question, the one we, you and I, anthropologists, ask of participants in two major Christian denominations in two adjacent cultures in the New World provokes dramatically different responses. In Spanish America, where the vast majority of people speak Spanish and are Roman Catholics, we are directed to the *iglesia* where Christ is an exterior form to be seen and often touched. In the American South, where the vast majority speak English and many profess to be Baptists, we are told that Christ is an interior presence, a voice perhaps, but in any case impossible to see, at least with ordinary vision.

Despite the difference in where the two denominations locate Christ, one in exterior form to be seen and touched and the other in interior presence to be felt and heard, both faiths, however, recite the story of Jesus, who, they say, was a man of humble circumstance—though of the lineage of King David—a carpenter who preached to the multitudes and who, because of that preaching, was condemned to death by crucifixion. Both insist at this point in the narration that though Jesus died, Christ arose from the grave and, furthermore, lives today. And both proclaim in their recitation that Christ is here, now.

To address the question of the where of Christ and to account for how the two, Catholics in Spanish America and Baptists in the American South, establish his presence are tasks of considerable magnitude. To address the question anthropologically augments the task even further, for to pursue the where of Christ we must first address the kind of creatures we humans are. Asking what kind of creatures we are brings us in full view of ourselves. And what amazing, wonderful, full of wonder, contradictory creatures we find ourselves to be: two-legged mammals who look with far-seeing eyes into the future and reach out with thing-seeking hands to build that future into the now; naked primates, cousin to the gorilla, sibling to the chimpanzee, who communicate with symbols and thereby create a reality that can be measured neither by the eye nor by the hand; flesh and blood organisms genetically programmed to die but equally programmed to transcend death. So to address the where of Christ becomes at the very first instance an aspiration to address an even greater issue: us.

In our eagerness to confront ourselves with the urge to find out who we are, our goal is not to resolve the contradictions we find—lest we resolve ourselves out of existence—but the goal is to bring the disparate elements into a single focus. What better way to accomplish this goal than to review how in fact we did it! In the forthcoming section, "From Hominid to Human," we trace the broad outline of our evolution. As we retrace our route through geological time, we discover too that our capacity to construct a symbolic reality evolved conjointly with changes in the biological component, with changes in our anatomy. At some stretch along the way, the process produced animals capable of saying to each other, "You are; I am." At that time, our hominid ancestors became us; at that time, we awoke. The emergence of the reflexive self, however, brought with it the capacity to recognize death. What we awoke to was each other but also death. With that recognition, we humans launched upon a struggle with death, a struggle fought wherever we find humans, a defining struggle, a struggle that tells us who we are.[2]

2. Do other animals know death? When I went out to the barn to pray for my soul, did Mulely, Dolly, Midnight, and Laddie pray with me? Or, even better, for me?

While our sibling apes may display severe grief upon the death of a close friend or relative, this experience, although clearly painful, is "quite different from having a sense of one's own

Although our review of how we did it clearly establishes that we are at one and the same time both creatures of flesh and blood and creators of symbolic reality, we still search for a concept to bring into sharp view these two disparate components. Given the widespread antipathy toward considering ourselves as part of nature, we need, particularly as anthropologists, to keep in the forefront of our concern the feeling, seeing, listening, laughing, hurting parts of us. Likewise, given the tendency of some to consider us little more than an appendage to molecular DNA, we must continue to celebrate the creating, metaphor-making, story-telling, poetry-dwelling part of us. The concept of being-in-the-world offers a possible solution to how to juggle both disparate components at the same time. In "Experience and Symbol," we explore the potentiality of the concept. With being-in-the-world we see a single condition divided into two components: *being*, which we should consider as experience, as be-ing, and *world*, which we should recognize as symbolic reality, or worldhood. Note that hyphens join the two components into a single phenomenon: To be humans, we humans have to have a world to be in, but the world in which we are, we create. Take this text, for example: To be readers, we have to have a text to be in. The text we are in, however, we create, I by writing, you by reading. (Parenthetically, please observe how dependent I am upon you. The text that I write requires your reading for it to be; my words need your eyes for them to speak.)[3]

---

mortality, a sense of self, a sense that life is more than one's self. An awareness of mortality requires at the very least that the individual be an object unto itself" (Pavelka 1991, 595). An accounting of the awareness of mortality leads some to a study of mortuary rituals, or how specific people bury their dead, for example, S. C. Humphreys and Helen King (1981), Maurice Bloch and Jonathan Parry (1982), and Peter Metcalf and Richard Huntington (1991). As María Cátedra (1992) would clarify, "specific people" often become distant "others," residing far from the personal life of the anthropologist. Such objectification encourages, at least among sardonic minds both within and without the field, an "exoticification" or "orientalizing" of people's grief. Yet anthropologists have attempted to address their own turmoil when a wife hurls herself to her death or a caring grandfather turns still (Rosaldo 1989, Behar 1991, and especially Panourgiá 1995). For my part, I, with your help, would travel a different route to ponder the significance of a single, recurrent mortuary ritual: that of Jesus.

3. Linguists of the Deborah Tannen school (1989) speak of you as the co-author of this text. Consequently, the text is not a prefabricated house into which you gain entrance; it emerges as you and I meet on the page. As coauthor of this text that we are in, you write in your reading and you do so as you see fit. You author in your own way, of course. I would not have it otherwise. But please, please, don't fuck up.

Being-in-the-world, then, conjoins experience and symbol, feeling and speaking, into a single phenomenon, us. Being the physical creatures we are, whenever we are, we are always somewhere; consequently, being-in-the-world means being-in-place. "Being-in-Place and Out," considers the implications of being-in-place and stresses the importance of the where in defining the who. Knowing where we are tells us who we are. Yet we discover that place, despite its rock-solid appearance, is not as fixed as we so blithely assume. Lurking in opposition to the in-place, like a horror in the basement of a Gothic novel, is the out-of-place. The out-of-place challenges, frequently to our dismay, our most carefully constructed demeanor. The loud rumbling of an angry stomach in the quietness of a holy moment interrupts our most transcendental flights. Indeed, as the ultimate in the out-of-place, death calls into question the very basis upon which we construct our humanity. In response, we attempt, continually and constantly, to put death in its place, to transform it from an ultimate challenge to that which we can live beyond or, at least, with. Such a Sisyphean aspiration can arise only in the dreams of a creature that itself is profoundly out-of-place.

To conclude this chapter, "The Anthropologist's Project" comments on the dual role of the field-working anthropologist as both a participant and an observer, an uneasy, slippery combination of sometimes incompatible components that makes the anthropologist always and everywhere out-of-place. The section also explains the rationale for comparing Catholics in Spanish America with Baptists in the American South and asks you, the reader, to consider my credentials for doing so. It finishes with a justification for why I want you in my text.

Now, let's turn to the beginning, to the beginning of how we came to be.

From Hominid to Human

The beginning of this endeavor that we have launched upon, this story that we wish to reread, you and I—the story of ourselves, of creatures, each with an identity, a name, a history, a destiny—extends far back beyond the Christian era, beyond the ancient civilizations, beyond the beginnings of agriculture and further still, into the period of great ice ages, the time of the mastodon and the cave bear, and further still, until when? At what point in the evolutionary process can we say the endeavor has begun? At what time can we state that here we said for the first time, "You are; I am"?

Was it with the appearance of the big brain? That you and I, *Homo sapiens*, have big brains has led many in the past and even today to argue that our humanity resides there, among the billions of neurons firing away in our craniums. Yet the facts speak otherwise. Table 1 compares the brain size of hominids, members of the biological family *Hominidae*, which includes you and me, plus our extinct ancestors. Hominids come in a number of different sizes and bear a variety of names, and in these days of intensive excavations and new discoveries, the varieties multiply and interpretations abound. For our purposes we must strive to balance the need to recognize the varieties against an even greater need to recognize the consistent trend in hominid evolution, that is, the process whereby hominids became human. In the Appendix, I attempt to present the contentious issues of classification and interpretation currently occupying the specialist literature. I believe the evidence strongly supports the humanization process offered here.[4]

TABLE 1. Brain Size of Hominids

Hominid	Average Brain Size in Cubic Centimeters
Homo sapiens sapiens (us)	1,350
Archaic *sapiens* (Neandertal and predecessors)	1,500
Pre-*sapiens* (*Homo erectus* and kin)	1,000
Australopithecines	450

4. The evidence emerges most clearly when the terminology employed emphasizes "grade" distinctions. A grade recognizes similarities in overall level of organization and adaptation (see Brace 1991; Clark 1992). My adaptation of the "grade" terminology is intentionally inclusive. The term "pre-*sapiens*" includes all those hominids, however classified into different species, who occur in the fossil record between the australopithecines and archaic *sapiens*. By and large, these hominids have, until quite recently, been included in the taxon *Homo erectus*. Calling these forms "pre-*sapiens*" does not imply they were on their way to becoming us. They were on their way to becoming them, and given that they occupied regions of the earth for over a million years, they were quite successful at being them. Evidence from a site in Siberia suggests that they may have ventured much farther north than previously thought (Morell 1994; see also Gibbons 1994), and the presence of Acheulean-like hand axes in south China demonstrates that the Asian pre-*sapiens* matched the symbol-making capacity of their African and Eurasian counterparts (Yamei 2000) and further supports the concept of grade. Archaic *sapiens* includes all hominids between *erectus* and anatomically modern hominids, that is, *sapiens sapiens*. In contrast to the pre-*sapiens*, we might suggest, any border between archaics and us should be blurred. Archaic *sapiens*

The average brain size of these earliest members of the hominid family was hardly larger than that of a chimpanzee. The brain of the chimp (which is a pongid, or a member of the ape family *Pongidae*, and our closest kin in the animal world) measures around 400 cubic centimeters. So something other than the brain got us started on this journey. That something else was the foot. The principal feature that separates all of the hominids—you, me, Neandertal, *Homo erectus*, and the australopithecine—from the pongids, the apes, is upright stature. We did not think our way across the boundary from nonhuman to human; we walked across.[5]

Walking upright as a normal mode of locomotion, as opposed to taking a few hesitant steps on one's back leg, requires a total reorganization of the body. For creatures of our lineage, the key to this reorganization is a pelvis that curves from the backbone around toward the front. This orients the hip joint in such a manner that the upper leg bone, the femur, angles into place the rest of the leg underneath the body. Such an orientation plants the foot firmly, and most definitely, on the ground. The foot itself becomes a walking platform balanced between an enlarged heel in the back and an equally substantial big toe in the front. Meanwhile, the curvature of the pelvis forms a basin to help support the guts, which would otherwise dangle down in a most disconcerting fashion.

Figure 1 compares the leg and pelvis of the two hominids (*Australopithecus afarensis* and *Homo sapiens*) with a pongid, or ape. The orientation of the leg of *Australopithecus afarensis*—better known as "Lucy," the lady from Afar, Ethiopia, a fossil skeleton that dates back to around 3.5 million years ago—

---

are us in an archaic mode. See Krantz (1980), who argues that archaic *sapiens* were simply *erectus* in transition.

5. Current assessments of the brain size of the australopithecines via computer imaging depict a range from 370 to 515 cubic centimeters (Conroy 1998; Falk 1998). Some argue that while these hominids were clearly bipedal, their wrist bones indicate their immediate ancestors knuckle-walked on the ground like the contemporary gorilla and chimpanzee. While the evidence solidifies our close kinship with the gorilla and chimpanzee, it introduces a greater complexity in explaining the origins of upright stature in hominids. If the immediate ancestors to hominids were adapted to terrestrial locomotion through knuckle-walking, how can we account for their abandonment of this mode to favor bipedality (Richmond and Strait 2000)? The most plausible scenario might be a feeding strategy based on provisioning males carrying meat obtained through cooperative hunting back to child-attending females with social bonds between particular individuals—bonds created and sustained through ritual, symbolic communication. See Appendix.

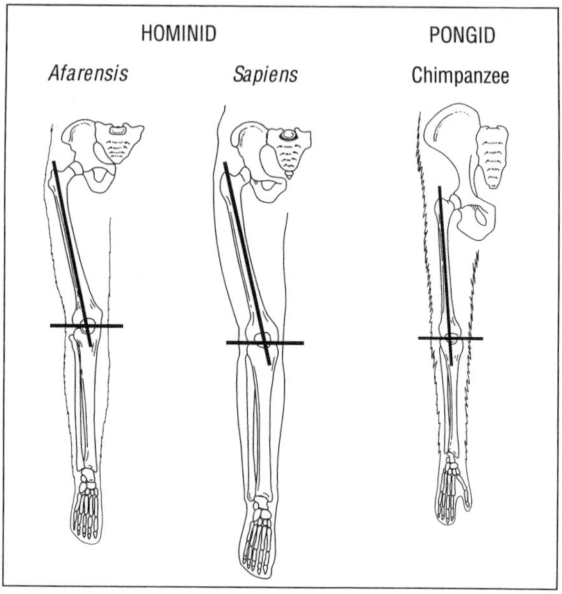

FIG. 1. Walking versus waddling. Adapted from Lewin (1998, 220), not to scale.

angles the foot directly under the body in the manner of *Homo sapiens*, better known as us. The leg of the ape, such as the chimpanzee, sticks straight down, so that when the chimp transverses bipedally, it waddles, like a gunfighter in an old Western movie. Additional material from other sites, including leg and foot bones, not to mention the fossilized footprints of two hominids walking across the savannah in Laetoli, Tanzania, clearly indicate upright stature evolved long before the highly touted big brain.

The foot started us out; the foot put us into the story we are still writing, but by putting us upright, the foot also endowed the eye, and its companion, the hand, with a special vision. Seeing has become for us humans, and especially for scientists, the premier faculty for discerning the truth. What we see we are ready to take for real. Seeing opens up. Enhanced seeing, the microscope and the telescope, reveals worlds hitherto hidden. But seeing is not restricted to the eye; the hand also discerns the truth. The two work together, for while the eye fixes, the hand manipulates. Many of our four-legged mammalian kin lead into the environment with the mouth; we, on the other hand, while still employing the mouth, reach out with the hand. The hand places before the eye (and the mouth and the nose) any object that arouses our curiosity and permits the eye to examine first one side and then the other. Furthermore, by tearing apart the object, the hand directs curiosity into the hidden interior. Indeed, the hand is curiosity at work, for it asks, when it encounters the world before it, "What is this?" More important, however, the hand locates us geographically and connects us socially. Seeking to reassure me that you are nearby, it asks "Where are you?" by reaching for you. And when your reassurance goes overboard and threatens to overwhelm me, the hand clears a space by putting you at "arm's length."

The foot, by placing us upright, enhanced our sensuality. Walking coupled with effective sweating allowed our ancestors to hunt down the swifter four-legged herbivores in the savannah heat. Effective sweating was tied to the loss of heavy body hair. The loss of a thick coat of hair made the skin especially sensitive to the hand and to the lips. Nursing offspring, a mammalian delight, became even more intense between a hominid mother and her baby. Sexual intercourse, also a recognized mammalian pastime, shifted from the front-ventral position, with the male plunging blindly into a crouched female, to the front-front position, and sex became a personal, face-to-face, eye-to-eye affair, a social act capable of great tenderness.

With upright stature, the mouth yields to the hand as the primary device for connecting the organism to the environment. The mouth moves to the forefront, however, in the production of sound. Vocalizing is a vital primate trait. To coordinate their movements, to warn of danger, to plead for help, to establish preeminence, our arboreal kin fill the forest canopy with hoots, whistles, and grunts. We continued the practice in our journey across the borderlands. Walking placed a premium on infant-mother communication. If they were to survive, babies had to be carried, in front, with their faces and arms in full view, engaging directly their mothers' attention. Joint infant-mother interaction of giving, sharing, and pointing provided the behavioral material from which natural selection constructed the genetic basis for our species-specific forms of crying, whining, fussing, smiling, and babbling (Borchert and Zihlman 1990). With subsequent development of specialized areas in the brain and with a reorganized vocal trait, as we walked across the border zone, our hoots, whistles, and grunts eventually became segments of contrasting sounds that conveyed arbitrarily assigned meaning, that is to say, speech.

Speech is a special aspect of the broader arena of symbolic communication, the nature of which I amplify below and the origin of which is discussed in the Appendix. Speaking has a dual aspect. As sounds flowing between us, speaking is the physical modulation of air currents, but these air currents now have arbitrary values that signify. What they signify is "you," "me," and "love." "You," "me," and "love" now have an existence of their own, not reducible to the air currents that physically compose them. They become objects that communicate our feelings and in the process shape those feelings. "You," "me," and "love" are symbols that we speak but that also, it seems, speak us. When you call my name, when you say, "Miles," do not I, whoever I am, appear? So when we walked across the borderland and our hoots, whistles, and grunts became segments of contrasting sounds that conveyed arbitrarily assigned meaning, we walked into a world of symbols that we ourselves created through speaking. With speaking came "you," "me," and "love." With speaking, also came, I am, at times, urged to say, the treasure of silence, the quietness of repose, the blessing of solitude.

Like the hand, the foot, an anatomical device for locomotion, is social, for in traversing the border country between animal and human, we walked in the company of others, holding hands, carrying babies, picking up those who stumbled and fell, and calling out to the young and adventurous. Thus, you can see, with just a glance down, as the part of our body that first and foremost connects us with the firm earth, the foot is fundamental to our being; soaring thoughts about the human spirit begin with the step of the lowly foot.[6]

For all of its steady pace, walking is a struggle against gravity, against falling flat on our faces. Consequently, to keep from falling, we rush ahead, further into the journey. Our journey has shaped the trajectory implied in Table 1. From our beginnings as small, two-legged creatures with brains of about 450 cubic centimeters (the australopithecines), we evolved into larger animals with brains of about 1,000 cubic centimeters (the pre-*sapiens* members of the genus *Homo*, such as *Homo erectus*). Further evolution led to the appearance of the archaic *sapiens* (such as the burly Neandertals), with a brain size of 1,500 cubic centimeters, and finally to our present composition, a slender,

6. Birds, our warm-blooded partners in today's world, followed a similar pattern in their evolution. The discovery of a fossilized nestling in Spain clearly demonstrates that wing evolution preceded skull evolution. As in the case of hominid evolution, changes in the mode of locomotion led the way to changes in the skull and brain in avian development. Birds did not think their way into the trees; they flew into them (Morell 1997).

more gracile form, with an average cranial capacity of 1,350 (anatomically modern *Homo sapiens sapiens*, that is, us, you and me).

What drove the trajectory? What evolutionary process accounts for the increase in brain size? Before we venture an explanation, we must note that in part the increase in brain size was due to the increase in the size of the hominids. Everything else being equal, bigger hominids have bigger brains. And with our crossing of the Pliocene-Pleistocene borderlands, we gained in size. The big increase may have come with the emergence of the pre-*sapiens*. The so-called boy of Turkana, Kenya, was a strapping youngster, already over five feet when he died at the approximate age of nine; at maturity, he would have stood higher than six feet (Lewin 1998). An increase in size is a trend that occurs in many of life's lineages, ranging from trees to mammals (Bonner 1988). Selection for increase in size in the case of the hominids presumably brought with it a degree of protection against a variety of predators prowling the African savannah. We note that an increase in size carries with it a number of features. Larger animals tend to have fewer offspring and a longer interval between offspring. Larger animals, in other words, have fewer young but invest more of their adult energy in caring for the ones they do have. They opt for the reproductive strategy of quality over quantity. At the same time, the young of large animals are precocious, that is, they are further along in their development than the offspring of smaller animals. When Dolly the mare had her colt, Seelum, though a bit wobbly at first, he practically hit the ground running, but when the neighbor's mamma cat had kittens, I had to wait several weeks before Midnight was big enough to leave his mother and his littermates.

Being among the larger primates (only the gorilla is bigger), we follow the rule of larger animals and the parent investment strategy of quality over quantity, with one child per birth being the norm (or such was the case until fertility drugs hit the market). Yet the increase in the hominid brain outstripped the increase in overall size. With the extraordinary increase in brain, we reverse the trend of larger animals to have precocious offspring. Human babies are notoriously (and beguilingly) helpless. And the reason is the big brain. Human birth remains one of the most severe of life's challenges because of the difficulty in getting a big-headed baby through a narrow birth canal. This can only happen, and even then with pain for all, if the development of the fetus's skull is retarded. With delayed maturation of the skull, it is sufficiently pliable to squeeze through the canal.

Thus, increase in size alone does not explain the increase in hominid brain dimensions. Furthermore, the brain doesn't come free. For its size, about 2 percent of the total body weight, it consumes an enormous amount of calories, around 18 percent of the overall energy budget (Lewin 1998).

To address the question of the extraordinary increase in brain size, we need to ask what else accompanied the increase? What else do we find in the record of our past?

The short answer: tools. Beginning at 2.5 million years ago, the record of our working in stone parallels the enlargement of the brain. So, you might wonder, What is a tool? An extension of the exploratory hand, one might reply, a device that allows us more effectively to exploit the environment, to dig up roots, to crack nuts, to slice through the thick hide to the fresh meat of a new kill, an instrument to increase our food supply, to be sure, and not simply an increase in bulk but an increase in quality. The shift into high-energy foods such as the "meat" of nuts and the true meat of animals fed the ever-avaricious brain and allowed selection for even further increase. But many animals use "extra-somatic devices" to enhance their food procurement. For wonderful examples ranging from seagulls to seals, I refer you to Benjamin Beck (1980); for a careful weighing of the evidence for our closest relative, the apes, I ask you to consider W. C. McGrew (1992). Hold up a human tool, however, and what do you see? Us. Human tools are like words; they have a dual aspect. They are sensible, that is, we make them, use them, and toss them aside when they break, but beyond being sensible, they are also intelligible; they signify. They are material signs that communicate a human presence. As physical words, human tools have a scriptlike quality that permits us to read a mind at work in the company of others.[7]

7. To say that human tools allow us to see the mind at work in the company of others moves us from the image of an individual knapper chipping away in splendid isolation to a more realistic scene of toolmaking as social activity. In this context the human tool becomes a communicative act, a point made by George Herbert Mead when he referred to socially constituted material objects as collapsed acts, as condensed symbols conveying social messages, and by Leslie White when he identified them as congealed human labor (see Richardson 1987). In addition, to refer to the archaeological record as "the mind at work" resonates with White's argument that the mind is not a thing but a manner of acting. Mind, he insisted, is "minding" (1949). Although the final outcome of their interpretation of the archaeological record differs from mine, William Noble and Iain Davidson (1996) also develop the position that mind is "minded behavior" rather than an interior entity and that mind is a social construction rather than an individual possession.

Papers delivered at the 2002 meeting of the Society for Paleoanthropology (March 19–20,

Figure 2 plots the trajectories of brain expansion and of stone-tool evolution. You can see how the development of tools more or less parallels the evolution of hominid brain size. To be sure, the oldest stone tools discovered to date appeared two million years later than a recently discovered hominid, *Australopithecus ramidus* (White, Suwa, and Asfaw 1994; renamed *Ardipithecus ramidus*, White, Suwa, and Asfaw 1995; see Appendix). Nonetheless, the appearance of these artifacts, called Oldowan pebble tools, corresponded to the temporal span of the later members of that genus.

When we look at a pebble tool, which is essentially a cobble about the size

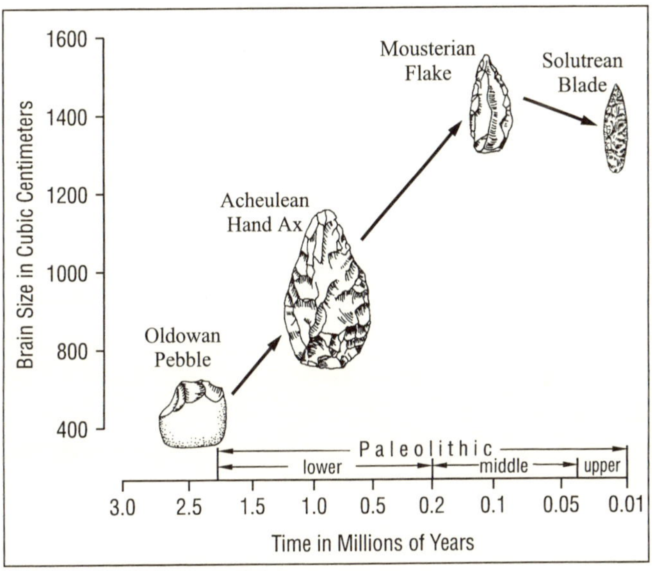

FIG. 2. Evolution of the mind at work

Denver, Colorado) gave a further glimpse at the "looseness" between hominid species and tool type. At the Dmanisi site in the Republic of Georgia, hominid remains belonging to *Homo erectus*, or, as some prefer, *Homo ergaster*—in any case, pre-*sapiens*—are associated not with hand axes but with Oldowan pebbles, the type ordinarily associated with earlier hominids, the australopithecines. Several possible reasons, all more or less speculative at this stage, suggest themselves. The one most consistent with the "social intelligence hypothesis" advanced here is that the increase in brain size between the australopithecines and the pre-*sapiens* is an adaptive response to the dilemmas posed by increased reliance on symbolic communication and that greater sophistication in tool type comes about later as a "spillover" from developments in symbolic communication that center on social relations.

of a fist, with flakes knocked off, do we see what *Australopithecus* saw? We see a dexterous hand, for sure, a hand that was capable of force and precision (Susman 1994, 1998). Even among the earliest tools discovered, ones that date back to 2.5 million years ago, we note an understanding of how stone splits and of how some stone splits better than others (Semaw et al. 1997). But in the thousands of years of unspecialized cores and flakes, we perhaps also see wishful thinking, aspirations that luck turned into an employable edge. One has the impression that *Australopithecus* banged away, one cobble against another, until something emerged that he, or she, could use (Wynn 1989).

When we look at the next tool type archaeologists have excavated, however, we see less wishful thinking and more controlled knowledge. These tools are generally larger than the pebble tools and are much more stylized. Many, particularly the later forms, have bilateral symmetry both in plan view and in cross section. Retouched by a knowing hand and a sharp eye, many have a long, straight cutting edge. Archaeologists suggest they were multipurpose tools, grasped in the hand to slice, stab, and crush; one innovative thinker has even argued the artifacts were hurled, discuslike, through the air to thump the heads of unlucky prey some yards away (O'Brien 1981). All agree the hominid using them—more than likely and for the most part pre-*sapiens* such as *Homo erectus*—did not haft them, so the hominid interpreters of today call the tool type a hand ax.

The next type, called Mousterian after an important site, Le Moustier in France, was likely hefted by its maker, the Neandertal. Unlike the hand ax, which is the core of the stone worked, the Mousterian tool begins with the flake knocked off the core. The flake is then retouched with a hammer stone or bone punch to produce a razorlike cutting edge.

While Mousterian tools are broadly, though certainly not exclusively, associated with Neandertals, the subsequent type of tool more commonly appeared in conjunction with the presence of anatomically modern people, like you and me. These Stone Age *sapiens sapiens* first reduced the core material into rectangular-shaped blanks and struck from the blanks long, thin blades, which they retouched to produce exemplary works of flint-knapping art. If you examine these tools, particularly those called Solutrean after the small village of Solutré, France, you gain the strong impression the tools were much finer than required for the assigned tasks.

The development of tools permitted the hand and the eye to produce other tools and material items not preserved in the archaeological record, so that gradually hominids created an environment built between themselves and nature. The production of this environment roughly parallels, as mentioned, the increase in brain size (and other anatomical changes, such as the decrease in the size of the face and the reorganization of the vocal tract). Furthermore, both tool development and increase in brain size accompanied the expansion of hominids from Africa (*Australopithecus*) to Asia and southern Europe (pre-*sapiens*), to northern Europe (archaic *sapiens*, such as the Neandertals), and then (with modern *sapiens sapiens)* throughout the Old World and, by at least 15,000 years ago, into the New. At this point, forgive me for taking an anthropocentric pause and asking: Is not this a record of achievement? Is not this a story of epic accomplishment? Is not this an account that we may feel honored today to contribute to?

Although I have tried to warn against it, the recitation of tool types seemingly shapes the understanding of ourselves as creatures preoccupied with getting food. Granted when the belly rumbles, it is hard to ignore. So if you are hungry now, go to McDonald's and order a Big Mac with double cheese, but hurry back because I need you. And surely along the way it will not be lost on you that even when the belly calls, you crunch on calories enriched with advertised meaning.

As critical as the food quest is to human welfare, a more difficult problem for us humans may be ourselves. Indeed, some argue that we need to replace the present labels that purport to encapsulate the distinctive qualities of humans, such as "Man the Tool Maker" and "Man the Hunter," with "Man the Social Animal" (Lewin 1998). They point to the apparent paradox of monkeys and apes being much smarter than they need to be to secure a full stomach. If such is the case, then what accounts for primate intelligence? In brief, the fluid nature of primate society. Individual primates, from baboons to chimpanzees, are constantly at work assessing each other's behavior, forming alliances, learning the subtleties of dominance hierarchies, sharing in the pleasure of grooming, and even devising ways to deceive those in power (Byrne and Whiten 1988; De Waal 1993). While this "social intelligence hypothesis" has its critics (Kummer et al. 1997) and even deflectors (Fischman 1993), it does have its strong supporters (Dunbar 1998). Criticism aside, most investigators would probably agree with an earlier assessment that to "do well for oneself whilst remaining within the term of the social contract on which the fitness of the whole community ultimately depends" (Humphrey 1976,

310) calls for considerable social skills. And those with the highest social skills, which may well include the maintenance of long-term friendships (Smuts 1985), will have the greatest reproductive success. Therefore, selection in the hominid line is likely to have centered on the more effective ways of creating social relations. Beck, for example, after his extensive review of animal tool use, concludes "that socio-economic and communicative behaviors were more important than tool behavior in the evolution of hominid intelligence" (1980, 246). Development in tool technology has been more or less a side effect—an extremely important one, to be sure—of that enhanced capacity to communicate what we want from each other, or maybe even how we want others to want, that is, to see us.[8]

Now, we see, I hope, the true importance of the big brain and its evolution in the hominid lineage. Broadly, and I feel correctly, interpreted, the development of tools points to a record of the brain enlarging in response to selective pressures for communicative behavior based on symbols. Throughout the journey from *Australopithecus* to us, evolution selected for those best equipped, in anatomy and temperament, to endow the experiential world of sounds, objects, and actions with social meaning. Arising out of the experiential world of the eye and the hand but always tied to it, the world of endowed meaning, the world of communicating with symbols, that is, culture, became our mode of being. The trajectory that we see in the hominid record is the trajectory of the humanization process, of hominids becoming more and more efficient at creating culture. The outcome of the journey is that without culture we would not be just another ape sharing the trees with the chimpanzee; we, in the sense of you who are reading this and I who am writing it, would be a turtle without its shell, an eagle without its feathers, a seal without its fur, that is to say, we would not be at all (Geertz 1973). In the classic statement of Sherwood Washburn, one of the major formulators of modern biological anthropology, "Our species only survives in culture, and in a profound sense, we are the product of the new selection pressures that came with culture" (1962, 28). For us today, for you and me, the symbol—cast as a tool,

8. Citing some of the same authors and in a manner paralleling the humanization process described here, Steven Mithen (1994) attributes the emergence of visual symbolism in the Upper Paleolithic, such as cave art, to the transfer of social intelligence to other domains of activity. Furthermore, accounting for such a transfer "is not dependent upon a change in hominid species or population replacement" (36) but is best thought of as an "across-the-board" process occurring throughout the hominid range. See Appendix.

performed as an act, or spoken as a word—is as fundamental to our being as the foot.

We have arrived, if you have stayed with me thus far, at the position where we can say that the emergence of upright stature launched us upon our endeavor. We can also say that the same evolutionary process that brought forth the foot transformed hominids into humans through selecting those hominids best equipped to communicate to one another with symbols. But at what point did we first say, "You are; I am"? To address that question, we need to consider the nature of symbolic communication. First, I must make sure you understand what I mean by "symbol" and "symbolic communication." By "symbol" I mean a unit to which an arbitrary value has been assigned. In speech, the unit is sound; in tools and other artifacts, the unit is material; and in action, the unit is behavior. By "arbitrary value," I mean that the value, or the meaning, of a symbol cannot be reduced to the physical properties of the unit that conveys the symbol. Take holy water, to use an example of Leslie White (1949), one of the first anthropologists to define culture as symbolic behavior: The significance of holy water, its "holiness," cannot be deduced from the physical composition of water. The "holiness" of holy water constitutes a reality both embedded in the medium of water but also independent of it. This "duality of existence" is the fundamental quality of symbolic communication. The symbol itself cannot exist without the physical medium; yet its value cannot be deduced from the properties of the medium. It matters, of course, and matters tremendously, what the medium is—water, sound, stone, or behavior—but the meaning of the value embedded in that medium cannot be reduced to the physical, chemical makeup of the medium. In sum, the medium is the conveyer and the meaning is the conveyed, and the two have a relationship like this page. On one side is the conveyer and on the other the conveyed; together they compose the symbol.

Haven't I heard this somewhere before? you ask. Yes, I reply. The formulation duplicates that of Ferdinand de Saussure, the founder, many would say, of semiotics and structuralism. In his original casting, the conveyer is the signifier and the conveyed is the signified, and the two relate together like the sides of a page to form the sign (1986). I use "symbol" rather than "sign" in conformity with White's earlier usage and with Clifford Geertz's later application. I also prefer "symbol" over "sign" because I do not wish to restrict symbolic communication to language, especially the language that many linguists are so fond of: a disembodied syntactic structure floating free of us speakers. Symbolic communication (which, by the way, is another term for thinking) is a trafficking in words, to be sure, but also in "gestures, drawings, musical sounds, mechanical devices like clocks or material objects like jewels—anything that is disengaged from its mere actuality and used to impose meaning upon experience" (Geertz 1973, 45).[9]

In imposing meaning upon experience, symbolic communication is not restricted to passing technological, how-to information from my head to yours. To be sure, I'd like you to know how to make an Acheulean hand ax, a Mousterian flake, or a Solutrean blade, along with many other things like riding a bike, driving a car, and "saving this text on your hard drive." Symbolic communication, in the sense used here and throughout our conversation, is "constructivist"; that is, it creates conditions, a setting, a place, where you respond to me in the way I hope, sometimes desperately, you will wish to respond.

So now, you ask optimistically, are we getting back to "You are; I am"?

We are getting close, I respond. To proceed we must make a dramatic switch from considering the earthy fossil record to pondering a contemporary philosophy widely cursed and blessed. Sounds like our cup of tea, you remark. Well, we'll see, I say with some necessary caution. The philosophy is known as deconstructionism, and its principal articulator is the French philosopher Jacques Derrida.

With the publication of *Of Grammatology* (1976), *Writing and Difference* (1978), and a series of later works, Jacques Derrida has enlarged our vocabulary with the likes of "logocentrism," "phonocentrism," and "the absence of the transcendental signified." Of immediate significance is his concept of "arche-writing." Arche-writing is that quality of symbolic communication that gives rise not just to writing in the conventional sense, which developed for the first time around 4000 B.C. in the Near East and independently in the New World around 700 B.C. in Mexico, but to inscription in general, including "cinematography, choreography [and] pictorial, musical, sculptural 'writing'" (1976, 9).

Linguists have long stressed that native speakers distinguish the sounds of

9. As you indicate in your question (Haven't I heard this somewhere before?), when you and I talk to one another, we do so in the intimacy of silence, without "". When others speak, and when we speak to them, that speech is public and so is placed between quotation marks.

their language by how the sounds differ. Saussure spoke in italics when he said, "*In the language itself, there are only differences,*" and added, "A linguistic system is a series of phonetic differences matched with a series of conceptual differences" (1986, 118). This means, for example, English speakers—and though born a Texan, I include myself in that category—distinguish the sound / p /, as in pill, not by any particular inherent characteristic of that sound but by the manner in which it contrasts with other sounds, such as / b / in bill, / t / in till, / g / in gill, and so on. Having recognized that the signification of / p / resides in the silent space between it and other sounds, linguists, nonetheless, proceed as if / p / has a presence by itself. They are guilty of "logocentrism" in that they privilege presence over absence. They do so, Derrida charges, because they, as scientists looking for objects to study, are enamored both with sound and presence. (Admittedly, as you point out, the possibility of a science based on silence and absence poses certain difficulties.) Because of their love affair with sound and presence, linguists privilege speech over writing in the ordinary sense. Writing, Saussure wrote, "obscures our view of language. Writing is not a garment, but a disguise" (1986, 29). Saussure and the rest, Derrida explains, are arguing that speech is primary and writing secondary. The insistence on the primacy of speech over writing, on being "phonocentric," carries with it a whole series of other privileged dichotomies, such as presence over representation, reality over image, interiority over exteriority. These dichotomies ignore that their properties come not from any inherent quality that each has but in the manner in which they differ from each other. What is that manner? The manner of differing?

To disclose the manner of differing, Derrida employs the concept of "differance." Differance is a neologism that combines "difference" and "defer." In symbolic communication, to put the matter in my simplified terms, the meaning of a symbol differs from the symbol itself; otherwise it would not be a symbol. Since the meaning cannot be derived directly from the symbol, it can be determined only by the presence of other symbols; that is, the meaning is deferred. And the meaning of *those* symbols? you ask. Their meaning is also deferred and dependent upon other symbols. And those *other* symbols? Likewise, their meaning is deferred and dependent upon subsequent symbols. Then there is no essential meaning? no core essence? Exactly. There is only differance. "This means that differance makes the opposition of presence and absence possible. Without the possibility of differance, the desire of presence as such would not find its breathing-space. That means by the same token that this desire carries in itself the destiny of its non-satisfaction. Differance produces what it forbids, makes possible the very thing that it makes impossible" (Derrida 1976, 143).[10]

Despite the protest of poets and other true believers, the meaning of symbols is never fixed in their sounds but is implemented in one another. Symbols yearn for presence; but in their presence, in their difference from what they purport to symbolize, and in their constant deferral of meaning, they convey absence. When we became human, we primates spoke and discovered absence (Richardson 2001).

So the question "At what time did we first say, 'You are; I am'?" asks another question in all its paradoxical reverberations: "At what point did hominids signify absence?" In other words, At what time did the dialectic between sound and silence, presence and absence, begin?, which is to ask, "When did hominids become human?"

In returning to consider the evolution of tools as indicators of humanization, we might suggest that the transition was underway certainly by the time pre-*sapiens* such as *Homo erectus* were producing hand axes and that by the time *Homo sapiens sapiens* was turning flakes into Solutrean points, the process had obtained its current, contemporary human state. So hominids became human somewhere in the interval between *erectus* and *sapiens sapiens*. Such a consideration points to the archaic *sapiens* and the Neandertals, and as a matter of fact, our first direct evidence of the capacity to signify absence comes from the Neandertal record.

From the time of the first discovery of Neandertal remains, in the valley of the Neander River in Germany in 1856, these hominids have caused consternation among the experts. One early assessment considered the Neandertal the carcass of antediluvian man, the type of man that failed to make it into Noah's ark when, according to Genesis, God wiped the world clean with a universal deluge. Another commentary, one somewhat unsympathetic to Gallic sensitivities, labeled it the skeleton of a French soldier left over from the Napoleonic Wars. Gradually, with additional discoveries of fossil homi-

10. Kenneth Burke (1966), from a position not unlike that of Derrida but advanced a decade or so before *Of Grammatology*, argued that as we are symbol-making, symbol-using creatures, we are consequently "inventors of the negative." Possessing the negative moves us to define what is by what is not, to exalt the virtues of saints by listing the characteristics of sinners. Thus, Burke concluded, the very ability to use words carries with it a sense of the not-there.

nids, recognition of the Neandertals' importance grew, yet they remained a caricature of ourselves (Figure 3).

Not until the 1960s did paleoanthropologists begin to see a greater affinity between Neandertals and modern *sapiens.* This reassessment led many to consider the Neandertals members not only of the genus *Homo* but also of the species *sapiens.* Their uniqueness warranted their designation as a subspecies, *neanderthalensis.* In this arrangement, their full scientific designation is *Homo sapiens neanderthalensis,* while ours is *Homo sapiens sapiens.* Among the fossil hominids, they are our closest kin, as you can see in Figure 4. (See Spencer 1984 and especially Smith 1997 for historical overviews.)

FIG. 3. The image of Neandertal that earned the epithet "Neanderthal." From Smith (1997); see also Moser (1992).

FIG. 4. The Neandertal as kin. Adapted from a painting by Maurice Wilson in Andrews and Stringer (1989).

Despite their classification in the 1960s as *sapiens*, Neandertals remain controversial. Even the spelling of the word is an issue: to modernize in accordance with German spelling reforms and drop the now archaic "h" in "tha," or to preserve tradition and retain the "h"? As you can see, I have followed the reforms, except in the case of the scientific name *neanderthalensis*. Beyond spelling, paleoanthropologists are sharply divided today, more than ever. Some argue that the Neandertal features, particularly those of the "classical Neandertal"—sloping forehead, bony ridges above the eyes, and general bulkiness, including an exceptionally large brain—place them outside our immediate ancestry, while others insist with equal passion that the Neandertals are a population component of the archaic, earlier *sapiens* from which we evolved. In the latter view, the late appearance of the "classical features," the 1,500-cubic-centimeter brain being one, is nothing more than ourselves subject to a particular set of evolutionary circumstances. I refer you to the Appendix, where I have attempted to present the current debate. I must warn you, however, that I am pro-Neandertal. Being from the South, how could I be otherwise?

The most noteworthy feature of the Neandertals, however, was not their physiognomy but their behavior. Judging by the excavation of Neandertal sites, we find that when a Neandertal died, the living prepared a pit, placed the body in it, and often positioned around it an array of other items, especially tools of flint or bone but also in separate cases goat horns and the lower jaw of a wild boar (Rowlett and Schneider 1974). The most arresting case of Neandertal behavior occurred some 60,000 years ago in a cave in Shanidar, Iraq, where, as indicated by pollen analysis of soil samples, a bed of flowers was laid around the dead body of a Neandertal man (Figure 5; Solecki 1971, 1989).

As you might suspect, given the controversies surrounding the Neandertals, the burials are not without their critics. In the eyes of some, what we see

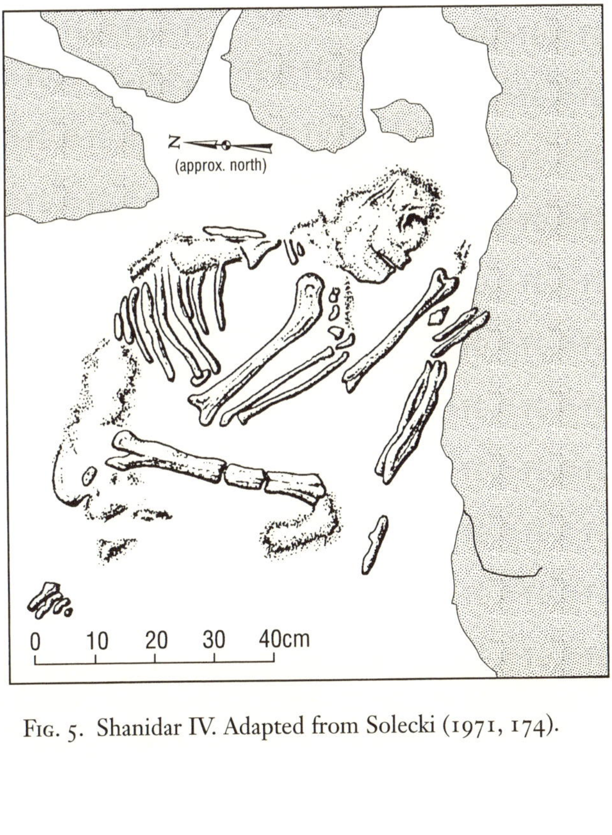

Fig. 5. Shanidar IV. Adapted from Solecki (1971, 174).

in these excavations are the random juxtapositions of artifacts and skeletal material produced by naturally occurring processes of deposition and erosion and thus are not evidence of Neandertal behavior. The grave goods, the tools, the goat horns, the jaw of the wild boar are simply coincidental accumulations brought together with the skeletal material by chance. And the bed of flowers in Shanidar? The pollen in the soil surrounding the Neandertal remains testifies not to loving care but to an idle wind that blew the seed into the cave. Others, however, argue the living Neandertals scooped out pits and positioned the corpses and artifacts into these pits and thus, in fact, buried their dead. Again I ask you to turn to the Appendix for an overview of the scholarly altercation, which continues even as you read these words.

If we accept the Neandertal evidence as burials, what do we see? Do we see in pit and artifact a belief? You might respond yes, a belief in an afterlife, a concern that the dead make their journey to a spiritual realm beyond both cave and grave. I would reply that we do indeed see a concern, but as at any funeral it is not a concern for the dead; it is a concern for the living.

When the Neandertals scooped out the pit and laid one of their kind into its embrace, they created a place distinct from surrounding nature. In their actions, they recognized their own, the dead, as being different from just another bit of smelly debris. In creating a place, they gave voice to a quality among themselves that was beyond the physicality of the body, dead or alive. This is the quality we recognized in prehistoric tools, at least since the hand ax and certainly in Mousterian flakes. It is the quality referred to earlier when I spoke of the duality of existence in symbolic communication. Symbolic communication, being a trafficking in symbols, creates meaning whose value cannot be deduced from the physical properties of the material medium in which it is embedded. The Neandertal burial differs from the dead remains in that it imposes its meaning upon the remains. Consequently, the burial speaks to us today and asks us to consider its significance.

Looking at the excavated graves, if we were among those so honored with the opportunity, or looking at the drawings of the graves, we can ponder the significance of the Neandertals' action. The fundamental significance of the actions, I submit, is that the actions signified *to* the Neandertals.

In saying that their actions signified to the Neandertals, I suggest that, having imposed meaning upon the body, they then reflected upon the meaning itself. The message of the graves is the Neandertal capacity to reflect upon and act toward meaning itself. In reflecting upon and acting toward meaning, the members of the burial group gave voice to their feelings. Giving voice to their feelings means they not only spoke to us across the millennia; they spoke to themselves. In speaking to themselves in deed and in sound, in proclaiming, "You are; I am," the Neandertals offer us the first direct evidence of a two-legged primate with a consciousness of self.

The self, you ask? Now what is that (if, indeed, it is a what)? The self is, in fact, a the; it is an object, but it is a who object, not a what object. Now, that's clear, you sarcastically insert. The self is a who object, not a what object, I, unfazed, repeat, and being such, it is the object of much thinking by thinkers in numerous fields, from philosophy to sociology. We will return to the self again and again, so let me say that the concepts presented here draw largely from the social behaviorist, George Herbert Mead (1972; Strauss 1964; Richardson and Dunton 1989). In Mead's presentation, the self is not an entity that is antecedent to action, but rather it emerges out of social exchanges. The meaning of me is located in your responses; likewise, the meaning of you, despite your insistence that you are you no matter what, resides in my actions. The self, in short, is the outcome of the capacity you have and I have to reflect back upon the meaning of our actions. When we reflect upon the meaning of what we are doing, we recognize that we each have an identity, called "Miles" in my case and "you" in yours. Our recognition imposes upon the experience of living an objectivity that transforms the experience into "You" and "me." "You" and "I" are bounded in some way. I recognize myself, just as you do, when I reach for a piece of your Big Mac, and you say, Stop it! That's mine. If you are hungry, go get one yourself. Note, again, that I recognize my-self in the context of your actions. Your response to my actions defines us both. The self, our individual identity, perhaps our most precious possession, is very much a social construct. Indeed, the proper way to say "You are; I am" is not with a semicolon that separates the two selves, but with a hyphen that joins them, as in "You are-I am."[11]

The self, created out of our capacity to act toward meaning, is the awareness that you and I have that we exist. We do not hide that awareness in some deep crevice in our brain, but with the hand and the mouth we place it out

11. Intriguingly, Mead stressed the hand in accounting for the emergence of the reflexive self. The hand stops the otherwise continuous stream of experience and permits us to reflect upon that experience and thereby objectify it. Mead went so far as to say that speech and "the hand go along together in the development of the social human being" (Mead 1972, 237). For an insightful, and still relevant, application of Mead's ideas to sociobiology, see Barkow 1978.

before us so that we may ponder its significance. The marvelous cave art and the carved figurines produced by anatomically modern humans, *sapiens sapiens*, toward the end of the Pleistocene Ice Age, provide abundant evidence of the awareness of self and its outward articulation. Yet this development of art rests upon the earlier discovery by the Neandertals.

Being aware that I exist means that I am aware of threats to that existence. The single most damaging threat is the awareness that I may, and no doubt surely will, die.

In the same manner that the self is a construct apart from the physical body, so the awareness of death is a construct apart from the biological process of dying. When the Neandertals laid one of their kind into his or her grave, they attempted to maintain that one's identity, even in the face of the biological process of death. In their actions, the body became not simply an object occupying space but an object with meaning, a presence. Perhaps it is not too much to say that in burying their dead, the Neandertals constructed a presence that is not-there, the presence of death.[12]

Experience and Symbol

When the Neandertals dug the pit and positioned objects of worked stone or bone within it, they created a material setting apart from the natural surrounding. The setting became a site for interaction as they collected the dead

12. The link between "self" and "death" derives in the first place from Hallowell (1960) and secondarily from Dobzhansky (1965) and Becker (1973). These ideas closely parallel Botscharow's argument that archaeological sites, and specifically Mousterian-Neandertal sites, may be read as text. When interpreted as text, sites become documents, documents that were created and read by the document makers. In the case of burial sites, burials mark a distinction between the living and the dead. "The unburied dead create a conceptual quandary for categorizing beings: they are both here and gone, both human beings and refuse. They are ambiguous because they cross boundaries. They must be put in their place. . . . One place is to bury them" (Botscharow 1989, 153). The Neandertal burials, I have argued, are our first direct evidence of the self-concept in the hominid lineage. The concept may have evolved earlier, with *Homo erectus*, as the reflexivity present in the crafted hand axes suggests (Botscharow 1990; see also Wynn's [1989] analysis that hand-ax knapping required an intelligence equivalent to our own). Conversely, given the great social changes occurring between the Middle Paleolithic and now, there is no reason to propose that we humans have not become more intensely conscious of our individuality. We modern, or even postmodern, types, however, have no monopoly on existential anxiety. The threat of not-being, of death, haunts any creature that carries the name "human."

body and laid it in the pit. The conjunction of the setting and the interaction produced an image that conveys the meaning of the place; the grave image told the Neandertals, as millennia later it tells us, that the self struggles to continue in the face of death. For the first time in the journey from hominid to human, the Neandertals, in burying their dead, attempted to put death in its place.

With the emergence of a reflexive self, Neandertals also came to know death, not only as a biological process, but also as a boundary of the self. The awareness of existence brought with it an awareness of nonexistence; self and death, I and nothing, became linked in a dialectic that haunts us today perhaps even more than it did the Neandertal. "To put death in its place" means our attempt to depict death as inoperative, to render its finality less final, to resolve the glaring contradiction that we are both creatures of flesh and blood and selves that strive for significance. No one has posed this paradox more eloquently than Ernest Becker: "Man has a symbolic identity that brings him sharply out of nature. He is a symbolic self, a creature with a name, a life history. . . . Yet, at the same time . . . man is a worm and food for worms. . . . Man is literally split in two: he has an awareness of his own splendid uniqueness in that he sticks out of nature with a towering majesty, and yet he goes back into the ground a few feet in order blindly and dumbly to rot and disappear forever" (1973, 26).

The human endeavor, then, is an ongoing effort to resolve the existential paradox in which we find ourselves a creature like any other but possessing a name and a destiny unlike any other. What kind of creature are we?[13]

As always when I seek reassurance, I ask, Where are you? To my relief, you announce, Here. In your reply, however, you demonstrate your likeness to the material world. You are an object like any other—pebble, rock, or star—and have geographical coordinates. You can be located on a map. People can point to you and say to each other, "What a curiosity."

Yet because you are alive, you are "there" in a manner distinct from an inorganic object, like a rock. To be alive, I know you will agree, is a wonderful experience: joy, grief, love, hate, and loneliness. Living is not easy, despite the song, but it's liv-ing, with a ring.

13. Thomas Henry Huxley, the eloquent defender of Charles Darwin's theory of natural selection, observed, "The question of questions for mankind—the problem which underlies all others, and is more deeply interesting than any other—is the ascertainment of the place which Man occupies in nature" (Huxley 1902, 77).

Yes, being alive is a wonderful thing, but even you may hesitate to embrace kinship with the snake slithering across the yard, the vulture ripping apart a road kill, or the female baboon glowing in estrus. The human reluctance to admit membership in the kingdom of life is widespread. Either we make animals like us and bestow upon them human properties of speech and thought, as in the case of animistic religion practiced by many of the hunters and horticulturists of world (and by cat lovers like my wife and me) or we seek to erect an impenetrable wall between them and us by reserving all of the "higher" qualities of reason and faith to ourselves. The latter argument was the one that Charles Darwin and his friend and spokesman, Thomas Huxley, had to face down. It was the one William Jennings Bryan used to persecute a high school biology teacher in the famous "Scopes Monkey Trial" in 1925. And it is the one that continues today in the guise of a scientific creationism that demands equal time for its biblical message in public classrooms.

Why this antipathy toward other life forms? After all, as we said, life lives. It's liv-ing, with a ring. A rock cannot hold the hand of a loved one or smile at a baby's delight. Nor can it see the sun rise through the sprawling oaks in late September, when the cool air of the first front tells me, once more, why I'm home in Louisiana.

But somewhere inside me, I hear a small boy say, Nothing hurts a rock.

Nothing hurts a rock; that's true, you tell me. But you are not a rock. We are intensely alive. And if it hurts, this business of being alive, you remind me of the gentle hand, the baby's delight, and the new dawn filtering through the majestic oaks.

As warm-blooded mammals, we come equipped with an array of sensory devices. In the course of our evolution, the foot, the hand, the eye, the mouth, and the skin flooded the brain with information, and the brain adapted to that flood of data by increasing in size. Today, we are continually organizing experiential data, and not uncommonly we use the body to assist us in that organization (Figure 6).

Let me say that the anthropologist in me resists the idea that everyone everywhere employs this model. And indeed many languages are said not to use the body to establish coordinates, nor do they use the symbolism of left and right (Levinson 1996). Yet the same anthropologist agrees that Christians are especially prone to its charm. In this particular model, space that is ahead, above, and to the right of the body has a greater positive value than space

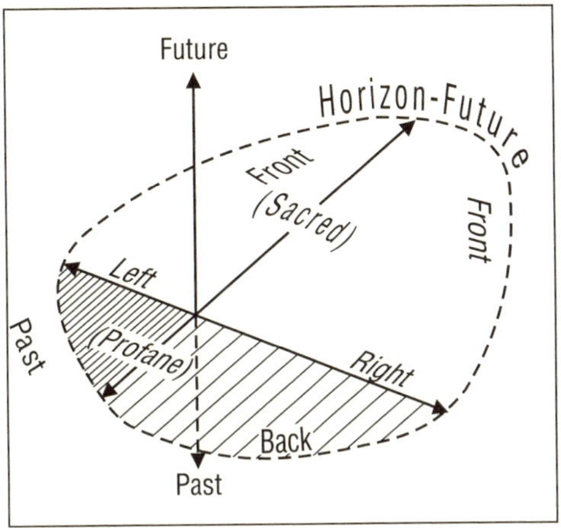

Fig. 6. A model of the body as an organizer of space and time. From Tuan (1977, 35).

that is behind, below, and to the left. Translated into time, the future beckons ahead and above, and the past fades behind and beneath. Translated into Christian cosmology, heaven rises above, hell resides below, and in the heavenly kingdom, Jesus sits at the right hand of the Father (Mark 16:19). And did not Jesus himself say to the tempter, "Get thee behind me, Satan. . . . [Thou] savourest not the things that be of God, but those that be of men" (Matthew 16:23)? And does not this mean that the things of God, the sacred sphere, extend ahead while the things of men and of Satan, the profane sphere, are best put behind our backs? To be sure, circumstances, factual and mythical, distort the model, as in the American South, where the chivalrous past, lost forever in defeat, becomes more sacred than the federally mandated future. Even the Christian schema is not straightforward. Not only do Christians look ahead to the second coming of Christ; they look behind to the first coming. As the later chapters explain, the aim of both Catholic and Baptist worship is to bring those holy days when Jesus walked on the Sea of Galilee (John 6:19) into the present. The very deviations of the model, however, show the model's claim upon our organizing of experience.

We use the body as a device to structure the experiential world about us; we also use each other. Being not only mammals but also close kin to the gorilla and the chimpanzee means being in the presence of one another. In our face-to-face encounters, we position ourselves spatially. We seek the appropriate distance to tell one another what we desire. If I want to share a secret with you, I don't shout it across the room for all and sundry to hear but approach your space, and you rightly anticipate by my stance that a secret is on its way. Conversely, sometimes we are too much for one another; the demands take more than we can give. In such moments, we long to flee the madding crowd. We seek the quiet so we may meditate on what it is we are about. In fact, we are often stretched between the near and the far, between the close and the distant, between sociality and solitude.

In replying Here to my question Where are you?, you announced yourself as an object and as a sentient being. "Here" established the physicality of your existence, the what of your being, but as a human, and at least since the Neandertals, you are also a who. Again, Ernest Becker: "But man is not just a blind glob of idling protoplasm, but a creature with a name, who lives in a world of symbols and dreams and not merely matter. . . . Society itself is a codified hero system, which means that society everywhere is a living myth of the significance of human life, a defiant creation of meaning" (1973, 3, 7). The who, of course, is another word for the self. When I asked, Where are you?, and you replied, Here, I took it that you meant not only that you occupied geographic coordinates as an animate object but also that the who, the self you claim to be, was presence.

Let me ask another question: Which is more real, the what of you, which I can see and feel, or the who, which I can neither see nor feel? The answer, in case you are still heavily into your materialistic phrase, is both. Yet how the what and the who, the sensible and the intelligible, occupy the same space (you!) remains mysterious, which is just another name for human.

To elucidate the mystery, to heighten its charm rather than to solve its puzzle, I want to turn to a man I do not understand but whose concepts are especially suitable to this endeavor of ours: Martin Heidegger.

As a young academic hoping to impress his senior professors in the late 1920s, Heidegger published a work that not only got their attention but made him famous. Arguably, *Being and Time* (1962) is one of the most important books in twentieth-century thought. In the turmoil of the 1930s in Germany, however, Heidegger joined the National Socialist German Workers' Party. He did so, his defenders insist, to protect his university, and despite public pronouncements, he soon became disillusioned with Nazism. His critics, however, point out that he never publicly repudiated his affiliation or addressed the question of German guilt for the Holocaust.

The issue, difficult and contentious, remains: How much of a person's biography should shape our judgment of that person's works? Are biography and work so tied that the mistakes of one destroy the contribution of the other? Frankly, I am unable to answer. My only solution at the moment is to suspend judgment about Heidegger's life—or let others more knowledgeable, and more ready with their stones, do the judging (Farías 1989; Rockmore and Margolis 1992; Harvey 1990)—and turn to the work itself.

In a manner that any anthropologist would applaud, in *Being and Time* Heidegger begins his explication of human beings as we are in our everyday mode of being. So the image of human beings is not that of the isolated philosopher sitting alone in his study in a house of thought where each room is occupied by other isolated and distant thinkers; rather, the image is of us in our most everyday, taken-for-granted, conventional life.

To convey this image of us engaged in the everyday task of being human, in *Being and Time*, which breaks new ground linguistically as well as conceptually, Heidegger rarely uses *menschlich*, human, or *die Menschheit*, humanity. Instead, he substitutes *Dasein*, as in: "The answer to the question of the 'who' of everyday Dasein is to be obtained by analyzing that kind of Being in which Dasein maintains itself proximally and for the most part" (153).

Dasein ordinarily translates as existence. If, however, we take the word apart, a technique permissible in German and one that Heidegger employs to great effect, we find *da*, which is "there," and *sein*, or "to be." Consequently, *Dasein*, the noun Heidegger substitutes for human, literally means "being-there." "Being-there" suggests that in the very act of existing, we are at work. Consequently, in our conventional life, the one in which we maintain ourselves "proximally and for the most part," we may describe ourselves as being deeply engaged in constructing our lives.

Being engaged in our work expands the spatiality of our being to an "aroundness," not unlike that drawn in Figure 6, that encompasses all that the hand touches and in particular the working tool that the hand reaches for. As the hand reaches, the tool makes itself, in Heidegger's words, "ready-to-hand." The tool, the hand, and the who conjoin in such a fashion that the who extends to the tool and perhaps even beyond. Let's take the carpenter that you have hired to build a shed in your backyard as an illustration. When the carpenter is at work, as he is now, the who extends out to the hammer that drives the nail through the siding that he is attaching to the shed's studs. The acts of building, erecting the studs, laying down the roof, nailing on the siding constitute the spatiality of the carpenter's self. In turn, the shed, as it rises, literally objectifies the acts of the carpenter's self. In the same manner that the hand ax, the Mousterian flake, and the Solutrean flake did for his predecessors, the carpenter's shed materially testifies to his presence.

Once the shed is finished and the acts of building are completed, however, the carpenter turns the shed over to you, throws his hammer into the toolbox, and moves on. He disengages from that work which defines him. His work is no longer that which he was involved in but now becomes something apart from him and distant. The shed he built is yours. And if he takes his hammer from his toolbox and sets it in front of him to examine in the manner of a dispassionate observer, who assumes no understanding of the carpenter's craft, a startling transformation occurs. Under such distancing gaze, the hammer ceases to be that which he uses to drive nails and becomes simply another object among the array of objects external to his being. The hammer loses its defining, artifactual character and becomes a naked object stripped of the carpenter's understanding; it becomes an object simply, again in Heidegger's words, "present-at-hand." Because Heidegger's disclosure of our ability to switch from being engaged in work that defines our existence, when what we hold is ready-to-hand, to being disengaged from it and its products so that they become present-at-hand is so central to this endeavor in which *we* are engaged, I need to address the distinction more fully.

First, the distinction relates to the earlier points made about the hand and the eye. The hand engages us with all that is around us. It establishes the spatiality of our selves as being beyond the interior of the body and, through the tools that it holds and the artifacts it shapes, beyond the fingers tips. The hand links us and our work. The eye, conversely, has the capacity to disengage us from what we do. It distinguishes between our selves and our work, and it positions the work as outside the sphere of our selves. Under its distancing gaze, what we have done turns into objects external to our being. Objects go from ready-to-hand to present-at-hand. What the hand joins, the eye separates.

Being engaged and being disengaged pairs also with the distinction between self and object, between the who and the what. When we are engaged in our everyday lives, we live in a rich context of taken-for-granted understandings. Upon seeing you, I extend out my hand and smile the joy of our friendship. It lies within you, however, to view my smile as the movement of facial muscles responding to nerve impulses. The treasured understandings are stripped from me, and I become a denuded object fixed by your baleful eye. Under such inspection, the who I claim to be devolves into a what, and the friendship I understood we had evaporates.

From this distinction, it is only a skip to the distinction between being a participant and being a scientist. Being engaged means we participate in life's events as we understand them to become. As pilgrims, we journey to a Christian shrine in Buga, Colombia, which we both understand to be the location where during early colonial times an image of the crucified Lord was found in a stream. The ecclesiastical authorities were so convinced that it was associated with witchcraft they ordered the Lord burned. Despite its raging flames, the fire could only blacken the image. Today, we travel to see with the pilgrim's understanding eye its dark presence, to touch, if we can, its miraculous being, and to thank it for healing the running sore in your leg. Being disengaged means we cannot see, much less touch, the understanding that the participants have, for we see them in the same manner that an astronomer sees the brief, intense luminosity of a supernova or that a microbiologist sees the rapid multiplication of the *Plasmodium* parasite in blood cells. To be sure, the disengaged vision of the astronomer or of the microbiologist discloses new understandings—the formation of the universe, the cause of malaria—but such a perspective turned upon us rather than upon wordless nature fails to do justice to the context in which we live our lives. For those determined to debunk religion, such a disengaged view pays great dividends, but for us anthropologists, whose job it is not to debunk but to present how participants construct meaningful lives, we seek a different perspective. This perspective aspires both to the skepticism of the disengaged and to the commitment of the engaged; we strive to be, in the language of the profession, both observers and participants. We stand at some distance from the believed-in basis of participants' understandings, but we want to see those understandings; we want to watch with a listening eye as we, too, travel to see, and even to touch, the dark Christ (Richardson 1995b).

Following Heidegger's disclosure of how we switch from being engaged in work that defines our existence to being disengaged from it and thereby stripping it of meaning has brought us to a view of the anthropologist's project. Later, I want to return to that project, for as you know, it is fundamental to *this* work; now, however, let us continue with Heidegger's disclosure of the who of *Dasein*.

As *Dasein*, Heidegger argues, we, in the acts of our existing, are "there";

we are engaged, and what we are engaged in is our work. This suggests a tie between us and our work. Indeed, the tie is of such nature that in our everyday life we and work are united, that selfhood and workhood are intertwined. To underscore that connection, Heidegger employs the phrase "being-in-the-world" (*In-der-Welt-sein*).

Being-in-the-world "stands for a *unitary* phenomenon. This primary datum must be seen as a whole" (Heidegger 1962, 78). Being-in is an active process that brings about the world in which we are. We are not in the world in the way the hammer is in the toolbox, inert and at rest, but we are in it in the way the hammer is in the hand and driving the nail through the plank to build the shed. We are-in-the-world actively, at work, creating our being.

You might think there is a great disparity between the writings of a German philosopher and the events engraved, as it were, in the fossil record. On the contrary, we see how this term of Heidegger's, being-in-the-world, aptly summarizes the humanization process reviewed earlier. Increasing efficiency with tools, as indicators of the broader process of symbolization, created an environment apart from nature. Symbolization distanced us from nature until, as evidenced by the Neandertal burials, we achieved capacity to reflect upon our own actions and to consider their creation. The outcome of the humanization process resulted in a two-legged primate who was, and is, condemned to create. For us humans to be, to be as humans, we must have a world to be in. But the world in which we are, we create.[14]

Being-in-the-world differs from other concepts social scientists have employed to describe the relationship between the human organism and its cultural environment. Some argue that culture is nothing more than a product of individual decisions, while others contest that culture is an impersonal force over which we have little control. Being-in-the-world, however, suggests that we employ culture to address one another's concerns, and out of that addressing we achieve a realization of who we are and an understanding of what we are up to. The world of being-in-the-world is neither the intrapsychic world of the idealist nor the overarching, deterministic sphere of the materialist but rather an intersubjective process. As an intersubjective proc-

14. "Condemned to create" is a paraphrasing of Jean-Paul Sartre's observation that in the absence of any external causality, supernatural or natural, we are, each of us, alone and consequently "condemned to be free" (1971, 34). Similarly, humanistic geographers, such as Tuan (1976), Buttimer (1976), and Ley and Samuels (1978), speak eloquently of worldhood, not as a system of abstract particles, but as a matrix for being.

ess, the world of being-in-the-world resides in the space between subjects, between you and me, like this text. In sum, culture is, in the words of Susan Parman, "a dynamic system of communication in which participants create, interpret, and maintain meaning in an ongoing dialogue with the anomalies of human existence" (1990, 26).

The world in which we humans are requires we are, together. As Heidegger expresses it, the "world of Dasein is a with-world" (1962, 155). In the same unitary manner we are in-the-world, we are with-each-other. As mammals, as I suggested earlier, and particularly as primates, we enjoy the physical proximity of each other, but beyond the physical intimacy, as self-conscious creatures, as possessors of names, we are, necessarily, together.

Hugh Duncan (1968), a student of Kenneth Burke's, summarizes how we are, together, in words especially resonant in today's postmodern discourse: "[We] create symbols in dialogue, not to measure space, but to name things, events, and relationships so [we] can act together" (104). "No social self exists, or exists in knowledge of itself, save in the responses of an other (real, fictive, or fantastic, as the case may be)" (100). "Even at the risk of suffering and death we seek out each other, for [we] are primarily *social* beings who must exist in terms of each other, even in destruction and death" (102). "We fear indifference more than hate, because we cannot address those who are indifferent to us, and we cannot be sure that if we do address them they will respond. Those who hate us *attend* to us, as we attend them" (104).

Words are the means by which we attend to each other. When we speak to one another and call one another's name, we are not simply transmitting technical information from one isolated entity to another, but we are establishing who we are in the context of our conversation. Words are equipment—tools—we employ in our day-to-day tasks of being you and me. In this respect, words build in the same manner as does the hammer in the hand. The mouth, when it speaks, and the hand, when it works, both create our human reality. Speaking and manipulating bring into being the world in which we are.

As Thiher (1984) makes clear, Heidegger sees language accomplishing its task in two ways. In our everyday life, we speak a conventional vocabulary of "How are you? I'm just fine, thank you." Because we are engrossed in the routine events of brushing teeth, leaving the house, greeting colleagues, having lunch, finishing classes, returning home, watching news, nodding off, and finally going to bed, we employ words that convey that routine. Indeed, we search for well-worn expressions that permit us to establish well-worn routines, for the last thing I want to do, while munching my salad at lunch with a mouth full of lettuce, is to respond to your self-important question: In light of September 11, 2001, do you believe that America has changed forever? At best, I might manage (with some subliminal sarcasm), We'll have to wait and see, but then I'd quickly move to They say the Tigers will go 8 and 3 this year and make the Sugar Bowl.

In contrast to the conventional vocabulary of the everyday, we find ourselves in moments that urge upon us a new way of speaking. This new way of speaking assaults the conventionality of our relationships and seeks to disclose a deeper understanding of what we are about. Heidegger believed that poetry is such a language. Poetry has the power to uncover relationships that we keep hidden or deny in everyday speech. It discloses the manner in which we seek to ignore that being-in-the-world is a with-world, a world in which we, you and I, require each other's presence in order to be. Other ways of speaking also claim a power to disclose a more fundamental reality. In subsequent chapters, we will see how religious speaking, particularly Christian discourse, claims such a power. I also want to reveal how in making such claims, the same discourse risks falling into a conventionality of its own.

Being-in-Place and Out

This process of being-in-the-world, particularly in our everyday lives, is not one in which an isolated, interior subject encounters an independent, exterior, objective reality. Rather, *Dasein* is being-there. The very phrase suggests an externality to our being. Being-in-the-world, in its hyphens, ties together the subjective be-ing with objective reality that be-ing establishes. Heidegger goes on to say that "If *Dasein* is, it already has . . . its own discovered region" (1962, 143). This means that the who of *Dasein*, the who I claim to be, by becoming has already found a region to be in.

Do you remember my question Where are you? And do you recall your reply? When you said, Here, you betrayed your physical existence as an object and as an animate being, you announced your identity as a person with a name, and you also located yourself both physically and socially. By placing yourself in "Here," you bring together the object and the subject of your existence; the what and the who come together in the where. Being-in-the-world becomes being-in-place.

As with being-in-the-world, being-in-place is a unitary phenomenon, a single process. The hyphens join the subjective (be-ing) with the objective (place) so that for us to be, to claim a who, we have to have a place, a where, to be. This where, this place, we create. With the work of the hand we create on the earth's surface an array of places, landscapes of significance that testify to our existence, defiant creations of meaning, Becker would say.

When people journey across the earth's regions, they build places that articulate their historical experiences and contemporary aspirations. Each place built has a particular configuration of material features that gives it a distinctive material setting. Each setting conveys to those who enter it, and to us who watch what others do, information as to what is happening around them and what they should be doing. As they respond to the information conveyed by the setting and to the actions of others, people draw upon that experience to provide themselves with an explanatory image of where they are and, consequently, who they are.

By rephrasing being-in-the-world into being-in-place, we shift from the general and the abstract to the specific and the concrete. In this engaged world of the everyday, where we are is our first clue to who we are. The individual who of *Dasein* gets disclosed by a particular where.

Everyday life, the life we lead during most of our waking hours, provides material for evaluating and communicating our experience. As the constituent of everyday life, place becomes a metaphor we extend to other realms. Here are some examples. Things fall into *place*, because there is a time and *place* for everything. She won first *place*, and her success put me in my *place*, but not being a good loser, I muttered, "God warns us about people in high *places*." Finishing in last *place* is a common*place* occurrence for those of us who cannot even find our *place* in line. Can you find your *place* in this text? I can't *place* him, but I'll *place* my bet that though we want to find our *place* in the sun, there's no *place* like home.

Note that we use place both as a noun, the home*place*, and as a verb, to *place* someone. Even more intriguing, note how we use it to convey both positive and negative experiences: my *place* in the sun versus putting you in your *place*. So deeply embedded in our lives, place takes on an ambiguity ranging from the comfortable to the stifling and from high achievement to the ordinary. This complex mix of daily life and conventional metaphor becomes even more convoluted in its permutations when we compare it to the out-of-place.

You have had that feeling before, haven't you? Acute embarrassment? Exposed? Nothing left to hide behind? The shell of yourself stripped away? You have found yourself out-of-place.

If place is the where of the who, then to be out-of-place is to endanger the who, to raise questions of the who's character and its strength, the who's claim to be. We have many whos and many places, so to find our place is not easy.

Paralleling Huxley's concern expressed earlier (see note 12), Max Scheler concludes a work titled *Man's Place in Nature* (1961) with this statement: "As soon as man has separated himself from the rest of nature and looks upon nature as an 'object'—this belongs to his essence and constitutes the very act of becoming man—he must, then, turn around with a sense of awe and ask: 'Where do I stand? What is my place in the universe?'" (88–89).

The uneasy alliance of the what, the body, with the symbol, the who, persists in challenging our efforts to find our place in the universe and, in much more specific ways, our stance with respect to one another. Often it is the body that does us in. Its unexpected rumblings, its foul odors, its spewing and dribbling, its mysterious urges, its determination to wrinkle and gray defy attempts to sweeten, to prettify, to render it angelic. On more than one occasion, when the body took it upon itself to emit a particularly unpleasant odor during your carefully sculptured performance designed to impress a really significant person, I have heard you say to a friend, "I was so embarrassed I nearly died."

Clothing, donned among so many people to turn a primate into a poem, may also turn against us. A run down a stocking, a bra strap peeking out, a fly unzipped, a suspicious stain appearing can bring us to a halt or even send us fleeing. Lapses of memory can produce the same effect, particularly among us older types, where memory, like clothing, may shred and tatter to leave us grasping at air. Words, even words, our best bid to transcendence, can fail us. They may refuse to come out when we need them most or, even worse, come out wrong and leave us red-faced and stuttering.

Our typical response to being-out-of-place is to rush to restore the conventional self that has been so mercilessly exposed. In our embarrassment we hurriedly put things, and our emotions, back in their places. We do so in the fondest hope that such a disaster will never recur. For, at the moment, we conceive of the in-place as the treasured mode of being. It is the one we might describe with words such as "ease," "graceful," "fluid." In contrast, the out-of-place evokes phrases such as "cumbersome," "heavy-footed," "knot-on-the log."

We might compare the two in the following manner:

In-Place	*Out-of-Place*
Being home	Being away
Being with	Being alone
Participant	Observer

When we are in-place, we are home with those we know and love, participating in stable and reassuring exchanges. When we are out-of-place, we are in foreign territory, alone among strangers, whose actions we observe from the outside of their zone of comfort.

Yet I know that you, especially you, and Tim Cresswell (1996) are not taken in by this easy contrast. Being the person you are, and Cresswell the geographer that he is, you are both quick to point out that the out-of-place renders the familiar problematic and by opening the windows to a fresh breeze of new possibilities it clears away the dense fog of our taken-for-granted, routinized life. In response to the above columns, you, if not Cresswell, suggest a revision:

In-Place	*Out-of-Place*
The world of the familiar	The world of the strange
Stifling, ordinary	Stimulating, exotic
To disappear	To stand out

The familiar world of the in-place stifles us to the point that the edges of our selves blur and mingle until we seem to disappear into the ordinary. In contrast, the strange world of the out-of-place stimulates us to the point that in such exotic surroundings each self stands out a clear and distinct shape. The in-place threatens to dull us into oblivion; the out-of-place refreshes our claims to individuality. In truth, the two, in-place and out, survive in an uneasy dialectic. Take the South, for example. Southerners are famous for their love of place, and I'm one. In my family, however, we have never died where we were born. The genealogy compiled by an unknown recorder with immaculate script in the family Bible begins in 1822 in Highland County, Ohio, and from there, it goes to Tennessee, Missouri, and Arkansas and ends in Falls County, Texas, with the death in 1913 of Miles Edward Richardson, the man whose name I bear. Since that day, the Bible itself has been discarded, with only the scruff-edged pages of the genealogy surviving while the family continues to disperse, a brother dying in New Mexico, another in Oregon, a daughter, born in Colombia, South America, living in New York City, and so the love of place and wanderlust, the rooted and the free, tug and strain against the constraints of the other.

Do you know Jimmie Rodgers, the father of country music? He was a white southerner from Mississippi who yodeled the blues. He sang, "longing for my Mississippi Delta home," but also bragged, "any place I hang my hat is home-sweet-home to me." He boasted, "I'm going to California where they sleep out every night. I'm going California because you don't treat me right," but riding the rails, he found himself at a water tank at night in the rain "a thousand miles away from home, waiting for a train."

You shrug and say, Well, what do you expect from the South? It's weird. The dialectic of the in-place and out, however, constitutes not a condition confined by any geographic region but one, as Heidegger argues, that is uniquely human. Being-in-the-world means that for us to be human we have to have a world to be in—a world that we create. Being-in-place likewise means that for us to be specific persons we have to have places to be in—places that we build. The construction of specific places, however, carries with it the chronic conventionalizing of our being. What once was an exciting experience now becomes a ho-hum repetition of the familiar. Furthermore, even with our most careful of careful arrangements, even in the most ordinary of ordinary circumstances, the threat of the out-of-place persists. Indeed, Heidegger argues that our ordinary, taken-for-granted reality comes about in response to the anxiety of the out-of-place. The out-of-place reveals to us how in some fundamental way we are uncanny creatures who "flee in the face of the not-at-home" (1962, 234). Although we pass our lives in the reality of the everyday, we do so in the baleful glare of the out-of-place.

Here the insights of Heidegger's existential phenomenology meet once more with what we learn from the evolutionary trajectory reviewed earlier. The trajectory, you recall, was that of a biped primate becoming more and more efficient at symbolic communication. Increased adeptness in using symbols, however, distanced us from purely natural processes until, at least by the time of the Neandertals, we achieved the capacity to reflect upon our actions. That capacity gained us both a presence and an absence, a self and death. We became a creature profoundly out-of-place.

The self of you, the self of me, the Neandertal self, the human self is the ability to reflect back upon our actions and upon what the actions mean. The self is the ability to be-there, to be-in-the-world. Death awakens the possibility that we may no longer possess the capacity to be-there. In death, we become no-where. We flee in the face of death, of the no-where, by putting death in its place. Yet death, being death, continues its pursuit, and the dialectic of in-place with the out-of-place moves forward. The struggle of culture with death proceeds.[15]

The Anthropologist's Project

You recall how earlier we talked of the distinction between participant and observer and how I promised we would return to the subject? Now, before we journey with the Christians on their way to the Crucifixion, is the time. As participants, we are engaged in the everyday work of being us. The who of each of us expands out into artifacts in our hands. We respond to each other's actions in the conventionalized forms that validate our presence. We take for granted this is the way the world should be. We are very much in-place. As anthropologists, on the other hand, our goal is to interpret what others are doing. Thus, we want to pull back from the taken-for-granted actions of the participants. We want to watch, with the distancing eye, what people are up to. The goal of our watching, however, is *not* to disengage ourselves to the point that we strip the actions of their meaning and thereby turn them into isolated things, into objects present-at-hand. Since humans have to have a world of word and artifact in order to be, since they have to have a there, and that there has to be "a codified hero system, a defiant creation of meaning" (Becker 1973, 7), and since we anthropologists study humans, we must take what people do and say seriously. It is their construction upon their lives we seek to understand and to describe. To accomplish this goal we must watch, not with the objectifying eye of a physical scientist, but with a listening, empathetic eye that preserves being-in-the-world as a unitary phenomenon. The purpose of our watching is not to debunk the conventional basis by

15. Bruce Knauft (1996) indicates the range of disagreement about Heidegger's notion of self and other. Part of the disagreement may stem from which Heidegger one emphasizes, the earlier Heidegger who spoke clearly—for Heidegger—of "being-in-the-world" and "being-with" or the later Heidegger who perhaps talked more of Being. Knauft's own interpretation of Heidegger's view of social life as "highly negative" (1996, 89) is diametrically opposed to mine. Yet, his formulation of "critical humanism" resonates, it seems to me, with much of this text.

which people live but to disclose how the participants create that basis. So in watching what Christians do, our task, yours and mine, is to disclose, that is, to elucidate, to make clear, how Christians bring about the world in which they are and how they ward off threats, both from within and from without, to their accomplishments.[16]

As Chapters 2 and 3 will demonstrate, the two Christian faiths have shaped, and in turn been shaped by, the surrounding secular cultures in which they are embedded. Spanish American culture and Catholicism and the culture of the American South and Southern Baptists have acted upon one another, sometimes in a hostile, critical fashion, on other occasions, in a supportive, reinforcing manner. Nevertheless, this project is not to show the impact of secular culture on religion in a cause-and-effect manner. If such were the aim, a better procedure might be to compare Catholicism in Spanish America with the same faith in the American South or Baptists south of the border with Southern Baptists. Instead, the effort is to illuminate the contrasting manner in which two distinct Christian groups in two different but similar cultures accomplish their work of being-in-Christ. This "method of controlled comparison" (Eggan 1954), in which the cultures of two people with similar traditions are juxtaposed, permits us to see more clearly those particular characteristics that each people employ to give their work its special attributes.[17]

16. Playing the role of the devil's advocate, one of your perennial favorites, you ask, Does not the eye, in its distancing, also lust? In the manner of a voyeur? And therefore, I complete for you, are we antrhopologists in our observing not guilty of voyeurism? To be sure, I forestall your ironic sneer, the qualities of the human eye extend into the mysterious. Many say the eye is the window to the soul. But far from being simply a window, the eye may indeed seek to possess. We have only to think of the lover who, in passion's gaze, "devours" the loved object. When we consider the pilgrim's eye in Chapter 5, when the pilgrim gazes on the shrine object, we encounter such desire. In contrast, the ethnographic eye acts phenomenologically to let the everyday show itself in all of its intricate elegance.

17. My more knowledgeable anthropological colleagues, which, of course, includes you, will recognize that the comparisons I am making are more in the idiographic, human science tradition of Ruth Benedict (1934) than the nomothetic, positive science tradition of George Murdock (1949). In these days when the postmodern knife is frequently raised in eager fratricide, what pleasure we can take, you and I, in citing the still relevant work of our betters: Benedict, Murdock, Eggan, and, earlier, Leslie White. In a similar mode, we point to the intriguing position, persistently if not frequently advanced, that New World countries invite comparison because the New World experience has shaped them into patterns distinct from those of their respective mother countries. Dating back until at least Herbert Bolton's call for scholars to address the

To watch with an anthropological eye for those characteristics and to listen with an anthropological ear for their soundings require that we document what we see and hear as people call out to one another and, occasionally, to us. To watch and to listen in this manner means we have to participate in the activities of the people whose meanings we are attempting to elucidate. This style of participation, however, necessitates that we write, photograph, and tape record. What we see and what we hear we must transcribe into field texts—written, pictorial, and audio. In addition, we collect documents the participants themselves use. These may include written texts, which in turn might range from mass-produced material to ephemeral pamphlets turned out locally, but they may also involve pictures and artifacts. The very act of documentation sharpens our watching and intensifies our listening. While the documenting distances us from the taken-for-granted world in which people are, that same documenting requires a participation that searches for the basis of that world. In brief, our anthropological project compels us to *Dasein*, to be there in a manner that parallels the being-in-the-world of those whose accomplishments we seek to understand and to describe.

My anthropological observations of Spanish American Catholicism began in 1962 in Colombia, South America. Since that date, during the summers (when anthropologists venture into the field) I have spent varying amounts of time, three months on some occasions, only a week on others, in Costa Rica, Guatemala, Honduras, and Mexico. During the summer of 1992, I returned to Colombia. Although I continue to travel south of the border, in 1996, I traveled along the United States side of the Rio Grande from near its mouth in south Texas to northern New Mexico.

---

issue of a greater America (1933) and subject to a critique under the heading *Do the Americans Have a Common History?* (Hanke 1964), the position finds more recent expression in Harvey Cox's juxtaposition of resurgent North American fundamentalism with Latin American liberation theology (1984), in Richard Morse's insightful essays on topics ranging from language to political ideology (1989), and in Gustavo Pérez Firmat's restated compilation, *Do the Americas Have a Common Literature?* (1990). Even more current is Deborah Cohn's *History and Memory of the Two Souths: Recent Southern and Spanish American Fiction* (1999). While these works may at times appeal to some common European substrate to explain their interpretations, for the most part, they want to engage the two Americas in a dialogue that promotes reflections on the peculiarities and similarities of each. As Cohn especially makes clear, comparing William Faulkner with Gabriel García Márquez, for example, is done not so much in the spirit of showing the influence of the former on the latter but rather to clarify how both portray the particular agonies of southerners and Colombians.

My observations of Southern Baptists, in some sense, go back to my childhood. Since becoming an anthropologist, I have attended Baptist services in Baton Rouge, Louisiana, where I live; in Princeton, New Jersey; Belfast, Maine; Winnfield, Louisiana; Austin, Texas; in and around Chapel Hill, North Carolina; Del Rio, Texas; and Española, New Mexico. This is not to suggest that I am a steady churchgoer; on the contrary, over the years, my attendance has been sporadic. I can only claim that I have learned from each visit and that the knowledge thus gained and augmented by my reading of anthropological and nonanthropological material on Spanish American Catholics and the Southern Baptists constitutes the basis of what I understand about how the two achieve being-in-Christ.

The presentations in Chapter 4 of the mass at the *iglesia* in Nueva Esperanza and of the worship service in the church at Mt. Hope are built out of incidents I have witnessed in both regions, but they are composite constructs. Nueva Esperanza as a town resembles to a degree Cartago, Costa Rica, but the *iglesia* on the plaza bears a resemblance to one on the central plaza in Querétaro, Mexico. Mt. Hope shows some attributes of Winnfield, Louisiana, where I spent a summer of fieldwork, and of Palestine, Texas, my hometown, but the church is a more modest version of the First Baptist Church in Baton Rouge, Louisiana, where my family and I have lived since 1965. By making the presentations composite constructs, I aspire to show you in vivid detail the different means employed by the Catholics in Spanish America and the Baptists in the American South to create their respective Christworlds. The task is not simply to offer a skeletal analysis of what transpires but to describe what occurs in such a full-bodied prose that you will exclaim, Oh, now I see. You understand, I hasten to add, that I am not after any sleight-of-hand prose; thanks to poststructuralism, we are even more aware today than in the past how texts may hide as well as reveal. To the best of my ability, I write to construct through your reading the experiential reality of the mass and the service. I am after immediacy; I want you in the text. But we both know being-in-the-text is some distance from the moments when Catholics and Baptists experience the ineffable. With that understanding, let us turn back to the beginning of the differences we see between Christ in Nueva Esperanza and Christ in Mt. Hope, back to the time when Spain, having (with the help of the sword-wielding apostle, St. James) cleared the Iberian Peninsula of Moors, was preparing to cross the Atlantic and England was awash with Protestantism.

2

THE PRESENCE OF CHRIST IN THE NEW WORLD DURING COLONIAL TIMES

Today, Catholics in Nueva Esperanza and Baptists in Mt. Hope continually tell a continuing story of Christ. At each telling, in sacrament and in word, Christ in Spanish America and Christ in the American South come to be. To the extent that Christ exists today in the experiential world of Christians, he exists in contemporary narrative. Yet Christians proclaim Christ today only in the context of previous proclamations. Contemporary narrative language, the only language that we, you and I, speak, is also a storytelling chained to a past, and the past to which Spanish American Catholics and Baptists of the American South are chained began, as do so many Christian stories, even the original one, with violence.

Toward the end of the fifteenth century, throughout the sixteenth century, and into the seventeenth, Christians in Europe fought one another in the pulpit and in the battlefield over how Christians might be with Christ. The dispute, in which Christians shed their blood on the sword of hate, or were blown apart by the newly invented cannon, ushered in the Modern Age by reforming Europe into a Protestant faith, located largely in the Atlantic north, and a Catholic rite, situated principally in the Mediterranean south (Map 1).

The differences between the two Christs in the New World originated in the differences that split apart the European homeland, and these differences sustained themselves during the separate encounters with the New World. So let us uncover these differences in their origins and trace their journey across the Atlantic. We start in the Mediterranean south at the end of the medieval period and then go to England and the origins of the Baptists. In

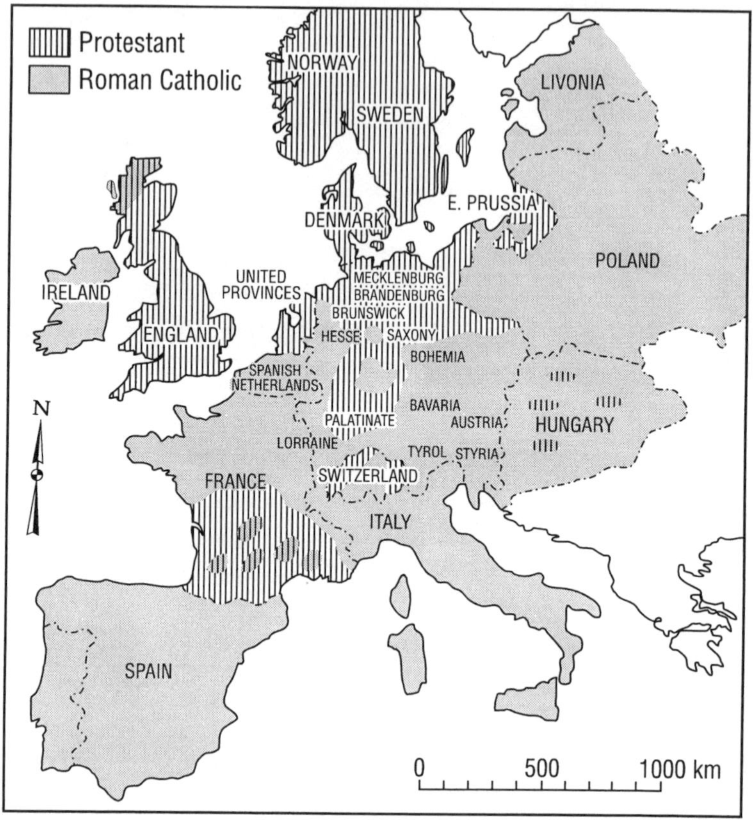

Map 1. The divisions of Christianity in Europe after the Treaty of Westphalia, 1648. From Searle (1973).

the second half of this chapter, we follow the conquistadores across the ocean to the south and then the pilgrims to the north.

Sacrificial Host and Divine Word

In the Mediterranean south, in Spain, Christians participated in Christ's sacrifice during the celebration of each mass, the central ritual of medieval Christianity. When the bread and wine of the mass, already symbolic of the bread and wine Christ shared with his disciples at the table of the Last Supper, were consecrated, "communal symbols of eating and drinking a meal with the Risen Lord [became] transformed into a ritual drama designed to

. . . instruct . . . the meaning of Jesus' passion and death" (Mitchell 1982, 51). The drama of the mass altered the bread and wine into the actual body and blood of the Savior, and on the altar of medieval Christianity, Christ was sacrificed anew to atone for the sins of his followers. The participation of the laity was neither required nor particularly desired. A screen between the nave, where the laity stood, and the chancel, where the priest presided over the altar, blocked the view of the ritual. Those parishioners who did partake in the commemorative feast, which they might do once a year, received only the bread and were not permitted to drink the wine (Searle 1973).

Despite the commonality of the mass, Spanish Christians, expanding southward to reconquer the Iberian Peninsula from the Islamic Moors the very year Christopher Columbus landed in the New World, were often at odds with one another. Throughout the peninsula, people were born into a local religion of relics and images, but an indigenous humanist-illuminist movement sought to purify this Christianity that most accepted so matter-of-factly. At the same time, the established church of the pope in Rome sought both to purge the local religion of its folk elements and to eradicate completely the reform movement.

The local religion of the village and the town itself had several layers. Prior to the eleventh century, as in the rest of Catholic Europe, local devotion focused on the relics of martyrs. The remains of St. Vincent, who in the fourth century refused to deny his Christian beliefs even when in the city of Valencia his Roman persecutors placed him on a fiery gridiron, and those of St. Eulalia, who likewise in the fourth century praised the Lord as iron hooks tore flesh from her young body during her persecution in Barcelona, were among the first to become objects of devotion throughout Spain. Through a type of emotional inversion, the suffering of St. Vincent, St. Eulalia, and other early martyrs became a blessing for the worshipers. The torturing of the saints made them powerful, and people sought that power for illnesses and other misfortunes (Brown 1981). Here, we see for the first time the recurrent, persistent notion of suffering as a quality that empowers.

The most famous of these early shrines, however, was that of St. James, one of the original twelve apostles, who, it is said, brought Christianity to Spain and thus became the patron saint of Spain. In the battles with the Moors, he sallied forth from his shrine in Compostela to appear as a warrior on horseback with sword aloft, ready to lead the Christian faithful on to victory. In this capacity, he was Santiago de Matamoros, St. James the Moor Slayer (Payne 1984).

Beginning in the eleventh and twelfth centuries, images in the form of statues possessing miraculous qualities replaced relics in popular devotion. While each image had its own devotees, they all had similar explanations for their appearances. The explanations typically began with an account of a herdsman searching for a lost bull or ox. In the uncultivated and dangerous wilds that surrounded his secure and conventional village, he encountered an image in a tree or in a spring or in a cave. The herdsman rushed home to inform the people of his village, and led by the parish priest, the herdsman and the villagers returned to carry the image to the parish church. During the night, however, it left the church to reappear at the original location. After several unsuccessful attempts to bring the statue into the village, the people constructed a shrine at the spot where the image first appeared, and the image, now pleased that the villagers had understood its wishes, responded by answering their requests for divine assistance (Christian 1981a).

With the veneration of images found in the countryside, local religion spread beyond the control of parish church and its relics. The multiplication of shrines, each with its miraculous image, led to a sacralization of the natural landscape. The statues provided people with the means to venerate saints not associated with relics, and consequently many shrines housed images of saints who specialized in the assistance they could offer their petitioners. In addition, the use of images permitted Mary, the mother of Christ—who, according to widespread belief, was bodily assumed into heaven after her death and therefore left few relics—to become increasingly important in local religion. Associated with the earth and thereby evoking fertility, Mary often appeared as a tiny figure, and the statues that represented her were commonly small themselves. She was not restricted to any particular specialization, so people appealed to her for whatever ill had fallen upon them. With the increased frequency of her appearance in the countryside, often in caves, shrines built to house her images soon outnumbered those of the specialized saints (Christian 1981b).[1]

1. One relic Mary left is her veil, housed at the famous shrine in Chartres Cathedral. Variously referred to as the Holy Tunic or the Holy Shirt, this garment adorned the Virgin at the time of the Annunciation, when the Angel Gabriel gave her the news that she was to give birth to Jesus (Luke 1:26–31). After being pressed against the reliquary in which the Holy Tunic lay, small replicas were given to soldiers to protect them in battle. Likewise, linens put in contact

The shrine devoted to the Virgin of Guadalupe in Spain exemplifies the concerns of the period. She appeared in the fifteenth century to a herdsman searching for a lost cow along the Guadalupe River in the province of Cáceres, Estremadura. In her apparition, the Virgin directed the herdsman to instruct the church authorities to dig at a certain location. Complying with the instructions, the clergy uncovered a small figure in a tomblike cave standing on a rock. According to one account, devoted followers had buried the image in the eighth century to protect it from the invading Moors. In any case, people, upon hearing how the Virgin had restored the lost cow and had indeed revived the herdsman's son who had been near death, journeyed to the location in great numbers. On arriving, pilgrims kissed the slab of marble upon which she had appeared and sought to restore their health by drinking water mixed with scrapings from the rock. As the result of their fervor, the shrine became the most popular one in fifteenth-century Castile and one favored by the monarchy (Christian 1981b; *Enciclopedia* 1925, 26:1509–16).

Another shrine the monarchy favored was the Christ of Burgos. Reputed to be the work of Nicodemus, the Pharisee (John 7:50–52), and brought from Rome to the northern Castilian city of Burgos at the end of the twelfth century, the crucified figure evoked the admiration of none other than Philip II. Looking upon the face that presented such an impressive resignation, such a sublime sweetness, Philip was said to exclaim, "Let he who would lose his faith come here, and he will find it" (*Enciclopedia* 1925, 9:1474–75).

In their pursuit of assistance from the Virgin of Guadalupe, the Christ of Burgos, or one of the saints, villagers made personal vows that if the shrine figure helped them overcome the illness that plagued them or the misfortune that threatened their livelihood, then in return they would make the pilgrimage to the shrines to express their devotion publicly. In a similar manner, participants in the humanist-illuminist reform movement sought direct communication with the sacred. Unlike their village brothers and sisters, however, these seekers turned their vision inward to establish a union with God himself directly, without intermediaries and without the material embodiment of the images.

The humanist strand of the movement came into Spain through the writ-

---

with the reliquary and worn by pregnant women eased the pains of childbirth (Mâle 1983). The ability of the Holy Tunic to transfer its power to objects touching it exemplifies "the contagiousness of the sacred," to which we will return in Chapter 5.

ings of Erasmus (1466–1536). A Renaissance figure, Erasmus satirized the ignorance of the clergy and pleaded for a more informed reading of the Bible. He asked, "Which are the true relics of St. Paul? A few small pieces of bone preserved in a reliquary, or his spirit that shines resplendent in the Epistles?" (Bataillon 1966, 199). In Spain, those intellectuals inspired by Erasmus argued against the authority of the church to administer the sacraments, but at the same time they scorned the popular devotion to local shrines. "They sought a 'spiritual life' centered on Christ and the Holy Sacrament, purified . . . of exterior practices, which they considered ridiculous in common people and reprehensible in the clergy" (Christian 1981b, 159).

Although inspired by the pietism in the Netherlands, the birthplace of Erasmus, the illuminists were Spaniards from varied backgrounds and included members of the Franciscan Order. They formed devotional centers to practice inner purification and total submission to the divine will (Elliot 1963). Known popularly as the *alumbrados*, that is, those who dispel darkness, the illuminists had no use for images; the clarity of their inner light let them see that in any woman Mary resided (Christian 1981b). This same light caught the eye of the Inquisition.

To the villager's veneration of the saints and Mary, to the humanist's preference for a learned reading of the Holy Scriptures, and to the illuminist's quest to merge with the divine—and to the Protestant faiths developing in Atlantic Europe—the Catholic Church in Rome attempted a twofold response. First, in 1478, Pope Sixtus IV issued the papal bull that began the Spanish Inquisition. The Inquisition had the power to conduct inquiries into claims made by villagers of their having seen divine figures. For example, in 1518 the Holy Office sought testimony from Juan de Rabe, a shepherd in the province of Cuenca who was said to go into trances and have visions. Upon hearing Juan confess that Our Lady, the Virgin Mary, had appeared to him as a tiny girl dressed in white riding a tiny burro, the Tribunal ordered that he be given a hundred lashes in public and returned to jail for further instruction necessary for the health of his soul (Christian 1981a).

The Holy Office was more disturbed by the humanist-illuminist argument that communication between the individual and God could be achieved apart from the sacraments administered by the church. Such an argument clearly undercut the authority of the church in a manner that the likes of Juan de Rabe could not. Consequently, the Inquisition vigorously pursued its investigation of humanist-illuminist activities, and by the closing decades of the sixteenth century, the Holy Office had either driven the humanists and the illuminists out of the country or persuaded them to renounce their errors (Elliot 1963; Kamen 1985).

Second, in its response to the perceived threats to its existence, the Catholic Church sought to address the disputes within its own ranks, and the Papacy issued a call for the bishops to gather in council at the city of Trent in northern Italy. Opening debate in 1546 and closing the third and final session nearly twenty years later in 1563, the Council of Trent issued decrees that characterized the Catholic position until 1962 and Vatican II.

The council reaffirmed the centrality of the sacraments as administered by the church's representatives in establishing the real presence of Christ. This doctrine of transubstantiation meant that during mass, in the words that only a priest sharing Christ's sacerdotal power could speak—"Hoc est enim corpus meum," "For this is my body," and "Hic est enim calix sanguinis mei," "For this is the chalice of my blood"—the bread and wine of the sacrament became the actual body and blood of Christ. The doctrine verified the medieval argument that at each mass "Jesus Christ himself is both priest and sacrifice" (Clark 1960, 77) and that at each mass Christ suffers his Crucifixion anew.

The council confirmed that Latin should continue to be the language of the Mass; it did, however, decree that preaching in the vernacular become a medium through which the church proclaimed the message of Christ. As they administered the sacrament of the Eucharist, parish priests were required to preach, that is, deliver a homily, on all feast days and on Sundays. So that the parishioners might better hear the homily and see the host being consecrated, the screens that in medieval churches had separated the altar from the nave were removed, and new churches were built so that the attention of the congregation might be directed toward the altar and the homily. At the same time, the Council of Trent argued that the church should continue to celebrate the ecstasies of the saints, the miracles performed at the shrines, and the occasions of martyrdom by the faithful. For worship of the saints, separate chapels were built along the side of the nave, and the statuary placed in those chapels attempted to portray the moment of mystic revelation (Searle 1973).[2]

2. In a review of Spanish Catholicism in preparation for his account of the Mexican Virgin of Guadalupe, Stafford Poole, C.M., insists that in spite of the Tridentine reforms worship remained strongly local and more focused on devotion than on dogma: "When the Council of

During the sixteenth and seventeenth centuries, the people of villages and towns throughout Spain worked to adapt the Tridentine affirmation of the sacramental presence of Christ to local, votive use. The outcome of their efforts was to enshrine the passion of Christ and to celebrate his suffering. Consequently, the veneration of the saints declined, and though devotions to Mary remained high, people sought her in her role as the mother of an afflicted Christ, as Our Lady of Solitude. By the end of the sixteenth century, brotherhoods of men filled the streets of the larger cities on Thursday and Friday of Holy Week to flagellate themselves in imitation of Christ's agony (Christian, 1981b). Among the religious orders, the Franciscans especially encouraged devotion to the Passion and to the Cross (Christian, 1981a). Continuing through the seventeenth and into the eighteenth century, the "morbid strain in Spanish religiosity" dwelt increasingly on death (Payne 1984, 56–59). Morbid or not, dying was a problem, for hell was no abstract entity "but, rather, a vividly pictured place of unspeakable horror [only] 1,193 leagues beneath the earth's surface" (Eire 1995, 517). Dying was a problem but a problem with solutions—solutions created in ritual processions. Throughout the streets of small towns and major cities, people in holy festivals carried images of the suffering Christ and the grieving Mary. In procession the boundary between life and death shifted; likewise the distinction between person and image blurred: "The people dressed and whipped themselves and wept so they looked like the images; and the images sweated blood and wept as if they were people" (Christian 1981b, 198).

The Counter-Reformation in Spain and throughout much of Europe emphasized the "dramatic miracle of the Mass, the intercession of the saints vividly represented in statues or stained-glass, and the pre-eminence of the Blessed Virgin as the first among the faithful and the Mother of God the Son." While in the seventeenth century, continental Catholic worship was religion on parade, "English Catholic worship was religion in hiding" (Davies 1975, 462).

Christians in England during the turbulent decades of the 1600s developed strong antipathies toward one another. Caught in and indeed contributing to the political tumult that included the beheading of Charles I in 1649, the

---

Trent legislated the preaching of sermons on Sundays, it was widely regarded as an intolerable innovation" (1995, 20).

establishment of the Commonwealth, the restoration of monarchy in 1660, the attempt of James II to promote Catholicism, and the "Glorious Revolution" of 1688 that brought William and Mary to the throne along with a measure of religious toleration, various Christian groups came to power to persecute others, only to find themselves being persecuted by their former victims as their power waned.

The contentious spectrum of English Protestantism ranged from the Church of England, or the Anglican Church, on the one hand to the Dissenters on the other. The Dissenters themselves varied from the more "established" dissent, as voiced by the Puritans—themselves composed of the Presbyterians and Independents—to the radical sectarians, such as the Baptists.

The Church of England removed the pope from its ecclesiastical hierarchy, eliminated most of the saints, translated the liturgy into English, and reduced the number of sacraments to two: baptism and holy communion. The Presbyterians abolished the bishops. The Independents established the autonomy of local congregations. The Baptists made church membership dependent on public confession of sins to be followed by a baptism that entailed full immersion of the now-cleansed sinner. Even more radical than the Baptists, the Quakers abandoned all the sacraments, elevated silence over the spoken Word, and awaited the presence of the Holy Spirit. In sum, paralleling the reduction of the Church from an international, authoritative hierarchy to a local, egalitarian congregation was a depreciation of the physical senses and an interiorization of the holy. Sacred reality moved from the host the hierarchical priest held aloft for all to see to the silence of a prepared heart, invisible to the viewer but resonant with the Spirit (Davies 1975).

The "meeting-houses" where Baptists and other Dissenters "gathered together" had no intrinsic sacred qualities. To worship did not require entering a holy place, for they believed Christ's assurance: "For where two or three are gathered in my name, there am I in the midst of them" (Matthew 18:20). Consequently, the meeting-houses had no towers, spires, transepts, apses, chancels, or other ostentatious protuberances that characterized the "steeple-houses," as George Fox, the Quaker founder, so contemptuously labeled them (Davies 1975, 518). The meeting-houses, "austere, scrubbed, and domesticated" (Davies 1975, 10), resembled large, middle-class homes, sober in color and rectangular in shape. Inside, the pulpit, where the Word was preached, replaced the altar, where the Word became flesh, as the chief architectural sign of the faith.

In the seventeenth century, the pulpit was an imposing three-decker; later, in the eighteenth century, it became even loftier. To ensure the delivery of the preacher's lengthy sermon, a sounding-board topped the uppermost deck. On the board's otherwise plain surface a carved dove, its wings raised in flight, clutched "an olive-branch in her bill, the symbol of the preacher bringing the news of reconciliation to the voyagers in the ark, itself the type of Church, bearing the souls of the saved" (Davies 1961, 46). Paired staircases led to the middle deck, where the minister stood to lead the prayers and read the lesson from the Holy Scriptures. Beneath him on the first deck, the "presenter" lined out either metrical psalms or hymns. At the designated time, the minister, like Moses climbing Mt. Sinai, ascended to the topmost deck to deliver a three-hour exhortation (Davies 1961).

For those Dissenters who practiced communion regularly, the other principal item of furniture in the meeting-house was a long table in front of the pulpit at which the members sat to partake of the Lord's Supper. For those among the dissenting groups who followed the teaching of John Calvin (1509–1564) that divine grace granted by a sovereign God to a depraved humanity was the only means of salvation, the Supper sealed the covenant between them and the Lord; for those who adhered more closely to the teachings of Huldreich Zwingli (1484–1531), eating at the Lord's Table remembered, in a purely symbolic manner, the First Supper. For neither Calvinist nor Zwinglist did the meal offer in sacrifice the Body and Blood of Christ.

The Dissenters replaced the annual liturgical cycle that tracked the seasons of nature and commemorated the feast days of the saints with a weekly cycle of work and the Word. They even rejected the christological cycle of Christmas and Easter. The "Sabbath," a term they claimed was more sanctified with Biblical authority than Sunday, was filled with "exhortations, sermons, prayers, and psalm-singing, and with only a minimal concession to the needs of the body" (Davies 1975, 246). Through its denial of the acts of the body (sports, festivals, and even work) and through its depreciation of the physical senses, the sanctification of the Sabbath made Sunday a day of earthly death. It declared the Dissenters ready for the day in the future, not so distant perhaps, when those filled with grace would rise to meet their sovereign God in heaven.

In the meeting-houses, people longed to pray with a full heart that no formulaic message could convey. Spontaneity in prayer spoke of inner conviction. Kneeling, especially during the Lord's Supper, seemed to imply the Catholic doctrine of transubstantiation, so the Dissenters instead sat, as Christ surely did at the First Supper. For the preacher to make the sign of the cross suggested that he had some power the congregation did not have; consequently, the Dissenters refused the gesture, and similarly, they rejected special garments for the minister. Music, in its full cathedral development of choir, soloists, and violinists alternating parts from an authored score, also suggested a hierarchy of sanctity and the substitution of human script for divine inspiration. Some Dissenting groups allowed the Psalms to be lined out in meter, but others criticized the placement of God's Word in the straitjacket of human rhyme, and John Smyth, an early Baptist minister, permitted only "charismatic solos" (Davies 1975, 272). As the seventeenth century progressed, however, ministers encouraged adding passages of the New Testament to the metrical psalmody, and by the last of the century, the Baptist Benjamin Keach convinced his church to sing hymns at the close of the Lord's Supper. So as the eighteenth century began, Charles Wesley, brother of Methodist founder John Wesley, discovered many congregations receptive to his songs (Davies 1975).

Among Dissenters in the seventeenth century, preaching replaced the presentation of Christ's body in the Eucharist as the principal sacred occasion. Preaching bridged the gap between Almighty God and puny man. The Word was proclaimed not to instruct the congregation with human knowledge, which might fill those who heard with false pride, but to impart divine revelation, which made all who listened humble (Davies 1975). Furthermore, all Dissenters rejected prescribed homilies, and each preacher composed his own sermon. While some preached directly from a written text and others from memorization, the more radical preachers, to ensure their sermons were the work of the Holy Spirit, preached the Word as it came to them in the presence of their gathered brethren.[3]

At the radical edge of the dissenting movement, the Baptists restricted

3. Margaret Miles (1985) points out that in contrast to visual imagery, which by privileging certain aspects of sight over others evokes hierarchy, speaking—especially speaking in the vernacular—promotes unity and egalitarianism. During the Reformation, several of the commonfolk communities quickly grasped the revolutionary implication of their unity, much to the distress of their rulers.

membership in a gathered church to those who publicly confessed their sinful state, professed a belief in Christ, and submitted to full immersion. The first Baptist statement on baptism, the London Confession of 1644, explained that it signifies "first, the washing of the whole soule in the blood of Christ; secondly, that interest the Saints have in the death, buriall, and resurrection; thirdly, together with a confirmation of our faith, that as certainly as the body is buried under water, and riseth againe, so certainly shall the bodies of the Saints be raised by the power of Christ, in the day of the resurrection, to reigne with Christ" (Lumpkin 1959, 167). By requiring the believer to be fully immersed in public, they risked persecution from that segment of their Protestant brethren in power at the moment and scorn at the spectacle of people floundering and sputtering on the muddy banks of a cold river with wet clothes plastered in a revealing manner to the contours of male and female forms. In the manner of radical groups everywhere, they constructed an identity out of behavior that appeared to others in seventeenth-century England as unduly antagonistic and most unseemly. A sainthood united in symbolic death, burial, and rebirth, they proclaimed their name Baptists, those baptized in Christ.

Apparitions and Voices

While the Baptists in England during the seventeenth century composed—in plain meeting-houses, in spirit-filled preaching, and in baptismal symbols—the ancestral narrative of the Southern Baptists, the story of Christ's presence in Spanish America was already a century or more further along in its telling.

The Spanish subjugation of the highly complex indigenous civilizations of the Aztec, Maya, and Inca and the conversion of their people to Christianity, two movements seemingly at odds, were in fact propelled by a similar vision: The lands on this side of the Atlantic were to become a *Mundus Novus*, a New Society in a New World, one to be more purely Christian than the old one the conquistadors, the priests, the merchants, the intellectuals, and the craftsmen had left behind.

How to make the new society more purely Christian became the issue. How to convert the Indians was the central debate. Should the road to utopia be one of peaceful persuasion? Or should it be one of forced indoctrination?

The humanists who survived the Iberian Inquisition to make the Atlantic crossing argued that Native Americans had the reasoning faculties that civilization required and that, therefore, a program of peaceful evangelizing would permit them to comprehend the superiority of Christianity over native religion (Greenleaf 1962). On the contrary, the scholastics argued, the Indians' rude nature prohibited the attainment of civilization and, therefore, of Christianity. Citing Thomas Aquinas himself, who had reasoned that war may be waged when it is done so in the right manner and in the right spirit (Hanke 1959), the scholastics sought to convince the Spanish crown that to spread the faith and, indeed, to prepare the world for Christ's Second Coming, the Indians must first be conquered. With an eye toward its own interest, the crown accepted the view of Native Americans as creatures without reason and the scholastics' argument for conquest. It urged upon the church a policy designed to hasten Indian submission, to promote conversion to Christianity, and to instill loyalty to the crown (Barnadas 1984). By the middle of the sixteenth century, the humanist visions of a New World utopia had all but vanished (Elliot 1987), and civilization became "a weapon of attack rather than a standard of measurement" (Jennings 1975, 8). The kindred light of the *alumbrados*, if, in fact, it had made the journey across the Atlantic, departed with the soul of Friar Francisco de la Cruz, burned at the stake in Lima, Peru, in 1578, for heresy (Góngora 1975).

The conquering of the Native American civilizations and the associated evangelizing required that the Indians be congregated in towns. Likewise, the administration of the hierarchical Spanish empire necessitated the establishment of focal cities to appropriate resources, including the primary one of Native American labor, and to implant government. Consequently, from Mexico in the north to Chile in the south, laying out a town articulated both the millenarian call for a City of God in the New World and the imperial design for hierarchical order. Whatever "the constraints of place and circumstance, a town founding was a liturgical act sanctifying newly appropriated land [and] exemplified the 'mystical body' that was central to Iberian political thought" (Morse 1987, 167). The liturgical act imposed the rectangular grid of rational urbanity drawn directly from Roman sources on the uncivilized, curvilinear nature of the New World. The articulation was not always perfect. In atypical, but always instructive Costa Rica, where there was an absence of large quantities of both precious metal and native labor, the Spanish colonists all but abandoned the colonial capital of Cartago to leave the grid pattern occupied principally by the royal governor, who spent his days complaining in letters to the Spanish crown how difficult it was to collect taxes with the population scattered across the mountainous countryside (Chacón de Umaña 1967; Richardson 1978; but see Gudmundson 1986). Despite the exceptions, implicit in early colonial town founding was the ideological equation, still voiced today, of civility, urbanity, Christianity, true humanity, and the grid. Those who lived within the grid were truly human; that is, they were civilized and Christian. Those who lived outside the grid and in nature's wilds were less than truly human, barbaric, and superstitious (Fraser 1990).

In separate ways, Indians and colonists participated in the labors of urbanization. The regular clergy—particularly the Franciscan, Dominican, and Augustinian Orders and, to a lesser degree, the Mercedarian and, later in time, the Jesuit Orders—established *doctrinas*, geographical units into which they moved the Indians. The secular clergy, under the ecclesiastical control of bishops, founded parishes within which they administered the sacraments to colonists. The urban nuclei of both the *doctrina* and the parish were laid out in a geometrical grid, with the center square converted to a plaza that was bounded by the church on one side and the state on another. The Indian grid was much less compact than that of the Spanish parish: The plaza was a vacant space, with the church (and, in many cases, the convent of the order responsible for that *doctrina*) the only buildings of architectural distinction. The single-room Native American house with thatched roof and wattle-and-daub walls was set in the center of a compound, isolated from its identical neighbor by a fenced square. In contrast, for the Spaniard, the central plaza was flanked with ecclesiastical, administrative, fiscal, and commercial structures that identified through their architecture the hierarchies of colonial authority and commerce. The Mediterranean courtyard house, with tile roof and thick brick and plaster walls secluding an interior patio, was set butted against adjacent houses in competition for a prestigious location fronting the plaza.

Within the open compound of the Indian *doctrina* of the monks and the compact grid of the colonist parish of the priests, Iberian Catholicism, as part of the conquest culture of the Spanish empire, reconstituted itself in the New World (Foster 1960, Lockhart and Schwartz 1983, Fraser 1990). In the *doctrinas*, the reconstitution began with a fortresslike monastery. The monks directed the Native Americans to construct thick-walled, near-windowless churches whose castellated roofs bespoke a militant Christianity on the move, recalling the manner that Rome had moved against the pagans and Spain against the infidel. Fronting the church was a walled space, an *atrio*, into which Indians were congregated to see and to hear the message of conversion, which might be performed at an open-air altar located in a niche in the building or in the wall of the *atrio*. Inside, a single nave, the public domain into which the Indians crowded, provided an unobstructed view of the sanctuary, the domain of the priest. Ornate vaulting distinguished the sacred space of the Spanish priest, the altar, and the host from the more profane space of the Native American nave (Kubler 1948; Ricard 1966).

In the Spanish parishes, the New World reconstitution of Old World faith occurred first in modest buildings of wooden beams and adobe walls, but as the sixteenth century progressed, as the conquest moved to the more distant frontiers, and as the centers in Mexico and Peru developed their hierarchies of church, state, and commerce, the restructuring of Iberian Christianity required massive cathedrals. With their huge, rectangular, central nave flanked by column-lined aisles, the cathedrals in the capitals of Mexico City and Lima and in the regional centers such as Guadalajara and Cuzco in the late sixteenth and early seventeenth centuries announced the final victory of the scholastic argument over the humanistic spirit (Kubler 1948; Wethey 1949).

Constructed by native labor to fit plans designed by Spanish architects and their Creole descendants, the cathedral was often "set on a stepped platform above the level of the plaza and boasted a broad atrium, or open court, before it. This provided a stage, a dramatic setting with the facade of the building as backdrop, for the various ceremonies and colorful processions that enlivened the religious life of the age. Decoration [particularly during the Baroque era] was lavished on this facade, with columns, pilasters, niches, and statues a part of the embellishment" (Keleman, cited in Greenleaf 1977, 240).

In both *doctrina* and parish, the church entrance was most commonly an arch. Flanked on either side by columns that rose to support a classical pediment, the arch became the preeminent signifier of Iberian Christianity in the New World. In a land where people had not known the arch, it brought together, in a manner no other single architectural feature could, the meeting of the triumphal arch of military prowess and the equally triumphal arch of Christendom. As the passageway between the grid pattern on the outside and the sacrament on the inside, the ecclesiastical arch restated to both Native American laborer and European colonist the conjunction of civilization and Christianity (Figure 7; Fraser 1990).

If the Spanish city, laid out in perfect rectangularity around a central plaza

FIG. 7. The triumphal arch of Christendom. From Fraser (1990, 131).

of ecclesiastical, administrative, and commercial hierarchies, and the Indian *doctrina*, a looser rectangle of familial compounds focused on a fortress monastery, were paired material components of the Spanish Christian empire in the New World, and if the cathedral itself, with its massive bulk organized in accordance with Counter-Reformation dogma, was a celebration of the holy establishment, then apparitions in the New World evidenced the continued vitality of the local religion of village and town. The Iberian visionary tradition of a herdsman finding a statue or seeing a holy figure that instructs the village to build a shrine so that people may venerate the object and thereby gain divine assistance crossed the Atlantic practically intact. The herdsman was replaced with a person of similar low status, such as an Indian, and the image or figure often manifested itself at a location previously sacred to Indians. Scarcely had the Spanish landed on the Caribbean coast of Mexico and on the Pacific coast of Peru, when the New World sprouted shrines to which both native and Spanish traveled on pilgrimage in gratitude for divine intervention into their troubled lives.

In an account widely accepted today, the Virgin of Guadalupe in 1531 instructed the Indian Juan Diego to take her cloak to the bishop so that he would be persuaded that she had indeed appeared at Tepeyac hill outside Mexico City. Shortly after, in 1540, she established her presence at Los Remedios in nearby Puebla, but as early as 1521, she is credited with appearing at Zapopán, in more distant Guadalajara. A century later, in 1626, she initiated her cult with a life-restoring miracle at San Juan de los Lagos, also near Guadalajara. In the highlands of Peru and Bolivia, following Francisco Pizarro's conquest in 1532, the Virgin appeared in 1583 in Lake Titicaca as the Virgin of Copacabana. Other Andean locations reported her manifestations, and at one, Pachakamaq, she was also known as the Virgin of Guadalupe. In the less contested terrain of Central America, she appeared at Costa Rica's colonial capital of Cartago in 1635 as the Virgin of the Angels (Map 2).

Again according to accounts that today are accepted as official, Christ also made his presence known shortly after the Spaniards arrived. In 1539, he appeared as Christ Crucified to Augustinian monks in a cave at Chalma, a location near Mexico City, and throughout the sixteenth century, Christ materialized on his cross at sites all around central Mexico. In the Andean regions, the revelations of Christ in material form are later and are frequently associated with earthquakes. In 1650, a previously unremarkable crucifix was given credit for saving at least a portion of Cuzco from an earthquake, and it subsequently became known as the Lord of the Earthquakes. Beginning in 1654 a mural in Lima of Christ Crucified withstood numerous earthquakes and became venerated as the Lord of Miracles. Among the many other, less widely known appearances of Christ was the image an Indian laborer saw, in 1675 near Cuzco, of a man tied to a post and being whipped. This image of Christ being scourged before his Crucifixion (commonly referred to as Christ at the Column) became known as the Lord of Huanca and functioned as the focus of a regional pilgrimage. Another regional shrine developed in Buga,

Map 2. The location of selected shrines in Spanish America

Colombia, near Cali, where in 1550 an Indian woman found a crucifix floating on a river. Despite being thrown on a fire by a suspicious clergy, the image survived to become the object of devotion known, like the Lima Christ, as the Lord of Miracles. In Central America, pilgrimages to Christ Crucified were reported to begin as early as 1596 to the town of Esquipulas in western Guatemala, where a statue of Christ on the cross acquired devotion under the title of Our Lord of Esquipulas (Map 2).[4]

Parish church, *doctrina* monastery, urban cathedral, and pilgrimage shrine were all opportunities for an architecture that conveyed the religious sensuality of a hierarchical, imperial Christianity. While architectural styles in the Spanish New World recapitulated earlier European Romanesque and Gothic designs (Kubler 1948), the most characteristic style of Spanish American colonial churches, and the style that still today provides the ambience of worship in many churches, was the Baroque. Developing out of more restrained Renaissance compositions around 1600, the Baroque flowered longer and with greater exuberance in Spanish America. In contrast to Europe, the emerging Neoclassicism did not replace it until the middle of the eighteenth century.

The sanctuary of a typical Baroque temple was made dramatic with the installment of figures of the saints, the Virgin, and Christ in doorlike settings arranged in tiers behind and above the altar (Figure 8). Standing in the threshold between their world and ours, each figure in these visual scenes, or *retablos*, adopted a pose: St. Anne, the mother of Mary, with her hand over her heart, or St. Paul, the Apostle, with a book and a sword. The doorlike quality of the niche from which the saint gestured was enhanced by columns that bracketed the niche and extended upward to support a cornice upon which another row of saints stood. At the beginning of the Baroque, the columns were as plain as those in any Greek or Roman temple, but they became spirals entwined with vines out of which tiny heads peeked. In the ultra-Baroque, architects turned the columns on end to form inverted pyramids so that the upper row of saints appeared to be sustained only by their ethereal sainthood. The results were that everything "is in movement, in flight. Cherubs hover suspended, angels flutter, stirring the garments of the royal saints by the wind from their wings. The very wall disintegrated, and heaven opens

4. Although critical to our understanding of the shrine's power, the dates of the founding apparitions are not necessarily, and probably were not, the dates when the shrines first achieved prominence. The founding narratives more resemble explanatory accounts that developed *after* visitation to the respective shrines became popular than historically verified chronicles. Furthermore, the interpretation of the founding narratives changes through time. As you surely know by now, nothing in these qualifications suggests that we can be dismissive of the founding narrative's explanatory power. Please wait until Chapter 5.

FIG. 8. The Baroque *Retablo.* From Wethey (1949, 321).

up, as it were, to receive the worshiper. It is one of the great religious arts, theatrical, perhaps, but a just setting for ecstatic devotion" (Weismann 1950, 130).

During the Baroque, the classical facade surrounding the triumphal arch of the early colonial portal became an exterior *retablo* (Figure 9). Spaces be-

Fig. 9. The Baroque portal. From Wethey (1949, 128).

tween columns were now occupied by the saints, above the portal another row was added, and the columns themselves twisted into spirals. The distinction between the secular street and the sacred temple, never a sharp boundary in the colonial world, nor even today, dissolved into a permeable passage through Baroque sensuality.

Liturgical space within the Spanish American temple developed a complexity of altars (Kubler 1948). The subsidiary altars, which in some locations threatened to rival the main altar in the sanctuary, lined the nave or formed separate chapels that extended off the main structure. These too featured spiraling columns resting, in some cases, upon disembodied heads, with other heads peering out of the intricate foliage of curves. Between the columns and above the altars, images of the saints, the Virgin, or Christ stared down at the supplicants kneeling in prayer (Figure 10).

In the early colonial period, the figures themselves, many near life-size, were carved from wood, covered with plaster, and then painted with flesh tints; later, statues were molded with cloth impregnated with plaster. The most common form during the latter part of the seventeenth and eighteenth centuries, however, was framed images dressed in real clothing (Wethey 1949). This permitted the statues to have a change of clothing for various occasions: "In Lent the Virgin must wear mourning; . . . but immediately after the Nativity, when . . . she must flee with the Child into Egypt, she must be equipped with traveling cape, pilgrim's hat, lunch basket, and water gourd. . . . It was unthinkable, when the poorest Indian had a change of everyday and Sunday clothes, that the Queen of Heaven should always appear in the same old garments" (Weismann 1950, 178).

Iconography adorned the pulpits as well. These were fixed alongside the nave at some distance from the altar. To deliver the homily, the priest left the altar, climbed the stairs lined with balustrades, and entered a box with a canopy. At his back, in raised relief on a wall panel, was often the Madonna, and on the panels of the pulpit, the four evangelists, Sts. Matthew, Mark, Luke, and John, addressed the multitude in raised relief, while overhead on top of the canopy, the saint to whom the church was dedicated lifted his or her arms in command. Rarely was Christ present on the pulpit (Wethey 1949).

The Neoclassic, with its return to the unadorned columns and triangular pediment of Greek temples, arrived in Spanish America toward the last half of the eighteenth century as the presumed antithesis to Baroque spirals. In Peru, at least according to one author, it brought a "tragedy of wanton destruction. . . . The churches of Lima and other cities were stripped of their magnificent Baroque altars, which were consigned to the fire" (Wethey 1949, 70). In Guatemala, earthquakes and the movement of the capital to the present location permitted the construction of a new cathedral in Neoclassic so-

FIG. 10. The Altar of the Crucifixion. From Wethey (1949, 328).

lemnity. In many places, however, it was simply added on to existing structures, as, for example, in Mexico City, where in the early nineteenth century workers erected towers and a cupola on a structure begun three centuries before (Weismann and Sandoval 1985). In the interior, clean, white columns replaced the entwined, rich darkness of the *retablo*, but between the columns holy figures continued to gesture at the doorways between their world and that of the parishioners, and above the main altar or in a side chapel, Christ continued, even in Neoclassic restraint, to suffer.

By the end of the colonial era, the transformation of Christianity into the religion of a conquest civilization was nearly complete. The conquered subjects of that Spanish-Christian empire, the indigenous people of Middle and South America, supported that empire with both their bodies and their minds. Within the confines of the *doctrina* they sought answers to their condition through a creative synthesis of aboriginal and European religions. The cult of the saints in particular seemed to provide a medium through which they could both retain aboriginal beliefs and articulate the emerging corporate character of their colonial villages. Their own anguish no doubt lent new poignancy to the anguish of Christ, yet the passion for Christ's suffering was, and is, a Spanish passion.

The images of the colonial Christ often depicted him in the final hours of his life: tied to a column and beaten, dressed in a crown of thorns and taunted, struggling with his cross and falling, and, the climax, crucified and dying. Today, the contemporary observer strains to cross the temporal gap. Harold Wethey, in his study of architecture and sculpture in colonial Peru, describes one scene of Christ at the Column as uniting a "feeling for beauty with a spirit of religious resignation, which is deeply moving," yet contrasts that scene with one from another church that depicts a "sadistically bruised Christ" (Wethey 1949, 243). Elizabeth Wilder Weismann, in viewing Mexican crucifixes, notices the details that rouse emotion: "the fingers curling . . . the straining toes, the lidded eyes and exhausted mouth." She explains further: "What is moving, and what is harrowing, is emphasized more and more. . . . Naturalistic detail is driven to the unnatural and impossible: arms become too strained, joints too torn, wounds too deep and too many, blood too red, anguish too violent" (1950, 164). Yet an observer of the time, Friar Miguel de Guevara (c. 1585–c. 1646), saw a different figure, as evidenced in this poem frequently attributed to his hand.

To Christ Crucified

I am not moved (O Thou my God) to love Thee
By Heaven which is Thy promise and my rest.
Hell moves not me, where fear is fearfulest,
To offend no more by mine iniquity.
Thou mov'st me (Lord), it moveth me to see
Even Thee Thyself mocked at, nailed on the Cross;
It moveth me to see Thy wounded Body's loss;
Thy death, their insult, much this moveth me.

(Flores 1961, 62)

Spanish Catholicism came to be out of the experience of the Spanish conquest of the New World and the subsequent establishment of a hierarchical control of native civilizations of considerable complexity. The New World experience was even more determinant in the origins of the Southern Baptists. Indeed, both literally and substantively, the Southern Baptists could not have come to be without a South to be in. The accounting for that joint birth, if not unholy alliance, will come subsequently, but to foreshadow it, I offer this brief synopsis.

Baptists came across the Atlantic with the early English settlers to North America. The most well known was Roger Williams, the founder of Rhode Island. Born an Anglican, Williams became a Puritan, but during his conflicts with the famous Puritan leader John Cotton, he rejected infant baptism to become an advocate of full immersion of adults, whose "outward profession of Christ was to include being *buried* with [Christ] in baptism" (Grenz 1983, 45). Baptists swelled in numbers during the Great Awakening of 1740–1742, and the conversion-centered, evangelistic fervor of that moment became an essential, permanent ingredient of their faith. Despite the increase in numbers, however, the Baptists remained a minority sect and the natural enemy of the establishment Anglicans of the Tidewater plantations (Eighmy 1972, 8). With the Second Awakening of the early 1800s, however, the Baptists, along with the Methodists, became the main form of Christianity among the plain folk of the southern frontier, and by the time of the Civil War, they, again in company with the Methodists, replaced the Anglican-Episcopalians as the principal Christian faith among the slaveholding planters (Rosenberg 1989). Thus, crossing the Atlantic from England, where their practice of total immersion of the adult believer in the cold waters of the Thames earned them the derision of the more conventional faiths, and fighting for a place within the New World, where even the freedom-seeking Puritans evicted them, the Baptists found a niche first among the plain folk of the southern frontier and, by the time of the American Civil War, a more commodious space within the hierarchical environment of the southern plantation. All these events, however, were predicated on the transformation of a peopled landscape into an "empty continent." So to this transformation, we now turn.

At the base, the English view of the indigenous peoples settled in North America resembled that of their Spanish counterparts. The derogatory label of "heathen" is derived from an Anglo-Saxon word for country dweller (Jennings 1975). Since the Indians did not, according to the English view, live in towns, they were heathens, that is, neither civilized nor Christian, perhaps not capable of being either (Mitchell 1987, Meinig 1986). The Native American food procurement strategy relied heavily on hunting, which, to the English, put their human status further in doubt, for the English (but not the plain folk of the South) considered hunting both idleness and savagery. Unlike the Spanish, however, the English devoted little effort to congregating the native populations into nucleated communities, and missionary work among the Indians, such as it was, yielded few converts (Axtell 1985). In contrast to the Spanish "civic-centered system" (Meinig 1986, 236) in which the colonizer was required to select the site, lay out the grid of streets, designate the square to become the plaza (to be bordered by church and council) and distribute lots to settlers, the English settlement process, especially after the development of the rectangular land survey system, resembled a vast lottery in which buyers purchased land with the hope that the lots they bought would have high value (Meinig 1986). While in Spanish America, the grid was a component in a "liturgical act," in Anglo America and in the South, gridding the wilderness was an element in a commercial act that allowed a national government strapped for cash to gain income from its individual citizens (Stilgoe 1982). The colonial pattern in which the "dispersed individual family farm and household formed the basic unit of social and spatial structure" (Mitchell 1987, 106) flourished with marketing of public lands in the newly independent republic. In fact, individual settlers often moved ahead of the formal sale of land to squat on a particular fertile location and later filed claim for its possession. Such a settlement process led inevitably to military confrontations with the indigenous peoples and, following the treaties the British and, later, the American governments negotiated with the various Indians groups, led equally inevitably to the Native Americans ceding land and moving westward (Hilliard 1987).

The European process of emptying the land in North America, as in Middle and South America, was greatly aided by the spread of Old World diseases. Whereas the densely settled areas of Central Mexico and Andean South America continued to support an indigenous population—even in the face of one of the "greatest demographic disasters in the history of the world" (Denevan 1992, 7)—in North America, with considerably fewer native inhabitants, the impact was even more devastating, which, in the Christian scheme of things, was a blessing. As exemplified in the observations of a prominent member of the faith, even the Quakers rejoiced that "the Hand of God was eminently seen in thinning the *Indians*, to make room for the English . . . it at other times pleased Almighty God to send unusual Sickness amongst them, as the Smallpox, to lessen their Numbers" (Archdale 1836, 89). Consequently, the "American land was more like a widow than a virgin. Europeans did not find a wilderness here; rather, however involuntarily, they made one" (Jennings 1975, 173).[5]

Ravaged by both disease and warfare, Indians in the South, nonetheless, sought to establish a viable culture in the interstices of an expanding European society. Indeed, modern scholarship suggests the frontier was less a boundary than a "middle ground" or a "regional zone," where, at least in the early stages of westward expansion, the exchange between European and Native American, however antagonistic, created a distinctive subculture (Eslinger 1999; but see Meinig 1993). The passage, however, of the Indian Removal Act in 1830, which forcefully relocated southeastern Indians to the territory that later became Oklahoma, terminated the Indian presence in the South. Or did it? Ask any group of southerners, white or black, who has "Indian blood," and watch the hands go up. In your cynical mode, you reply, Yes, the world is full of wannabes, people who want to be Indian, especially on their "mother's side." True, yet the historian James Merrill (1989), in a sweeping indictment of fellow historians for continuing to talk of the "peopling of North America" when referring to the arrival of Europeans, insists

5. William Denevan suggests 3,790,000 as the size of the native population of North America, north of Mexico, at the time of Columbus's landfall. Although this figure is much more accurate than earlier estimates of 1,000,000, the overall density remains considerably lower than that of Central Mexico, with over 13,000,000 native people, and of Andean South America, with over 11,000,000 (1992, xxviii).

that until we grasp the simple fact that native peoples were an integral part of early Atlantic America, our efforts to grasp the nature of that colonial world will continue to fail (see also Jordan and Kaups 1989).

With Native Americans being "removed" though disease, war, acts of Congress, and the words of Eurocentric historians, the region became the habitat of a "people who never stayed in one place for a very long period of time" but who, in a perpetual quest for opportunities, might in a series of restless starts and stops traverse the region from North Carolina to Texas in a single generation (Bruce 1974, 14). In the South, particularly, the centrifugal forces of the frontier launched a frontal assault on formal institutions and created a society with such a "minimal civic order," with such "frailty of community" (Meinig 1986, 414), that what kept people "together was their ability to live apart" (Wiebe 1975, 46).

Among the plain folk of the South, the ability to live apart preadapted them for the rapid spread from Appalachia to Texas (Newton 1974). Economically, they practiced a blend of stock raising, agriculture, and hunting that led them to seek the appropriate combination of corn land, timber, and water. Socially, they lived in loosely grouped, egalitarian settlements of neighbors, with whom they visited and with whom they fought. Ethnically, though they might later be referred to as "good Anglo-Saxon stock," many in fact were of non-English origin (Mitchell 1987). In addition to those of Germanic ancestry, the Celtic background of many settlers contributed, at least according to one historian, to the southern plain-folk love of hunting and fighting and to their disdain for urban life and authority (McWhiney 1986). Similarly, the Finnish element among the first settlers in the Delaware Valley contributed to the wood craft and shifting cultivation techniques of plain-folk life (Jordan 1986; Jordan and Kaups 1989).

Baptist evangelism launched by self-governing churches transcended these ethnic divisions. It permitted a social diversity that corresponded to the dispersed settlement of southern plain folk but promoted a commonality in belief that cut across ethnic divisions. Furthermore, the lingering Calvinistic allegiance to a sovereign God with the Baptist election as God's people prepared the psychic groundwork for the emergence of a regional consciousness, which became the South. Central to Baptist evangelism was the conversion experience.

Earlier, in England, the Dissenters had rejected the sacramental nature of infant baptism. If baptism is not a sacrament, then, the Baptists concluded, infant baptism should be abolished altogether and replaced with the full immersion of the adult believer, which would signify the believer's wide-awake commitment to join the "company of saints." Furthermore, the congregational movement among the Dissenters rejected any religious authority higher than the individual band of baptized believers. In colonial North America, during the Great Awakening of the 1740s, Calvinism contributed the requirement that any candidate for membership in a church "give verbal evidence of a religious experience which had made him aware of his elect status. [This] meant that church membership now required an experience which was totally beyond the power of man to produce by his own efforts" (Grenz 1983, 39).

The account of Isaac Backus, a Puritan who in the Great Awakening became the father of the American Baptists, which was what the Southern Baptists were before they became the Christianity of southern slavery, is exemplary:

> As I was mowing alone in the field, August 24th, 1741, all my past life was opened plainly before me, and I saw clearly that it had been filled up with sin. I went and sat down in the shade of a tree, where my prayers and tears, my hearing of the Word of God and striving for a better heart, with all my other doings, were set before me in such a light that I perceived I could never make myself better, should I live ever so long. Divine justice appeared clear in my condemnation, and I saw that God had a right to do with me as He would. My soul yielded all into His hands, fell at His feet, and was silent and calm before Him. And while I sat there, I was enabled by divine light to see the perfect righteousness of Christ and the freeness and riches of His grace, with such clearness, that my soul was drawn forth to trust Him for salvation. And I wondered that others did not also come to Him who had enough for all. The word of God and the promise of His grace appeared firmer than a rock, and I was astonished at my previous unbelief. My heavy burden was done, tormenting fears were fled, and my joy was unspeakable. (Grenz 1983, 64–65)

In this narrative, Backus was, as with the Spanish American seers, away from the thick culture of the center of settlement and in a pastoral setting. In contrast to those seers, however, Backus did not see an external figure in a cave or on a rock; rather he "saw" an interior realization "that God had a right to do with [him] as he would." Nor was the divine light that engulfed Backus something that he stumbled across, but it came after a long period of anguish and questioning; yet despite the extensive mental turmoil, the vision was not an achievement of Backus. The calvinistic strand that it was God who dispensed grace and that human effort could gain nothing permeated Backus's telling.

Further dramatized through the vigorous outdoor preaching of John Wesley, the founder of Methodism, and of his colleague, George Whitefield, both of whom had crossed the Atlantic from England to bring the message of salvation to North America, the Backus-type conversion experience gained popularity throughout the several colonies. With its spread, the number of Baptists (and Methodists) multiplied, and by the end of the century, in 1792, the Baptists had 891 churches with 65,345 members. The Great Revival of the early 1800s, which came to have an even greater impact than the first Awakening, quickly doubled membership (Eighmy 1972; Hill 1980).

For the South and its emerging Christian faith, the Great Revival created a unique form of spiritual ecstasy: the camp meeting. Although similar to the miraculous visions of Spanish American pilgrimages in its threat to conventional Christianity, the camp meeting was much more an American creation. In "both belief and practice it was something quite different from its European antecedent" (Bruce 1974, 7). Too, the object of the evangelizing was not the American Indian but the participants in the plain-folk culture. The camp meeting, born out of southern plain-folk experience, sought to convert its own culture.

The camp meeting created a holiday of religiosity, a suspension of the workaday loneliness of the dispersed farmstead, an interval in which the plain-folk participants might exclaim an interior vision—a sight of Christ on the cross, continuously dying, bleeding great drops—or a voice calling their names. More frequently, they felt the power of God descending upon them like a storm and threw themselves to the ground, jerking, barking, crying in rapturous joy (Eslinger 1999). And they sang:

> I am bound for the promised land,
>   I'm bound for the promised land,
> O, who will come and go with me?
>   I am bound for the promised land.

To the formal hymns, the plain folk added a chorus in which they, together, challenged in strong, sectarian voice the established world of the hierarchical South with an otherworldly message:

O come, and join our pilgrim band,
Our toils and triumphs share;
We soon shall reach the promised land,
And rest forever there.
(Bruce 1974, 103, 117)

As an interval of heightened social exchange, the camp meeting counteracted the solitary and often contrary individualism of the plain folk. The plain folk stressed cooperation and hospitality. They welcomed new arrivals to their dispersed settlements with food and offers of assistance. They joined together to accomplish tasks, such as house construction or crop harvesting, that were beyond the capabilities of any single family. Their constant search, however, for openings within the oppressive structure of southern society, also fostered competition and hostility (Eslinger 1999).

The fight to get ahead created the mythic figure of the self-sufficient man, which, in the context of a drinking bout, translated into the challenge of the crossroads bully, who declared himself ready to kick, bite, and gouge anyone foolish enough to stand in his way. "Posing the threat of defiant noncooperation, the acts of the brutal antisocial hero represent the last stand of [the plain folk] against an oppressive system" (Bruce 1974, 33). By attacking the vices of gambling, drinking, swearing, and fighting—vices that in fact often erupted along the peripheries of the camp—and by calling for the complete surrender of the individual to the conversion experience, which implied a capitulation to group conformity, the camp meeting sought to transform the antisocial bully into a more cooperative, and docile, Christian.[6]

The taming of the antisocial bully and the evangelizing of the South did

6. A lighter side of the crossroads bully is told in the song "I'm the Man Who Rode the Mule Around the World," in which the singer brags about all the things he has seen and done. He recounts the day he spied on Adam and Eve in the Garden and the time he helped Noah load the ark. He finishes up with

I'm the man who rode the mule around the world.
I'm the man who rode the mule around the world.
I saw Peter, Paul and Moses playing ring around the roses,
And I'll whip the man who says it isn't so.

Another brag I heard in my drinking days at county-line joints back among the pines at the end of gravel roads was: "I'm a fighter, fucker, and a wild-horse rider." This was usually proclaimed after several beers. The speaker might add a certain luster to the point by crushing a beer can—the real, pre-aluminum kind—with one hand.

not, and still does not, occur without rifts among those who placed salvation of their own individual souls ahead of family, friendship, loyalty, and a live-and-let-live ethic. Among the tensions caused by the evangelical assault by the born-again upon their fellow southerners were those between a younger generation of cock-sure, beardless preachers and an older generation of weathered frontiersmen, between husband and wife about just what the pursuit of glory demanded, and between the austere, evangelical life-style and the festive one of dancing, partying, drinking, and group hunting. None of these were greater, however, than the "association of evangelical loyalties with unmanly dependence" (Heyrman 1997, 214). Conversion seemed to require the loss of mastery of self and, particularly for men, a turning away from slaps on the back and mock exchanges of blows that might suddenly become serious and a turning toward embracing, hugging, and crying in the arms of an effeminate preacher.

Despite these tensions, and maybe even in some strange way because of them, the camp meeting so successfully converted its own culture that in the 1830s, the Baptists, striving to move up the social hierarchy, abandoned the campground and its physical spirituality to seek respectability in a more decorous, textual proclamation of faith. Their success gave them entrance into the established world of the slaveowning South.

Yet open-faced egalitarianism did not fuse well with hierarchical nobility, and though the South became color-conscious and white, there remained two Souths, the lowland South of the slave plantation and the upland South of the independent plain folk. Although proudly and militantly Southern Baptists, the Baptists of the upland South continued to speak the language of sectarian dissent, a language that condemned sacramental ritual as an impediment between God and his "priesthood of believers."

The churches in which the "priesthood" gathered to hear the Word distinguished themselves only by their names. Located in settlements strung along waterways frequently named after the first settler, the churches took on those names—Gilbert's Creek, Tate's Creek, Swanson's Springs—thereby contributing not to a sacred landscape of saints and apparitions but to a secular one of people.[7] Built of logs, square or rectangular in shape, with a chim-

7. The churches might also carry the name of a natural feature, such as Pine Grove or Fall's Chapel. One such church, Sandy Creek in North Carolina, carries the reputation of being the first Baptist church in the South. Begun in 1755 through the work of Shubal Stearns, a missionary from Connecticut, the congregation was composed of New Light or Separate Baptists. Hav-

ney for warmth in the winter and one or two windows to catch a breeze in the summer, the churches expressed a simplicity that sprung from the Baptist suspicion of the sensory mode as much as it came from frontier austerity (Figure 11; Sweet 1931, Dillenberger 1988). Inside, the ranting voice of the preacher filled the empty walls, and in tune with his vocal rhythms, the congregation shouted aloud in ecstasy or murmured in silent conviction, "Now, I see!" (Dillenberger 1988, 15).

The Baptist insistence on interior conviction over exterior sacrament infused the plain-folk life-style, already plain as an adaptation to their sojourn across the southern frontier and to their marginal position in a hierarchical society, so as to make the plain even plainer, to sanctify the plain with the glow of true spirituality. Limited in their access to education, plain-folk

FIG. 11. The plain-folk frontier church. From *Encyclopedia of Southern Baptists*, Vol. I (1958, 68).

---

ing "separated" from the Congregationalists because of being bathed in the "new light" of the Holy Spirit, these Baptists worshiped enthusiastically, with tremblings, screams, and acclamations, modulated in a nasal, holy whine (Stroupe 1983; see also Purefoy 1858). Such a plain-folk beginning for the Southern Baptists is often laid alongside the more restrained development in Charleston, South Carolina, where gentlemen theologians stressed the importance of unadorned but formal piety (Leonard 1990). In the spring of 1995, James Peacock, a student of Appalachian Baptists (Peacock and Tyson 1989), and I visited the grave of Reverend Stearns, who lies in the cemetery next to the church he founded.

preachers saw exceptional virtue in being called rather than being trained. They "farmed during the week, lest someone should accuse them of preaching for money," and "their preaching was almost entirely exhorting, [and many] seemed to be exponents of the philosophy that 'schoolin ain't necessary as long as I've got good wind'" (Dale 1958, 18). Plain-folk Baptists rejected the logic that civilization and its urbanity provide the proper matrix for Christianity, and they distinguished their Christianity from the southern planter's image as the pious cavalier. Civilization, among the more Baptist of the Southern Baptists, became suspect; rural humility, they argued, perhaps out of necessity but certainly out of conviction, is closer to God.

The conviction that plain is more godly gained its authority from the widespread belief that the people knew best. And if the people knew best, then preaching must reach them. The audience became an arbitrator of truth, and consequently the "colloquial sermon" became the genre of choice (Hatch 1989, 133–41). It featured a poetics of storytelling, strident attacks, gross humor, ridicule, and the revelation of intimate experience. Plain-folk preaching drew its strength through its constant denigration of the "worldly ways of the high and mighty." Individual preachers strove to combine the image of John the Baptist shouting, "Repent, for the kingdom of heaven is at hand," with that of Thomas Jefferson proclaiming, "All men are created equal." Competition among these "men of God" for their audience furthered the proliferation of churches, and consequently, in the opinion of one scholar (Hatch 1989), evangelical religion had a darker side, a side that, instead of integrating plain-folk society, frequently caused its disruption and fragmentation.

Furthermore, despite their fondness for denigrating worldly riches, congregationally sensitive plain-folk preachers soon developed a strategy for accommodating themselves to the "high and mighty." While the first generation of preachers, filled with the Holy Spirit of liberty, condemned slavery, the second generation stifled their dissent, and the third found slavery ordained in the Holy Book itself.

In Spanish America, European hierarchy rested on an indigenous American base; in the American South, European stratification sat on the backs of transported Africans. On the eve of the Civil War, cotton plantations based on slave labor dominated the landscape from Virginia, around the Appalachians, through the central Carolinas, piedmont Georgia, the black belt of central Alabama and Mississippi, the natural levees of the Mississippi floodplain, and westward into East Texas. Tobacco plantations continued to flourish in Virginia and North Carolina, and rice cultivation extended along the coasts of North Carolina and Georgia. Sugarcane estates, reinforced with refugees from the Haitian revolution of 1791 on the island of Santo Domingo, occupied South Louisiana (Map 3).

This agricultural empire was economically tied to the manufacturing centers in New England and Europe and, as such, was part of the developing world capitalist system (Wolf 1982). Ideologically, however, it cloaked its exploitation of land and people under the cape of the Cavalier myth. In the Cavalier myth, the antebellum southern plantation was headed by a well-born father / master, who, along with his sons, governed the structure; beneath these men came the women, the wives and daughters, then the children, white dependents, and, at the bottom, black slaves. Furthermore, a code of manners, behavior, and deportment permeated the system (Pyron 1989). For a society, however, "that was still largely frontier even in 1860 and hardly more than a single generation removed from personal and immediate contact with hoe and plow, the myth was more aspiration than a reflection of social reality" (Degler 1977, 56).

By 1845, the Baptists of the United States, despite their centrifugal na-

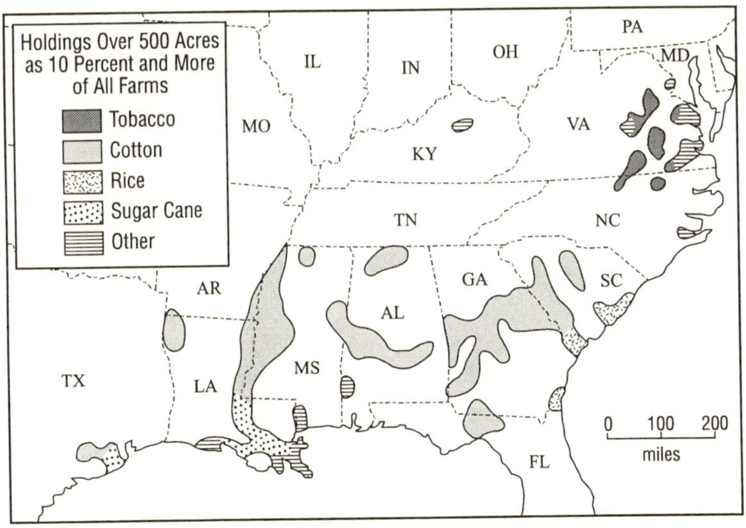

Map 3. Large agricultural holdings and crop specialization in the American South, c. 1860. Adapted from Hilliard (1990, 106–107).

ture, had organized themselves into a national body that, among other things, promoted missionary—that is, evangelistic—work within the country. At the meeting of the Baptist Triennial Convention in 1845, the northern, controlling half of the convention refused to accept a southern slaveholder as a missionary. Consequently, the southern churches withdrew to form their own convention. The Southern Baptist Convention was born on this particular question: Could a slaveholder also be a missionary? In saying yes, the Southern Baptists committed themselves to the defense of slavery and to becoming the Christianity of the South. "The preachers . . . did their best to Christianize, humanize, soften the attitude of the masters toward their slaves, while they quietly reaffirmed the divine sanction of slavery as a social system" (Genovese and Fox-Genovese 1988, 21). "Because southern life appeared particularly Christian to those churchmen whose theology allowed them to overlook the social evils of slavery, threats against the South were interpreted as threats against the last remaining stronghold of Christian civilization" (Boles 1976, 32). The equality of salvation confronted the inequality of slavery and lost.

At the time of the organization, there were some 350,000 Baptists in the South; those Baptists who had slaves owned a total of some 100,000 (Redford 1958). Paradoxically, because slaveowners wanted both to spread the gospel among their slaves and to keep an eye on how that gospel spread, southern churches were more integrated before the Civil War than afterward (Boles 1976). The relationship, of course, even when well-intended, was asymmetrical. For example, to encourage religious instruction among local blacks, Baptists in Alabama sought to have Caesar Blackmoor, a popular black preacher, devote himself completely to preaching. Because it was unlawful for Blackmoor to be a freedman in Alabama, three trustees of the state association assumed the role of master, and thus the Alabama Baptist Association acquired a slave (Redford 1958).

However contentious the marriage, frontier egalitarianism and plantation nobility joined to make the South a region that stood in dialectical opposition to the North. "By mid-century people in all levels of society generally accepted the views of evangelical religion. . . . the South [was] solid religiously before [it] became solid politically" (Boles 1976, 32). In its opposition, the South became solid and equal, solidly white and equally noble. The plain folk, in their restlessness, claimed identity with the slaveholding planters. They so thoroughly bought into the paradoxical ideology of a white republic supported by black slavery that they died in disproportionate numbers on the battlefields during the "War Between the States" (Harris 1998). For their part, the planters, some of whom found ways—quite justified, no doubt—of avoiding the front-line slaughter, cloaked the inhumanity of slavery in the garb of the manners, behavior, and deportment of *gentil*—"genteel"—civilization.

Thus was born the South and the Southern Baptists.

3

THE PRESENCE OF CHRIST IN THE NEW WORLD DURING MODERNITY

¡Viva Cristo Rey! and the Bible Is True, Jim Crow

In Spanish America, independence from Spain introduced a time of great expectations, of imperfect achievement, and even of despair, all summed up in the embittered words of Simón Bolívar, the Liberator, who, at the end of a life dedicated to freedom and reform, observed, "He who follows the Revolution plows the sea." By the late nineteenth century, however, the political instability of the postindependence era, marked by the rise and fall of various ruthless, intimidating, physically courageous *caudillos*, had congealed into regimes of greater permanence in which the telluric *caudillo* had to share space with the aspiring technocrat, whose commitment to positivistic efficiency often engendered similar ruthlessness (Safford 1987; Bushnell and Macaulay 1994). The political change was accompanied, if not led, by a bustling export of commodities produced by agriculture and mining and transported by an equally burgeoning railroad network to ports for shipment via steamships crossing the Atlantic to an apparently insatiable Europe, whose appetite for beef, bananas, and nitrate continued unabated until the world economic crisis of the 1930s (Glade 1989).

The political agenda and the export economy changed the countryside. The symbiosis of the Spanish hacienda and the indigenous village established in the colonial period, always hostile, entered an era of greater conflict. Prior to 1870, the hacienda, in general, was an ill-defined extension of territory inhabited by both rangy livestock and an abundance of resident workers. It was, nonetheless, profit oriented and actively, if inefficiently, engaged in a market economy (Bauer 1989). The indigenous community, which supplied the hacienda with labor for seasonal harvesting of crops and cattle, had synthesized Spanish and aboriginal culture to form an encapsulated society that was more or less successful in resisting intrusion. The worship of the saints carried out by religious brotherhoods, or *cofradías*, which the colonial missionaries had introduced during the founding of the *doctrinas*, articulated and sustained the closed, corporate character of these *pueblos de los indios*.

Liberal ideology of the nineteenth and early twentieth centuries, with its glorification of the rationality of the egalitarian individual, disparaged the corporate community as an impediment to progress. Legal reforms, designed to encourage the assimilation of Native Americans, opened community lands for a more efficiently organized hacienda. Under the twin attacks of governmental policy and global capitalism, Native American communities lost land and, through acculturation, individuals. Many, however, proved to be amazingly resilient, and in those areas where the work on the hacienda provided an alternative source of income without absorbing community lands, the walls of cultural separatism may have grown even stronger (Grieshaber 1979; Donghi 1987).

On the peripheries of the former colonial core, where the aboriginal population was less dense and had succumbed quickly to European diseases, the European demand for Latin American commodities brought extensive areas into production. Agrarian industries of coffee, sugar, fibers, and bananas operated on an economy of scale that required a low-cost, efficient work force that responded to the scheduling of an impersonal management. Within this enclave economy, labor became a commodity, and former peasants, a rural proletariat. Yet in certain areas associated with coffee production, as in Costa Rica and the Antioquia region of Colombia, the export economy permitted the development of family farms cultivated by independent yeomen (Bauer 1989, but see Gudmundson 1986). Communities composed of these farmers differed from the closed, corporate Indian villages in their closer proximity to national institutions with concomitantly less cultural encapsulation. The cult of the saints, for example, was less a village activity and more an individual preference; furthermore, the saints themselves more nearly approximated orthodox models and in any case assumed a role secondary to the worship of Mary and of Christ.

Nineteenth-century liberalism worked to change the cities as well as the countryside. Requirements of the export economy "encouraged the replacement of the individual strong man or caudillo with institutionalized government composed of all-powerful executive named by elite consensus and a largely advisory legislative branch staffed and controlled by the same elite" (Scobie 1989). This elite, residents of the national and regional capitals, desired urban landscapes that expressed their opulence. Toward the end of the century, the wealthy began to move away from the congested central plazas of the major cities in search of higher ground and more space. They left behind the Mediterranean courtyard house and built multistory mansions of French, Italian, British, and, by 1930, U.S. designs with grand entrances and sweeping balustrades. Having departed from the central plaza, they insisted that it be beautified with gardens, trees, benches, fountains, and commemorative statues. Public buildings—cathedral, executive mansion, supreme court, and ministries—received major facelifts or were completely rebuilt, and new palaces of fine arts, theaters, clubs, and operatic houses whose massive doors opened to imposing foyers, marble balconies, and velvet upholstery offered new vistas of social splendor, places to see and, especially, to be seen by an admiring and appreciative populace (Scobie 1989).

In the nineteenth and early twentieth centuries, classical liberalism in Spanish America defined itself through the promotion of secularization. In Mexico, for example, as part of the "La Reforma" program of the 1850s, marriages, cemeteries, hospitals, and the recording of vital statistics were removed from control of the Church, and nunneries were suppressed. Liberals everywhere argued that ecclesiastical wealth had to be extracted from the dead hand of the Church and permitted to circulate freely and thereby stimulate business. "A modern secular state," the liberal agenda promulgated, "was made up of free individuals, equal before the law and unrestrained in pursuit of their enlightened self-interest" (Hale 1989, 236). Such an agenda proved favorable for the ascendancy of positivism, the scientific sociology of the French philosopher Auguste Comte, which, when imported to Spanish America, favored the economic over the humanistic, central control over regional autonomy, and, at least in some cases, authoritarianism over democracy (Hale 1989).

In its response to the liberal agenda, the Catholic Church drew its doctrinal inspiration from Pope Pius IX's encyclical *Quanta Cura* and its *Syllabus of Errors*. Promulgated in 1864, the encyclical condemned secular education, freedom of thought, and religious toleration (Lynch 1989; Fremantle 1963). Pope Pius IX also convened Vatican Council I (1869–1870), which promulgated the doctrine of papal infallibility: by virtue of his apostolic authority as the successor of St. Peter, "the rock" upon which Christ built his Church, when the pope speaks on matters of church doctrine, his statements are free of error.

In the early twentieth century, priests continued the attack on modernity and from pulpits urged greater participation in the sacraments. Formal observance, private piety, and individual morality were the chief concerns voiced by many clergy and laity (Lynch 1989). Piety in the face of a hostile world found articulation in the increasingly popular devotion to the Sacred Heart of Jesus.

The wounds that Jesus received during his crucifixion were popular objects of devotion during medieval times. The torment they spoke of became, paradoxically, a place of refuge and solace. The wounds appeared to people in visions, and masses were dedicated to them (Rubin 1990). The image of the lacerated heart of Jesus that forms the modern cult emerged from this medieval "passion." In the 1670s in France, Margaret Marie Alacoque reported that Christ revealed to her his heart encircled with thorns, pierced by a spear, and crowned with flames. With his heart thus revealed, he spoke of his love for humanity and how much he had suffered from the ingratitude and indifference shown toward the Blessed Sacrament. He instructed her to make reparations by promoting the devotion to his Sacred Heart on the Friday of the week that follows Corpus Christi (Moell 1967). The placement of the feast day of the Sacred Heart so close to the one dedicated to Corpus Christi indicates how the newer one plays off the earlier, medieval sacrament.

As it developed in the late medieval period, the feast of Corpus Christi was celebrated on Thursday following Pentecost (which exalted the day the Holy Spirit descended "as tongues of fire" upon the disciples to fill them with evangelical zeal) and centered on the presentation of the host, the wafer of unleavened bread used in mass, to the congregants. After sanctifying the host, the priest placed it in a monstrance, an ornate, sunlike disk with a glass enclosure in its center and mounted on a hand-held pedestal (Figure 12). Elevating the monstrance, the priest then visually offered the Blessed Sacrament for the adoration of the congregants. Later, he might position the monstrance on the altar or in a special chapel to which individual worshipers could retire to honor the Sacramental Christ or to pray for a special favor. As communion for the ordinary worshiper was observed infrequently, this "feasting by seeing," or "ocular communion," supplemented the "feasting by eating" (Mitchell 1982; Rubin 1990). During the late medieval period in Spain, the

FIG. 12. Monstrance

priest, holding the monstance aloft, led the populace through the streets in an elaborate procession to display the Real Presence of Christ. Such a public display of the central Catholic principle of transubstantiation heralded through the land the triumph of the true Church (O'Shea 1967b; Foster 1960).

Following the Counter-Reformation, in both the Old World and the New, the pomp of earlier processions became more modest (Foster 1960). Yet the popular saying "Hay tres Jueves en el año que causan admiración, Jueves Santo, Jueves Corpus, y Jueves de Ascensión; There are three Thursdays in the year that cause admiration, Maundy Thursday, Corpus Thursday, and Thursday of the Ascension," repeated in Spain and in Spanish America, voices support of Corpus Christi as a cult of continued and extraordinary importance to the Hispanic world (Chevalier 1977).[1]

Both Corpus Christi and the Sacred Heart, one closely following the other, depict the sacrifice of Christ. The iconography, however, is strikingly different. While the sacramental wafer within the monstrance is the core symbol of Corpus Christi, the symbol of the Sacred Heart is the lacerated heart crowned with thorns and shooting flames (Figure 13; Morris 1967). While the image of Corpus Christi is Christ "Sacramentalized," *Cristo Sacramentado*, the image of the Sacred Heart is far more physical and portrays the incarnate aspect of Christ, Christ Embodied, as it were, or *Cristo Encarnado*.

In its imagery, the Sacred Heart brings together the bloody, physical heart with the metaphorical heart of suffering and love. It also ties "the theme of suffering love with the theme of protective veneration in the face of hostility" (Taves 1986, 35). In so doing, the Sacred Heart responded to the threat of nineteenth-century liberalism and to the emerging hostility of twentieth-century socialism. As Catholicism shifted from being the de facto center of the Spanish American world to becoming an alternative among other alternatives, Catholics moved to protect the Sacred Heart from additional mutilation. In the last year of the nineteenth century, Pope Leo XIII dedicated the entire human race to the Sacred Heart, and Spanish American countries soon followed the papal lead: Venezuela dedicated itself to the Sacred Heart in 1900, Colombia in 1902, Nicaragua in 1920, Costa Rica in 1921, and Bolivia in 1925 (Carroll 1989).[2]

In the early twentieth century, an additional ceremony, the Enthrone-

1. In translating from Spanish to English, my goal is to make the switch as if the Spanish voice gave way immediately to the English voice. Consequently, I avoid the usual practice of putting the translation in brackets, and, instead, I begin the Spanish sentence or phrase with quotes and close the quotes at the end of the English translation.

2. Carroll (1989) and Kehoe (1979) offer two divergent explanations for the popularity of the Sacred Heart. Carroll, in a psychoanalytical interpretation, argues the position of the Sacred Heart on the outside of the chest of Jesus recalls the infant fantasy that in sexual intercourse the mother absorbs the penis of the father; consequently, the stated directive by the Sacred Heart to make reparations for the hostility shown toward the Blessed Sacrament draws its emotional strength from the subconscious desire to atone for the mutilation of the father. Kehoe, taking a cultural historical view, raises the question of why the Sacred Heart devotion is so strong in Mexico and, by extension, Spanish America. She explains that the Aztec practice of eating the

Fig. 13. The Sacred Heart of Jesus

ment of the Sacred Heart, continued the prevalent movement toward formal observance, private piety, and individual morality (Larkin 1967). In the Enthronement, a devout family places a small statue of Jesus pointing to his Sacred Heart on a shelf attached to the wall of the front room. The shelf becomes a small altar, to which the family might add a candle, flowers, perhaps a statue of the Virgin, and even, more recently, a Bible, as in Figure 14 (which is based on a photograph taken in Buga, Colombia, in 1992). In so

heart of the sacrificial victim provided the necessary cultural substrate to turn a more or less inconsequential European practice into a popular passion.

FIG. 14. The enthronement of the Sacred Heart on a household altar

consecrating themselves to the Sacred Heart, family members promise love in the face of hostility and recognize "the social sovereignty of Christ the King" (Larkin 1967, 820).

Although the ecclesiastically endorsed cult of the Sacred Heart became the most popular response among laity to the perceived threat to the Church, other activities of the faithful, activities with far less papal support, also responded to the felt condition of powerlessness. In Spain, since the thirteenth century, the people of Madrid have venerated the Virgin of Atocha, so-called because the Virgin appeared in a field of *atocha*, a grass hemp, growing near the city. In the late eighteenth century, an effigy of the Virgin of Atocha with the Christ Child attached to her hands was installed in the newly built church dedicated to Christ Crucified in the mining town of Plateros, near Fresnillo, in northern Mexico. At some time in the nineteenth century the Niño became detached from his mother and acquired his own following.

The iconography of the image at Plateros is as distinctive as its history. The *Niñito Moreno*, Little Brown Child, as the Christ Child is affectionately addressed, wears a long robe and over the robe a cape decorated with cockle shells. On his head is a wide-brimmed hat, and on his feet, sandals. In his right hand, he carries a staff and a water gourd, and in his left, a basket (Figure 15). This distinctive attire purports to be that of a pilgrim of earlier days. According to the founding story, the Moorish conquerors of the city of Atocha, Spain, imprisoned many Christian men under harsh circumstances of little food and no spiritual consolation. One day, a child dressed as a pilgrim of the time, with a staff and gourd of water in one hand and a basket of bread in the other, appeared at the prison gates with a request to administer to those kept so cruelly within. Once they consented, the Moorish jailers were astonished to discover that after the child had served each prisoner water and bread and had given each a blessing, the basket was still filled with bread and the gourd with water. Christ, in the form of a child on a pilgrimage, had responded to the prayers of those so sorely in need.

Since Lange (1978) offers documentation that the veneration of the Holy Child of Atocha originated in the New World and did not reach Spain until the early decades of the twentieth century, both the distinctive dress of the Niño and its founding story appear to be applications of earlier forms to late nineteenth-century Mexico. The image of Christ as a child who nonetheless acts on his own, independent of his mother, is a particularly evocative combination of innocence and power. In the Niño, the impeccable virtue of a child, scarcely more than a babe in arms, combines with the discriminating capacity of a mature adult to become a miracle worker that offers no direct confrontation with the antagonistic secular establishment. Furthermore, the faithful gain access to this transformational vigor through channels outside the normal workings of ecclesiastical potency. As a consequence, the popularity of the cult at Plateros has turned the small town into a shrine city of pilgrims whose devotion to the Christ Child has superseded the veneration of the Mother of Atocha and even of the Christ Crucified to whom the church in Plateros was originally dedicated. The veneration has spread as far north as the New Mexico town of Chimayó, where a shrine dedicated to the Niño stands next to the more famous one venerating the Christ Crucified (Figure

FIG. 15. The veneration of the Santo Niño de Atocha, showing the location of the shrines, the image of the Niño, and plaques on the shrine wall at Plateros

15). The popular cult of the Niño, as mentioned, went across the Atlantic and reached Madrid in the 1920s.

Yet for all of its stress on sacramental observance and individual piety, as the nineteenth century drew to a close, the church hierarchy began to address social issues. In 1891, in the encyclical *Rerum Novarum*, Pope Leo XIII recognized that though the right to own property was in accordance with the law of nature, unions had the corresponding right to organize. In fact, from a perspective vastly different from the condemnation of the world contained in the *Syllabus of Errors* issued less than twenty years earlier by his pious predecessor, Pope Leo observed that in 1891 the "condition of the working classes is the pressing question of the hour" (Fremantle 1963, 194). For all of its concern for the plight of workers, however, the encyclical did not prevent the Church from becoming the enemy of Mexico's social revolution of 1910. "The new Church, independent of the state and caught up in the winds of change of *Rerum Novarum*, was on its way to becoming an instrument for social reform. Yet many revolutionary leaders were as convinced as had been their liberal fathers that Mexican Catholicism was a congenital enemy of progress. By the same token, the new Catholic leaders, like the old, were certain that a liberal secular State was a perversion of true Mexicanism and a foe of basic human values" (Bailey 1974, 22).

The revolutionaries acted first. With the new Constitution of 1917, they successfully extended the control of the state over the church far beyond its "Reforma" predecessor of 1857. In the new Mexico, monastic orders were forbidden, religious bodies could not acquire property, worship in the existing church structures required permission from the federal government, and public worship outside the church buildings, that is, street processions, was declared illegal. The clergy could not vote or hold public office, nor could they criticize, either publicly or privately, public officials (Bailey 1974).

In this context, the emergence of a new feast day on the Catholic liturgical calendar devoted to *Cristo Rey*, Christ the King, took on wider significance. A further development of the veneration of Christ's embodiment in the host consecrated in mass and tied, too, perhaps, to the devotion of the Sacred Heart of Jesus, the feast was instituted by Pope Pius XI in 1925 in response to a "crisis of faith in the Savior's authority, exercised by the Church" (Hardon 1980, 104). The celebration of Christ the King explicitly articulated the theme of "the authority of our Lord to rule all nations" (Attwater 1958, 95).

"Jesus is the King who has obtained His sovereignty through His blood. He is the Redeemer King" (O'Shea 1967a, 627).

Before the official institution of the feast in 1925, a huge statue of Christ with his arms outstretched was erected in the approximate geographical center of the country on top of Mt. Cubilete, north of Mexico City. The papal delegate, Ernesto Philippi, led some 50,000 pilgrims up the mountain to crown Christ king of Mexico. Recognizing this act as a challenge to their authority, Mexican officials declared the act a violation of the Constitution of 1917 and evicted the Vatican delegate (Wilkie 1966).

Concurrently, in southwestern Mexico, a militant Catholic movement composed largely of farmers revolted against the revolutionary presidency of Plutarco Elias Callas, who swore in turn to "defanaticize the masses" (Lynch 1989, 367). Supporters of Callas contemptuously referred to the members of the armed rebellion as *cristeros*, "Christers," but the rebels rushed to accept the term and took the pennant of Christ the King, along with that of the Virgin of Guadalupe, into battle.

At first, the papacy lent support to the *cristero* movement, but anxious to reach an accommodation with the Mexican government, "Rome withdrew to narrowly spiritual ground as the only feasible position. It sacrificed everything else" (Bailey 1974, 307). Despite earlier successes, the *cristeros* met final defeat in 1929 in a confrontation with the army of General Saturnino Cedillo, whose force consisted of *agraristas*, landless peasants to whom the government granted or promised to grant land. Thus, the conflict pitted members of the rural lower sector against one another to the benefit of the federal "revolutionary" government (Ankerson 1984).

Prescient, perhaps, of the lack of support from the established church and of the duplicity of the government, Anacleto Gonzáles Flores, a convicted leader of the *cristeros*, when placed before a firing squad in 1927, shouted, "I die, but God does not die, ¡*Viva Cristo Rey*!" (Figure 16).

In the American South, the Civil War brought both defeat and freedom and the vision of a new day dawning. What the region got was the "New South" and Jim Crow. The "New South," the one officially celebrated by Atlanta journalist Henry W. Grady's address in New York in 1886, was the first of the many "new Souths" that bid to replace a forever "dying" Old South. The New South looked north for capital to industrialize itself out of its agrarian past, and in return it promised northern capitalists social stability, that is, low

Fig. 16. Execution of the *cristeros.* Adapted from Brenner (1971).

wages, no unions, and disfranchised African Americans. Jim Crow legislation, beginning in the late 1800s and with a name derived from the buffoonery of blackface minstrelsy (Wilson 1989), reverberated through the state legislatures during the first decades of the twentieth century. The legislation mandated separate coaches on trains, separate schools, separate public facilities (toilets and water fountains), and separate parks for white and black southerners. Even prisons had separate chain gangs. Works of social theorists, such as William Graham Sumner's *Folkways*, were cited to bolster the claim that these recent legal inventions expressed something intrinsic in southern race relations. Calling upon the fiction that segregation was an inevitable part of the "southern way of life," white-dominated state legislatures passed literacy, property, and poll-tax requirements to prohibit blacks from voting. In Louisiana in 1896, nearly twenty years after the end of Reconstruction, there were 130,334 registered black voters; less than ten years later in 1904 following the restrictive legislation, there were 1,342 (Woodward 1974).

As the New South became segregated, it became a region of "courthouse towns." The increase in rail traffic toward the end of the nineteenth century connected cotton planters directly to northern markets and thereby shifted the focus of urbanization from the coastal and river ports of the pre–Civil War South toward the interior locations of the post-Reconstruction South. Innovations in the ginning and baling of cotton and in the extraction of oil from cotton seed encouraged the development of small, nucleated centers, so that by 1900 urban places of five thousand to ten thousand inhabitants dotted the landscape from southern Georgia to eastern Texas (Goldfield 1982, 1997).[3]

As the seat of government of the surrounding countryside, the courthouse town constituted the hub of the county political system. Within its grid pattern of streets resided the governing elite, "men of the word, who peopled and maintained the civil order of the town and the county." Occupying the streets adjacent to the courthouse were "law offices, surveyors' offices, stores, a market, a printer, banks, a Masonic hall, and a post office" (Newton 1974, 151). A block or so from the civil square stood the urbanized evangelical churches, the more literate ministries of old-line churches, and in the larger towns perhaps an academy of learning where young boys conjugated Latin verbs. With the exception of Maryland, portions of Kentucky (where church parishes were founded by immigrants from Maryland), and South Louisiana (with its French-speaking population), Catholicism counted itself lucky to find an empty block near the edge of town to erect an inconspicuous chapel.

White people, particularly those of substance, lived in central hallway homes or in more recent Victorian structures. Across the railroad tracks, in the "Quarters," in much more modest houses and packed in much less space were the blacks, their churches, and, locked in a continuously uphill battle to

3. Edgar T. Thompson, a South Carolina planter's son who became a sociologist, observed that as part of the plantation system, the southern county developed as a social as well as a governmental unit. "The township as a functional unit," he insisted, "was a Reconstruction imposition" (1972, 73).

secure support from a white board of trustees, their schools. With the exception of the large landowners, few farmers lived in the county seat; "it was not an agricultural village" (Newton 1974, 151).

Out in the countryside, in the upland South, where the custom of open range permitted cattle and hogs to graze and scavenge widely, roads conformed only to the lay of the land. Branch roads often bisected the farmsteads of the white plain folk and the less common black landowner, both of whom arranged house, barn, garden, and stock pens according to notions of convenient access. This resulted, in the eyes of more aesthetically minded travelers, in a landscape untidy, if not downright "trashy," with moral implications. Where small roads crossed the more important routes, dispersed hamlets, made up of a store, a wooden-frame church, a cemetery, and a few houses of people related by descent and marriage, appeared. Without central greens or public spaces, the hamlets, called "settlements" in the vernacular and named after the dominant family—thus, "Hilliard's Settlement"—also struck the sensitive outsider as disorderly and uncouth (Newton 1974).

In the changing New South of the late nineteenth and early twentieth centuries, the Southern Baptists emerged as a powerful denomination behind a thoroughly white Christ. Becoming powerful meant also movement toward respectability, away from the county's ill-bred peripheries to the hierarchical civility of the county seat. Having long ago superseded the Episcopalians and Presbyterians and closing in on the Methodists, the Southern Baptists claimed space near the law-and-order center of the courthouse, where the founding congregation erected an imposing edifice, the First Baptist Church. The congregation constructed, immediately adjacent to the worship hall and filling out the remainder of the church property, another structure of equal size and demeanor: the Sunday School.

A Protestant institution that emerged in the nineteenth century with the new middle-class vision of a democratic society (Boylan 1988), Sunday School did not develop as a major component of Southern Baptist worship until the very end of the century (Barnette 1958). Once underway, however, and under the control of the denomination's Sunday School Board, Sunday School became an integral part of Southern Baptist life. During the first quarter of the twentieth century, from the passing of Jim Crow legislation and the rise of the southern small city through World War I, the 75 percent increase in Sunday School attendance outdistanced even the spectacular 55 percent rise in church membership. In the second quarter, a time when southerners, along with other Americans, suffered through the Great Depression and then fought the Axis powers in World War II, church membership increased by 48 percent to stand at slightly over seven million, and Sunday School enrollment, compared to the earlier leap, grew a less spectacular 46 percent to reach slightly over five million at midcentury (Table 2).

By 1950, Sunday School consisted of age-graded classes extending from toddlers to adults, with a nursery provided for babies. An hour before Sunday morning worship service, the high point of the Baptist liturgical day, children gathered in an auxiliary auditorium in the Sunday School building for a period of singing, prayer, and announcements. Segregated according to sex, the groups then dispersed into individual rooms for classes. Volunteering their time, church women taught the earlier grades of both girls and boys, but church men took over the classes of adolescent boys. The minister often assumed responsibility for the adult men. Teachers taught from Sunday School lesson booklets prepared by the Sunday School Board and distributed to classes. Each student was expected to bring a Bible.

In Sunday School, children learned about the sins of dancing, drinking, smoking, gambling, playing cards on Sunday, and swimming in the company of the opposite sex. They also heard about the evils of liturgical sacramentalism and ecclesiastical hierarchy (i.e., Roman Catholicism). Above all, they were instructed in the virtues of instantaneous conversion from a life of depravity. Education in Sunday School taught "for a verdict" (Chapman 1958, 1147), demanding a public confession even from a ten-year-old.

As children grew up and moved from the juvenile classes to the subadulthood of the Young People's Group, they made their way through the Bible several times, even including the "begats": "Abraham begat Isaac; and Isaac begat Jacob; and Jacob begat Judas and his brethren. . . . And Jacob begat

TABLE 2. The Growth of the Southern Baptists in the First Half of the Twentieth Century

	Church Membership	Percent Increase	Sunday School Enrollment	Percent Increase
1900	1,658,000		671,000	
1925	3,649,000	55	2,692,000	75
1950	7,080,000	48	5,025,000	46

SOURCE: Adapted from Storer 1958, 1256–57.

Joseph the husband of Mary, of whom was born Jesus, who is called Christ" (Matthew 1:2–16). The teacher frequently began class with the request that the students take turns in reciting their favorite verse of Scripture. Inevitably, a city boy, impeccable in coat and tie, pronounced, "For God so loved the world, that he gave his only begotten Son, that whosoever believeth in him should not perish, but have everlasting life" (John 3:16). Not to be outdone, a kid from the country, to cover an ineptitude of unruly hair and scruffy shoes, tried for snickers with the shortest verse in the Bible, "Jesus wept" (John 11:35). Throughout the Sunday School journey, from nursery to adolescence, in lesson, story, and song, children were reminded that "Yes, Jesus loves me. Yes, Jesus loves me. Yes, Jesus loves me. The Bible tells me so." And when the Bible spoke, it—like the Roman Catholic pope—was infallible and, for nearly all, inerrant, or without error.

The term *inerrancy* came into vogue after the Civil War among biblical conservative scholars. Drawing upon the school of Scottish Realism, they argued that, like nature, the Bible was a storehouse of facts; consequently, reading the Bible consisted of gathering together the facts contained within it, much in the manner an inductivist scientist, in the tradition of Francis Bacon, collected the facts of nature. Furthermore, the Bible was a plain-speaking document, which meant what it said; therefore all people of common sense (as opposed to the Germanic professors of the Higher Criticism) had access to its truth (Marsden 1980).

Although some members of this common-sense philosophy reached a more moderate position that while God inspired the Bible, humans wrote it, and therefore, being human, they made mistakes; biblical conservatives insisted the Bible, even with human writers, remained without error (Marsden 1982). The Southern Baptist Convention, responding to the growing controversy between biblical literalism and evolutionary theory, opted for the more radical position. Specifically, on the matter of the inerrancy of the Scriptures, the Confession of Faith accepted by the convention in 1925 stated, "We believe that the Holy Bible was written by men divinely inspired and is a perfect treasure of heavenly instruction; that it has God for its author, salvation for its end, and truth, without any mixture of error, for its matter" (Lumpkin 1959, 393).

Inerrancy tied the Baptists to the written infallibility of the Holy Scriptures and moved them away from spirit-filled revivalism. Plain-folk revivalism had treasured the emotional experience of God moving among believers;

authority came from the voiced sense of the divine, barking, shouting, crying, "Lord God Almighty!" Now that Southern Baptists had become planters, doctors, lawyers, and merchants and had turned a whole city block of the county seat into the First Baptist Church with its Sunday School, they found knowing God through reading an infallible Bible more amenable to their station than the emotional excesses of the "lower sort." Conversion narratives and fiery exhortations from the pulpit continued, but the road to salvation now found textual direction: "O wretched man that I am! Who shall deliver me from the body of this death?" (Romans 7:24).

As true conservatives, the Southern Baptists embraced the doctrine of inerrancy. In so doing, they chose to ignore the historical process that selected, from among competing documents during the first centuries of the modern era, those biblical texts deemed canonical by the church fathers, that is, those that constitute the present-day Bible. Such a dismissal of history stems from the vision of Baptist exclusivity. This vision is most clearly pronounced in Landmarkism.

"Landmarkism" refers to reasserting what its proponents insisted were the truths that purified Baptists from the mistaken practices of all other Christian faiths. Principal among these truths was the assertion that Baptists were not Protestants. Prior to the Reformation, Landmarkers insisted, there were Baptists, and prior to the Roman Catholic Church itself, there were Baptists. Baptists today, they claim, are lineal descendants of the original church, the Jerusalem church, Jesus established upon being baptized by John in the river Jordan. "Christ declared," Landmarkers argued, "that he builded, founded, called into existence his own church, and the gates of hell were not to prevail against it. . . . If Christ's words be true, His church has had a continuous existence from His days until our own, and if His words are not true, He is not the Christ of God, and we have no Savior" (quoted in Wamble 1964, 439). Protestants, on the other hand, "are modified Catholics in the sense that they retain and are branded by certain Catholic characteristics. . . . Throughout history, Landmarkers held, the true church (Baptist) and the false church (Roman Catholic church and offsprings) have existed side by side, with the former being persecuted and the latter persecuting" (Wamble 1964, 443).

Landmarkers also argued that while all who have accepted Christ as their personal savior constitute the invisible kingdom of Christianity, only those who undergo full immersion at the hands of a particular Baptist-ordained minister in the company of a specific Baptist congregation can claim membership in a Christian church. Since other Christian groupings did not have these qualifications, those groups formed "societies," not churches. The marrying of radical exclusivity and local autonomy eventually led the Landmarkers in 1905 to form their own organization, today known as the American Baptist Association, which has particular strength in Arkansas. Despite the splintering, "Landmark emphases and methods encouraged the growth of denominationalism and resulted in Southern Baptists becoming more committed to their own distinctive principles and methods than ever before" (May 1958, 335). In 1969, in a critical review, one Southern Baptist writer observed that the successionist view of Baptists as the direct descendants of the Jerusalem church remained popular and, in fact, "is probably the prevailing one among Baptists in the South" (Patterson 1969, 5), and in 1972, another Southern Baptist, not sympathetic to Landmarkism, observed "that you do not have to travel far in Southern Baptist life to find Baptist Church Successionism advocated" (Shurden 1972, 30).

The doctrine of inerrancy, with its promotion of a flat reading of the Scriptures, and the concept of successionism, with its jumping of history from the Jerusalem church to the present, encouraged Baptists to be comfortable with the now. And the now of the first half of the twentieth century for Southern Baptists was a social structure compatible with their emergence as the dominant Christian church in the South. Not surprising, the Social Gospel movement, a growing concern within American Christianity for "raising wages, fighting political corruption, housing the homeless, and feeding the hungry" (Thompson 1982, 29), failed among the Southern Baptists. Service to improve social conditions, a Baptist state convention committee advised, "is temporal and material; the work of the church is eternal and spiritual. Social service seeks to improve the housing problem in the slums; the church points to mansions in the skies. Social service deals in soap as the means to cleanliness; the church contends for the cleansing through the blood of Christ" (quoted in Eighmy 1972, 109).[4]

With its emphasis on the divine authority of the printed word, inerrancy

4. Anne Firor Scott points out that the "demand of Christianity in the South was such that women were persuaded to apologize abjectly for the very qualities which make a woman (or a man for that matter) an interesting and rich personality—for spirit, for a roving mind, for pride to think well of themselves. . . . Perhaps the vision of heaven was comforting . . . but the price of admission was high" (1972, 101–102).

suggests a social conscience that is conservative and elitist. In contrast, revivalism, with its emphasis on the immediacy of the divine call, brings forth an attitude that is potentially radical and populist (Marsden 1980). Before World War II, while the courthouse crowd looked down an inerrant road to a self-congratulatory bliss, out in the countryside, at the forks of the creek, where the poorly educated, jackleg preachers raised hell and where the revivalist spirit still descended, congregations of tenant farmers, coal miners, or mill workers found themselves shouting "amen" to mixtures of unionism, socialism, populism, and Divine Love. They joined radical organizations such as the Populist Party and the Farmers' Alliance, and they fought for women's suffrage and against alcohol. One church woman vowed, "I am going to work for prohibition, the Alliance, and for Jesus as long as I live" (quoted in Flynt 1988, 139).

The road out of poverty in the rural South, however, led infrequently to social justice and more commonly to salvation. J. Frank Norris, a leading crusader in the battle for souls, for example, grew up in a sharecropper family headed by a father who responded to his own misery by drinking and beating up his children, in one violent episode breaking Norris's nose. Suffering from psychic wounds all his life, "along the way [Norris] also learned how to inflict them" (Marty 1991, 195). He turned the violence into fundamentalism, and from his pulpit in Fort Worth, Texas, he repudiated social reform by urging his listeners to prepare their souls for the Second Coming of Christ, an event Norris apparently believed, given the sordid record of diabolical modernity, was not far off (Flynt 1988; Taylor 1958).

Yet even in the solid South of evangelical inerrancy, some Southern Baptists spoke for earthly justice. As president of the Baptist-supported Wake Forest College, Dr. William I. Poteat assured the reform-minded Southern Sociological Congress that "the Kingdom of God . . . is a social spirit which will transfigure all institutions" (quoted in Flynt 1988, 149). Dr. Archibald T. Robertson, a biblical scholar at the Southern Baptist Theological Seminary who was not known for his liberalism in biblical interpretation, nonetheless insisted that the "rights of labour are unquestioned and the labouring man must have the opportunity of educating his children" (quoted in Flynt 1988, 150).

Jim Crow racism, however, with its carefully tended fear of African Americans, kept Southern Baptist churches white and under the control of conservative leaders. As ministers to their people, these pastors of the "First

Churches" emerged as a sort of Bourbon aristocracy. These were men "who supplied desperately felt needs among Southern whites for dignity, refinement, and consolation," and as such, they were much admired. Charming, "even courtly in manner, they practiced tolerance and eschewed crudeness or bombast. But they were wed to the *status quo*, or at the very most were gradualists in their desire for change in church and community" (Hill 1972a, 204).

Liberation! and Fundamentalism!

We emerge from the nearby metro station to see, through the perpetual smog that shrouds Mexico City, the swayed dome of the new basilica where resides Mexico's most famous sacred personage, the Virgin of Guadalupe. The dome, gray and green, as ugly as the atmosphere, catches me off guard. How different was the scene in 1973 when I came through on my way by bus to Costa Rica. Then, women with dark shawls over their heads inched their painful way on their knees across a wide stone patio. Awaiting them in sacramental patience stood a rectangular structure with twin towers and a rounded cupola. Flanked on either side by the towers, an ornate facade rose above massive wooden doors through which pilgrims, many of the women remaining on their knees, made their way toward the Virgin encased above the altar under a domed sanctuary. From their niches on the outside of the facade, weathered saints viewed the piety in their accustomed silence, while within the rectangular, compact space of the interior, additional brightly colored and dressed figures along the wall blessed the painful worship with the stares of generations.

Today, blocked off from public access by a wall of tin, the old structure stands in the rebellious silence of pre–Vatican II. "Rather than tear it down," a sympathetic cab driver later explained, "they are letting it collapse according to its own will."

In a manner not far removed from that of an athletic stadium, the oval roof of the new, circular basilica swoops up to an off-centered pinnacle. At the summit stands a short, stubby cross. Visually in line with the cross on the top, a similar cross, also empty, adorns the lintel over what purports to be the main entrance into the seamless structure. Inside, lights encased in hexagonal shades hang in clusters from the rising ceiling. To the left of the expanding panorama, flags of many nations drape from slender poles, and to the right organ pipes ascend in key. In the middle and above the elevated altar the image of the Virgin of Guadalupe is framed into the wall. So distant she stands that the worshipers kneeling at the altar rail can barely discern the features of her brown face and the famous roses that wreathe her body. Above her, no figure hangs from the stylized cross, and no statues stare from the unadorned walls that circle back to the several exits.

Outside, we look again at the old basilica collapsing in solitude behind its barrier of tin. In puzzled irony, you remark, Behold what Vatican II hath wrought (Figure 17).

In 1962, some four hundred years after the Council of Trent, Pope John XXIII, the so-called caretaker pope who proved to be more progressive than the cardinals who selected him, called the bishops together in a council that became known as Vatican II. Following John's death in 1963, Paul VI, the newly elected leader of the Church, proved as vigorous as John in promoting reform. By the end of the final session in 1965, the Catholic Church was on a trajectory that is still ascending today.

The change in liturgy the council called for was designed to bring the

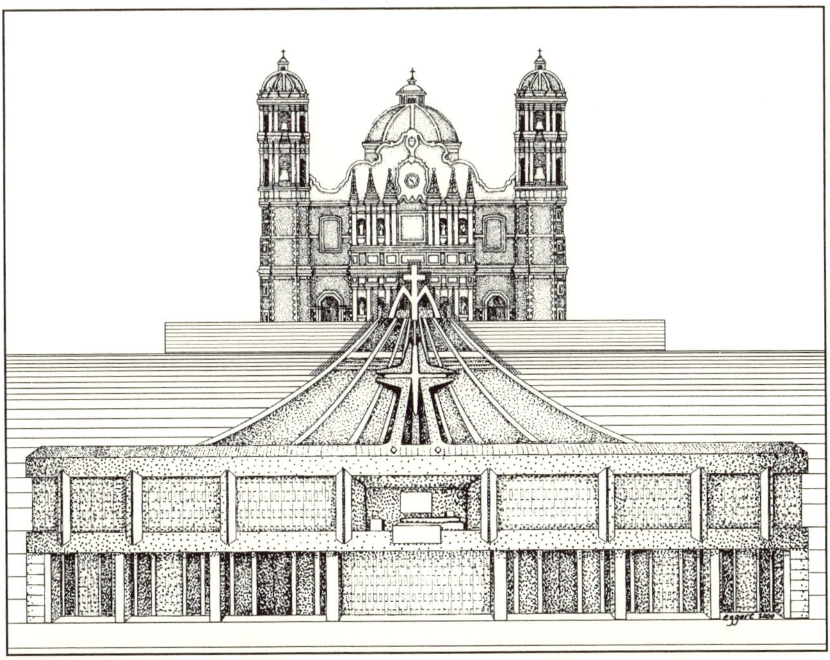

FIG. 17. Basilicas Guadalupanas, pre– and post–Vatican II

priest and parishioners together as a unit, to move the ritual of mass from being a collection of contemplative individuals to a more congregational union. Liturgy was to be a corporate act whenever "the People of God," that is, the Church, assembled. Thus, the language of the mass should be the language of the people, and Latin, a universal but dead language, was to give way to particular but living vernaculars.

To accomplish these liturgical aims, the high altar, the one located at the other end of the rectangular church, opposite the entrance, came forward from its position against the back wall, and the priest, who formerly stood in front of the altar with his back to the parishioners, moved to take a position behind the altar facing the people. So that Christ, the universal Savior, became the visual focus of the parishioners' eyes, the rich array of saints that filled the niches around the main altar and presided over the small altars along the sides vanished to leave only those who had significance to the Church as a whole. The feast days of the remaining saints were not to overshadow those of Christ. The principal liturgical day, Vatican II reiterated, is Sunday, and only feasts of the highest order, such as Good Friday or Christmas, might take precedence. Parishioners should gain access to God through the Holy Scriptures, particularly the New Testament, and during Mass, the reading of the Holy Word had to be from a lectern clearly visible and audible to the seated listeners. During Sunday masses the priest was obliged to deliver sermons that were thematically linked to the biblical reading cycle (Klauser 1979, 153–60).

The transformation required by Vatican II in the interior architecture related to equally strong innovations of exterior form that modernist styles in architecture were promoting. The restrained Neoclassical styles that had replaced the exuberant Baroque continued into the twentieth century. To be sure, here and there the pointed archways and the lanceolate spires of the Gothic Revival disrupted the restraint. The Gothic Revival, with its evocation of the mystical forest (Stanton 1968), however, was linked more to northern Europe than to the Mediterranean and consequently succeeded more in Anglo America than in Latin America. After World War II, churches constructed in the 1950s preferred the minimalist lines of modernity and the offsetting angles of asymmetrical roofs. It was almost as if these churches were awaiting Vatican II to rid themselves of voluptuous statuary. Indeed, the new basilica of the Virgin of Guadalupe sits as a conjuncture of architectural and religious modernity.

Replacing Latin with the vernacular introduced more than simply saying the pre–Vatican II mass in Spanish or English. It laid stress on Scripture, on its reading and on its preaching. Thus, while the council preserved the centrality of the Eucharist with the statement "wherever the Eucharist is celebrated, there is the Church present" (Hastings 1991, 58–59), it also reopened the Bible. With that act, it opened the debate on whether the emphasis on the Word might detract from the basic Catholic position of the Real Presence of Christ in the Eucharist. For some, the resolution was that Christ is present both in the liturgical reading and in the sacrament: "The truth is that *all* sacramental thinking and language are symbolic, and precisely thereby, they work in a way not weaker but actually stronger than the way the naive realist calls 'real.' . . . Scripture itself works *sacramentally*, especially when it is made actual by effective reading and preaching in the liturgy" (Murray 1991, 79). Opening the Bible also opened the door that Pope Leo XIII, in *Rerum Novarum*, unlocked. It opened the door to liberation theology.

Liberation theology, the most progressive, even radical, development of the post–Vatican II era in Catholicism, found articulation during the 1968 conference of Latin American bishops in Medellín, Colombia. The conference amplified the Vatican II definition of the Church as the people of God into an expression of solidarity with the poor, whereby the suffering of the poor was to be the suffering of the Church. At the same time, the poor became, not simply a stratum to be pitied, but a people in whom resided faith, a faith to be treasured because, to paraphrase Matthew 11:25, what God had hidden from the wise and the learned he had revealed to the poor (Berryman 1987).

Further developments in the liberation theology movement equated sin with social injustice. Thus, the elimination of sin required political action, and critiques of the establishment classes, at times honed to a Marxist edge, were unsheathed. In the attack, sympathetic parish priests and members of the religious orders launched a program of *concientización*, consciousness raising, so that the masses would realize they "may become the true agents of their own liberation" (Poblette 1980, 46).

To promote consciousness raising—and in concert with the larger definition of the Church as the people of God—priests, nuns, and lay leaders organized grass-root groups, *comunidades de eclesiales de base*, or, more simply, base communities. In a poor barrio in the large Colombian city of Cali, for example, sisters of a religious order bought a house, found jobs to support themselves, and in dress and speech identified closely with community. With the help of a group of foreign priests who were staffing the local parish, they set up a cultural center, installed a lending library, and held short classes in theology, community affairs, and practical skills. They attempted to reorient the pattern of traditional Easter activities by redirecting vigils, processions, decorations, and offerings in a more community-focused direction. Particularly, the "symbols of Christ's suffering, death and resurrection were given a more direct social and political interpretation" (Levine 1986, 209).

As the activities of the sisters demonstrated, "going to the poor" and consciousness raising based on biblical reading within a congregational setting led the progressive movement into a troublesome relationship with the beliefs and practices of the poor. On the one hand, since the poor possessed a knowledge hallowed by their experience, the progressives sympathized with the poor's dedication to particular saints, their desire to make costly pilgrimages to distant shrines, and in general their personal piety. Yet these traditional modes of popular religion prevented the poor from becoming agents of their own liberation. For many progressives and outside observers as well, the popular image of Christ in Latin America represented "weakness, pain, even emasculation. He [symbolized] not triumph and salvation but patience and resignation" (Nelson 1986, 219). To them, such a Christ appeared mute. Consequently, the task of liberation theology was to give voice to the dead icon, to open the Bible so the poor could read together "Bienadventuras vosotros los pobres porque el Reino de Dios es de vosotros; Blessed are you poor, for yours is the kingdom of God" (San Lucas 6:20; Berryman 1987).

A sympathetic commentator cautioned that for the progressives to serve "as the 'voice for the voiceless' is not the same as listening to what the hitherto voiceless may have to say" (Levine 1990, 71); yet the same commentator agreed with many that successful "development of strong associational life and shift of popular culture from passive resignation, fatalism, and powerlessness to equality, activism, and organization would be changes of truly heroic proportions in Latin America" (Levine 1990, 73). In the meantime, the rapid increase of aggressive, evangelizing groups such as the Baptists, the Mormons, and the Pentecostalists, in an otherwise solidly Catholic region has led some to wonder *Is Latin America Turning Protestant?* (Stoll 1990). In Guatemala, 20 percent of the population may have already converted, and by 2010 the entire country may shout "Jesús es el Señor," the evangelical trademark cry that Jesus is Lord (Stoll 1990, 337).

Catholic progressives consider the evangelist message of individual salvation at odds with the progressives' communitarian accent and their commitment to social justice. Catholic hard-liners, especially those filled with *hispanidad*, with a sense of Spanish heritage, see Protestant growth as a cultural invasion, on a par with rap music and McDonald's fast food. Both groups of Catholics suspect the growth derives mainly from North American organizations flooding the countryside and the urban barrios with money, in essence, buying souls. And indeed, Oliver North, a member of the charismatic Church of the Apostles, in his White House–based strategy to demonize the Sandinistas, assisted a number of Pentecostal groups to strengthen their operations in Nicaragua (Stoll 1990).

While the causes of conversion may vary from region to region and even from village to village and from barrio to barrio, the liberationists' attack on popular Catholicism may have hastened the day their Protestant rivals win the battle for Latin American souls. "What outsiders interpret as resignation [in popular religion] can serve as a protective mantle for vital traditions of cultural resistance." The confrontational style of the liberationists contradicts how the poor "prefer to deal with oppressive situations: a subtle combination of deference, footdragging, and evasion" (Stoll 1990, 313).

Both the liberationist base community and the evangelical church have great faith in the spiritual potentiality of the ordinary person. Both use the Bible to awaken that potential. For the liberationist, however, saving souls makes little sense apart from transforming the social order. For the evangelist, the first step to transformation, and perhaps the only step, is individual salvation. Once people accept Jesus as Lord, other changes will surely follow, and if they do not, Jesus is still King. In this competition between social justice and salvation, liberation "theology may be better at filling faculties, bookshelves, and graves than churches" (Stoll 1990, 313). For the peasant or the urban poor, it is easier to stop drinking than to confront the powerful. Converting to evangelical Protestantism allows—perhaps demands—individuals to change their personal behavior, which, while not always easy, is much safer than leading a strike. If one cannot control the price of coffee, one can stop cursing.

The bishops of Latin America met again in 1979 in Puebla, Mexico, and the Latin Americanization of Vatican II took a conservative turn. The turn began with the reassertion of hierarchical control over the base communities with the justification that in their push for social justice, these were neglecting the purely, and uniquely, religious message of the Church. Under Pope John Paul II the conservative swing became pronounced. He appointed Joseph Cardinal Ratzinger, described as a "Vatican hard-liner," to head the Congregation for the Doctrine of the Faith, the office responsible for maintaining orthodoxy, and Ratzinger "pursued his work with fervor" (Stewart-Gambino 1992, 7). Cardinal Ratzinger warned of "the case of faith [being] transformed into 'terrestrial messianism,' the experience of men being therefore 'amputated' and 'brought down to the level of temporal fulfillment [which results] in the betrayal of Christianity and the betrayal of man'" (quoted in Calvez 1990, 192). Presumably, the cardinal had in mind the emerging argument of "graced nature." Expressed by liberation theologian Míguez Bonino, the argument asserts that "Jesus Christ does not come to superimpose a different, transcendent, or celestial reality on top of the realm of nature and history, but to reopen for man the will and the power to fulfill his historical vocation. He has not come to make man into superhuman beings, or a religious creature, but to open to him the will and power to be man" (quoted in Cleary 1985, 85). This is what the good cardinal called "the betrayal of man."

In 1992, as part of the quincentennial celebration of Columbus's discovery of the New World and in conjunction with Pope John Paul's visit, the Latin American Conference of Bishops convened in Santo Domingo, Dominican Republic. The conservative turn veered right still again. "Liberation theology" was much too materialistic-sounding for the conservatives in charge, and they replaced it with "evangelical," as the Church's option for the poor. Instead of evoking the "graced nature" of an incarnate Jesus, the documents that finalized the conference gave voice to an abstract, transcendent Christ, a Christ seemingly closer to and therefore more capable of confronting *el Señor Jesús* of the *evangélicos*, the Lord Jesus of the born-again Protestants (Serbin 1993).[5]

5. The culmination of dramatic changes in the relations between the Vatican and Mexico also came in 1992. A year earlier, modifications in the Mexican constitution moved it away from the anticlerical 1917 document. Churches gained legal status, and with that status, they could hold property, open schools, and have access to the mass media. Priests and ministers could now vote, even if they were prohibited from partisan campaigning. In 1992, Mexico reestablished diplomatic ties with the Vatican, yet as if to avoid the accusation of reinventing through these momentous changes a Catholic state, the government required all religious bodies to register. Requiring all to register suggested that Catholicism was only one faith among many, that the smallest, spirit-filled Pentecostal church enjoyed legal parity with the Papal See.

* * *

As the Word became inerrant and as the Baptists moved into the center of southern society, with "the embourgeoisement of Evangelicalism" (Williams 1997, 119), they faced the question of what type of structure they should build. Inheritors of the egalitarian, plain-folk meeting rooms and of the Dissenters' disdain for "steeple-houses," they were now settling in a block or two from the courthouse. Could they continue to build the simple, rectangular structure they erected at Sandy Creek, at Shady Grove, at Lone Pine, at Swanson Springs? Would such a building adequately testify to their newly found place in the southern hierarchy? What were others doing?

At the time the Southern Baptist Convention convened in 1845, the more prosperous Christian denominations were trying to decide between the older Neoclassical, Greek Revival architecture and the newer, Neo-Gothic, Gothic Revival style (Dillenberger 1988). The Neoclassical architecture featured both a monumentality and a simplicity that caught the prosperous Baptist eye. It was a rectangular structure similar to what they had built in their frontier settlements, but it had an imposing portico. Placed at the top of steps that brought the congregation up from the street, four to six huge columns rose to support a pediment that announced to people, as they climbed the steps and passed through the columns, a message both bold and complex.

The message of the Neoclassical portico connected the Baptists to secular institutions, such as banks, post offices, and the courthouse itself, all of which had similar columnar entrances. Here the message seemingly was the proclamation of a republic, of a learned, textual civilization that harkened back to classical antiquity. The portico also tied the Baptists ever closer to the plantation South, to the porticos of the Greek Revival mansions of the planter elite, and to the nobility of the South. Thus the portico's message was at one and the same time republic and noble.[6]

Both Anglo America and Spanish America were recipients of the multitudinous contributions of Neoclassicism. The political philosophy of the associated Enlightenment profoundly affected the political ideas of Thomas

6. On the other hand, disputing the close connection between the South and Greek Revival, Roger Kennedy argues that historians writing in the late nineteenth and early twentieth centuries interpreted Greek Revival mansions as giving imperial dignity and legitimate authority to the plantation. "This was Reconstruction reconstructed," he complains (1989, 30). Despite Kennedy's protest, the myth of the South's affinity for Greek Revival and for classical antiquity continues, I suspect, to be part of the message of Greek Revival First Baptist churches.

Jefferson in the north and Simón Bolívar in the south. In Spanish America, however, Neoclassicism's architectural antagonist was the earlier Baroque period, which the Neoclassic replaced. In North America, Neoclassicism's competition was the newly arrived Neo-Gothic, whose spires threatened to darken the white gleam of the Neoclassic colonnade.

Southern Baptists and Gothic? If preaching the divinely inspired Word of salvation fits uneasily with Greek Revival, at least the Baptist doctrine of separation of church and state relates to the idea of a secular republic. The Gothic Revival, however, with its affinity to Anglicanism, evokes an establishmentarian church. Furthermore, in its inception, it was considered appropriately mysterious for the mystery of the Eucharist, certainly an anathema to the Baptist's Lord's Supper of remembrance. Indeed, one assessment maintains that in building Neo-Gothic churches, Baptists have missed an architectural opportunity. "Throughout America, towering pseudo-Gothic edifices house a faith that lies at the opposite pole of belief and practice from that of the Roman Catholic that inspired this style. Until very recently, Baptists have remained oblivious to this contradiction" (Christ-Janer and Foley 1962, 239).

While it may be true that in building Neo-Gothic churches, with their pointed arches, stained glass, and levitating towers, Baptists have demonstrated an absence of understanding of their own worship, you know that as an anthropologist, I am reluctant to agree that people lack explanations for their own actions. Consequently, let us consider the question more carefully.

First, we may note that Southern Baptists insist in a Calvinistic manner that good works do not Christians make; only the experience of personal surrender to an almighty God, as Isaac Backus discovered, accomplishes salvation. Similarly, you recall from Chapter 2 that church buildings are not required for Baptist worship: "For where two or three are gathered together in my name, there am I in the midst of them" (Matthew 18:20). Yet how many times have we attended a Baptist worship service in which the pastor urged support for the building fund? It seems congregations everywhere are constantly raising money to renovate, expand, or to build anew. And hasn't it always struck you as odd to have Jesus, who was after all born in a manger, dwell in a house the construction of which necessitates the membership go into debt? These are matters, however, that trouble any Christian group that aspires to build an imposing church of whatever architectural design. There remains the question: Why Neo-Gothic?

Despite its professed kinship to the Eucharistic mystery and despite several noteworthy exceptions—St. Patrick's Cathedral in New York City, for example, and La Ermita in Cali, Colombia—Neo-Gothic was not particularly popular among Catholics, neither in Anglo America nor in Spanish America. It was Anglican, that is to say, English, and it was rural. The rurality of the Neo-Gothic lay in its bid for the image of an Anglican parish church in a village setting. The bucolic setting was not the howling wilderness of the frontier, but a tamed rural, a husbanded rural, a gentrified rural, the rural of Romanticism (Stanton 1968). Congregations emerging out of the American backcountry and settling down amid middle-class urbanity found the appeal nigh irresistible. The Methodists, with their historical links to the Anglican Church, could voice a legitimate claim to the Neo-Gothic, and if the Methodists, why not their closest competitors, the Baptists?

Being juxtaposed to Greek Revival, Neo-Gothic quickly became a sign in its own right. While Greek Revival housed banks, post offices, and courthouses, Neo-Gothic came to possess a particular spiritual aura. Driven by the arguments of its ardent supporters, Neo-Gothic transformed itself into being *the* architecture of Christian culture. Even the less passionate agreed that it promoted a sense of awe appropriate for an Almighty God (Turner 1979; Dillenberger 1988).[7]

Raleigh, the state capital of North Carolina, vividly illustrates these relationships. Completed in 1840, the capitol building is a classic example of governmental, republic Greek Revival. *All* the churches—Methodist, Presbyterian, Baptist, Episcopalian, and Catholic—that compete for space near the seat of government feature an architecture that in one version or another is Neo-Gothic. The Baptists in Raleigh organized a church in 1812, a year after the Methodists. The membership grew in fits and starts, but it gradually got to the point where the pastor decided they should be more decorous in their

7. One of the few Neo-Gothic state capitol buildings is the Old State Capitol in Baton Rouge, Louisiana, described by Mark Twain as a "sham castle" more at home in the medieval romances of Sir Walter Scott than on the banks the Mississippi (Twain 1968, 270). It has since been superseded by the New State Capitol, a Huey Long obelisk decorated with the most social realism this side of the former Soviet Union. Events and buildings take peculiar turns in Louisiana, my adopted state. Likewise in North Carolina, things are not always straightforward. As in Raleigh, Neo-Gothic emerged as the favorite architectural style for older churches in nineteenth-century Wilmington; but here, the Wilmington courthouse, which was built after the churches, is a "High Victorian Gothic structure . . . the sole area representative of a strong national style, although seldom used in the South" (Wrenn 1984, 72). Interestingly, the courthouse annex, completed in 1925, returned to Greek Revival.

worship and requested they stop "shouting" during the service. Some years later, in 1859, the present Neo-Gothic structure was completed (First Baptist Church 1987). Thus, urbanity and decorum joined under Neo-Gothic awe (Figure 18).

Throughout the nineteenth century and into the twentieth, Southern Baptist congregations built churches in Neo-Gothic. The First Baptist Church in Wilmington, North Carolina, is an imposing Neo-Gothic structure, begun before the Civil War and completed in 1870; but arguably the most famous Neo-Gothic Baptist building is the First Baptist Church in Dallas, Texas. Reputed to be the largest white Baptist church in the world and claiming to be the home church of Billy Graham, Dallas First Baptist began construction of its "Americanized Gothic" in 1891 and remodeled it in 1908 and again in 1924. Since then it has expanded into several blocks of downtown Dallas (McBeth 1968). At the time of its construction, other congregations continued building in Greek Revival: the First Baptist Churches in El Dorado, Arkansas, and in Durham, North Carolina, for example. You must also remember that Greek Revival or Neo-Gothic notwithstanding, not every newly built church emerged as an imposing edifice of stone. In the less prosperous churches and in those more closely related to plain-folk egalitarianism, porticos were modest wooden pediments supported by squared posts in two-by-eight-inch pine, and Gothic verticality was imitated with longitudinal board-and-batten framing, the so-called Carpenter Gothic.

Today, Baptist architecture is, if anything, eclectic. Some congregations have chosen modern functionalism and have built churches with plain fronts and detached steeples. Some have abandoned the rectangle for a circular plan. Some continue to build in versions of the Greek Revival; Neo-Gothic, in contrast, seemingly has all but disappeared. Perhaps, however, the most recurrent style, popular even today, is one vaguely reminiscent of a Currier and Ives painting. A portico with pediment and columns extends out from the rectangular plan, but a steeple rises from the pitched roof behind the portico. The steeple may be no more than a spire rapidly coming to a point, but in the more elaborate and, one is tempted to say, more ostentatious forms, the steeple is a three-part structure that begins first with a square tower, goes to a "bell tower" without the bell, then ends in a spire. The style is often called Colonial. The contemporary construction apparently hearkens back to the Georgian and Federal styles popular in the late eighteenth and early nineteenth centuries, particularly in New England (Kennedy 1989; Williams

Fig. 18. The First Baptist Church in Raleigh, North Carolina, in ascending Neo-Gothic

1997), a time and place much removed from today's Southern Baptists (Figure 19).[8]

In sum, Southern Baptists, as they have made their way into the center of southern society, have accommodated themselves to prevailing architectural styles much in the same manner they accommodated themselves to slavery and, after the Civil War, to racial segregation. As we have seen, this accommodation is not without significance. The Greek Revival portico points to the republican civilization of the county seat and betokens the presence of a southern aristocracy; the Gothic Revival spire elevates frontier wilderness to English countryside and brings into the boisterous congregation a meditative awe; and contemporary eclecticism parallels Baptist experiments to address the diversifying aspirations of modern times. Accommodation to the public, however, stops at the door. Once inside, even the most ascending Neo-Gothic ceiling or the most nostalgic Colonial spire turns Baptist.

While the exterior of a Southern Baptist church conforms more or less to the generalized picture of an American church, the inside remains close to the distinctive Baptist message. In a manner closely paralleling the division between good works and salvation in Baptist belief, the outside of the church is the good works side, and the inside is the salvation side. It is what is inside that counts, inside the heart and inside the church, for the inside is where the congregation gathers together in the Lord's Name.

Then again, you point out, the inside is more under the control of the congregation. The location of the pulpit, the Lord's Supper table, the piano, the organ, the American and Christian flags, the floral display, the hymnals in the pews: all these matters (which will gain our attention in the next chapter) are more subject to the wishes of the pastor, deacons, and congregation than the fixed, conforming appearance of a portico, an arched window, or a steeple tower. The inside, however, is also subject to accommodation. Crosses, once the sure sign of Romanism, are, in fact, still rare, but they do

8. These observations about Southern Baptist church architecture come from trips made at various times ranging from Wilmington, North Carolina, to Española, New Mexico. For summaries of trends in religious architecture in North America, see Williams 1988, 1997; for examples of Baptist churches, see the illustrations in the *Encyclopedia of Southern Baptists* 1958, 1971, 1982. Nostalgia continues here in Baton Rouge, Louisiana. In 1991, the Jefferson Baptist congregation, whose pastor never turns down an opportunity to lambast the evils of modernism and of the moderates, took out a full-page advertisement in the *Advocate* to announce the dedication of its massive "new auditorium" of Colonial colonnade and spire.

Fig. 19. The First Baptist Church in Greensboro, North Carolina, in nostalgic Colonial

appear—plain ones with no figure—in front of or over the baptistery, and during the increasingly common Maundy Thursday service (the Thursday before Easter), some churches place a large cross on the platform near the pulpit.

Although you may be tempted to seek it, a connection between high-style architecture (Neo-Gothic, Greek Revival, or Colonial) and a high-church liturgical style among the Southern Baptists is difficult to establish. Architecture and liturgical style appear to vary independently of one another. Again, however, once inside and through the foyer, a connection, albeit a loose one, between the interior and the individual church's stance on theological and social concerns does indeed emerge. Those churches having crosses, a minister in academic gown, Communion instead of the Lord's Supper, services on Ash Wednesday and Good Friday, a fixed cycle of biblical readings (or a lectionary), and an order of service in which the offertory follows the sermon will likely self-identify themselves as moderates on theological matters, support women in the ministry, argue the case for minority rights, and speak out on issues of social justice. Thus, the paradox: The more high style and formal the church, the more likely it will address issues of inequality; or conversely, the more observant of plain-dress worship the church is—the more Southern Baptist it is—the more likely it will regard questions of poverty and injustice as secondary to salvation. To this continuing paradox we now turn.

Born out of the region's convulsions and achieving prominence during the heyday of Jim Crow, Southern Baptists opted to face the second half of the twentieth century with a conservative stance. The shape of this decision first appeared during the civil rights movement of the 1960s in which there were Baptists on both sides of the struggle: black Baptists at the lunch counters and in the marches and Southern Baptists in the White Citizen Councils.

The march to civil rights began in the South and was directed toward the white power structure. The Southern Baptists, very much part of that structure, found themselves the object of attack. In 1954 the Southern Baptist Convention passed a resolution supporting the Supreme Court ruling that "separate but equal" was inherently unequal, but this "was not an accurate measure of Southern Baptist feeling about desegregation. Some pastors openly criticized the Court's ruling, the most prominent being W. A. Criswell of Dallas, Texas, pastor of the convention's largest church." In 1969, he became president of the convention (Eighmy 1972, 191).

Today in the larger churches and particularly in those inclined toward the "moderate" position, it is not uncommon to see one or two immaculately dressed African American couples. The major effort, however, of white Southern Baptists and of the convention toward the incorporation of African Americans is to assist in the development of a separate ministry for them, as well as for Hispanics, Koreans, and other minorities.

Here you remind me about the Douglas Avenue Baptist Church. Douglas Avenue is a small street in north Baton Rouge near the city's mammoth petrochemical industry. From the time Standard Oil (now Exxon Mobil) first located its refineries in the area, the housing that developed near the plants was white and blue-collar. During World War II and into the 1950s and early 1960s, white, working-class "North Baton Rouge" became the self-conscious counterpart, and antagonist, to white, middle-to-upper-class, and professional "South Baton Rouge." Radio stations, movies, schools, and churches divided accordingly. The prep-football season peaked when Istrouma High School from "North Baton Rouge" played Baton Rouge High School from "South Baton Rouge." But then I-10, linking Baton Rouge to the nation's interstate system, sliced through the city, and by 1981, when I first went to Douglas Avenue Baptist Church, the transition was underway. Preaching "I Have Decided to Follow Jesus," the minister did his best. He even threw off his coat and added a joke about cleaning bills, but he could not stem the tide of white flight and in fact no longer lived in the neighborhood himself. Ten years later I was back at Douglas Avenue Baptist to attend a dramatization of the Resurrection. The structure was the same, but the congregation was completely black, completely black and Southern Baptist. The minister, seemingly aware of the denomination's heritage, had become a Southern Baptist during his attendance at a nearly all-white Southern Baptist college. Taking up his role as both African American and Southern Baptist, he observed, "If we're going to live together in heaven, we have to begin here" (*State-Times* 26 January 1989).

By 1980 there were approximately 600 predominantly black Southern Baptist congregations with an estimated membership of 100,000 (Smith 1982, 2124). By 1989, according to Sid Smith, the manager of black church development for the Southern Baptist Sunday School Board, the number had climbed to 1,200 black churches with 200,000 members (*State-Times* 26 January 1989). The rise of this new "separate but equal" division notwithstanding, Leroy Fitts, the black pastor of the First Baptist Church in Baltimore and author of *A History of Black Baptists* (1985), wrote that he looked forward to the time when all gain true understanding of fellowship in Christ, when salvation in the South becomes color-free.

Given the largely lily-white composition of the Southern Baptist churches, Fitts's vision, on the one hand, may be overly optimistic. On the other hand, listen to the words of T. B. Maston: "It is difficult for peoples of the world to understand why Christians will send missionaries to proclaim Christian brotherhood and yet many of them will not practice that brotherhood in their churches and communities" (1958, 1128). These words appeared in the *Encyclopedia of Southern Baptists* in 1958, several years before the major push for civil rights. Listen, too, to the affirmation of basic religious principles signed by fifty-three clergy in Baton Rouge in 1961: "God condemns all acts of injustice, all hatred, all abuse, and all persecution." Among the signees were fifteen Southern Baptist ministers, many from the smaller churches in the white neighborhoods in North Baton Rouge (*Morning Advocate* 7 May 1961). And listen, still further, to a Baptist minister from Winnfield, Louisiana, during an interview in the summer of 1978: "I was raised with a hatred of Negroes. It wasn't until I was converted and started studying the Bible that I realized that the Bible doesn't teach there's one kind of Christian for whites and another kind for blacks. We're all one." But isn't it interesting that this minister was not pastoring at one of the big churches in town but was preaching in a rural settlement and had to work outside his ministry to support his family? And that the pastor of the First Baptist Church in Baton Rouge was conspicuously absent from those who signed the 1961 affirmation of religious principles? Nonetheless, perhaps it is the voices of Southern Baptists such as these that Fitts has heard and that provide his hope for the future. Historian David Goldfield, in his latest assessment, believes that urban whites and blacks get along better in the South than they do in the North. He goes on to observe, "The burdens of history seem lighter today" (1997, 7). Can we believe that such is the case? Could it truly be?

The conservative stance the Southern Baptists have taken toward civil rights has, if anything, become more conservative with respect to the affairs of their own denomination. Pushing a strict version of the doctrine of inerrancy, the more conservative of the conservative Southern Baptists have taken over the leadership of the Southern Baptist Convention and purged the seminaries of those hapless moderates who argue for tolerance and civility. The conservatives are said to be, and indeed often act as, fundamentalists.

What is fundamentalism? A truly multivocalic symbol, fundamentalism evokes different assessments. James Thompson (1982), for example, distinguishes it from religious conservatism and associates it, perhaps "stigmatizes" would be a more appropriate word, with largely uneducated, rural masses. George Marsden (1980, 1982), to the contrary, denies that it is a product of rural backwardness and argues that it presents the Bible as a book of plain facts, open to a Baconian-like inductive reason available to all. Fundamentalism's scorn toward professors of Bible criticism and of science is that neither possesses the common sense of the ordinary reader and thus both miss the obvious truths the Bible tells. So again, what is fundamentalism? Is it the unlearned faith of the uneducated rural South, the last hallelujah of the upland South plain folk? Or is it the crafted ideology of a highly sophisticated, urban mainstream?

Fundamentalism entered the lexicon in the 1920s, when Curtis Lee Laws, the editor of a northern Baptist newspaper, the *Watchman Examiner*, wrote that a "'fundamentalist' is a person willing to 'do battle royal' for the fundamentals of the faith." The term functioned as "both a description and a call to action" (quoted in Ammerman 1991, 2). While there may be, and quite possibly are, Catholic fundamentalists, the movement has flourished among nonsacramental brands of North American Protestantism. The physical presence of the sacraments and of icons are no match for the verbal realism of the biblical literalist, for whom the Resurrection was a historical event, the blood of the Atonement flows red, and trumpets will blare forth the Second Coming (Marty 1991). Spoken with the fervor of fundamentalism, the language of the Bible achieves a mystical reality that transcends the print on the page and cuts across the divisions among Protestant groups. At the same time, that language draws hard and fast boundaries. No pussyfooting around. When a fundamentalist shakes the Bible at you, the intent is to offend (Marty 1992).

A typology of North American Protestant fundamentalism, derived from Nancy Ammerman (1991), may clarify the logic of exclusion and inclusion:

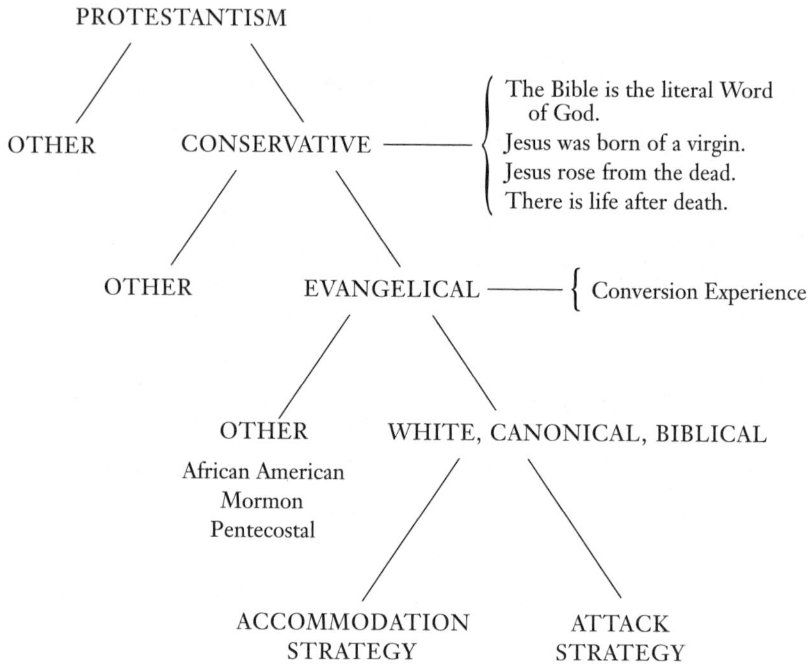

Biblical literalism separates conservatives from other Protestants. In addition, conservatives insist that Jesus was born of a virgin, that on the third day following the Crucifixion he rose from dead, and that today he has prepared a place for us in heaven when we die. While other Protestant groups may hold to one or more of these beliefs, none assert them with the vehemence of the conservatives. Among the conservatives, evangelicals insist that you must be born again, and, consequently, it is the evangelicals' duty to convert you lest you die in sin. Race separates the African American evangelicals, the Book of Mormon places the Mormons apart, and revelatory experiences that cause the recipient to prophesy in unknown tongues divide off the Pentecostalists. Finally, those white, biblical evangelicals who have no desire to get along with people who profess to be evangelists but want to be accommodative, those "attack evangelicals," those are the fundamentalists.

Social science commentaries on fundamentalism have often implied it is a soon-to-disappear minority reaction of a highly conservative, rural culture to a modernizing, increasingly secular, urban world. Such characterization conveniently overlooks the fact that the leadership of the fundamentalist movement in the Southern Baptist denomination comes largely from the huge, urban churches, such as the First Baptist Church in Dallas, the Second Baptist Church in Houston, and the First Baptist Church in Atlanta. Here, especially, you can see that fundamentalism, in its no-holds-barred attack on what it proclaims as modernism, uses the latest techniques of mass communication to persuade people and politicians as to the righteousness of its message. Further, fundamentalism is fervently nationalistic and capitalistic. Indeed, along with the leadership of the Southern Baptist Convention, it has appropriated "the American Way of Life" as its own (Kaplan 1992).

With the 1979 election of Adrian Rodgers as president of the Southern Baptist Convention, the fundamentalists, or, as they prefer to be called, the *real* conservatives, gained control of the national organization. Given that each Baptist church is an autonomous organization, free to choose and to dismiss its own pastor, free to raise and spend its own money, and free to argue and to heal its own disputes, control of the convention would seem not to be a matter of great import. But the fundamentalists proved otherwise. By controlling the presidency, they controlled who became the directors of the various convention agencies, and by replacing the trustees at the several Baptist seminaries, they either fired or put into early retirement the current administrators and replaced them with men not hesitant to tell the faculty what message to teach, and if the faculty did not care for that message, well, it being a free country, the faculty were free to leave.

In 1988, in a clear departure from the Baptist radical heritage of the Church as a priesthood of believers, with the truth of salvation available to all, fundamentalists got the convention to proclaim that the pastor has special abilities in that regard. After all, they declared, pointing to the inerrant text, the Bible itself said, "Obey them that have the rule over you" (Hebrews 13:17). All men are equal in the eyes of God, but apparently some are more equal than others. Certainly in the fundamentalist agenda, men are more equal at pastoring than women, and the convention went on record as opposing women in the pulpit.

The moderates among the Southern Baptists, as is the case with moderates everywhere, tried to moderate the debate. But the real conservatives would have none of it. "Moderate" was just another name for "liberal," and Pastor Criswell of the First Baptist Church in Dallas reminded the convention that a "skunk by any other name still stinks" (Shurden 1993, xv).

In 1994, Jim Henry of the First Baptist Church of Orlando, Florida, who described himself as a conservative and as strongly committed to inerrancy, defeated an even more conservative candidate, and in 1995, he was reelected. Some suggested that his reelection would indicate an amelioration of the fundamentalist agenda. And, in fact, a momentous event occurred in the 1995 meeting. By nearly unanimous vote the delegates passed a resolution stating that Southern Baptists "lament and repudiate historic acts of evil such as slavery" and ask "forgiveness from our African American brothers and sisters" (quoted in the *New York Times* 21 June 1995). Gary Frost, an African American and first vice president of the convention, joined Jim Henry at the convention podium to lead the convention in prayer, and Billy Graham, seventy-six and recovering from an illness, gave the closing address in which he commended the convention for the resolution.

Larry Lewis, of the convention's Home Mission Board, proudly announced that in 1995 there were 1,900 predominately black congregations affiliated with the convention and the number was growing at 200 congregations a year. In addition, the convention had 3,000 Hispanic, 800 Korean, and 700 Native American churches (*New York Times* 21 June 1995). Along with the resolution, such figures may indeed support Reverend Leroy Fitts's hope for the day coming when all, black and white, Hispanic and Asian, may dwell together in Christ, though perhaps separately.

At the end of the second millennium, the "real conservatives" remained solidly in control of the Southern Baptist Convention. In 1998, at their meeting in Salt Lake City, where they took the opportunity to launch a mission to convert the Mormons into "real Christians," the delegates elected Paige Patterson, one of the principal architects of the conservative takeover. And in Texas, the state convention ousted the University Baptist congregation because the congregation, located across the street from the University of Texas in Austin, had openly embraced gays and lesbians. Thus, upon entering the third millennium, the current Southern Baptist Conference message remains clear: While members of ethnic groups may come together "in Christ," albeit separately, homosexuals need not apply.

As the conservative express rolls down the road to Glory (and you, being you, want to add, Yes, even hell-bent), certain gray, if not dark, clouds gather. For one thing, the last half of the twentieth century saw the growth of the Southern Baptists going at a much slower pace than the first half. In the twenty-five years between 1950 and 1975 church membership increased 44 percent and enrollment in Sunday School by 31 percent. In the twenty-four years between 1975 and 1999, membership grew at only 20 percent and Sunday School enrollment at 10 percent (Table 3). The debate over who are the real Baptists may be taking its toll, and indeed many moderates, banding together to form the Cooperative Baptist Fellowship, have all but left the convention (Shurden 1993). Indeed as time passes, more and more moderates are following former president Jimmy Carter's lead and abandoning the convention to its fate. The position of the other former president who was also a member of a Baptist church affiliated with the Southern Baptist Convention, William Jefferson Clinton, remains murky.[9]

In addition to a slower rate of growth, another challenge for the denomination is the dilemma facing the downtown churches: what to do when the formerly all-white neighborhood becomes "inner city"? In Baton Rouge, in the late 1970s and early 1980s, the Istrouma Baptist Church, located in a formerly white, working-class neighborhood in north Baton Rouge and a longtime competitor to the First Baptist, found itself surrounded by African Americans, declining property values, and an interstate highway at its doorstep. After what no doubt was a difficult time for the membership, with pleas to "follow the will of God," the church relocated in 1988 in the growing suburbs to the southeast of the central city. Paradoxically, the membership chose a spot with immediate access to the same interstate system that did them in at their former home. At their new location, however, they self-consciously switched from being a "neighborhood church" to being a "commuter church." In the old home in the old days, you walked to church; in the

TABLE 3. The Growth of the Southern Baptists in the Second Half of the Twentieth Century

	Church Membership	Percent Increase	Sunday School Enrollment	Percent Increase
1950	7,080,000		5,025,000	
1975	12,736,000	44	7,283,000	31
1999	15,852,000	20	8,147,000	10

SOURCE: McClellan (1982, 2473) for 1975 figures; Strategic Information and Planning Section, LifeWay, for 1999 figures.

9. I gratefully acknowledge the assistance of the Strategic Information and Planning Section, LifeWay (formerly, the Baptist Sunday School Board), in obtaining the enrollment figures for 1999.

new home in the new days, you drive—Glory! (Cadwallader 1994). In the meantime, the First Baptist in Baton Rouge clings to its place in the old core, with the most recent new pastor asking the congregation not to remember where they were twenty years ago but where they want to be twenty years from now.

Other downtown churches more prominent than those in Baton Rouge, such as the First Baptist in Greenville, South Carolina, have left the center, but perhaps the most poignant was the move of the First Baptist in Augusta, Georgia, for it was at the Augusta First Baptist in 1845 that the Southern Baptist Convention was born. From the particular site it had occupied since 1817 and from its massive, modified Greek Revival edifice built in 1902, the church in the late 1970s relocated to the end of a major thoroughfare in Augusta, where it now occupies acres of suburban green. There, it has erected a complex of buildings and a cruciform sanctuary with a towering Colonial steeple. Stained glass windows depict the life of Christ and the history of Christianity, including the founding of the Augusta First Baptist Church.

The Southern Baptists are not the only major Christian denomination to find that it is growing more slowly than in the past. As reported in the popular press, old-line established churches, such as the Episcopal, the Presbyterian, and the former competitor of the Baptists, the Methodist, are actually "experiencing negative growth," that is, they are losing members. On the other hand, Mormons and Pentecostalists lead the pack in rate of growth. The changing American economy, which is currently producing an uneasy generation of "baby busters" to follow the affluent generation of "baby boomers," further compounds the mission of the churches. In response to the changing economy and to competition from the Mormons and Pentecostalists, Baptists, along with other mainline denominations, have created the "megachurch."

The megachurch builds its foundation upon the marketing principles of American consumer culture, to wit: before you can communicate to people, you must entertain them. To entertain, you market the product. Thus, you offer aerobics, basketball, movies, and a rock band—something for everyone: dates for singles, advice for young marrieds, videos for the family, and even a few old hymns for the sentimental. The "mega" means what it says, which includes a budget in the millions, seating in the thousands, and a choir in the hundreds, lifting their voices in a high-tech architecture designed not for Greek nobility or Gothic awe but for visual consumption. Yet the theology from the pulpit, televised with state-of-the-art cameras, affirms hell is hot, heaven is sweet, and Jesus saves! The Southern Baptist megachurch is a fundamentalist's triumph; "Prophecies of doom [have become] songs of victory" (Turner 1993, 119).[10]

Jordan's Uncanny Tides

For two chapters we have pursued the twists and turns of two streams of the Christian presence in the New World. You, like me, cannot help but be impressed by how the streams, both branches of the river Jordan, have flowed in paradoxical currents.

During the European Renaissance, the humanists and the printing press opened the Bible. In Spain, the orthodoxy in its counter-reforms moved the Word toward a more central place in its liturgy but kept the Body of Christ visible. In England, the Baptists, the apparent radical inheritors of an open book in a community of believers, verbalized the Body and made the Text an object of adoration.

In the New World, to the south, Mediterranean Christianity reconstituted its corporate splendor in the massive cathedral fronting the plaza, where stately processions displayed the Corpus Christi. To the north, Atlantic Christianity, already asunder, fragmented further under the impact of the centrifugal settlement process, and periodically the wilderness rang with campground shouts of glory. In the New World, too, Christianity—stretched between freedom and slavery, between the oppressor and the oppressed—carved a new cross, and two minorities, Native Americans and transported Africans, came to haunt the Halls of the Kingdom.

In the nineteenth and on into the twentieth century, Spanish American

10. While the First Baptist Church at Dallas is huge, it has a more restrained persona befitting its status as the Papal See of the South. A more characteristic megachurch can be found farther south, in Dallas's antibody, Houston. There, in Space City, at her desk, the receptionist answers the phone with a lilting "Exciting Second" and directs callers to various offices of the complex that constitutes the Second Baptist Church. The pastor of Second Baptist, H. Edwin Young, was among those who charted the course of the Southern Baptist Convention back to the inerrant Word, and for his labor, he was elected president of the convention in 1993. One final example of computer-age technology at the service of fundamentalism is the Internet. The Southern Baptist Convention now has its own website, www.sbc.net.org, with links to "God's Plan."

Catholicism fought to maintain its preeminent position against the growing secular state, and the Sacred Heart bled in retribution. Southern Baptists, bred in the South, sought nobility and offered up the Confederate Soldier, who stood on the courthouse lawn ever ready to die for the Lost Cause.

In the post–World War II world, Vatican II opened the Bible to liberation and to the notion of injustice as sin. During Sunday School, where each attended with a Bible, the conservative Southern Baptists closed the text around a reenforced notion of inerrancy. Now, in the twenty-first century, just as Catholics in Spanish America may be turning conservative, perhaps the Southern Baptists, with their apology, are inching toward a more moderate position. But, you say, don't hold your breath.

In viewing the twists and turns of the dual narrative streams, we must remind ourselves the matter is not simply how we place the two Christianities in their past but, more importantly, how they place their past into the present. We must recognize how from the present, they labor at times against the flow of the past and how, at other times, they rejoice in its rapids and in going over its waterfalls or, in still other moments, how they are content to float gently upon its wide expanse disregarding the distant cries for help or the clouds darkening on the horizon.

The past does not carry them willy nilly. For all the impact that the New World experience has had on the presence of Christ in Spanish America and in the American South, Christ's presence arises from people's actions. The argument of this anthropologist's account is not one of passive determinism. Let us, then, leave history (as if we ever could!) and return to search for the Christ of Nueva Esperanza and for the one dwelling in Mt. Hope, but before our departure, let us remember two separate dates, March 24, 1980, and January 16, 1991, and how Christ was made present on those occasions.

On the evening of March 24, Oscar Romero, archbishop of San Salvador, the capital of the tiny Central American country of El Salvador, entered the chapel of the Divine Providence Hospital at the nation's capital to say mass. From the time he became archbishop in 1977, Romero had spoken out against the atrocities of war, the war going on in his own country. The week before, during the homily of his Sunday morning mass, he addressed the members of the Salvadorian National Guard: "Brothers, you come from our own people. You are killing your own brother peasants when any human order to kill must be subordinate to the law of God which says, 'Thou shalt not kill'" (Romero 1982, 31). This evening, he had scarcely begun his homily when a single shot from an assassin's gun ended his life.

On the evening of January 16, 1991, the Reverend Billy Graham, America's most famous Southern Baptist, was at the White House watching the news from the Persian Gulf. President George Bush, who had earlier that day begun Operation Desert Storm with an order for massive air strikes against Iraq, entered the room. The two talked at length. The next day, at a prayer service at Arlington National Cemetery, with the president in attendance, the Reverend Billy Graham delivered a short sermon in which he reassured his audience, "There comes a time when we have to fight for peace" (*Daily Telegraph* 18 January 1991).

Thus, the Cross in San Salvador, and the Bible at Arlington.[11]

11. Ten years later, September 11, 2001. Another war and another Bush. The events unfold around us in their horror, and my own feelings are as muddled as anyone's. Consequently, at the time of this writing, I can only ask: Will the events move toward the cross of suffering or toward the Bible of glory?

The answer may reside in the apparently contrastive meanings of "Support Our Troops" and "God Bless America." These are the signs that both conflicts produced across the South and across America. "Support Our Troops" was the Gulf War's call to arms, the "just" war. But what does "God Bless America" say? It is the line with which every U.S. president ends his appeal for us to follow his lead. So is it also a call to arms? God is on our side, so who can be against us? But it seems to lack the coercive element in "Support Our Troops." It evokes solidarity and often is joined with "United We Stand." United how? In our "get-'em-dead-or-alive" anger? Or in our "Pray for Peace" redemptive suffering?

Just as he had at the outbreak of the Gulf War, Billy Graham spoke to the nation. This time, however, at the National Cathedral following President George W. Bush to the lectern, old and infirm, he started out with puzzlement: "Why does an almighty God allow evil?" He added that though he had dwelt on this question many times, he had no answer. He then proceeded to say we can implode and disintegrate or we can rebuild on God's firm foundation; the choice is ours. Amen, Brother Billy.

Behold, I shew you a mystery.

—1 Corinthians 15:51

4
THE TEMPLE AND THE HOUSE

You, having traveled with me down the twists and turns of the Christian story in the New World, rightly grow impatient. I have promised, you remind me, I have promised that we will find how they find Christ. We will participate as they participate in their worship. I cannot but agree. So, now, rather than wondering (and wandering about) in the subjective and asking ourselves, as we did back in Chapter 1, Were we to go to Nueva Esperanza or to Mt. Hope?, here we present ourselves in the present indicative and in full expectation of a realization of how Christians in both locations come to be in an image of Christ they themselves bring about.

To-be-in-Christ, Christians have to have a Christ to be in, which they bring about. They bring about Christ in places, which means they place themselves in-Christ, in his divine presence, but in the empirical, experiential world of sight and sound. They establish a where in order to accomplish a who. Using the warm-blooded, mammalian body, vertically erect on two feet, they employ the eye, the mouth, and the hand to position themselves in space and with respect to each other. The future unfolds ahead, the past (don't we wish!) fades behind; transcendence beckons above, but inertia drags from below.

The organizing of flesh-and-blood, primate experiential space becomes informed and transformed by the material settings around which the two faiths have built their worship. Each setting, the *iglesia* in Spanish America and the church in the American South, has a particular array of material features that contrasts with other settings, and in that contrast (not unlike the manner in which, as we saw earlier, the / p / phoneme defines itself in opposition to the / b / phoneme) the settings define, in a preliminary fashion, the who, the self, that is about to emerge. Thus, our first step toward the realization of their being-in-Christ is to approach the material settings and allow the settings to inform us as they inform the participants.[1]

In being so informed, we soon realize that the settings of the *iglesia* and church are themselves set in larger settings and these in turn in still larger ones and those in ones larger still. At the widest levels the settings become "defiant creations of meaning" that the people of Spanish America and of the American South have in the course of time constructed across their lands. Indeed, expanded to their true height, the local settings constitute the record of human endeavor on this planet and give voice to our "central calling": the heroic. Keeping in mind that we always lose something in the process, we can, however, enter the record at different levels. What we lose in perspective, we may gain in focus, though frankly I'm not sure about the terms of the trade-off. In any case, in the next section, "The Altar and the Pulpit," we enter at the level of the *municipio* of Nueva Esperanza and the county of Mt. Hope, proceed down to the individual structure of *iglesia* and church, and go still further into the interiors of each.

As we enter the *iglesia* and the church, in the following section, "The Host and the Call," we follow at an anthropological distance the counterposing

1. In addition to the general insights provided by archaeologists such as Tilley (1994) and sociologists like Gottdiener (1995), particularly relevant in clarifying the role of the material setting in Christian worship is Colleen McDannell's *Material Christianity: Religion and Popular Culture in America* (1995). She rightly insists that the "material world of landscapes, tools, buildings, household goods, clothing, and art is not neutral and passive; people interact with the material world thus permitting it to communicate specific messages" (2). Furthermore, to understand these material worlds, we must not "merely analyze their symbolic qualities, we must also look at how they fit into a system of exchange organized and given meaning by individuals" (3).

At the risk of beating my own drum—a risk you never dodge—I began the attempt to illuminate the process whereby we use the material setting, the where, to create ourselves, the who, in the 1970s (Richardson 1974b, 1974a). I suspect my more successful clarifications are Richardson (1982), where I first used Heidegger's concept of being-in-the-world, and Richardson (1995b), where I first found Derrida.

That's well and good, you comment so innocently, and the "so" in your voice tells me you've got payback in mind. Well and good, you repeat, but how do you react to this assessment of earlier, that is, 1970s, studies of material culture: "After several decades in the academic doldrums [the study of material culture] has re-emerged as a vanguard area liberating a range of disciplines from museum studies to archaeology" (Miller 1998)? Decades "in the academic doldrums"? Is he talking about you? Well, I grit my teeth but manage to say, bravely, We who reside in the doldrums, we also stand and serve.

acts of worship in Nueva Esperanza and in Mt. Hope that recast the settings into distinct performances. The performances in which we participate marginally and observe intensely are the early morning; the weekday mass, where the priest at the altar holds aloft before individuals kneeling in solitude the emblem of sacrifice; and the Sunday morning worship service, where the preacher at the pulpit calls out to the congregation sitting before him for the lost to accept salvation.

Having been informed by the contrastive settings and having seen and heard the distinctive performances, we step out of our role as participating observers in the final section of this chapter, "The Living Christs," to reflect back on the experience. In doing so, we review the concept of being-in-the-world and its relationship to being-in-Christ. We move from there to specify the ways in which the participants join setting and performance to constitute the distinct Christworlds in which they are. I argue that in their constituting, they, Spanish American Catholics and Southern Baptists, recreate the mystery of a Christ who lives. In Spanish America, he lives as the "Christ of the Touch," and among the Baptists of the American South, he rejoices as the "Christ of the Word."

But what is all this *they* stuff? you interrupt. Christians though they may be, are not they part of the "we?" Are we not with them? And you are right, or nearly so. My written text, invigorated by your reading eyes, attempts to create its own understanding. Our place-in-the-text is that of participating observers; we are in their world as anthropologists. The time we enter their world is the early fall.[2]

The Altar and the Pulpit

During the rainy season, which the people called *invierno*, winter, though it comes in May and often extends into September, the winds from the ocean roll the mist up the valleys that dissect the mountain ranges to wrap Nueva Esperanza in diaphanous lace. The mist swirls around the hills long ago denuded of their oaks and now covered with coffee trees loaded at harvest with

2. Material in the forthcoming section is also used to examine the much-cited concept of *habitus* of Pierre Bourdieu in "The Speech of *Habitus* in the New World: Divergence and Convergence in Landscape Practices of Administrative Towns in Spanish America and the American South" (Richardson 2002).

cheerful red beans. The mist lies along the sides of Mt. Yrcazú, which, though it periodically spews the air with ash, is relatively benign, for a volcano. Some years back, a mudslide, speeding down from the denuded hills, wiped out a nearby community, and the mist, as a last act before the morning sun burns it away, kindly thickens to hide the lingering scar.[3]

Over the next range toward the interior part of the country sits a regional city of several hundred thousand inhabitants, and still farther inland, far from the reach of the ocean's mist, the nation's capital and the country's largest city dominates the heartland with its millions.

Nueva Esperanza, whose full name is Nueva Esperanza de San Pablo, is the *cabecera*, or administrative head, of the *municipio*, or territorial unit, of the same name. Coffee is the principal source of sustenance for the area's economy. A few individuals own large tracts, but here, as in Costa Rica and portions of Colombia, smaller owners can harvest a good crop. The large growers, however, own the *beneficios*, the coffee processors, and that may give them leverage over their smaller neighbors, who by necessity are their clientele. The recent decline in world coffee prices, however, has descended upon the large and small alike.

In the plaza this early weekday an old man, who rises with the sun, has already uncovered the high-backed chair upon which his clients sit while he polishes their shoes to an incandescent glow. Over at the market a few blocks away, barefoot men pushing and pulling carts of all descriptions—some carts with iron wheels that slice through the debris of fallen bananas or melons, others with solid wooden wheels that wobble unevenly across the market floor—have finished unloading the produce hauled in from the countryside and wait to collect their pay. Shopowners raise the metal curtains they had locked down to protect their windows during the night and get out brooms to sweep the sidewalks in front of their stores. Toyotas and Mercedes jockey

3. In this part of Spanish America, the highland tropics, seasonal variation in temperature is very much secondary to variation in rainfall. Generally speaking, May to October are the wetter months and November to April the drier ones. In Spain, the wetter months are in winter, the *invierno*, and the drier ones in the summer, the *verano*, so when the Spanish arrived in the tropics, they called the wet season *invierno* and the dry, *verano*. Thus, on a particular rainy week in June, people in the streets, scurrying from one sheltered overhang to another, remark to their neighbor, "Mucho invierno; A lot of winter," meaning "It's been pouring down all week." Likewise, on an exceptionally dry, dusty day in December, a man from his post on a plaza bench may observe to his cronies, "¡Qué verano! What a summer!" and kick the dirt to show how dry it is.

with Chevrolets and Fords to find space in the narrow streets, and buses, converted from gasoline to diesel, spew black smoke as they rev up from depositing passengers at the plaza corners. Scooters move in and around the traffic, their drivers perched upright and steady. More than a few are women, immaculately dressed for the office in short skirts and stockinged legs. Clearly expert at negotiating their way, they rise slightly from the seats to take the numerous bumps with their knees.

Still the hub of this enduring and lively downtown, the plaza provides a green respite from the fumes of the streets. In the center, a fountain spirals water upward on the occasions considered sufficiently celebratory, such as October 12, still called here *el Día de la Raza*, "the Day of the Race," the day Christopher Columbus brought the flag and the cross to the New World. Over toward a corner stands a kiosk where the *municipio* brass band plays a selection of Sousa marches and Strauss waltzes on Sunday evenings, while small children race around the fountain in a furious chase, cutting in between clusters of teenage girls who stroll in presumed ignorance of the admiring eyes thrown their way from separate groups of their male age-mates. While their wives chat on the benches lining the walkways, the older men lounge against the commemorative busts, including one of Simón Bolívar, who fought to liberate the region from Spanish domination, but also one of Andrés Bello, a contemporary of *El Libertador* and an educator, humanist, and poet whose epic stanzas earned him comparison with Virgil.

Among the restaurants and banks that line the plaza sits a large, older, two-story structure that resembles a stately courtyard home. This is the seat of *cabecera* government, called, despite Bolívar's attempt to introduce democracy, the *palacio municipal*, the "municipal palace." Although it is early, several of the clerical workers are already pushing their scooters through the huge doors that open onto a spacious patio. Like the plaza, the patio has a fountain that already sparkles and greenery that rises up to the second terrace. There is talk of tearing down the *palacio* and replacing it with one of more progressive design, but at the moment, it and the offices that open their doors to citizens crisscrossing the patio continue to serve the administrative needs of La Nueva Esperanza, both the town itself and the larger territorial unit that bears the same name.

Crossing the plaza on their way to school, kids shout greetings to one another. Led by their older siblings, some are scarcely bigger than their booksacks. Among them are classic Mediterraneans, with coal black hair and pearly white skin; others are redheads from northern, Celtic Spain. Most of them, however, are shades of brown from colonial mixtures. For adults, the shades of color deepen from merchant to bus driver to barefoot men in the market and come to rest in the dark bronze of the old man in the plaza awaiting his first customer. Nowhere, however, do we see anyone dressed in the colorful blues or the solid blacks of Native Americans. If any live in Nueva Esperanza, they are indistinguishable in dress and demeanor. Likewise, African Americans, tied as they are to the coast and to bananas, rarely appear here.[4]

When the Spanish came through the region in search of gold, Native Americans to mine it, and pagan souls to convert to Christianity, they first located a town at the juncture of a smaller stream and the larger river they had followed up from the coast. Their leader, the conquistador Gil de Soto, reputed to be a distant relative of the more (in)famous Hernando, named the town after the patron saint of his birthplace in Estremadura, Spain, and because they all, soldier, missionary, and colonist, anticipated a bright unfolding in the New World, he added "Esperanza," thus La Esperanza de San Pablo, "The Hope of St. Paul." They quickly discovered, however, that the heavy rains during the *inviernos* turned the site into a disaster, so they moved farther up the slope. Here, located within the protective arms of the Santa Madre Cordillera, with access to the fertile valley below and the oak forest above, and with fresh water supplied by a more amenable stream, they successfully established a new settlement. This new community they christened, appropriately, La Nueva Esperanza de San Pablo, "The New Hope of St. Paul." Today, a few bedraggled huts of bamboo linger at the original site, which carries the title of "El Viejo" (Map 4).

The Spaniards never found much gold in the region, and, decimated by epidemics of what the Nahuas in Mexico called *matlaltotonqui*, the Spanish *tabardillo*, and the English typhus during the demographic collapse of the late sixteenth and early seventeenth centuries (Cook and Lovell 1991), the Native Americans dispersed to establish scattered settlements in the fastness of the Cordillera they, too, called "Holy Mother." The town, reduced to what the

4. In Nueva Esperanza, height, like skin color, varies socioeconomically. The bigger the load, the smaller the person. The men straining against the weight of the carts in the market, though muscular, are short, while the merchant rolling up the metal curtain in front of his store is at least a foot taller. The tallest of all are the politicians.

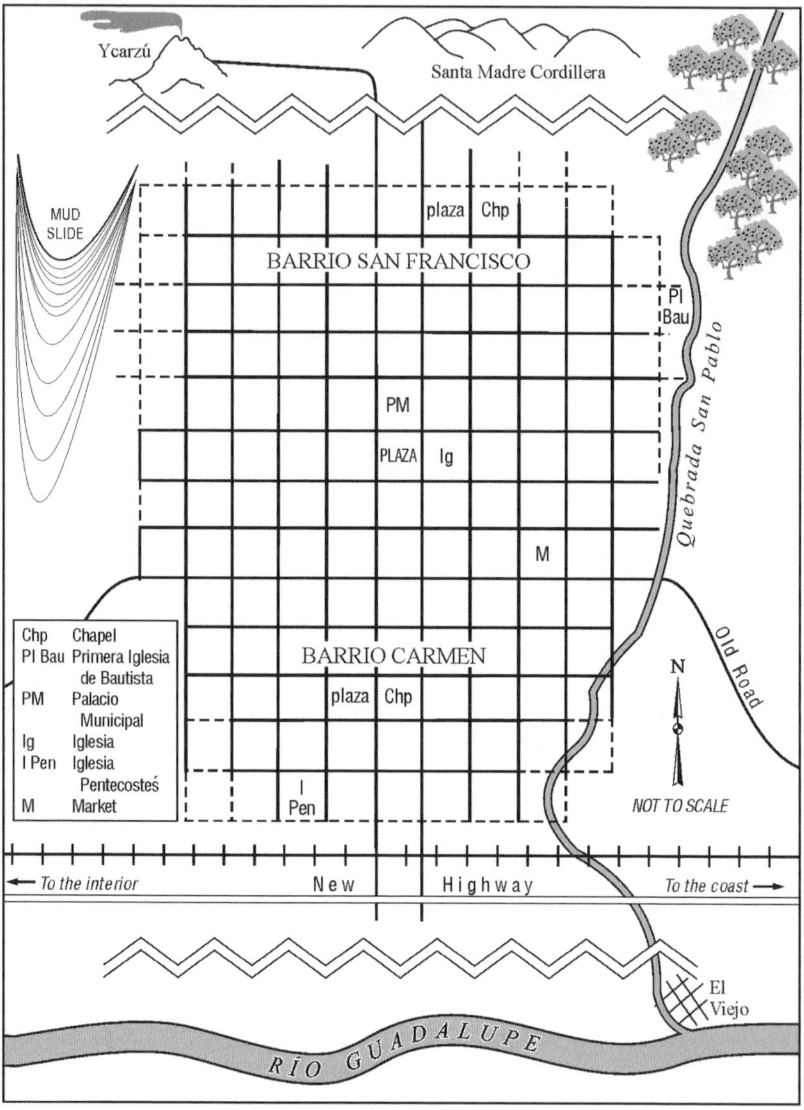

Map 4. Nueva Esperanza

Spanish governor, embittered by his unfortunate appointment, referred to as "sin la iglesia, hay solamente algunas chozas miserables; apart from the church, there are only a few miserable huts," nonetheless endured. Its lack of luster shielded it from the turmoil of the decades following independence, and with the introduction of coffee in the 1840s, it began in a modest way to prosper. The railroad, descending down the Rio Guadalupe, linked Nueva Esperanza to the interior cities and to the coastal port, where steamships awaited to carry the stimulant to the growing market among the working masses in Europe and the United States. Positioned in the transportation networks of the railroad and, later, of the new coastal highway, Nueva Esperanza found a niche in the hierarchy of the country's settlements. Today, with around 40,000, it belongs to the third rank of urban places, between the regional center in the interior and the smaller towns and hamlets toward the coast.

During the early colonial period, when there was still gold to mine and Indians to mine it, the Franciscans established a *doctrina* above the town and tried to ameliorate the disaster descending upon the Native Americans, but their laboring proved futile against the twin evils of disease and greed, so, eventually, they abandoned the location. Today, at the apparent site of the Franciscan effort, a small chapel built from the remains of the monastery fronts a plaza to serve the population of the Barrio San Francisco. In contrast to its earlier spread upward, in this century Nueva Esperanza has grown downslope toward the river. The recent completion of the new coastal highway between the river and the town has pulled development farther in that direction. For the parishioners living in this newer part of the city, the Catholic authorities have built a chapel dedicated to the Virgin of Carmen; consequently, the neighborhood has become Barrio Carmen.

At the edge of the new barrio, a Pentecostal preacher, arriving only a few years back from the regional city, has successfully converted a sufficient number of townspeople to build a modest, concrete-block structure, and each Sunday, tongues of fire descend upon the *hermanos y hermanas* gathered at La Iglesia Pentecostés, and the walls resound with Spirit-filled voices. During the same Sundays, the somewhat more restrained Baptists collect at a slightly more elaborate church but one situated precariously on the banks of the Quebrada. Outside, the sign reads "La Primera Iglesia de Bautista," the First Baptist Church, and inside, *pastor* Juan Jiménez, dressed in suit and tie, opens La Santa Biblia to preach the everlasting Word, "*Jesús salva*; Jesus saves."

For centuries, *la iglesia de San Pablo* has dominated the skyline of Nueva Esperanza. Even the disgruntled Spanish governor admired it. His predecessors, marshaling their resources in face of impending disasters, were determined to build an enduring monument, and as we cross the plaza on this bright weekday morning in early September, with the ascending sun turning the dome and its tower into gold, we are forced to agree that they succeeded (Figure 20).

The structure rises directly from the sidewalk. And no matter if they are on their way to the market, to the shops, to the bus stop, wherever they may be going, people encounter the *iglesia*. Rarely are they out of sight of it or out of hearing. No lettered sign disturbs the sheer mass to name its presence. There's no need, you observe. There's no competition, I add. And between the fluted half-columns that rise to support the horizontal cornice above the door, weathered icons, secured in their doorlike niches, voice in visual silence a statement more direct than writing of where we are and prepare us to present who we claim to be. Centuries of repetitive *inviernos* and *veranos* have so scrubbed the figures that their features are difficult to discern. The one on the right appears to be holding a book and a sword, so perhaps he is St. Paul, the *santo patrón* himself, the patron saint. Paired with him on the other side of the door is another figure with a bald head and flowing beard who is also holding a book but with a pair of keys. St. Peter, you suggest, not displeased at my confusion.

As he passes in front of the *iglesia*, a man about our age lifts his hat in a gesture of deference. And before you can stop me, I call, "Señor." He politely stops. "¿Quién es?" I ask, "Who is it?" and gesture toward the first figure. He looks at both me and the figure and, in a tone that suggests that any fool should know, replies, "Un santo, señor; a saint, sir." "Sí, pero, ¿Qué santo? Yes, but what saint?" I insist. As he continues to gaze at me, impeccably noncommittal, I reply to my own question. "Es San Pablo ¿verdad? It is St. Paul, isn't it?" "Sí señor," he seemingly agrees. And I motion to you in triumph, See, I told you. But as the man turns to go, he adds, "Sí, es un santo; yes, it is a saint." And you can barely restrain your glee at my chagrin.

Off to the right, in her own niche by the corner of the *iglesia*, an elderly lady sits at a table. She offers candles and prints. You compare the prints on the table with the ones we saw yesterday in the market. All glow in the same bright, if not lurid, reds and blues: Jesus pointing to a heart aflame on his chest, St. Francis talking to the animals, and even one of the now-banished St. Christopher carrying the Christ Child across a stream. Among the prints

Fig. 20. La Iglesia de Nueva Esperanza

is a small, brown figure barely visible in her finery, and I recognize the Virgin of the Angels, the patroness of Costa Rica.

In the market stall, which was near the medicinal plants, you were attracted to a small booklet with the title *Oración a la Santísima Muerte*. Inside was a prayer to Most Holy Death and instructions on how and when to recite the words. You ask the woman about it. She vigorously wags her finger back and forth in front of her face, "Eso no vendo yo; *I* don't sell that. *Es brujería, pura brujería*; it is witchcraft, pure witchcraft." To mollify her, you buy an *oración* to the Virgin of Carmen.

On Sundays and important feast days, beggars flank the entrance. One has a huge, running ulcer on his leg that he points to (with some glee, I can't help but think), so people will be moved to give more. But an early weekday mass is hardly worth the effort. People are in a hurry, and those who aren't don't have any money. The other evening in the plaza, we struck up a conversation with a young man in a Dallas Cowboys jersey. It turned out that he was a priest. He urged us not to give money to the beggars. Often they force children to beg, he said, and added that some even pour acid on their wounds to evoke greater sympathy and get more money.

The sound of bells pulls our attention upward, and the hands of the giant clock positioned beside the tower move toward the hour. As we pass through the arch of the massive door, the arch of Spanish triumph, I look up and remark, How about that? Above, carved in relief, a man sits astride a charging stallion, sword in his hand, turbaned figures falling beneath the hoofs: Santiago de Matamoros, St. James the Moor Slayer. Just being a good Christian, you observe, cynically I hope (Figure 21).

Elizabeth Wilder Weismann and Judith Hancock Sandoval, in their *Art and Time in Mexico: From Conquest to Revolution*, speak of the *iglesia* as a historical *conjunto*, an ensemble of time: "Starting with a hand-me-down Renaissance retable over the high altar, the congregation may have added a pair of fashionable pieces every half-century for two hundred years, and moved them about, and reassembled them, and installed old forgotten saints from the lumber room, and introduced new cults, and electricity, and added brocade dresses here and there, with artificial flowers and false pearls, as well as sheaves of real tuberoses in oil cans" (1985, 60). Inside the one at Nueva Esperanza, we see and, even with our opaque eyes more than half-blinded by our anthropological ineptitude, we become part of the *conjunto*, the ensemble. Behind is the street and its world of noise, merchants, and beggars; in front,

FIG. 21. Santiago, the Moor Slayer, over the entrance

extending out before us until we are surrounded by it, is the world of the temple and its silence. Below is the brick floor, so worn that our feet, seeking out its crevices and ridges, discover a presence. Above begins with the altar, the place of sacrifice, and above the altar is the tabernacle, where the Host is stored, or "reserved," and above the rounded roof of the tabernacle is the retable, the *retablo*, which extends upward until the curvature of the dome commands our view and promises to transport it still higher, perhaps to eternity.

Even with electricity, conveyed by wires strung haphazardly along the walls, there is much that remains in the shadows, a half-darkness that beckons. On either side we become aware of figures, each residing in a niche above a small altar. Below each is a rack for candles. Some are glowing; others have melted down to dark stubs. The sight of the orange flame and the smell of the wax draw us farther into the interior of the temple.

A middle-aged woman, her head covered with a shawl, approaches one of the figures with a candle she has secured from the stall out front. She lights her candle from one already burning and positions it in one of the holders. She then kneels, places her hands together, and bows her head. The figure, only a few feet above her head, wears a purple robe. He has fallen under the heavy cross he attempts to drag forward. His head is turned toward us, and blood from the crown of thorns runs down his forehead. But it is his eyes that haunt us. They are frightened, scared, agonized eyes. They peer out at us, and even as we look hastily away, we cannot avoid returning to their pain. The figure, found in *iglesia* after *iglesia* throughout Spanish America, is *Jesús el Nazareno*, Jesus the Nazarene.

In the center aisle, immediately in front of us, a man, the one in the business suit whom we have seen before, stops at one of the rows of plain wooden benches. He kneels, crosses himself, and then moves to a place on the bench. There, he reaches forward to the bottom of the bench in front and turns downs a long, narrow plank. He kneels on the plank.

Unexpectedly, I find myself doing the same, first dropping to one knee, then crossing myself as I have watched others do, to the head, to the chest, to the left, and to the right. You look at me, puzzled.

The benches are barely wide enough for a medium-sized rear end, and the back is equally austere. Taking my cue from the man in front of us, I reach forward and turn down the kneeling rail. You are not sure what to make of all this kneeling, but you join me. From our knees, balanced on the thin rail, we watch other people arrive.

Some of those appearing we have seen before: the ancient, enduring ladies in black, the young girls in their fresh, green uniforms, the man in the business suit. And there are others: a woman in the crisp blouse and skirt of an office worker; in front of her, an older lady with lots of makeup—red lips, powdered cheeks, penciled brows—and her hair pulled severely back; an elderly man, poorly shaven and bent, sitting at an angle to her; and a young woman who at first wanders about the side altars as in a daze but who finally sits behind us and prays in a loud voice. There are still others: a worker with a coil of rope slung over his shoulder, a young boy with a crippled foot, a small girl with a rag for a dress. People in all their variety are here as individuals. Family groups—a young married couple with a child at their side, a mother with a teenage daughter, an older couple so similar they look like twins—more frequently attend the Sunday mass. Even then, at that principal mass, among the groups the solitary worshiper is the archetypical figure.

Our knees give out, so we cross ourselves and sit back on the narrow bench. The center aisle leads to the altar rail that separates the nave, the part where we sit, from the sanctuary proper, the space between the rail and the curving wall of the apse. Raised on a platform, the altar sits in front of the *retablo*, which stretches across the apse. In front of the *retablo* and hanging from the ceiling is a figure of the crucified Christ. Not too long ago, perhaps as part of the impetus that led to Vatican II, someone had decided to place Christ in front of the *retablo* so that it may command our view. Perversely, we ignore Vatican II and look behind the Christ to the *retablo*. In a manner similar to the facade surrounding the entrance, two layers of figures gesture from their doorways. The scene is not as ornate as a Baroque drama, but here and there I believe I see an angel fluttering and a cherub peeking.

The Christ suspended from the ceiling is smaller than the figures in the *retablo*, which are about half the size of an average person. Although from where we sit the details of his passion are obscure, we can discern he is a more curvaceous, full-bodied Christ than the angular, flat Christ of folk carvers. Conversely, even at this distance, the bend in the knees, the reach of the arms, the slump of the thorn-crowned head are much more lifelike than the minimalist Christs of modern, if not postmodern, production.

Below the figure the altar, more recent than even the Christ, is a polished wood table resting upon two equally polished pillars. Like the *iglesia* itself, the altar is a holy place, for it "stands as a sign of Christ himself, who is the priest, the victim, and the altar of his own sacrifice" (International Commission 1991, 346). The corner of my eye catches sight of the pulpit rising alongside the wall, near the figure of St. Martin of Porres. With the four evangelists proclaiming from its panels and with St. Paul, the patron saint, atop the canopy, it is pure Baroque, or at least it was. Now its dilapidated stairs indicate it has been abandoned for the microphone and the lectern.[5]

An older priest, overweight and arthritic, emerges through a door to the right of the altar and moves in short, painful steps down the far aisle to the confessional booth located midway along the wall, between the side altars devoted to the Lord of Esquipulas and the Virgin of Carmen. He swings open

5. According to Theodor Klauser, after World War I innovation in church architecture ran ahead of the liturgy, and the altar "looked once more like a table, for the [traditional] attempt to make it look like a monument had sometimes led to it looking all too much like some gigantic tomb" (1979, 150).

the half-door to the small, boxlike structure and lowers himself gingerly on the bench along the back. A few people move to form jagged lines on either side of the booth. The priest knocks against the right wall, and a lady on that side kneels down and slides partially open a small door in the wall. Through the narrow slit, she recites her sins, and the priest, upon hearing her words, grants absolution and assigns penance. He turns to his left, knocks to indicate readiness, and the person on that side, also a lady, kneels, slides open the door, and makes her confession. With the completion of that confession, the priest turns back to the other wall and knocks. However, the person who is more or less next in line, a man, hears something by the entrance that draws his attention. Others, wondering at the man's interest, also turn to see what might be occurring. The priest, impatient at the delay, sticks his head out and urges people to attend to their turns. With his urging, people proceed in a more orderly manner, and in any case, only a few participate, and the whole matter is over in less than five minutes. Perhaps there are confessions that resemble the Hollywood version of the anguished sinner and the calm, wise priest. In Nueva Esperanza, however, it is, as is much of the worship, a matter-of-fact, no-nonsense affair. On the other hand, I myself have never knelt at the partition and have never slid open the door to address my sins. Have you?

While the priest attends to the last person, a young man in shirt sleeves appears with the vessels for the mass. He is partially paralyzed but efficiently arranges them on the linen-draped altar. His task completed, he passes in front of the altar, kneeling as he does so. At the other side of the sanctuary he flips on the lights and adjusts the audio amplifier. He passes again in front of the altar and kneels once more. And you note that everyone, with rare exception, does likewise whenever they cross in front of the altar. The attitude corresponds to that of the man out front—the one who "explained" the stone figures—who doffed his hat as he passed the doorway. Klauser tells us that this genuflexion is to the Son of God hidden in the eucharistic bread stored in the tabernacle above the altar (Klauser 1979). In Nueva Esperanza, as part of its lingering Baroque, the tabernacle is a miniature structure of columns and a dome that resembles more than anything a throne.

The young man, having completed his checks, leaves. A bird by an open window bursts into song. A bus screeches its brakes at the corner to deposit its passengers. The worshipers, scarcely more than thirty for this early morning weekday mass, sit scattered among the pews, all engrossed in their own thoughts.

On this hot Sunday morning in mid-September, the town of Mt. Hope sits among rolling hills of pines awaiting the season's first cool front (Map 5). *Weekend Edition* has a special on saying goodbye to summer, and the sound waves are full of Midwestern voices bidding the season a reluctant farewell, while people in Mt. Hope can hardly wait for it to go. On this Sunday, as with all Sundays, and Saturdays too nowadays, downtown Mt. Hope is deserted. Not even a stray cat prowls its solitary streets. The Jefferson Davis Hotel, built during the heyday of the railroad, when the Great Southern discharged its daily measure of passengers and freight, emptied its rooms and shut its doors several years back. Even the adjacent restaurant, the Dixie Do-Drop, sporting deer heads over marble counters, came to an end, despite its brag that "We Never Close." Both buildings await the wrecking ball of "urban renewal."

Down a weed-infested spur of the Great Southern, the remains of a cotton gin are being devoured by the kudzu vine, a "New South" plant introduced to control soil erosion that now has run amok throughout the region. If I shut my eyes, I can hear the creak of harness and the ring of hoofs as drivers maneuver their teams to haul cotton into the yard.

Before World War II, farmers throughout Fredonia County raised cotton as a cash crop, and both whites and blacks earned a living sharecropping the larger holdings. Except for the bottom land along the Trinity River, however, the county's red clay soil was at best marginal for cotton, and after the war, the smaller owners, the "one-mule farmers," sold out and moved down to Houston, over to Atlanta, or up to Chicago. The big owners, with help from the federal government, which paid them an allotment *not* to grow cotton, converted their land to pines. Table 4, based on data from Winn Parish, Louisiana, is also indicative of what happened in Fredonia County.

With the land in pines and the small farmers moved to cities, New Jersey and Atlantic (NJ&A) set up shop at the edge of the Quarters. It was a good location for such a lumber company: The land was cheap, the nearby railroad and, later, the interstate highway carried logs in and products out, and the black inhabitants of the adjacent Quarters accepted jobs in exchange for pollution, or at least they had until recently. For about the last year, Reverend Jackson, pastor at the Greater King David Baptist Church, has inserted in his

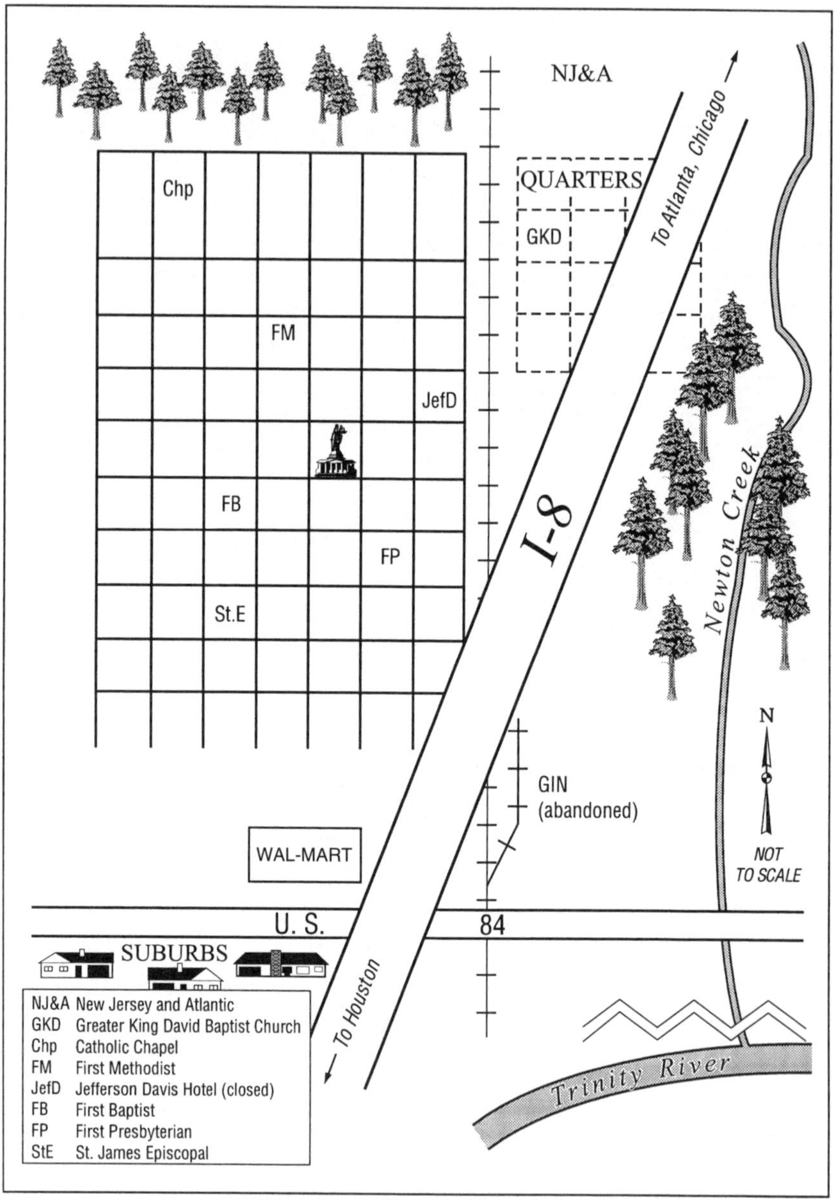
NJ&A
To Atlanta, Chicago
QUARTERS
GKD
Chp
FM
JefD
FB
FP
St.E
I-8
Newton Creek
N
GIN
(abandoned)
WAL-MART
NOT
TO SCALE
U. S.
84
SUBURBS
To Houston
Trinity River
NJ&A New Jersey and Atlantic
GKD Greater King David Baptist Church
Chp Catholic Chapel
FM First Methodist
JefD Jefferson Davis Hotel (closed)
FB First Baptist
FP First Presbyterian
StE St. James Episcopal

MAP 5. Mt. Hope

TABLE 4. Post–World War II Decline in Cotton Farming

	1940	1960
Number of farms	1,641	750
Number of owners	1,103	673
Number of tenants and sharecroppers	459	34
Amount of acreage in cotton	8,585	315

SOURCE: U.S. Department of Commerce 1943, 1961.

sermons not-so-veiled allusions drawn from Jeremiah about "a den of robbers." Consequently, the executives at NJ&A are getting a little nervous. For the moment, however, the logs roll in, and the products—telephone poles, pulp, and lumber—roll out.

Here, however, in the empty cotton gin, at the other end of town and in the shadow of its past, I hear along with the creak of harness and the ring of hooves a young mule driver, holding his head against the bars of the county lockup and, upon reconsidering his run-in with the law, advising his kind to "drink only a half a pint and stay in the wagon yard."[6]

The mule driver, his sharecropper daddy, and the sheriff who put him in jail, all looked like what you think the descendants of Scotch-Irish should look like, especially with an admixture of German and English. Not uncommonly, family members might claim "Indian blood," Cherokee, usually, and always on their "mamma's side." None spoke of African heritage, though veiled allusions were sometimes inserted into conversations about certain families, and I suspect in Mt. Hope and throughout the South there are as many "black" genes as "red" genes in the "white" gene pool. The African American side of town probably had in those days and still has in these a greater range of physical type, from as dark as any Congolese in the rain forest to as light as any Berber in the desert. Yet in the racial classification of the segregated South, any "Negro blood" in the genealogy of any family made and still makes that family black.

6. These words come from a song, familiar to the longtime listeners of the Grand Ole Opry, sung by David Akeman, much better known as Stringbean, the Kentucky Wonder, whose own tragic death in the streets of Nashville in 1973 at the hands of robbers seemed somehow foretold by the song. Another Kentucky comedian from the old "hillbilly" days, the "Duke of Paducah," who worked with Roy Acuff, always ended his routine with a signature closing relevant to the times: "I'm going back to the wagon, boys, 'cause these shoes are killing me." (See Malone 1985.)

While Mt. Hope as a place dates back to the Civil War, it remained a crossroads community until the latter part of the nineteenth century, when the Great Southern Railroad came through. Upon considering Mt. Hope's location in the network of regional settlements and upon having friendly, if not cozy, chats with local politicians and merchants, the executives in the Great Southern boardroom in St. Louis decided to place repair shops for their locomotives in the town, and as a result the town grew considerably. It became the county seat of Fredonia County and boasted an impressive courthouse that featured Greek porticoes on all four sides. In each pediment the face of a clock provided time in all four directions. A dome rose from the center, and on top, the highest point in town, blind justice balanced her scales. Although the Civil War was fought and done before there was even a Fredonia County, those in charge opted for a statue of a Confederate Soldier to guard the grounds, with an inscription at its base for those who might be so prone: "Lest We Forget." During the heyday of the Dixiecrats, when Strom Thurmond came through on his presidential campaign for states' rights, a Confederate banner was hoisted alongside the U.S. flag. And it's still there. As you toil the stairs leading up to and through the massive columns, the thought comes to you that justice might be more blind for some than for others.[7]

By the time the Great Southern switched from steam to diesel, it had merged with the Northern Pacific. The boardroom in Minneapolis paid little attention to small-town pleas from distant Mt. Hope, and the shops were moved. Now the fast-trekking diesels scarcely pause to sound their horns at the forlorn Jefferson Davis. Despite the appointment of a mayor's commission on downtown development, the town's center continues to die. A new Wal-Mart out by the interstate on land said to be owned by the mayor's brother-in-law has pretty much sealed the coffin.

Today, the faithful continue to attend the downtown churches and drive from their suburban homes to worship. Those who exit I-8 onto US 84 see right after

Mt. Hope
Pop. 38,459

7. In the days of World War II, the city fathers erected a large billboard in front of the courthouse and placed on it the names of all those in the county serving their country and put stars by those killed or missing in action. There was talk that the names of Negroes ought to be segregated, maybe put down last, but wiser heads prevailed, and for about the first time in Mt.

a veritable gaggle of signs: "Rotary International," "Lions Club," "Kiwanis," and a somewhat faded "Mt. Hope: Come Watch Us Grow." A sign proclaiming the First Baptist a family-oriented, Bible-based church looms over a smaller and more restrained announcement for the First Methodist, and crowding in at the edges are ones for the First Presbyterian and St. James Episcopal. This noisy clambering for attention brings back the image of the tower of the *iglesia de San Pablo* rising above Nueva Esperanza in splendid silence.

A few streets over from the courthouse, the First Baptist Church, or FBC, as it is known in the vernacular, occupies a city block and more. Although the Methodists got to Mt. Hope in 1852 and the Southern Baptists did not arrive until 1871, today it's no contest: the Baptists are bigger. And despite the growing popularity of the suburban Kennelworth Baptist out in Villa del Rey, in Mt. Hope, the downtown church remains the premier congregation. To provide parking space for the lingering minivan set and the upsurging SUV crowd, the church has bought out the adjoining properties, torn down the Victorian houses, and paved yards over with asphalt. In the remains of its own front lawn a sign in a churchly motif of black letters on white background announces the Sunday event (Figure 22).

While high-church Baptists frown upon the custom, the FBC at Mt. Hope follows the widespread practice of displaying a monthly word of wisdom on their "marquee." In addition to one appearing currently, other good ones are:

FOR PURPOSES THAT LAST PUT GOD FIRST

GOD SEES YOU AS A "KEEPER"

ALONE WITH GOD BRINGS YOU HOME

But my favorites are:

THERE'S
HELP
HOPE
HOME
HERE

Hope, sight became color-free. Recently, a veterans' group has petitioned for a memorial to honor those killed in Vietnam, but Korea—"our war," yours and mine—remains unrecalled.

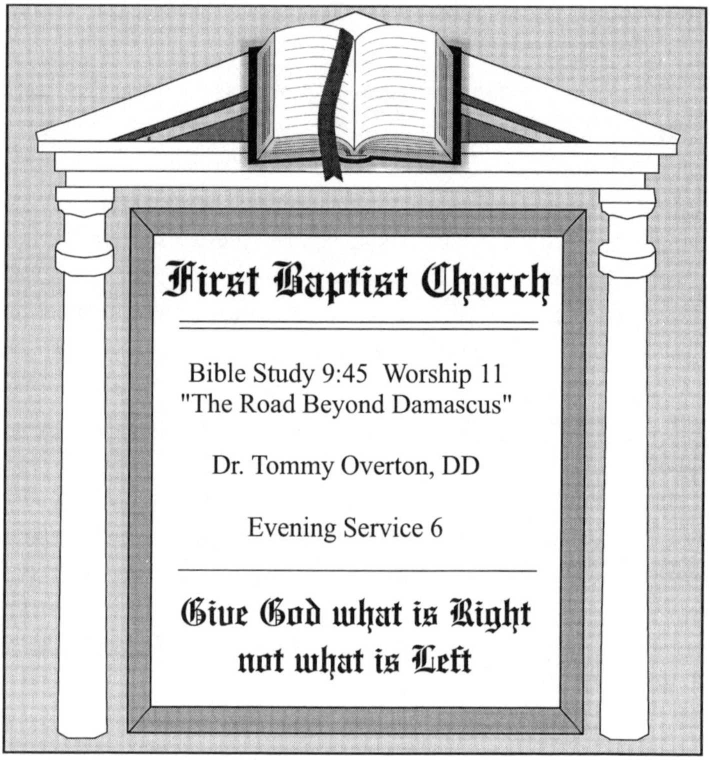

FIG. 22. What is coming Sunday at First Baptist in Mt. Hope

and

SOMETHING'S MISSING
CH CH
UR

When the Gulf War broke out, churches all over Fredonia County went red, white, and patriotic. And FBC had

SUPPORT OUR TROOPS

PRAY FOR VICTORY[8]

8. That was in the last century. In this century, the twenty-first, after September 11, many Southern Baptist Churches put up "God Bless America" and some, "Pray for Peace." One even had "Anger Is Only One Letter from Danger." At the FBC in Mt. Hope, our lady in the blue

I notice that changing life-styles have eliminated "Baptist Training Union" from the list of advertised events. This was sort of a night Sunday School that preceded the evening service but was more freewheeling. I cannot help but feel a bit sad. When I was a Southern Baptist, training union was my favorite occasion. Waxing with my fellow teenagers over the evils of alcohol, which none of us had ever tasted, or lambasting the Catholics, whom few of us had seen, joined us in a solidarity on a summer's night that superseded for the moment our adolescent torments.[9]

As we approach the steps, I stop. I can't do it. The emptiness of Sunday weighs too much. The fresh sounds of dawn have long since fallen silent; only the mourning doves call. The cicadas in the sycamores add a desolate shrill to the stillness. In the distance a single car circles the courthouse. It is, as Johnny Cash sang, "Sunday Mornin' Comin' Down":

> On a Sunday morning sidewalk, I'm wishing Lord that I was stoned.
> 'Cause there's something in a Sunday that makes a body feel alone.
> And there's nothin' short of dyin' that's half as lonesome as the sound
> Of a sleepin' city sidewalk and Sunday mornin' comin' down.

I am in Chapter 2 and in the Reformation Sabbath and back in the Prologue and in my childhood and in the Sunday of no work, the day of death.[10]

You are annoyed with me and look away. You are all too familiar with the debates being batted back and forth in my head—so familiar as to be irked. Are we going in or not? you snap. Your anger stirs my own, and recklessly, I gesture forward and climb the steps (Figure 23).

As befits a congregation that explicitly identifies itself with the South and in a town that until quite recently has uniformly done likewise, the First Baptist fronts a Greek portico that any plantation estate would envy. Six gleaming columns rest on a raised platform and rise to support a pediment of pure white. The present structure dates back to 1950 and replaces a smaller one of similar design. At that time, the steeple-crowd argued for a Colonial-Federal

---

dress with white trim wanted "Love Covers a Multitude of Sins," but she lost out to Brother Tommy's "United We Stand."

9. To be sure, some of the larger churches have a Discipleship Training Program before the evening service. However, more than one church has found attendance so thin on Sunday night that they have had to cancel the entire evening program.

10. Few country singers, and none of the new ones, can match Johnny's "Buddy, I know what it's like" voice, especially on this song written by Kris Kristofferson.

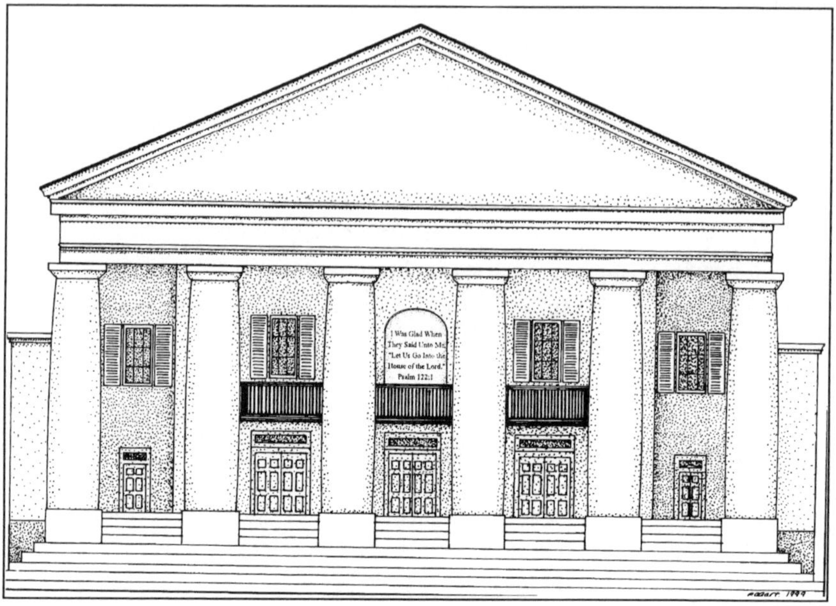

FIG. 23. The First Baptist Church at Mt. Hope

style, but the First Methodist had just replaced their old Carpenter Gothic structure with a sanctuary of such a design, and no one at First Baptist wanted to be accused of following the Methodists. Still, the steeple-crowd, a dedicated minority, is now pushing to add one above the pediment. Thus far, the antisteeple folks have successfully held the line. Renovation in the 1960s installed air-conditioning, and further improvements in recent decades have brought in a sound and lighting system, along with a television production unit. Next on the list is the enlargement of the educational plant. Reverend Overton is a firm believer that if you are not growing, you're falling behind, and even if he wasn't, the booster types among the deacons, such as the mayor and his brother-in-law, would keep him hopping.

At the top, you pause to make sure my anthropology is back. Seeing it return, you motion first to the right and then to the left. No beggars with running sores; no vendors with candles and images. Going through the columns, we read the message overhead (Figure 24).

You point above, No clock; no *Santiago*. There's one inside, I explain. Only the preacher can see it. The clock, I mean. There is no *Santiago*, or even a St. James, but only James, and he's in a book.

FIG. 24. Psalm 122:1 over the entrance

We enter the foyer, and a man in a gray suit with matching tie and an extended hand advances to greet us. We recognize him as the man we first met in Chapter 1, descending the courthouse steps. "Hello. My name is Womack. We're so glad to have you join us today." You are overcome by the enthusiasm of his pumping hand and can only mumble a response. From the stack he clasps in his left hand, he passes a program to each of us and repeats, "We're glad to have you."

With our programs in hand, we pass through Mr. Womack's enthusiasm and enter the church proper. Sunday School is over, and people are coming through the doors that connect the educational building to what more and more people, particularly the steeple-crowd, call "the sanctuary," though other members, scornful of such liturgical pretense, continue to insist on "auditorium." And it looks exactly like an auditorium, you remark. I can't resist being professorial: "audio," from a Latin verb meaning "to hear." Auditorium, the place for hearing. Hearing the Word. Not to be outdone, you add: "sanctuary," from the Latin verb meaning "to set apart, to make holy." Sanctuary, the place of the holy. And we look at one another and add together, A place for hearing the Holy Word, the place the Word makes holy.[11]

From where we stand, the carpeted floor slopes down to the front. The rows of pews curve slightly to the sides so that the aisles between them converge in amphitheater fashion. As we are not eager to get close to the front, we take a pew in the back. The light brown carpet, freshly vacuumed, carries no trace of previous steps. The back of the pew curves to fit the spine, and cushions, color coordinated with the carpet, pillow our weight. There are no kneeling rails. Being good southerners, Southern Baptists don't kneel. In front of us, on the back of the pew ahead, songbooks are strung along rails, and jutting periodically from the back are small shelves with circular indentations. You can't resist running the tip of your finger along the edge of one and glancing at me for a comment.

"Good morning." A well-groomed lady in a light blue dress with white lace trim descends upon us. Being taught to do so from childhood, we rise in her presence. "We are so pleased you could come this morning." She does not offer her hand, so we keep ours down. "Is this your first time at First Baptist? Well, you just make yourself at home. And do come back again."

The general color scheme is white walls and brown carpet. The long, narrow windows on either side, sealed shut since the introduction of air-conditioning, are stained with what might optimistically be called gold. Although the steeple-crowd, persistent if nothing else, longs for pastoral scenes and rays of light streaming down on storm-swept seas, the windows remain free of liturgical, that is to say, papist, designs. Conversely, the walls also remain free of the brightly colored banners shouting in vivid letters, "Rejoice" or "Hallelujah," that are the fashion of the more "dynamic" suburban congregations.

11. The captions under the photographs of churches in the 1958 edition of the *Encyclopedia of Southern Baptists* refer to the church building proper as "the auditorium."

Down at the front a man runs a last-minute check on the sound system. To the left stands the Christian flag next to the piano; across to the right stands the American flag next to the organ. Centered between is the Lord's Supper table. Across the front of the otherwise plain structure of dark, polished wood, inscribed in biblical Gothic, is "This Do In Remembrance of Me." On top is a large, opened Bible, and next to it are the velvet-lined collection plates. Immediately above the table and centered on a raised platform that elevates it above eye level is the largest, most imposing piece of furniture in the church, the pulpit. Its width is such that Reverend Overton can dramatically extend his arms to grab either side, its depth is such that he can stretch forward across its surface or conversely pull back away, and its strength is such that it can withstand a pounding fist or a Bible slammed down upon its surface. On either side of the pulpit are high-backed chairs where the preacher and the music director sit when the other is addressing the congregation. Behind the chairs in stacked rows are the seats for the forty or so members of the choir. Above the choir, framed between organ pipes, at the exact spot where in Nueva Esperanza Christ hangs on his cross, is the baptistery. The curtains are parted to reveal the river Jordan flowing in bright pastels through a green valley while a white dove flies overhead. And sure enough, beneath the river but above the choir, in large block letters, is Luke 24:5: "WHY SEEK YE THE LIVING AMONG THE DEAD?"

The church buzzes with exclamations of "Hello there. How are you today? So glad to see you." Inevitably, there are hopeful declarations about the University of the South's football fortunes:

> "This might be the year for the Foresters."
> "The way they played yesterday makes me think 11 and 0."
> "A bowl bid for sure."

More than one person discovers us sitting there, in the back, underneath the balcony overhang. We rise to meet each extended hand, and so we are up and down a lot. The men are in suits, and the ladies, in stockings. A few young men wear sport shirts and slacks, but the young women appear in fresh dresses that bedeck their vivacity. Several families sit together. The small children, however, the toddlers and preschoolers, are deposited in the nursery in the educational plant. Right in front of us, as far away from adults as they can get, is a pew packed with teenagers. You nudge me and point to a thirteen-year-old, scruffier than the rest, without a tie and with hair in his eyes. That's you in 1945.

No street noises penetrate the hermetically sealed inside. No African Americans appear in the doorway. The congregation focuses upon itself. The last-minute stragglers come through the vestibule and through Mr. Womack's greetings. Attendance will be good on this bright Lord's day, close to five hundred.

The Host and the Call

"In el nombre del Padre, el Hijo, y el Espíritu Santo." At the invocation of the name of the Father, the Son, and the Holy Ghost, the worshipers stand, make the sign of the cross, and mutter "Amen."

You nudge me, and I reply in kind. The priest celebrating the mass is the same young man in the Dallas Cowboys jersey who warned us against the beggars. Why is he here? The older priest has served the parish of Nueva Esperanza for years. Why two priests? At this early, weekday mass, there are at best thirty people. In any case, here he is, in green vestments, the color for this interval in the liturgical year, the interval called "ordinary" because it falls between the mysteries of Christ's birth and his Crucifixion.

"El Señor esté con ustedes," the priest snaps out in crisp vowels. "May the Lord be with you." The worshipers reply, "Y con tu espíritu," each in a soft, private manner, so the response is not in unison, but more like a rippling murmur, "And with your spirit."

The performance of the mass is tightly scripted. What is to be said, who is to say it, and when it is to be spoken are written in the missal. Particularly since Vatican II, the Church has attempted to make the missal more available to the public. Catholic bookstores offer the complete volume, with its alternate cycles progressing though the liturgical year. Commonly, vendors, such as the lady out front, sell a monthly missal, and even more commonly, a sheet containing the particular responses and readings for that Sunday's mass is distributed on the spot, which is the way it is done in the *iglesia* at Nueva Esperanza. During the course of such a mass, the young man with the limp may appear with a clump of sheets that he attempts to pass to those who seem interested. Most people do without. Thus, though the mass is tightly scripted and notwithstanding the written missal, in the celebration of the mass, in its coming to be in Nueva Esperanza, the verbal script takes precedence over the written one. The priest speaks from the missal, but the audience, the worshipers, speak from experience. Likewise, I speak to you in these written words you see so that we both may be part of the coming-to-be of Our Lord's Sacrifice on an early morning weekday mass in Nueva Esperanza. Consequently, while my words stay loyal to such a mass, they do not duplicate the script of the printed missal but aspire to convey a performance in their own performing.[12]

The priest, facing the worshipers, requests that we, *hermanos* (we, he, all of us standing together), to prepare ourselves for the celebration of the sacred mysteries, recognize our sins. Having made this request, he then switches to the I, to the individual that he is, to say, "Yo confieso. . . ." And we, each of us individually, also say, "Yo confieso. . . ." And saying it in Spanish allows us to double stress the *I*, in the *yo*, the pronoun, and in the verb form, in the terminal *o* of *confieso*. He and each of us confess we each have sinned greatly in thought, word, deed, and omission. Raising our fists to our hearts, we hit ourselves in the rhythm of "por mi culpa, por mi culpa, por mi gran culpa."

Mi culpa, mi culpa, mi gran culpa. You like that, don't you. Remember when we first heard it, in Colombia, in Latin: "mea culpa, mea culpa, mea maxima culpa"? And how later, now always in Spanish, we heard it in Costa Rica, in Honduras, in Guatemala, in Mexico, "mi culpa, mi culpa, mi gran culpa"? *Culpa* in Latin and *culpa* in Spanish sound the same, don't they? They should; they are from the same Mediterranean source. *Culpa* translates as "guilt" in English, but "guilt" comes from northern Europe, from the Old English *gylt*. The major difference, however, between *culpa* and *guilt* is in the *gran*. *Gran* or *grande* can mean large or great. Coming after the noun, it indicates size. *Un hombre grande* is a big guy; but *un gran hombre* is a great man, a hero, a Bolívar. So *mi gran culpa*? "My grand, marvelous guilt"? "My heroic guilt"? Having beat our breasts, if only with a light touch, we, each of us, continue to say that because of my grand guilt, "ruego a santa María, siempre Virgen, a los ángeles, a los santos, y a ustedes, hermanos, que intercedan por mi ante Dios, nuestro Señor; I ask blessed Mary, forever virgin, the angels,

12. Honesty, and I am nothing if not honest with you, requires that I report that I found the written missal, whenever I had one, a great aid to my understanding of what both the priest and the people were saying. This is partly due to the fact that I read Spanish better than I hear it, but also it is because, as a compulsive professor, I am a person of the book more than I am a person of free-flowing, untethered speech.

the saints, and you, my brothers and sisters, that you intercede on my behalf before God, our Lord."[13]

Having gotten through the introductory part of the mass, the priest moves into the Liturgy of the Word, the first of the two major segments of the celebration of Christ's sacrifice. The performance is scripted, but there are alternative scripts, and there are moments of spontaneity.

In an unexpected move that makes me want to rethink my first impression of him, the young priest asks the oldest of the school girls sitting up front to read the first scriptural passage, which is almost always from the Old Testament. She enters into the altar space, the sanctuary proper, where before Vatican II, she, not only as a lay person but as a woman, could not have entered for risk of ritually polluting the sacred domain. Her voice hesitant, she announces the reading: "Lectura del libro del profeta Isaís; Reading from the book of the Prophet Isaiah, chapter 35, verses 4–7." Taking courage from the prophet's words, her speech gains strength: "Digan a los de corazón apocado: ¡Animo! No teman. He aquí que su Dios, vengador y justiciero, viene ya para salvarnos; Tell those faint of heart. Be strong! Do not fear. Behold your God, conqueror and arbitrator, comes now to save us. Then the eyes of the blind shall be open and the ears of the deaf unstopped."

With a nod from the priest, the girl remains at the lectern to direct today's responsorial reading from Psalms. She announces, "Ven, Señor, a salvarnos." She waits while we repeat, "Come, Lord, and save us," and then reads the first passage: "The Lord is always true to his word and it is he who brings justice to the oppressed; he distributes bread to the hungry and liberates the captive." She pauses, and the response, coming from each of us in different rhythms, is a murmured, "Come, Lord, and save us." She continues, and at each pause, there is the murmur, unsynchronized, individual, and quiet. "Come, Lord, and save us." Finished, the girl solemnly rejoins her schoolmates. If it were Sunday, there would be another reading, from one of the

13. When these words are written down, either in the missal or in the sheets passed out on Sundays, the second person plural, the *vosotros* form, appears, so the words read "ruego a santa María, siempre Virgen, a los ángeles, a los santos, y a **vosotros**, hermanos, que **intercedáis** por mi ante Dios, nuestro Señor." Because of its near absence in the everyday speech of Spanish Americans, the second person plural in the discourse of the missal assumes a liturgical status, but the young priest in Nueva Esperanza will have none of this stuffy formality, and so we say "ustedes . . . intercedan."

New Testament's Epistles. But since it is a weekday, the priest moves directly to the Gospel, which only he, the priest, reads.

"Lectura del Santo Evangelico . . ." At the sound of his voice, we rise, and hands flash over faces to weave intricate crosses that often end with thumbs raised to the lips for a signature kiss. "En aquel tiempo," the priest begins from the Gospel according to St. Mark, chapter 7, verses 31–37, and proceeds to read how in those days, Jesus, traveling along the Sea of Galilee, astonished even his disciples with his actions. "Hace oír a los sordos y hablar a los mudos; He makes the deaf hear and the mute speak." Upon finishing the reading, the priest raises up the ornate volume, kisses it, and returns it to the lectern.

Preaching, delivering the homily that follows the reading of the Gospel, has become a more important component in the contemporary celebration of the mass. It was Archbishop Romero's hard-hitting homilies that provoked his assassination. Here in Nueva Esperanza, however, in the morning mass on a weekday, the priest does not often offer a homily. Yet today, with the young priest in command, you know he is not going to pass up the opportunity.

He unhooks the microphone from its stand, comes around in front of the altar. "Why do you sit there like rocks?" And we blink at him. "Why do you have to sit scattered about?" And it is true, there are no more than two people per bench and often only one, with empty benches in between. "If the *iglesia* reached from here to the plaza, you would spread from here to there, wouldn't you?" And looking about, you agree he is probably right. Still holding on to the microphone, he moves from the altar, out of the sanctuary area, and into the central aisle. He's coming straight at us! He stops and raises his free arm. "We should sit together like a family," he pleads and swoops his arm as if to collect us. "Like the disciples around Christ, we should gather together. Like a family," he repeats.

His pleas, no doubt straight from a youthful heart, fall on less-than-attentive ears, partly because of the amplification system. The amplifier, not a particularly sophisticated instrument to begin with, cannot cope with all the centuries-old nooks and crevices of the *iglesia*. Even in the best locations, the words get distorted, and some spots are completely dead to sound. Looking at the old pulpit, rising above the heads of the parishioners in its faded splendor, I wonder how his words would sound coming from there.

"Ir a la misa no es como ir al cine; Going to mass is not like going to the movie. You don't just sit and watch. You participate. When there is singing, you sing. When there is a response, you respond."

Now he pulls himself erect and gestures, somewhat disdainfully, it seems to me. "Ustedes deben entender; You must understand," he shouts. "Las imágenes allá y allá," and he points to the *Nazareno* and to the Virgin of Carmen, "y allá y allá" and he swings to point to the ones on our other side, to San Martín de Porres and even to Nuestro Señor de Esquipulas: "Esas imágenes no son más que imágenes; Those images are nothing more than images. They are symbols. At times, people confuse them with *La Santisima*, with the Most Holy." He stares at us, us in our stupidity, us in our lack of understanding, us in our lack of *cultura*, and we return the stare. Before he moves back to the altar, he gives it one more shot: "Esas imágenes no son más que imágenes."

In other words, you whisper to me, what he desires is a congregation in a church where icons are banished. Billy Graham could not ask for more. And I think of the older priest and wonder, Does he feel, as I do, when I stand in front of a class of freshly scrubbed undergraduates, ancient? an out-of-place artifact? something left over from an earlier day?

As the young priest turns to lead us in saying the Creed, the nearby worker with the rope strung over his shoulder gets up from his bench, goes over to the Virgin of Carmen, briefly kneels before her, crosses himself, and leaves. He, perhaps even more than either priest and certainly more than either of us, believes "en un solo Dios, Padre todopoderoso, creador del cielo and de la tierra; in a single God, Father all powerful, creator of the sky and of the earth," but he worships, as many do in Nueva Esperanza, according to his own agenda, and he comes and goes to the rhythm of that personal ritual cycle. Central to his agenda is the expression "Es la fe que vale": It is faith that has value, or, more broadly, it is faith that works. *La fe*, the faith in question, is his own. It is his own personal faith that establishes a social tie between him and this particular image of the Virgin of Carmen, to the Virgin of Carmen herself, and ultimately to the Virgin Mary, and, through her intercession, to God. Without faith, without his own, personal faith, kneeling before a statue gains nothing. The young priest, in his eager denunciation of images, apparently is unaware of this capacity that belongs to each of us, the capacity of *la fe*.

The Liturgy of the Word ends, and the priest prepares the altar for the Liturgy of the Eucharist, arguably the high point of the mass. As part of the offertory, the young man with the paralyzed side appears with a basket on a long stick. Unannounced and without fanfare, he goes down one side of the benches and comes back up the other. He extends the basket in front of people if they appear to have coins or bills in their hands. If they do not, he passes them by. Even with his bad leg, he's done in a minute or two.

The priest steps to where the school girls are sitting and leaning over the altar rail, he asks them if they would sing. The one who read the *primera lectura* nods, and after a brief consultation, they begin. Too soft for my dull ears to decipher the words, the song, fraught with youth and purity, offers both joy and a curious lingering regret.

The altar becomes a table, as the priest, acting in our behalf, prepares the bread and the wine: "Bendito seas, Señor Dios del universo, por este pan; May you be blessed, Lord God of the universe, by this bread, which is the fruit of the earth and the work of man." "Bendito seas, Señor Dios del universo, por este vino; May you be blessed, Lord God of the universe, by this wine, fruit of life and of the work of man."

With our murmured responses tailing after him, the young priest moves quickly. Suddenly we are on our knees, bells sound, and the priest, speaking directly to God, asks that these gifts of bread and wine be converted "en el Cuerpo y en la Sangre de Jesucristo, nuestro Señor; into the body and blood of Jesus Christ, our Lord." Now the altar becomes the table of the Last Supper, and priest, holding the host above his head and to the sound of bells, speaks in the voice of Jesus, as written in the Gospels:

> Tomad y comed todos del el
> porque esto es mi cuerpo
> que será entregado por vosotros.
> Take and eat all of you
> because this is my body
> that will be delivered up for you.

Here is the moment when the Word becomes Incarnate, when the wafer becomes the Host. Here is the moment the table becomes an altar. Here is the time many say Christ is sacrificed once more and a few, in heresy, that Christ dies once again on the cross. Here is the sight, the celebration of the physicality and externality of the sacred, that radical Protestants such as the Baptists refused to see. Here, now, also appears my first mass in San Pedro, Colombia, when years ago, I watched how the casual coming and going halted and all went to their knees, even the men standing reluctantly in the doorway and even the young boys, dropping to one knee on the dusty church tile after first putting down a handkerchief so as not to soil their freshly pressed pants. Here, in Nueva Esperanza, though few went to confession and few will take communion, all kneel.

Now the lifted chalice, the bells, and the words:

> Tomad y bebed todos de el
> porque este es el caliz de mi sangre,
> sangre de la alianza nueva y eterna,
> que será derramada por vosotros
> y por todos los hombres
> para el perdón de los pecados.
> Take and drink all of you
> for this is the chalice of my blood,
> blood of the new and eternal covenant,
> that will be shed for you
> and for all men
> for the pardon of sins.
> Haced esto en conmemoración mía,
> Do this in remembrance of me.[14]

Now, in my kneeling, the sounds of the street, ever present, become distant. Now, the bird on its perch by an open window trills softly. Now, my eyes go from the priest to the saints along the walls, their darkened countenances flickering in the candles' glow. My gaze goes from saints to the kneeling figures around me. Now, I take each person into my sight; each appears before me, each unique. Now, I hear the sound of my own breathing. Ahora, aquí en Nueva Esperanza, yo soy; now, here in New Hope, I am." "Ven, Señor Jesús; Come, Lord Jesus."

We stand to join the priest in saying the prayer recited by all since childhood and recognizable, even in Spanish, to any Sunday School kid in Mt.

14. Please note that the young priest, his breezy informality notwithstanding, when speaking the voice of Jesus, reverts to the liturgical *vosotros* for the verbs "tomad, bebed, and haced." In this context, the Spanish second person plural functions in the same manner as the archaic second person singular (thou) in Southern Baptist prayer speech. Both priest and preacher distinguish ordinary, profane speech from extraordinary, sacred speech. In so doing, they both aspire to speak the holy.

Hope, as Matthew 6:9–13, the Lord's Prayer: "Padre nuestro, que estás en el cielo; Our Father, who art in heaven, hallowed be thy name. . . ."

"Líbranos del mal," I murmur to myself, while you watch with your favorite quizzical smile. "Deliver us from evil."

The priest continues, "Señor Jesucristo, you who said to your Apostles, 'I leave you peace; my peace I give you.'" The priest's voice itself becomes a murmur, but no matter, I know the words he is saying: ". . . concédele la paz y la unidad, tu que vives y reinas por los siglos y siglos; grant peace and unity, you who live and reign for centuries upon centuries."

It was in Cartago, Costa Rica, when the hand of peace first touched my own. It was the first mass in Spanish America I had attended since the Vatican II reforms. For reasons still unclear, I had to fight myself to attend that day: "Miles, go, damn it, just go." Once inside, I found familiar solitude in the company of others in their solitude. I was still tied to the Latin mass I knew from Colombia. The lady standing next to me, a complete stranger, reached over and grasped my hand. What was she doing? I stood in near-panic. She said, "La paz del Señor." The peace of the *Señor. La paz* of the Lord. The words repeated themselves in my head. She looked at me expectantly, and I replied, "La paz del Señor." A reassuring smile, a tiny squeeze, and she dropped my hand to join others saying, "Cordero de Dios, que quitas el pecado del mundo, ten piedad de nosostros; Lamb of God, you who take away the sins of the world, have pity upon us." I was alone once more.

Nowadays, in Nueva Esperanza, I'm ready. I shake your hand, then the hands of those in front, and turn to the person in back of me and even go a few steps to the next person standing a little ways down the bench. "La paz del Señor. La mano de paz." Those around me respond in turn. The more eager types go up and down the aisle. The whole affair threatens to become infused with "the spirit of fellowship" so dear to the Southern Baptist congregational heart. But, for one thing, there are not enough people, and it subsides. And for that I am grateful.

While most of us remain in place, our knees gripping the hard, thin rail in front of us, several individuals leave their seats to walk to the front to take the Body of Christ in their mouths, the young girls in uniform, of course, the older ladies in their black shawls, and one or two more. The majority remained in their places, at first on their knees, and then, as knees go numb, easing back in their seats. How different, you observe, from communion in a U.S. parish, where in orderly fashion, beginning in the front and moving toward the rear, people move in line to the priest in the front. The whole church partakes; communion equals community. Given such logic, the ritual of communion emerges as the culminating event of the mass.

Here in Nueva Esperanza, however, the veneration of the Host, the Corpus of Christ, remains the focus. It is a visual event, a relationship established through sight, between self and object, between you on your knees and the Host elevated above the priest's head. Thus, it is a dyadic relationship, a two-party tie between the self and the sacred, and it is established in the presence of other two-party ties. The result, consequently, even with the reforms of Vatican II, is not a community but a collectivity of individuals.

While the priest returns the leftover but still blessed wafers to the container in the tabernacle, let me pause to stress how in Spanish America the feast of Corpus Christi, even though shifted from Thursday to the following Sunday, continues as a premier visual event. You remember the last time we were in Querétaro, Mexico? Because the official anticlerical opposition of "La Reforma" and of the Revolution of 1910 persisted, the procession had been forced indoors, but it was taking place nonetheless. With the Host in the center eye of the sunburst monstrance, the priest moved from side altar to side altar, all of which were adorned with symbols associated with the feast. Another priest threw open the entrance doors to allow more people to squeeze into an already packed *iglesia*. In other communities in other countries where the streets remain open to the Real Presence, a procession typically follows a path of colored sawdust and flowers laid down from the doors of the *iglesia* through streets around the town. In the middle of the procession, the priest, under a canopy supported by several men, holds the monstrance ahead of him in hands carefully wrapped in ecclesiastical cloth. The procession periodically stops, and the people kneel, while the priest chants in a barely audible voice. After an hour or so of winding its way past homes where the inhabitants come to the door and cross themselves, the procession returns to reenter the *iglesia*. It may well be, as you suggest, that as in the days of the Counter-Reformation when the procession of the Corpus Christi heralded the triumph of the true church over the threat of Protestantism, today the same procession of *Cristo Sacramentado* holds the line against the biblical Jesus that the young priest and his contemporaries love to recite.[15]

15. As mentioned in the notes to Chapter 3, in 1991 the Mexican government pushed through a repeal of restrictions on processions and other constraints placed on the Church dur-

But the morning mass in Nueva Esperanza we are attending is drawing to a close. If it were Sunday, the priest would likely give news of the parish, including what special days are approaching, such as the feast of Nuestra Señora de Dolores, Our Lady of Sorrows, and the times masses would be celebrated in the chapels in the barrios. On this weekday, however, the priest quickly brings the mass to a close. He inscribes the air before him with the sign of the cross and asks that the blessing of the all-powerful God descend upon us. He requests that we go in peace, for "la misa ha terminado; the mass has ended." At the abrupt conclusion, you repeat the more distant words, from San Juan 19:30, in the voice of Jesús, upon the completion of his Crucifixion, "Todo está consumado; It is finished."

The two priests, the older one hesitantly because of his arthritic knees, the younger one behind, fretting, his impatience scarcely concealed, make their exit. The girls quickly leave for their school, but the old women, with less to anticipate, are reluctant to depart. Several seek out their favorite *patrón* or, in the case of the Virgin, *patrona*. While we linger, engrossed in watching others, from a side chapel a beautiful female voice, alone and unaccompanied, fills the emptying space. We hear

> Ya venido el Señor
> a traernos la paz.
> Now comes the Lord
> to bring us peace.
> Te alabamos, Señor
> por tu cuerpo hecho pan.
> We praise you, Lord
> for your body made into bread.

Again, the voice repeats,

> Ya venido el Señor
> a traernos la paz.
> Now comes the Lord
> to bring us peace.

---

ing "La Reforma" and codified in the revolutionary constitution of 1917. In the following year, 1992, diplomatic relations were reestablished with the Vatican. At the same time, the changes may have provided Protestant groups with a legal identity they previously did not have when they were all grouped under the category of "sect" (See Samson 1995).

A man kneels in front of Nuestro Señor de Esquipulas, Our Lord of Esquipulas. I nod toward him and whisper to you, Someone from Central America? Could be, you reply. And we both recall the times we traveled to Esquipulas, a small town in western Guatemala to visit the famous shrine devoted to the "Black Christ," as he is commonly called, a Christ crucified but distinctive because of his dark color (Richardson 1995b).

We go to the side chapel in search of the beautiful voice. But it has finished its song, and we find only an ancient woman in black. Was it hers? you wonder in amazement. Incredulous, I stare at her. She stands by the tomb of Christ. The tomb is embedded in the wall at about waist height. If you were to kneel, which you did not do, your eyes would be on level with the naked figure visible through the glass. In contrast to the crucified figure over the main altar, and certainly distinct from the dark Lord of Esquipulas, the stretched-out body is pale white. Even the puncture wounds in the feet and hands and the slash in the side, which on crucified figures generally glow a brilliant red, are here barely pink. A lettered sign positioned near a collection box for donations announces what we already know, that this is El Santo Sepulcro de Nuestro Señor Jesucristo, the Holy Sepulcher of Our Lord, Jesus Christ. "¿Este es la paz del Señor?" you ask in Spanish. And recalling words from my Sunday School childhood, I ask in turn, "Is this the peace that passeth all understanding?"

Back out in the main space of the nave, we pass *El Nazareno*. I see a note pinned below the feet of the icon. Did the lady who was here earlier leave it? Throwing caution and decorum to the wind, I kneel to read it. The penciled words are in large block letters on tablet paper. "Le doy gracias al Señor; I give thanks to the Señor that my two sons are now married. Once I thought they never would be. Now they both are. Cecilia María de Urueta"

Just before we exit the *iglesia*, you discover a large painting on the wall and drag me over to examine it. Darkened with age, it probably dates back to the construction of the *iglesia*; nonetheless, we see its message across the centuries: San Pablo struck down on the road to Damascus (Hechos 9:3–8).

We emerge through the great doors in time to see the old priest leave in a chauffeured black sedan, while from around the corner, the young priest, already in his Dallas Cowboys jersey, roars by on a motorcycle.

Later that day we pass by the open door and glimpse something going on. We can't resist going inside. Between the pews and the altar, a small cluster of people gather with a tiny baby. The priest, the old one, sprinkles water on the baby's head. We are too far back to hear, but we know from your incessant questioning that it is a baptism. The man holding the baby is the godfather, the *padrino*, and woman beside him, the *madrina*, the godmother. The two promise to attend to the spiritual upbringing of the child and even assume the responsibilities of the parents should the parents die. In many communities, the more important tie is that between the godparents and the parents. Through this ritual they become *compadres*, co-parents, and among the traditionally minded and the poor, they become sources of support for one another. This is a bond that dissolves when people convert to evangelical Protestantism, which rails against infant baptism. But an upwardly mobile Protestant doesn't want poor relatives, ritual or otherwise, clinging on with requests for a helping hand. And you shake your head to say that is harsh. And I observe it to be part of the famous, or infamous, individualism that capitalists exalt.

In the space occupied by the *retablo* in Nueva Esperanza, where the saints from their niches peer out over the sacrificial altar, in Mt. Hope that same space has become for all the world a stage for the choir and the preacher. The wide border that runs along the outer edges of the raised platform further enhances the appearance of a proscenium arch.[16]

You fiddle with the church bulletin Mr. Womack has given us (Figures 25.1 and 25.2). On the cover it announces its presence, and on the second page it gives the morning order of worship. The opposite page provides the order of worship for the evening service, and when you flip the bulletin over to the back page, you find listed under the heading "About Our Folks" the names of those recently admitted for surgery and those now convalescing at home. Among the latter is Thomas C. Overton Jr. Beneath are various announcements, such as "There will be an orientation for the young men's group going to Mexico next week" and "The Stewardship Committee will hear a report from its chairman about meeting the goals of the fund-raising drive." The page ends with a urging for all to attend the Wednesday evening Prayer Service at 6:30.

16. In Baton Rouge, at the Family Worship Center, the church of the (in)famous Jimmy Swaggart, hangs a theatrical curtain down from the arch. Another example, more appropriate in that it is a Baptist church, is the Northside Baptist Church, a megachurch on the outskirts of Charlotte, North Carolina. At the stroke of the hour, music sounds, the curtain rises, and the service begins.

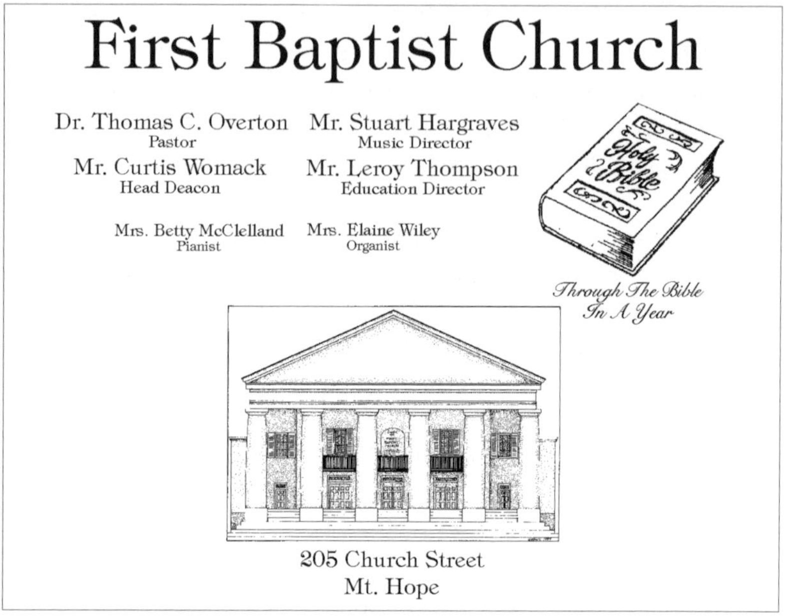

FIG. 25.1. Cover, bulletin of the First Baptist Church, Mt. Hope

Some urban churches, especially those in university towns, such as Austin, Texas, and Chapel Hill, North Carolina, succumb to the desire for formality and begin their services with a prelude from Johann Sebastian Bach. As a commentator noted years ago, there is in all, be it Austin, Chapel Hill, or Mt. Hope, a tension between fellowship and reverence (McGlothlen 1958). At Mt. Hope, where Bach remains too ecclesiastical, if not popish, the organist opens the worship with a softened version of a standard hymn. As she plays, the ceiling lights grow dim. The choir, robed in flowing garments of tan with red trim, files in, the high-voiced ladies in front, the deep-sounding men in the rear. With the choir in place, two men in business suits enter; one, tall, slim, and young, strides to the pulpit, while the other, older, heavier, graying, sits down on one of the two, large, red-cushioned chairs that flank either side of the pulpit.

Dr. Thomas C. Overton, D.D. Were did he get his D.D.? His Doctor of Divinity? The Dallas Theological Seminary? Even for a conservative Southern Baptist who believes in the infallibility of the Scriptures and who preaches from the King James Bible, the Dallas Theological may be too fundamentalist. Maybe he got his training and his degree from one of the seminaries affil-

Morning Worship

Prelude	Mrs. Elaine Wiley
Before the service, talk to God. During the service, let God talk to you. After the service, talk to each other!	
Call to worship	Mr. Stuart Hargraves
"All Hail the Power of Jesus' Name"	Hymn 202
Invocation	Dr. Thomas Overton
Welcome	Dr. Thomas Overton
Announcements	Mr. Leroy Thompson
"What a Friend We Have in Jesus"	Hymn 182
Offertory Prayer	Mr. Curtis Womack
Doxology	
Special Music	Miss Jane Wiley
Sermon . . . . . "The Road Beyond Damascus"	Dr. Thomas Overton
Invitational Hymn . . . . "Just as I Am"	Church Choir
Benediction	Dr. Thomas Overton

Please do not leave the service during the invitation.
Remember your own moment of decision and pray for those trying to come to Christ.

Fig. 25.2. First page, bulletin of the First Baptist Church, Mt. Hope

iated with the Southern Baptist Convention: the New Orleans Baptist Theological Seminary, perhaps, or the Southwestern Baptist Theological in Fort Worth. If so, it was some years ago. Nowadays, all these seminaries have modernized to offer a D. Min. (Doctor of Ministry) and even, heaven help us, a Ph.D.

The tall, slim man speaks, "May we stand in prayer?" The earlier glad-handed enthusiasm silenced, we rise, and he begins, "Oh, Lord, Our God, we come before you burdened with sin. . . ."

With "We ask these things in Jesus name, Amen," the slim man completes the short prayer and immediately switches to fellowship. "Turn," he commands, with bubbling joy, "to page 202 in your hymnal. 'All Hail the Power of Jesus' Name.' We'll sing verses 1, 2, and 4." With arms high, he glances to the left, to Miss Betty at the piano, and then quickly to Miss Elaine at the organ on the right. Satisfied, he gets them underway, then turns to the choir, then comes back to us, arms swinging a vigorous beat and tenor voice ringing.

The man is Stuart Hargraves, known to his friends, of which he has many, as Stu. He pairs off well with Dr. Overton, who is older and, as befitting a pastor, more restrained. Hargraves waxes and hardly ever wanes. He plays several instruments, including the musical saw, on which during the relaxed evening service, he can be enticted to perform "for the glory of God."

After the first verse, Stu urges us to newer heights. "I don't care if you sound like a frog in the bucket. God doesn't care. He said, 'Make a joyful noise.' That's what you do when you sing. Now, with a smile on every face, here we go. . . ."

You and I are standing without a hymnal, so the lady next to you (I'm sitting by the aisle with an escape route planned) passes hers over, already opened at the designated page. While our mouths pretend, the congregation follows Stu through the remaining verses and brings the song to a rousing finish: ". . . and crown Him Lord of all" (Forbes 1991).

Reverend Overton approaches the pulpit, and the mood switches back to reverence. "Let us pray. And as we pray, may every head be bowed and every eye closed. 'Our Father, we come before you today, humbly and contritely. . . ."

You point out, rather smugly I think, that not every head is bowed, not every eye is closed. Most women comply, but a few men stare ahead. And the more daring of the teenagers in front of us exchange nudges and grins, much to the pained dismay of their sensitive friends. But only Reverend Overton's voice sounds. The sealed windows block and cushioned floors absorb any extrinsic noise. We are sealed off. The coo of the doves, the shrill of the cicada, the shifting gears of an occasional car cannot penetrate the air-conditioned sanctuary. We are sealed off, together.

Reverend Overton prays aloud, but he leads us in prayer. We pray silently, together. The occasion is not one in which we repeat words directed toward us, nor is it a prayer spoken in solitude from bent knees with opened eyes fixed on a icon. Despite only one voice sounding, in standing together with heads bowed and eyes closed, we pray communally.

When Reverend Overton prays, not only does he pray aloud, but he prays orally. He scorns the high church minister's practice of crafting a written prayer and praying from that script. He prays a King James speech, full of "thy's" and "thou's," such as "In thy love for us, thou sent thine only begotten son to die for our sins." As an oral presentation, his prayers pile one stock phrase upon another. The phrases come from a lifetime of participating in Baptist verbal culture, some from favorite biblical passages, some from sermons Overton heard as a boy, and some from southern daily life. Having, in the tradition of plain-folk worship, rejected written prayer as artificial, he faces the task of using these stock phrases to convey a sincere heart truly open to God. On some occasions, he is so successful as to astonish himself, and he is moved to say, "God has spoken to me." On other occasions, for all his efforts, the words fall flat, and he fears, "God has turned his face from me." Regardless, he always concludes his prayer, as he does today, "in the name of our Lord and Savior, Jesus Christ. Amen."[17]

"Welcome to the House of the Lord," Reverend Overton switches from solemnity to joviality, as the congregation settles in their seats, but Overton has a surprise. "We especially want to welcome our visitors. Usually, we ask our visitors to stand. But today, we're going to ask our members to stand while the visitors remain seated." You and I feel obligated to stay in our seats, and so we are descended upon by glad hands and bright smiles. And there's more. "Will the ushers pass out our visitor cards to the visitors? We ask you to fill out the card and to drop it into the collection plates when we take the offering."

We each receive a folded card, with a pencil conveniently inserted, and a tiny red rose, cleverly done from cloth, pinned to a corner. I finger the rose, uncertain. Overton takes care of my uncertainty. "Pin the rose to your suit or dress," he commands, "and members, when you see someone with a rose, go the extra mile to receive them into our fellowship." Fighting back surges of childhood-born resistance to such bullying, I open the card. It requests name, address, phone, and answers to: Are you a Christian? Would you like the minister to call? The card also states,

If we meet and you forget us,
you have lost nothing;
but if you meet
JESUS CHRIST
and forget him
you have lost everything.
GOD BLESS YOU — WE CARE

17. Bill Leonard calls this verbal culture the "language of Zion." It is the language that assures "the listener that the speaker is a person of faith whose heart-felt religion is genuine and sincere" (1990, 129). All Southern Baptists talk it, but some are better at it than others. When dealing with contentious issues, the language of Zion becomes a kind of doublespeak that evokes piety, orthodoxy, and community, even though all understand, especially the speaker, that nothing has been resolved.

I want to sneer and say, Big deal!, but I'm an anthropologist, and so I say, I'm not certain if welcoming the visitors has more to do with enhancing congregational solidarity at the expense of outsiders than it has to do with being open to all. You reflect back to Nueva Esperanza and to the coming and going during mass. Here we see a group in action; there we saw individuals in the presence of one another.

"I call on Brother Thompson, our education director," Reverend Overton announces, and a man seated by his wife and married son climbs the stairs from the floor to the pulpit. "I ask you to note the activities listed in your program, and I especially want to encourage your support of our trip to Mexico. Yes, I'm going too. It will be my first trip. Brother Crutchfield promises to take care of me. Seriously, we look forward to a wonderful week, working for the Lord and carrying the message of salvation. Pray for our success."

Reverend Overton returns to the pulpit. "The lovely arrangement of flowers you see before you is given by the Baker family in honor of their dearly departed mother, Miss Josephine." Overton points to an array in a large vase near the Christian flag; gladioluses flown in from Colombia, you whisper, with a nudge.

Stu is back with another hymn. "Number 182, 'What a Friend We Have in Jesus.' Let's stand. This time we'll sing all three verses." And this time, we are ready and raise our own voices, pitifully sounding as they are, and before we know it, we are into the "third and final stanza":

> Are we weak and heavy laden,
> Cumbered with a load of care?
> Precious Savior, still our refuge,
> Take it to the Lord in prayer:
>
> Do thy friends despise, forsake thee?
> Take it to the Lord in prayer;
> In his arms He'll take and shield thee.
> Thou wilt find a solace there.
>
> (Forbes 1991)

Twelve men, an appropriate number, leave their wives and file to the front. We recognize Brother Womack. He takes the collection plates stacked on the Lord's Supper table, next to the opened Bible, and passes them to his fellow deacons. (There are no women deacons at the First Baptist; nor are there likely to be any, anytime soon.) At the request of Reverend Overton,

Brother Womack leads the offertory prayer. "Dear Lord, we just want thou to know how much we love thee for all that thou hast done for us, who are so unworthy . . ."

Raising money at the First Baptist is serious business, as it must be because, as a free and independent fellowship, it has only the pocketbooks and purses of its members to draw on, so at the conclusion of Brother Womack's prayer, the deacons, each with a plate, spread out, some in front, others midway up the aisles, and still others in the balcony. In alternative rows, they hand the plates to people seated at the ends. These place contributions, frequently in bills but also in envelopes taken from the back of pews, in the plates and pass them on. Parents give their young children change so they can "get in the habit of giving." Nearly everyone puts in some amount, even those who have signed pledges and mail in monthly checks. As the plates reach the far ends, the deacons standing there pass them to the first persons on the next row. The plates, made of highly polished wood with purple velvet centers, measure more than a foot across, yet at completion of the last aisle, most are piled high with contributions. Brother Womack takes the plates into the back, where he, assisted by several other deacons, immediately counts and secures the morning's offering.

Without a word, Hargraves signals the choir, and the familiar words of the Doxology come forth: "Praise God from whom all blessings flow . . ." After singing the Doxology to its concluding "A-men," the choir along with Hargraves take their seats, while a young lady from the second row steps out to stand before us. At the imperceptible nod from her, the man in the balcony working the synthesizer fills the church with orchestrated sounds. I can't make any sense out of it. With all the musical talent the church has, why has it chosen to import the tinny, artificial sound of the synthesizer into the sanctuary? It makes me mad, and I get madder because I don't understand my anger. It's their church, you tell me. It's their service. You're right, as usual, but I'm glad when the soloist, who delivers the song in the same confident manner and with the same body movements of a pop star, finishes and returns to her seat on the second row.

The special music ends the first half of the service. In a rough fashion, it parallels the Liturgy of the Word we see in Nueva Esperanza. Now, corresponding to the Liturgy of the Eucharist, but only in a structural sense, comes the sermon. Like the Eucharist, it is the main event, and the congregation shifts about in the pews to prepare itself to be attentive.

Reverend Overton approaches the pulpit at a leisurely pace. "Amen," he compliments the special music with gestures toward the soloist and Hargraves. "Amen."

He beams out at us. "It's still hot, isn't it? But just you wait. I predict in another two weeks, it'll be pig-sticking weather." By that phrase, Overton hearkens back to days of a more rural South, when, once the days turned cool so the meat wouldn't spoil, small farmers slaughtered their hogs and salted away the hams to eat off the rest of the year. It's not that he lived those days, but many of his father's generation had, as had the parents of older members of the congregation. Speaking the language of a bygone rural life seeks after a genuineness that, in the stock opinion of many, the urbanity of today fails to possess.

Not only does Dr. Overton occasionally use the rural vernacular in the morning service, but every now and then during the evening service, when he is free of the constraints of decorous broadcasting, he may go in even further pursuit of that old-time, plain-folk past by breaking into the rapid-fire, sucking-air delivery that his father, a lay preacher up in the mountains, employed.

> Now speaking at rates often exceeding two hundred words per minute, intoning his message in staccato bursts of rhetoric similar to the irregular lines of unrhymed verse, with an occasional phrase that rises like an auctioneer's chant and approaches song, the preacher pours out such a torrent of words that at the end of each linear segment he emits a sharp "huuh" or "haah," as he quickly exhales and inhales preparatory for his next flow of rhetoric. This "huuh" or "haah" constitutes the dominant beat of his rhythm and is usually thought of as the hallmark of the Southern Appalachian sermon style. (Dorgan 1987, 59)

The rural metaphors and the sucking-air sounds make the upwardly mobile, status-aspiring members of First Baptist nervous. But the others, grateful that the lost past has once again been restored, if only for a moment, applaud with amens and nudge one another, "That's Brother Tommy."

This morning, having evoked the past, Reverend Overton continues, "I want to thank all those who have asked about my son. As many of you know, Tommy Jr. was shot in a hunting accident during a recent trip to Texas. We're thankful the Lord spared his life. If he hadna bent over to light a cigarette, the bullet woulda gone right through his temple. I never wanted him to smoke and tried for years to get him to stop. But maybe this one time was okay.

"Turn with me, if you will, to the Book of Acts, Chapter 9, verses 3 through 10. 'And as he journeyed, he came near Damascus, and suddenly there shined round about him a light from heaven. And he fell to the earth. . . .'"

As Reverend Overton reads, many in the congregation, even the teenagers in front of us, take up their own personal copy of the Bible, turn the thin, onionskin pages to Acts, and read along silently. Reading is the other half of writing. In reading, we enter the written world of the text. And the text we enter here, the Bible, is without error; we are in the infallible Word. In the same manner that the text we enter differs from secular text, so also our reading differs. We read from a lifetime association with the Bible—an association that began long ago in nursery school, when we sang, "For the Bible tells me so," and has continued on through the Sunday School grades and into the "Adult" and "Senior Bible Study." While we may agree that such reading is ritualistic and therefore evokes an aesthetic experience more commonly associated with reciting memorized poetry than with interpreting science (Barr 1966), we must not use the label "ritualistic" to dismiss the effort we see occurring around us. The reading going on about us is imbued with the notion that the Bible was written for plain folk. It is not necessary to know Hebrew and Greek to understand its message. The most untutored among us, one whose literacy skills are minimal, may gain more than the highly trained scholar, for that untutored and uncouth person, in a direct and simple manner, can call upon the Holy Spirit. And all agree that the Holy Spirit is a far better guide to reading than a Harvard degree (Weber 1982).

Reading the Bible together separates the congregation from the world outside. Reading together separates the congregation by connecting it today, this September Sunday, in the Mt. Hope First Baptist Church, to the time of the original Autographia, when the Holy Spirit inspired the human authors. Their writing transcribed their revelations, and our readings, inspired in turn by the truth that is Jesus Christ, bring those revelations into the present (Blum 1980).[18]

18. As a conservative, Reverend Overton very much adheres to the fundamental Southern Baptist position, described in the 1950s, when he was a young man, that the Bible, the very breath of God, is sufficient, certain, and authoritative (Mullins 1958, Colson 1958).

The Word is literal, and its eternal being, through reading, becomes present. The object, the artifact, the element, however, is only symbolic and remains a remembrance. You recall we were here the other Sunday night when they had the Lord's Supper. At Mt. Hope First Baptist, they hold the Lord's Supper about four times a year. Under Reverend Overton's direction, only those who are members of the Mt. Hope church can sit at the Lord's table. This policy stems from the implicit Landmarkian stance Overton takes. Landmarkians, as we saw in Chapter 3, hold that the Baptists are not Protestants of the Reformation but are the straight and lineal descendants of the first Church at Jerusalem. Other religious organizations, such as the Methodists and, of course, the Catholics, are not churches but societies; therefore, those who are members of such societies may not share in the Supper of the Lord. Indeed, there is no Church as such, only individual bands of baptized believers. Consequently, each individual congregation partakes of its own Supper. Reverend Overton also repeats, as he does on every occasion as the deacons distribute to each of us first the crackers on flat plates and then the grape juice in tiny glass vessels (about "shot" size), that the occasion is one of remembrance, not of sacrifice. The things, the crackers and the juice, are "only symbolic" of the body and blood of Christ. The Scripture, however, the God-breathed-upon Word, is literal.[19]

Overton tells us that God speaks. And we who are made in his image speak. Dogs don't speak, cattle don't speak, mules don't speak, though they sometimes sing. God speaks. He uses language to talk to us. The Bible is God talking. (See also Packer 1980.)[20]

19. The First Baptist at Mt. Hope never refers to the Lord's Supper as communion. Other Baptist churches may have a more ecumenical attitude. During Christmas seasons, for example, the more liturgically upscale Baptist churches in Baton Rouge announce in the daily paper that they "will observe a candlelight communion service at 6 P.M. on Christmas Eve." Incidentally, now the purpose of those small shelves with circular indentations attached to the back of every pew is revealed: They hold the empty vessels from which we drank, together, the *symbolic* blood of Christ.

20. The value Southern Baptists place on speaking comes through vividly in these words of a preacher delivering a sermon in a rural Louisiana church: "Part of the likeness that we have with God is that we have the ability to speak. . . . Now, man was made to talk. Man was made to talk from creature to creature. Man was also made to talk from creature to God. And, man was given the ability to create with his words. Words would become mighty tools in the mouth of man" (Gregory 1992). Somehow, reading this calls to mind from the days of my childhood in

"And there was a certain disciple at Damascus named Ananias; and to him said the Lord in a vision, 'Ananias.' And he said, 'Behold, I am here, Lord.'" With the reading of the final verse in the selection, Reverend Overton closes his Bible. He begins his sermon in a conversational tone. "The story of Paul is a familiar one to us all. As Saul, he was making havoc of the early church, going into the places of worship, hauling men and women off to jail, condemning them to misery, if not death. He got permission from the high priest to go north to Damascus and bring all the Christians he found down to Jerusalem for trial. That was what he was doing on the road to Damascus. But the Lord has other plans for Saul."

As he talks, Reverend Overton moves our eyes from the page to the pulpit, from text to speech. In the act of reading aloud, while we read silently, he seeks to bring the world of the divinely inspired Word into the now, to unite the holy days of the Autographia with this September Sunday in the South. In closing the Bible, he moves from the discourse of the inerrant text to the more immediate, the more intimate discourse of speaking. He seeks to turn the collection of people sitting out in front of him into a congregation listening. His prominence as a preacher and as a pastor depends upon how well he succeeds. In Nueva Esperanza, should no one come for mass, the priest, though no doubt distraught, could carry through the sacrifice. The efficacy of the moment of consecration does not depend upon people listening. In Mt. Hope, however, to preach the Word, Overton needs, at the least, the appearance of attentive ears. Always aware of the delicate nature of his position, he periodically reminds us that coming to church won't get us saved. But—and this is a big "but"—we won't like heaven if we don't like church.

"What about Ananias?" he asks from a friendly position alongside the pulpit. "We know much about Paul. How much do we know about Ananias? Now, don't get confused. There were two other Ananiases. People in those days often had the same name. Just like today. But we do know that this Ananias was a servant of God. How do we know that? The Lord said, 'Ananias.' And Ananias replied, 'Behold, I am here, Lord.'

"When the Lord told Ananias to go to Saul of Tarsus, he was scared. He had heard of the evil Saul had done, of his persecution of Ananias's friends

East Texas an opposing, plain-folk view: "Too much talking (like too much loving) weakens a man."

and loved ones. You have to remember that the early Church was small. People knew each other. The people Saul was persecuting Ananias knew. These weren't strangers. These were Ananias's neighbors, friends, loved ones.

"The Lord explained that Saul was a chosen vessel and that Saul was to suffer great things in the name of the Lord. Ananias didn't say, 'What about me, Lord? Why can't I be your chosen vessel? Why can't I suffer great things for your namesake.' What did Ananias say? 'Behold, I am here, Lord.' "

In telling the story of Ananias, Reverend Overton takes us on the road to Damascus and beyond. The conversion of Paul tells us that our background won't save us, that our education won't save us, that our following the righteous laws of the Pharisees won't save us, that what will save us is a personal experience with the Lord. He also reminds us that Paul needed help. He was blinded by the glory of the Lord.

"So the Lord sent his servant, Ananias. When Ananias came before Paul, he said, 'Brother Saul, the Lord hath sent me that thou mightest receive thy sight.' And immediately there fell from his eyes as it had been scales; and he received sight forthwith, and arose, and was baptized."

Like other storytelling preachers, Overton commonly embeds his incidents in another time and place, some distance from the present. However, this morning, he comes home. "Many of you, especially you old-timers, remember John McCraney. His shoestore there on Main? 'McCraney Footwear. A Shoe for All Occasions.' John's gone, his family's left, and his store's closed. But Brother John lived the good life. He told me one day, right before he died. Right before he died, he said to me, 'Preacher, I want you to tell people God has blessed me.' There he was, suffering from that awful disease that came like a thief in the night to lay him waste. John had been a big man. 'Big John,' they called him. Now he was skin and bones. And he said, 'I want you tell them God has blessed me. In my life,' he said, 'I put God first. God first, family second, and shoes third.' Won't you put God first?"

Deep into his sermon, Reverend Overton preaches. And he preaches with body and voice. In telling the story of John, the shoe merchant, he changes his stance at the pulpit and varies the tone of his voice to convey John's words. He increases the volume and moves back from the pulpit: "God first, family second, shoes third." He drops the volume to a near-whisper and leans forward. "Won't you put God first?" He pauses and lets the silence accumulate. Then he is off again, not always logically. He's off into a story I heard years ago.

"There was a certain rich man, who was clothed in purple and fine linen and whose table was always laden. At the gate of his mansion lay the beggar, Lazarus. He was dressed in rags and lived on crumbs from the rich man's table. And dogs came and licked his sores.

"And it came to pass that both died. Lazarus was taken up by the angels into Abraham's bosom. The rich man descended unto hell. There he lifted up his eyes and cried out. 'Father Abraham, have mercy on me. Send Lazarus so that he may dip his hands in water and cool my parched tongue. I am tormented in this flame.'

"But Abraham denied his plea. And the rich man asked, 'Send Lazarus to my five brethren that he may testify unto them, lest they also come to this place of torment.'

"But Abraham replied, 'They have the words of Moses and the prophets. If they will not hear, they will not be persuaded.'

"We have the word of Moses and the prophets. We have the Word of Jesus Christ. Let us hear His Word, before it is too late."[21]

Reverend Overton lifts up his Bible with his left hand and gestures toward it with his right. "The Word of God is not just print on a page. Jesus spoke, and his Church came to be. The Word of God is the Body of Christ." Overton lifts the Bible high above his head and shakes it at us. "Feed on the Body of Christ.

"They want to take the blood out of the Bible. The Words of Jesus are in red. Look at your Bible. Are not the Words Jesus spoke in red? Stained red by His Precious Blood. The Blood He shed for you and me.

" 'Know ye not, that so many of us as were baptized into Jesus Christ were baptized into his death?' Romans 6:3.

" 'I am crucified with Christ; nevertheless I live; yet not I, but Christ liveth in me; and the life which I now live in the flesh I live by the faith of the Son of God who loved me, and gave himself for me.' Galatians 2:15."

21. In Reverend Overton's paraphrasing of Luke 16:19–31, I hear across the decades the voice of Reverend Summerall from the pulpit of the First Baptist in Palestine, Texas. At both pulpits, both men are speaking the voice of Jesus preaching. How true it is, as you say, that our voices are scarcely our own; they are inhabited by so many others. Our house of self gets crowded with "invisible guests," "social ghosts" who haunt our determination to "find our true self" (see Gergen 1991). Naturally, the older we get, the more occupants, invited or otherwise, our house has, and with each demanding a say, the place gets so noisy sometimes it's hard to think.

In quoting the Bible with the exact references, Reverend Overton demonstrates his close familiarity with the Holy Word: By inserting the words of Paul among his own, he joins the past to the present.

"A few years back, the so-called experts on the Bible got together in the nation's capital, in Washington, D.C. They got together to debate the question: Did Jesus arise from the tomb? The Resurrection Summit they called it. I'll tell you what to call it. The Devil's Summit. The Lord Jesus arose. He sits today in heaven, at the right hand of the Father. Jesus is alive."[22]

In the plain-folk tradition of the Southern Baptists, religion is not real if it is not felt, if it is not from the heart. Thus, as a self-proclaimed keeper of that tradition, Overton's job every Sunday is to deliver his heart. This Sunday, he asks, "How many of you can remember the day, the hour, the moment, when Jesus entered your life? When you said, 'Yes, Lord, I am thine'? How about a show of hands?" And the congregation becomes a sea of hands, waving enthusiastically.

"It seems like only yesterday. I remember it so well. I was raised in a God-fearing family. But I strayed. As a young man, with an education that my family sacrificed for, I got smart. As in smart-aleck. I got smart like only young men can. I got ashamed of my family. My mother didn't dress like the other mothers of my group. She didn't go to the hairdresser's every week; she didn't do her face up every night. My father was up before daylight and didn't get in till dark, so he didn't shave every day. He didn't put on new clothes until the old ones fell off. I got ashamed of my family. But friends, you can't rise above your raisin'. I was smart, oh, how I was smart. But then I learned about Jesus.

"There was a quietness in that evening, in the cool of that evening. I went out in the fields. I had strayed from the path my daddy set. But now I was coming home. Coming home, O Lord. Coming home, never more to roam. I knelt there, between the rows of corn. The old dog, Laddie, had followed me out there, and he lay down beside me. I could hear the cows lowing in the barn. But around me, it was still. Not a sound. And I said, from knees, 'O Lord, I'm lost. I'm lost. You are my one and only hope. I don't have much of a life, but I'm giving it all to you. Let thy will be done, O Lord. I am thine.'

22. The reference is to the Easter week of 1996, when three major weeklies, *Newsweek*, *Time*, and *U.S. News and World Report*, all featured a picture of the resurrected Jesus on their covers.

"I went straight back to the house. Gave my mother a big hug and said how lovely she looked. I told my father, 'Daddy, today I gave my life to Jesus.' And tears came to his eyes and flowed down his line-creased face. O happy day, when Jesus washed my sins away.

"Has Jesus washed your sins away? Have you washed your sins in the Blood of the Lamb? Can you say, 'Let thy will, not my will, but thy will be done?' Can you say, 'I am thine, O Lord?' "[23]

As the clock moves toward noon, just before people get fidgety, Reverend Overton wraps it up. "When you forty, you recall being young. When you fifty, you start slowing down. When you sixty, you remember all the things left undone. And when you seventy, you better start packing.[24]

"What a friend we have in Jesus. 'Do thy friends despise, forsake thee?' Does the world turn away? Let it turn. Let it turn. Let the world go. You have a friend. Not a fair weather friend, but a friend forever, 'a friend so faithful, Who will all our sorrows share. . . .' "

Reverend Overton is issuing the invitation, the altar call. He is at the point, structurally, that corresponds to the moment in which in Nueva Esperanza the wafer becomes the Body of Christ.

"There may be people here whose names are on the church's roll but who are not genuinely part of the Body of Christ, who have not truly accepted Jesus Christ as their personal savior. Examine your hearts. Let God in. Jesus knocks. Open the door, and let him in. If you know not Christ, this is the time. This is the time. Don't wait. And the Lord said to Ananias, 'Ananias.' And Ananias replied, 'Behold, I am here, Lord.' Say to Jesus now, 'Behold, I

23. You recognize the parallels between Reverend Overton's conversion account and my own. Even the dogs have the same name and do the same thing. The difference lies in the outcomes. While Overton may have found, in his conversion, "the peace that passeth all understanding" (Philippians 4:7), thus far it has eluded me, and for that I can be grateful. You will recognize too that the words "I am thine, O Lord" come from the hymn of the same title. The chorus is perhaps even more familiar:

> Draw me nearer, nearer, blessed Lord
> To the cross where thou has died;
> Draw me nearer, nearer, nearer blessed Lord,
> To thy precious bleeding side.
>
> (Sims 1956, 349)

24. As you see, Reverend Overton, especially when he feels the need to communicate plainly, leaves out, intentionally or otherwise, his auxiliary verbs, particularly, his "ares."

am here, Lord.' Now, while the choir sings our invitational hymn, won't you come?"

Stu, subdued and somber, steps forward, to lead.

> Just as I am, without one plea,
> But that Thy blood was shed for me,
> And that Thou bidd'st me come to Thee,
> O Lamb of God, I come, I come.
> (Forbes 1991, 307)

Reverend Overton leaves the pulpit, descends the steps to the level of the congregation, and spreads out his arms. "Listen. Jesus said, 'Behold, I stand at the door and knock. If any man hear my voice, and open the door, I will come in, in to him, and will sup with him and he with me.'[25]

"Just as you are. Without one plea. Without any reservation. Won't you come?"

At the altar call, in a church that has no altar, the preacher spreads out his arms, waiting for you to step forward into his embrace. As I watch, it occurs to me that the preacher is Christ, who opens his arms for you. If that is the case, then you are the sacrifice. When you step out into the aisle and walk down to the front of the auditorium, in front of the congregation, you offer up yourself.

In truth, as in many Sundays, today the altar call is anticlimactic. You stay put. Others turn their thoughts toward Sunday dinner. Indeed, one or two, saved many years ago, slip out the door, always with a good excuse and despite the plea at the bottom of the program. In the end, one couple who has recently moved to Mt. Hope comes before the congregation to request membership. Under the direction of Brother Womack, who is a busy man, the congregation votes to accept their letter of transfer. There is a certain amount of shuffling about, and you ask what has happened to Reverend Overton, who has strangely disappeared. We look up, and suddenly, there he is, in the baptistery.

Coming after the television broadcast and unannounced in the bulletin, the baptism is very much an event for, and of, the congregation. Reverend Overton, protected by a rubber suit, has waded out to the middle of the tank. He occupies the precise spot where, in Nueva Esperanza, Christ hangs on

25. Revelation 3:20.

the cross. In front of the painting of the river Jordan, he raises his right arm and again quotes Acts 9:18: "And immediately there fell from his eyes as it had been scales; and he received sight forthwith, and arose, and was baptized." From the opposite side, a young teenage girl, dressed in a white gown appears. Overton reaches out his arm and helps her to the front. I can tell you are tempted to make an irreverent remark about sacrificial virgins, but fortunately you don't.

I can also tell that Reverend Overton is tempted to use the occasion to deliver a sermonette on believer's baptism, but fortunately he restricts himself to telling us that the Greek word for baptism appears in the New Testament seventy-three times, and each time, it clearly means to dip, or to plunge. He quotes from Paul one more time, from Romans 6:4: "Therefore we are buried with him by baptism into death: that like as Christ was raised up from the dead by the glory of the Father, even so we also walk in newness of life." He turns to the girl. "Mary Frances Duncan, upon your profession in Jesus Christ as Savior and Lord, and in obedience to his command, I baptize you in the name of the Father, the Son, and the Holy Spirit. Amen." As he lowers her backward upon his arm into the water, I cannot help but recall my own immersions. Should I wish her better luck than I had?[26]

From his position in the baptistery, Reverend Overton gives the benediction, and when he is finished, people collect their belongings, put the hymnals back in their racks, and move toward the door, many chatting as they go. The milling about that occurred before the service characterizes its ending. Somehow, through some very quick movements, Reverend Overton is at the door, shaking the hands of those filing by. We spot a side door and break for it, only to find Brother Womack standing guard. He urges us to return. "We're always glad to have you."

The Living Christs

Having crossed the threshold of the giant doors at the *iglesia* of Nueva Esperanza and passed through the portico at the church in Mt. Hope and having

26. The London Confession of 1644, which we reviewed in Chapter 3, first described baptism as the reenactment of Christ's death, burial, and resurrection. In 1958, the words of the Confession reappeared in this forthright statement in the *Encyclopedia of Southern Baptists:* "The convert is immersed into the water. This means a dying with Christ. He remains there for a moment under the surface. This means being buried with Christ. He emerges from the water.

joined (in our peculiar anthropological manner) in the consecration of the Host and in the altar call for the lost and damned, we now arrive at the point of wanting to account for what we have seen and heard. In preparation for that task, we might well recall the words of San Pablo, "Fui crucificado con Cristo. Ya no vivo yo; es Cristo el que vive en mí" (Gálatas 2:20), and also Paul, "I am crucified with Christ; nevertheless I live; yet not I, but Christ liveth in me" (Galatians 2:20).

"Cristo vive en mí; Christ liveth in me" are words that reverberate throughout both the *iglesia* and the church and, indeed, wherever Christians gather. Theologians, far more learned about such matters than either of us, refer to the words as expressions of San Pablo / St. Paul's mysticism, the mystical union with Christ. One interpreter suggests the words reveal "at once the intimate relationship with Christ and the resultant redirection and reconstitution of the self. The self is neither annihilated nor merged with the divine as a stream in absorbed into the ocean; the 'I'-'Thou' relationship is retained" (Purdy 1962). What is the I-Thou relationship? How may the union with Christ be constituted as an I-Thou bond? Let us hold on to these intriguing questions for later consideration. Albert Schweitzer, he of the many talents and saintly heart, insisted that at least as far as the Apostle was concerned, the issue of the union with Christ was not a matter of subjective belief but of an objective condition based on the corporeity of the Body of Christ. Be that as it may, what grabs our attention in Schweitzer's discussion is the term he uses for describing the union with Christ: "being-in-Christ" (1931, 116). Upon seeing Schweitzer's "being-in-Christ" we immediately recognize Heidegger's "being-in-the-world," and "being-in-the-world," we recall from Chapter 1, is the human condition. Consequently, "being-in-Christ" is a specific application of being human.

Wait! Wait! you say. Where am I going? you ask. Off the deep end, once more?

Very well. Let us pause a moment and review the argument of Chapter 1.

Being-in-the-world, I remind you, is a unitary phenomenon. The hyphens so indicate. Being, the experience of be-ing, establishes the world, the symbolic construct, in which we are. As truly naked, unfinished creatures, we

---

This means being raised with Christ" (Smith 1958, 108). Now, Reverend Overton's acts reproduce what he believes occurred on that fateful day in the river Jordan when the heavens opened and the Spirit of God descended like a dove, saying, "This is my beloved Son, in whom I am well pleased" (Matthew 3:17).

cannot be without a world to be in. But the world in which we are, we bring about. To repeat my favorite example: You and I cannot be in this text without a text to be in, and you with your reading and I with my writing create our textual reality. Again I stress, it is your reading that makes my text live. So read carefully, so that I, the pronoun before you, may be!

Being-in-the-world is unitary but, as Heidegger insists, not solitary. The world in which we are is a with-world; we are always with-each-other. We create in the company of others, ones now in front of us and ones now dead, who remain, even in death, all around us. The gestures we make and the words we say, holding the Host aloft and proclaiming Jesus saves, are our gestures and our words; we do them, we say them, but often in the dialectal voices of ghosts.

Each time we gesture, each time we speak, we create; all of what we do and say are unique events that belong to us, you and me. They are our creations. But the gestures and voices are historical; they are in the past, yet we bring them about. We vivify them. We create them in the present. We give them presence. We are not pawns of the past; we restore presence to the past, but the past lives, especially in the South.

Christ is a historical figure and, as a historical figure, resides in the summaries of Chapters 2 and 3. But Christ would not be, here, now, today, alive in Christians without the gesturing of the young priest in the *iglesia* at Nueva Esperanza and the preaching of Reverend Overton in the church at Mt. Hope. Consequently, I agree with Schweitzer that being-in-Christ is not purely a matter of subjective belief; being-in-Christ cannot be reduced to individual psyches. However, being-in-Christ is objective only in the sense that it is socially constructed by today's Christians inhabited by the past.

Being-in-Christ, the union between us and Christ, is an aspiration that Christians both in Nueva Esperanza and in Mt. Hope share. The Christ whom they are in, however, is not an abstract Christ. He cannot be reduced to a generalized belief stored away in individual heads. Christ is public, social, out there, in the creations of his people. And these creations occur in places. In Chapter 1, we insisted that flesh-and-blood creatures such as you and I are never simply in-the-world but that we come to be in particular places. Likewise, to-be-in-Christ, Christians create specific Christs in specific places. Therefore, the *iglesia* in Spanish America and the church in the American South are sites for the construction of Christs.

Sites for the construction of Christs, you repeat querulously and with disbelief. In response, I again ask you to recall Chapter 1 and, indeed, the introduction to this chapter. On their journey across the earth, people build places that articulate their historical experiences and contemporary aspirations. Consequently, each place they build has a configuration of material features that gives it a distinctive setting. Each setting conveys to those who enter it—and to you and me as we watch—information as to what is happening around them and what they should be doing. As they react to the information conveyed by the setting and to the actions of others, people create an explanatory image of where they are and, consequently, of who they are.

All right, you insist, still in a state of disbelief. How does that generalized pattern fit what we have just found in our visit to the *iglesia* in Nueva Esperanza and the church at Mt. Hope. Show me, you dare. Just show me.

Fair enough. Let's begin where they begin, there in Nueva Esperanza and there in Mt. Hope, with the material setting. As we look at the material setting, let me insist once more, along with Colleen McDannell (1995), that we must consider it neither as simply an inert mass without meaning nor as a passive reflection of core symbols, but as calling out to us to respond to its message.

Settings

What do we see when we approach the outskirts of Nueva Esperanza? The tower of the *iglesia*. No other structure competes for our understanding of where we are. In contrast, what do see when we get near Mt. Hope? The courthouse, I, as a native son of a courthouse town, might be hurried into saying, but then I realize, as we exit from I-8, what we first see are words. Remember the gaggle of signs? And how the First Baptist sign dominates the Methodist, the First Presbyterian, and the St. James Episcopal? And later as we approach the church structure, the sign of words out front: "First Baptist Church, Dr. Tommy Overton, DD"? And at the *iglesia*? Not a single sign, not a single, solitary, written word. Instead, the weathered countenances of two saints stare back at us, while overhead Santiago rides triumphantly over the Moors and nearby at the elderly vendor's table, in lurid blues and reds, Jesus points to his burning heart. Thus, we anthropologically see our first significant contrast: icon versus written word. Icon versus written word, I repeat, and other contrasts tumble out: sensing versus reading, intimacy versus distance . . . Stop! you interrupt. Or at least slow down!

Very well, consider this: At the *iglesia*, there's no sign along the front to tell you where you are or who the priest is or when mass is to be heard. If you are truly a citizen of Nueva Esperanza, such knowledge you and the shopowner down the street, the old man shining shoes in the plaza, even the kids on their way to school already have. And if for some obscure reason you want to know these things, you ask. In other words, knowledge that would be written down in Mt. Hope is lodged in the people's verbal culture in Nueva Esperanza.

What about the priest's name? Does everyone know that? Some do. The school girls in green do, especially that of the young priest. The old women in black perhaps do as well, but they have seen so many priests come and go that they aren't concerned. The man with the rope, the business man in the suit, the lady who lit a candle beneath *El Nazareno*, however, may not even care. Knowing the name of the priest is not a necessary prerequisite to entering the *iglesia* and worshiping. Conversely, among the Southern Baptists, where the pastor serves at the pleasure of the congregation—in contrast to the Catholics, for whom the priest is appointed by the bishop—the pastor's name, his reputation, and his credentials stamp the Sunday service with a mark that few priests can duplicate in their celebration of the mass, nor should they.

The two images in their niches on either side of the doorway carry no signs to announce their names, and this they have done for centuries. We readers of culture feel compelled to know their names. I ask the man passing by, and he assures me they are indeed saints, and what idiot would not know such things? He supplies no names. What may we conclude from his disdain for the names of the saints he passes nearly every day and to whom he lifts his hat in deference? Verbal culture is closer to the conventionalized, taken-for-granted understandings that we have of the world and of one another. It is also more unreflective. Writing introduces sight and privileges the distancing eye over the more intimate ear. Consequently, writing enhances the objectivity of words. Writing makes available knowledge to a reading stranger.[27]

Yet verbal culture and written culture do not exist in separate, sealed con-

27. A visit to the graveyard of any small church in the South will often find you in front of graves without any names. You wonder, Who is buried there? If a longtime member of the congregation, a deacon, say, is with you, he will gladly point out who lies where. Thus, in a curious manner, the presence of a tombstone with a name may indicate a lesser familiarity with the dead person than would its absence.

tainers; they interact. Writing easily takes on the conventionality of speaking, and speaking may gain the objectivity of writing. Likewise, the distinction between verbal culture and written culture is not a division between people. Southern Baptists have verbal culture; the conversion narratives and prayer styles are perfect examples. Likewise, Spanish American Catholics have written culture; one might point to the missal itself as an exemplar, and, of course, the liberation theologians constantly have their fingertips at the keyboard. Consequently, the division is not one between illiteracy and literacy. People who can read may participate more completely in a verbal culture than in a written one. My father, whose fourth-grade education gave him the ability to read, read only the newspaper and the Bible. If he wanted information about matters not covered in these two texts, he would ask someone he thought might know such things.

Beneath this discussion of verbal and written cultures rests the status of Catholicism in Spanish America. Until recently, and still the case in most areas in most such countries, being Catholic in Spanish America is a fact of life. It is something you are born with as naturally and as inevitably as being born with a head. If you have a head, you are a Catholic. In the everyday world of conventional understanding, being Catholic is equivalent to being human. People in Spanish America commonly distinguish between the height of humans and the height of animals with different hand signals. The palm of the hand turned edgewise is the height of a *cristiano*, a Christian; the palm turned flat is the height of a *bestia*, a beast, an animal. *Cristiano* here translates as human, which translates as Catholic. In contrast, even in the "solid South," being Baptist is more iffy. In competition with their fellow Protestants, Baptist churches have to distinguish themselves, just as Rotary International must let everyone know it is different from the Lions Club. It's the American way. Consequently, and as the result of the emphasis on conversion experience, being Baptist is not such a sure thing. It always carries with it the potentiality of uncertainty, despite the belief Reverend Overton so fondly preaches: "Once saved, always saved."[28]

Getting into the spirit of things (as it were), you exclaim, Just look at how much we can see when we anthropologically view the material settings of the

28. Samson reports that in Guatemala, Protestant *evangélicos* have appropriated *cristiano* to designate themselves and thereby to imply Catholics are not Christians (Samson 1997). In doing so, they follow the arrogance of their born-again brethren in the United States.

iglesia and church, and we have not even got through the doors! Precisely. The material setting is not simply a collection of isolated objects, present-at-hand; but as material culture, the setting is equipment ready-to-hand. The significance of artifacts that constitute the setting is not determined by their Cartesian coordinates but by how they bestow context to action and inform the worshiping acts.

Once inside the massive doors of the ancient *iglesia* and through the portico of the 1950s Neoclassical "House of the Lord," the contrasts in the spatial contours of the two different Christworlds continue to appear before our participatory eyes. We enter the *iglesia* silently and alone. There is no glad hand at the door. In the shadows along the sides, figures with eyes aglow in the candles' light stare down at us. We smell the wax of the candles and other scents we cannot identify. Am I being too romantic if I say I feel the presence of centuries? As we join the silence of the people kneeling, we hear the bird at the open window and the buses at the plaza's corner. These everyday sounds suggest a worship that is more in place with the outside. After all, it is only a step from the street to the interior. And through the doors people enter and depart at their own rhythm. Yet the *iglesia* proclaims itself as holy, a sacred temple. Its proclamation resides in the rituals performed to consecrate it, to establish it as an "image of the Church itself, which is God's temple built from living stone" (International Commission 1991, 346), and in an architecture that stands distinct from that of the surrounding stores and governmental edifices. Rich in sight, silence, and smell, the *iglesia* whispers. What is it saying? Does it sigh, "Mystery"? I want to say, Yes, yes, yes. But the man with a coil of rope strung over his shoulder comes and goes in a manner that reminds me the mystery here in Nueva Esperanza, like Catholicism in general, is a fact of life, which may make the mystery even more mysterious.

Once past the welcoming hand of Brother Womack, our view in the church quickly follows the slope of the floor to the front. No figures hover in the shadows; indeed, the overhead illumination ensures there are no shadows. The only smell is the lingering perfume of the lady in the blue dress with white trim, and its pleasure dissipates into the smell of artificial carpets and artificial air. No outside sounds enter from the street, which in fact is some distance across the lawn from the front of the church. Baptists, especially Southern Baptists, have always prided themselves on being at odds with the secular world. Even today, if Reverend Overton had his way, there would be no movies, no dominoes, and certainly no bridge on Sunday and no mixed bathing any time. So the sharp boundary between the street and church, particularly the sealed interior of the church, suggests an equally rigorous separation between the sacred and the secular. What then are we to make of the American flag, along with the Christian flag, bracketing the Lord's Supper table? Our puzzlement takes another turn when we recall the Baptist doctrine, not always recalled so readily in these days of the Christian Right, of separation of church and state. Furthermore, in the several hundred *iglesias* I have entered in five Spanish American countries, countries where traditionally the Catholic Church has enjoyed close ties with the state, only once have I seen a national flag. The patriotism of the South and of the Southern Baptists Ellen Rosenberg (1989) attributes to a mode of being she calls hyper-American, an Americanism squared. Remembering that little more than a century ago the region seceded from the Union and in so doing gave birth to Southern Baptists, I wonder how that could be? But you nod your head in favor of the Americanism theme and remind me that during the Gulf War, Southern Baptist churches rang with prayers for victory, if not for peace.[29]

What Weismann and Sandoval, in their *Art and Time in Mexico* (1985), said about the Mexican church being a historical *conjunto*, an ensemble of time, applies to the *iglesia* in Nueva Esperanza. The weathered images, the faded painting of San Pablo on the road to Damascus, the lingering flutter of Baroque angels that even the more restrained Neoclassical could not still, the full-bodied and bloody crucifix, the abandoned pulpit, the modernistic altar, and the wiring for sound speak centuries of worship.

And what of the "House of the Lord"? Where is the past in a structure built in the 1950s? Where indeed? Yet the building is not blind to history. There's history in its name, for example; it proclaims that here worships the first Baptist congregation organized in Mt. Hope, back in the 1870s. But history is more present in the very absence of sensuous objects, an absence that speaks of the plain-folk tradition, of Puritanical origins, and of the time when

29. The one time I saw a Latin American country's national flag displayed in an *iglesia* was in Mérida, Yucatán, Mexico. Someone had draped a Mexican flag over the corner of an image of the Virgin of Guadalupe, thereby uniting two core symbols of Mexican life. In Baton Rouge much of the patriotism displayed during the Gulf War burst forth in song. One Baptist church presented a "Liberty Musical" that featured a hundred-voice choir dressed in red, white, and blue and several minidramas with representatives of each branch of service dressed in full uniform. That occurred in the last century; in this century, after September 11, praying and reflection has, at times, replaced singing and chauvinism.

"worshipers were expected to live as angels, as bodiless spirits, using ears, but neglecting the senses of touch, of scent, of taste, and above all, of sight" (Davies 1975, 532). *Church* comes from the Greek word *kyriakos*, "belonging to the Lord," that is, the house of the master or lord. As the inscription above the door at the Mt. Hope church tells us, Baptists use the phraseology, but like so much of Baptist speech, the phrase is, in their own attribution, "purely symbolic." The structure is not sacred itself. A new church might be "dedicated," or, with the final payment, the mortgage papers burned, but again these acts are "purely symbolic." Going to church is a special occasion, marked by time and "Sunday dress," but people come to hear the Word spoken, not to see it incarnated.

And there is the matter of clocks. In Nueva Esperanza, the clock mounted atop the *iglesia*'s facade announces the time, more or less correctly, to an exterior populace. Keeping public time is a function, not of a secular structure such as a courthouse, but of a sacred one. The clock at the First Baptist, which is accurate to the millisecond, is invisible except to the preacher (and the choir behind him). So, you say, big deal. It's there to keep him on time. It's there to do that, I agree, but it also measures time within the church, and that time is an interior time. Here, within the church, worshiping "is delineated by a vivid sense of interiority: one *is* a forgiven sinner; one *hears* God's call; one *knows* he is going to heaven; one *talks* to God in prayer; one *deepens* his devotional life; one *reads* his Bible; one *becomes* the vehicle for the recurrence of all this in the interior of others" (Hill 1972c, 35).[30]

In the *iglesia*, our vision and our senses curve among the statuary along the sides and on to the altar. We look beyond the priest, who, until Vatican II, joined us in looking beyond, to the thorn-crowned figure on the cross. But still contemplating his stillness, our eyes go past the figures in the *retablo*, to follow the curvature of the dome ever higher until our sight, as if by a miracle, escapes earthly walls. In the Baptist church, we look to the front, and the choir looks back. Their looking keeps our vision fixed. Has the choir become a living *retablo*? Sooner or later, however, our sight, as if by its own volition, moves upward to the river Jordan, the white dove, the empty tomb, and the inscribed Word: "WHY SEEK YE THE LIVING AMONG THE DEAD?"

30. Hill also points out that Southern Baptist theology, by dwelling upon Christ's sacrifice, resembles European, more than American, theology. But in Europe, where "concepts like Christendom and Christian civilization prevail," God's kingdom is more external (Hill 1972b, 21).

Having come this far, you will now agree, I believe, with the argument that the material setting of the two places, the *iglesia* of Nueva Esperanza and the church of Mt. Hope, bestows context to the respective actions by the two Christian groups in their aspiration to create Christworlds so that they may be. Let us proceed and address the matter of the differences in the actions themselves, in the worshiping performance, in the performance of worship.

Performance

When we speak of the worshiping performance or the performance of worship, we recollect Joel Sherzer's stressing the centrality of discourse. While in previous analyses, scholars treated discourse as the invisible glass through which the reality of social relations appeared, Sherzer insists that the glass itself, the discourse employed, requires our attention. For discourse (or human symbolic communication in its widest sense) is "an embodiment, a filter, a creator and re-creator, and a transmitter of culture"; consequently, "in order to study culture we must study the actual forms of discourse" (1987: 306).

Performance requires a script, to be sure, but it also requires performing, which means organizing the senses, positioning the body with respect to other bodies, articulating by gesture and by word the script, in brief, acting. And the reality of the performance is in the acting.

A religious performance, then, you ask, is nothing more than acting? Whenever you talk like that, I can hear by the tone in your voice—a worry hidden under brave assertions—that you are remembering your high school Shakespeare and how you dismissed the very idea that "all the world's a stage" whereon in the course of our lives we play many parts, entering and exiting many times over. I know too that you recall that sociology course on social interaction in which the professor, herself a hard-headed, quantifying positivist, nonetheless quoted Erving Goffman (1959), the foremost dramaturgicalist of everyday life, to the effect that life on the stage and life in the real are clearly different, but the differences are not always easy to specify.[31]

31. It comes to me that rather than recalling the lighthearted *As You Like It*, you remember *Macbeth* and

> Life's but a walking shadow, a poor player
> That struts and frets his hour upon the stage,
> And then is heard no more; it is a tale
> Told by an idiot, full of sound and fury,
> Signifying nothing.
>
> (V. v. 24–28)

By "performance" I simply mean that if you want to hear Ludwig von Beethoven's *Fifth Symphony* (and it is one of my favorites, too), you have to go beyond the historical author, beyond the score, beyond the instruments, beyond even the musicians, to the performance itself; likewise, if you want to understand what people are up to, you have to watch their doings (including their makings) and listen to their sayings, for it is in their doings and sayings that they become the who they claim to be. That is to say, the who we claim as our own, the self we purport to be, "is not an organic thing that has a specific location [in the body] . . . ; it is a dramatic effect . . . and the characteristic issue, the crucial concern, is whether it will be credited or discredited" (Goffman 1959, 252–53). If it, the self, is credited, we're home free; if it is discredited, we're out-of-place, all at sea, with our work cut out for us.

Traditionally, scholars have argued that drama developed from ritual (for example, Raglan 1956) and in the ritual of the mass we see the tie quite clearly. We note the manner in which the priest prepares the altar to become the Last Supper and, with the bread and wine transformed, speaks the words that reenact Christ's gift to us all. The mass is the drama of Christ's sacrifice. In contrast, the tie between the Sunday Service and performance seems less obvious, especially when we run square into the protests, spoken from the plain-folk tradition, that the Baptists don't do ritual; when we speak, they say, we speak from the heart. Yet compared to the more diffuse weekday mass, where people come and go and the street sounds mingle with the candle smoke, the Sunday Service seems much more orchestrated. Between the first prayer and the final altar call, the sharply bounded Baptist service focuses upon itself.

Granted that, you wonder, but *what* is it focused on? In response, I would agree with Samuel Hill Jr. (like me, a former member of the baptized flock, but who, unlike me, became an Episcopalian) that Baptist evangelical preaching aims to create estrangement (Hill 1980). Not only does it aspire to create distance between people within the church walls and the world of the street outside, but, with even greater enthusiasm, it also strives to create an existential crisis inside you. It awakens the realization that you're born a sinner and are headed for hell; it heightens the sense of self in the face of death. Having created estrangement, it offers unification "in the bosom of Jesus." You're born a sinner and headed for hell but "once saved, always saved." So here we have in speech, in the preaching of the lost and saved, a performance, a drama, a drama of sin and salvation, a drama of existence. The focus of the Baptist service, then, is not the reenactment of Christ's sacrifice, unless it is the confessed sinner who, Christ-like, walks the aisle to sacrifice self to perpetuate the congregation. The focus is the destruction of the old, sinful self and its reconstitution as the new, saved self.

Jean Heriot, in her fine-grained ethnography of a South Carolina Baptist church, goes so far as to argue that the drama of salvation is never finished. The goal is personal salvation, to be sure, but she insists the attainment of that goal is never certain; it remains ever out of reach of even, or especially, the most dedicated seeker. Drawing on the ethnography of communication and citing Richard Bauman's work on verbal art as performance, she carefully details *how* sermons, as speech genres, work to create a "constant state of uncertainty" (Heriot 1994, 132): Am I really saved? She adds that it is in the preacher's vested interest to perpetuate that state of doubt. If none respond to his heart-rendering plea "To come forth, now, confess your sins," and "Turn your life over to Jesus," then he judges himself and is so judged by others as a failure. As nearly all of his congregation have already made a public confession, he cannot hope to fill the aisles with newly converted, so he has to raise the doubt that salvation has been attained. Consequently, the drama of the lost and saved is compulsively reenacted Sunday after Sunday. The only route out of performing the perpetually unfinished play is to gain assurance through the Christian life one leads. To act like a Christian, to do visitations, to care for the shut-ins, to serve on fellowship and stewardship committees, to support the pastor means one must be, surely, a Christian. Yet even here doubt remains, for good works alone cannot gain you the kingdom of heaven. Thus, the play goes on.

In the performance of the mass, the priest must, first and foremost, act the role of priest, whatever his individuality. The priest, as priest, is central to the construction of the visible mass. Even with the reforms of Vatican II, only he can offer up the Body and Blood of Christ. Reciting the scripted discourse, positioning the crafted artifacts on the altar, lifting the wafer and then the chalice are movements into which the particular, unique biographical self disappears. To be sure, in Nueva Esperanza, no one confuses the old priest with the new one. But the successful unfolding of the weekday mass requires the two to perform the same priestly office. The office, the acting, subsumes the biographical actor.[32]

32. Of course, there are other acts priests may perform. While the charismatic movement has not entered Nueva Esperanza, no doubt because of the still influential opinion of the old priest, in those places where it has, priests may, in the manner of the Pentecostalists, become

Reverend Overton skirts on dangerous ground if people get the notion he is acting. He runs the serious risk of being discredited. To avoid any suggestion that he does not feel what he preaches, he must present himself as himself. Thus, to assure the congregation—and in his heart of hearts, himself—he periodically recalls the plain-folk heritage in Baptist preaching and comes across as Brother Tommy, the genuine article that continues despite seminary training. "Yea, woe is unto me," he shouts with Paul from 1 Corinthians 9:16, "if I preach not the gospel!"

Priests become priests in an ordination ritual that includes the bishop in direct, apostolic succession from St. Peter, the first bishop of Rome, laying his hands upon them. Baptist preachers likewise go through an ordination ceremony in which the local church licenses them to preach. The ceremony may actually include a laying-on of hands: The candidate sits in front of the church while the members of the congregation pass by and congratulate him with a touch of their hands on his shoulders. Of course, all of this is preceded by the local minister carefully explaining that such "laying on of the hands is purely symbolic."

Assuming the office of priest requires an inward conviction followed by a lengthy period of instruction and acculturation into the priesthood. Even in Reverend Overton's youth, Southern Baptists encouraged the formal training of preachers, and today a preacher cannot hope to occupy the pulpit of a church of any size without seminary instruction. Yet formal instruction pales in light of the "call to preach." Reverend Overton understands that his call to preach, when God spoke to him about the plan God had for him, is second in importance only to his original conversion experience, which he places above his marriage. Like the conversion narrative, the account of the call to preach becomes part of his stock-in-trade to be inserted from time to time in sermons to convey the sign of conviction, which no preacher can preach without.[33]

---

filled with the Holy Spirit and speak in tongues. The weekday mass remains distinct from such verbal fireworks in its sculptured objectivity.

33. The verbal "call to preach" is also employed to describe a preacher's acceptance of the ministry at a particular church. While the search process for a new minister may proceed along quite secular lines, such as the one I stumbled into at Del Rio, Texas, where the church heard the chair of the search committee explain the compiling of résumés in a manner that reminded me of my academic department's search for new professors, sooner or later, when the congregation decides on the pastor and the pastor on it, everyone will agree that "Reverend Bob is here today because God spoke to his heart."

In the Catholic performance, it is not a verbal narrative that conveys the sign of authenticity, but rather it is sight. Seeing objectifies; it "discriminates and defines" (Tuan 1982, 118). It establishes a world outside the interior body. As we discussed in Chapter 1, seeing distances, but it also connects. Seeing the wafer elevated above the altar establishes the object presence of Christ, but seeing also relates the self of the viewer to the Host. The resulting relationship is a dyadic, two-party relationship between self and holy presence. In Chapters 2 and 3 we found that both in Spain and in Spanish America, the visual mode of establishing the presence of Christ constitutes the principal method of communication between the sacred and the ordinary. In the next chapter, we will find that the visual mode is also fundamental to pilgrimages in Spanish America.

Southern Baptists, true to their Puritanical heritage, have abandoned seeing as a mode of communicating with God. They consider the physicality of the sacred next, if not equal, to idolatry. The verbal mode is the medium through which God speaks to them and they to him. The spoken words of Jesus, as recorded, are the literal words he spoke. They privilege writing over seeing; the text over the visual. The visual, the Lord's Supper or the laying on of the hands at ordination, is "only symbolic."[34]

In the seeing, the mass becomes a visual performance in which the movements of the priest, highly controlled and liturgically dictated, parallel the scripted discourse. The movements themselves signify. The priest rhythmically claps his fist against his chest when he intones, "Por mi culpa, mi culpa, mi gran culpa." In his preaching, the movements the Baptist minister makes, leaning forward over the pulpit, pulling back from it, lifting high the Bible, are subservient to the speaking.

In the performance of mass and Sunday service, the Bible figures prominently in both as icon and as text. Despite their many and important differences, as Christian faiths both are religions of the Book. In both, reading the Bible is a central, performative act. The manner of reading, however, is quite distinct. The distinction, we may say, is one between a sacramentalist versus a literalist reading. In the mass, the selections to be read are predetermined

34. The rise of the "only symbolic" in Baptist discourse appears, in a curious way, related to a wider movement in European thought that sees surfaces, what we see or hear, as superficial phenomena, expressive of a more profound causality underneath. From this perspective, the goal, in either religious or secular effort, is to reduce the multitudinous reality around us to a more certain, universal, explanatory truth: God or deductive science.

by the liturgical cycle. Although nowadays, it is common that a lay member read the Old Testament selection, only the priest reads the Gospel, and upon his reading, he and the parishioners cross themselves on the forehead and over the face. And although the selections read are printed in the missal, few in an early morning weekday mass have the printed text. Thus, the reading is spoken, with an emphasis, at least in part, on sound, rhythm, and beauty. This is particularly true in the responsorial reading. In the Baptist Sunday Service, however, the preacher himself selects the text as part of the sermon's message. He reads from the pulpit, but he invites others to turn to their Bibles and read silently along with him. This is a gesture toward an open Bible for all and toward a literalist reading for facts. In both the mass and the service the Bible reading aims to create an authoritative, sanctified context for subsequent action. This is particularly true for the Baptist service, since Baptists have rejected any physical, iconic manifestation of the sacred, and consequently, Reverend Overton reads the passages with considerable vigor, as if the sound of his voice alone would establish the presence of the holy. Finally, we note that apart from the responsorial reading, reading in the mass is each individual sitting silently listening to the priest (or the lay reader); reading in the service is, ideally at least, each individual sitting silently reading along with the preacher: the first, a more dyadic tie, the second, more congregational.[35]

Reading as a performative act grades into speaking. Here, we need to pause and recall the important distinctions scholars draw between writing and speaking. We especially need the pause, given the importance of the written text, the Sacred Scripture, the Holy Bible, in the two faiths. We begin our pause, paradoxically, by noting that both writing and speaking are forms of discourse. Discourse, in Heideggerian language, is the "house of being." We are, as humans, caught up in discourse, in symbolic communication. Not

35. I am indebted to Jill Brody for the distinction between sacramentalist and literalist reading. A liberationist reading may constitute a third type, in which the reading is less sacramental but is more open to social interpretation than a literalist's reading and is more congregational than the sacramentalist's. A scholarly reading constitutes a fourth type, seemingly quite distinct from the others. We often consider reading to be the solitary (and treasured) act of a single individual physically isolated from others, but as communicative behavior, reading varies greatly. I have suggested that in addition to an ethnography of speaking, we need an ethnography of reading (Richardson 1995a), and you, helpful as always, point to an edited volume by that very name (Boyarin 1993). Thank you.

simply labeling that which is already there, discourse, like tools, brings worlds into being (Thiher 1984). Of the two forms, speaking, because of its coupling with face-to-face interaction, brings into being immediacy and the possibility of spontaneity. Writing, connected to more distant interaction, increases the possibility of objectivity and reflection, even, some say, of rationality. Speech carries with it the likelihood of repetition, while writing sustains the possibility for revision. Speaking imparts ephemeralness and life; conversely, writing is partnered with preservation and death. Yet here, as in the juxtaposition of verbal and written cultures, we note that the two interact. On the one hand, some writing resembles speech that has been written down. Such writing is usually considered poor; it is full of "very's" and "really's." Some speech, on the other hand, has a crafted quality to it and is said to be eloquent.[36]

Speaking in the mass, except for the homily, which is—the young priest at Nueva Esperanza to the contrary and notwithstanding—commonly absent in an early morning weekday celebration, belongs to the special genre of ritual discourse (Chafe 1982). Ritual discourse is stylized and repetitive; consequently, the speaker is present but removed at the same time. It has features of speech, such as: personal pronouns, "yo confieso, creo en un solo Dios"; dialogue, "El Señor esté con vosotros" (or, as the young priest says, "ustedes"), "Y con tu espíritu"; and, as a special case of dialogue, speech directed toward God, "Cordero de Dios, que quitas el pecado del mundo, ten piedad de nosotros." But the words are scripted and, thus, polished. Ritual discourse has little of the hesitations of speech, a lack that is appropriate for words that are ecclesiastically sanctioned. It has the authority of the written word, but it is spoken; it is speaking writing.

It follows that given its status as a sanctioned ritual, the mass can be performed regardless of attention or even attendance. While no priest would personally enjoy celebrating the mass in front of an empty nave, theoretically, at least, he could do so. In a narrow, but specific and crucial sense, the ritual efficacy of the mass does not depend upon the parishioners occupying the benches.

The responses the people make to the priest's speaking the words from the missal are not always uniform and vigorous. As we have heard, the responses have a murmuring quality to them. That quality, plus their individual

36. A thorough review of the research on issues of speaking and writing, orality and literacy, and the interpenetrating of one with the other is Chafe and Tannen (1987).

movements about the *iglesia*, suggests the members are not closely involved in the speaking. However, the murmuring response produces a contemplative, quiet air that suggests, in turn, a closer connection to the priest's speaking than one might at first glance assume, perhaps more at the experiential level than at the cognitive.

At the point of the commemoration of the Last Supper, of Christ's sacrifice, the eyes and the bodies of the people focus, often dramatically, on the priest's actions. At this moment, he shifts from the other forms of speaking to quoted speech, to Jesus' words as written in the Bible. Repeating the words of the Last Supper, the words Jesus spoke, "Tomad y comed; Take and eat," makes possible the visual event of Christ's body residing in the Host. The spoken words of the priest perform the inscribed words of the Bible, and consequently, they reenact the recorded event but not in literal fashion. What we see is not the occasion as depicted in Leonardo da Vinci's *The Last Supper* but the present altar. Direct speech vivifies the wafer in the priest's hand and through the union of the "Word of God and the Body of Christ" seeks to establish the presence of Christ's sacrifice in the present (Murray 1991, 79).

Speaking in Sunday worship service is a special genre of oral discourse called preaching. Preaching has an array of discourse features that we all recognize and indeed may unkindly caricature. A goal common to these features, however, is immediacy. What is written in the Bible is the divinely inspired Word of God, a text without error, inscribed during the days of Moses and the prophets and during the time Christ walked on earth, the time of healing the halt and the blind, the time of casting out demons, the time of feeding the five thousand. Preaching aims to make the eternal, divinely inspired, written Word of God present among us, to bring the time of Christ into the momentary blinking of the now.

The use of discourse features means that preaching is "always oral rather than literary in style." Being oral means that preaching "seems to be the overflow of a full heart—spontaneous and fervent." Preaching "operates more in the area of spiritual than logical decisions. . . . The object of the sermon is to create the mood most helpful in the decision time at the end of the service" (Allen 1958, 1109). These words, though written in 1958, aptly characterize the importance today of speaking a sermon, talking the language of Zion, the plain-folk speech of Canaan's land, the verbal culture that all Southern Baptist preachers know, even those who, being theologically more moderate, reject it.

A particular discourse feature is speaking the words that Jesus spoke, or, more technically, "reported speech." Reported speech is speaking to a party in the language of a third and absent party. As we have heard, Reverend Overton's sermon is filled with words others, not present, have said. His voice is pervaded with the voices of others; its sound is truly polyphonic (Tannen 1995). Specifically, his voice is filled with the scriptured voices of the Bible. In his sermon on this Sunday, the voice we hear in Overton's voice most frequently is Paul's: "Know ye not, that so many of us as were baptized into Jesus Christ were baptized into his death?" and "I am crucified with Christ; nevertheless I live; yet not I, but Christ liveth in me. . . ." But we also hear Ananias's "Behold, I am here, Lord." And Big John's "I put God first. God first, family second, and shoes third." And Jesus speaking in the voice of the rich man, "Father Abraham, have mercy on me. . . . I am tormented in this flame."

Tannen refers to reported speech as constructed dialogue. She does so to underscore that the displaced nature of reported speech—that someone else said what I'm saying to you—hides the "active, creative, transforming" role it has in establishing the reality of the present (1995, 201).

Let me take another verse that Reverend Overton is fond of, one that is printed in red, the direct voice of Jesus: "For where two or three are gathered together in my name, there am I in the midst of them" (Matthew 18:20). In claiming to speak the words that Jesus spoke, the preacher is (1) asserting Biblical literalism, that the words attributed to Jesus in the Gospels were in fact spoken by him, and (2) pointing to Jesus and not himself as the author of these words. In the latter case, Reverend Overton and we, the audience, overlook that though the words are said to be Jesus', it is Overton speaking to a listening us for his, and our, own purposes—purposes conceivably quite distant from those of Jesus. In constructing this dialogue, he and we cross the distance between the days of Christ and those of the present, and in so doing, he calls forth, particularly with this verse, the Landmarkian claim that Baptists were the original church, and other organizations such as, and particularly so, the Catholics are at best societies.

Preaching is turning text into speech, or perhaps we could say preaching is a "re-oralization" of the text. But it is not speaking writing; it is not ritual discourse, and consequently it lacks the self-contained character of the mass. While the priest in Nueva Esperanza could celebrate mass in an empty *iglesia*, no Southern Baptist preacher, and certainly not Reverend Overton, can preach to an empty church. Since his speaking, even in the voice of Jesus, remains his own and carries no sanctification, for the sermon to be preached, a congregation, a band of baptized believers, those gathered in Jesus' name, must be in attendance.

Among the discourse features Reverend Overton and other Southern Baptist preachers employ, few are more central to preaching than the conversion narrative. In Overton's account we hear across the centuries Isaac Backus's voice recounting how under a tree beside a mowed field he understood that "God had a right to do with me as he would" (Chap. 2). So in speaking of his own conversion, Overton verbalizes the historical experience of the Baptists, their rejection of infant baptism and the acceptance of the Calvinistic position that only Jesus saves; that is, one must undergo an experience that requires the surrendering of the self to God. That personal experience is the alpha and omega of the Baptist being-in-Christ. But the personal experience is articulated in words. It "is the Word . . . written, spoken, heard, and read that converts the unbeliever" (Harding 1987, 168).[37]

The narrative parallels the biblical account of Christ's Crucifixion. As the Gospels tell us that Christ died and was resurrected, so the conversion narrative relates how a sinner has died but now has been reborn. The blood of Jesus makes possible our new birth. From the womb of Christ, covered in his precious blood, we are born anew (Harding 1987).

Although the conversion narrative points to the past, to that day when Reverend Overton went out alone into the fields, to the day that Isaac Backus realized the power of God, and to the day when from the grave Christ arose, the telling constitutes the now. Although told in the past tense, the narrative addresses the present (Stromberg 1990). By offering up his own experience, Overton uses the power of narrative to invite us into his story. Once in his story, we may discover his story is ours, and we start on the path to salvation. We join a speech community that talks the rhetoric of salvation, the language of Zion.

Closely related to conversion narratives are testimonials or rededications. These are occasions, often during the night service when feelings of solidarity

37. Few anthropologists know the language of salvation better than Susan Harding (1987). This is because she sees: "Among fundamentalists, church service and revivals are stripped of overt, imagistic, and sacramental material; . . . spiritual realities are not communicated through sensuous, nonlinguistic means" (169). And she listens: "We cannot understand fundamental Baptist conversion by looking only at what causes a person to listen to the gospel; the causes are innumerable. We must listen too, and we must explore the consequences of listening" (168).

run strong, when, at the request of the preacher, individuals will stand and recall their own moments of salvation and in so doing reclaim those periods of purity for the present. Here are examples from a rural Louisiana church.

> That night I came up and made a personal commitment, and I was baptized into the church.
>
> And we went down the aisle together, her and I. She went accepting Christ as her Savior, and I went rededicating my life.
>
> But the Bible showed me how Christ came off that cross and he came to live in me.

As Wayne Gregory, the linguist who collected these examples, makes clear, these testimonials aim not simply to recount a past event but to establish a presence now. In their dramatization, they seek to become an enactment in which the speaker and audience experience the transcendence of the original conversion (Gregory 1992).

It is important to note that the conversion narrative seeks a dramatic effect, and we should not confuse that dramatic effect with the actual event. Yes, you agree, and you go on to observe that those who walk the aisle to confess their wicked ways are more commonly children raised in the church who are fulfilling a cultural obligation. That's true, I reply. Yet we cannot forget, or at least I can't, that children sometimes take what adults tell them to heart. When Reverend Summerall in Palestine, Texas, preached the story of the rich man burning in hell, I believed him. When he said the lost are doomed for eternity, I knew he meant me. Well, you say, with a shrug, you were just a kid. Precisely, I snap back.

How different is the occasion of First Communion in Spanish America. Occurring at almost the same age at which Baptist children in the South accept Jesus as their personal savior, First Communion is one of the sacraments of initiation. Having sat through the mass as a group, young boys in suits and young girls in starched white dresses line up to receive the Body of Christ. The event is as much social as spiritual. I know you are thinking of our last trip to San Pedro, Colombia, in 1992, and how the priest, trying his best to accentuate the transcendence of the moment, became exasperated as the fathers crowded around him to take photographs and videos of their children receiving the host. He stopped, went to the microphone, and complained, "Me dan pena ustedes; You are aggravating [literally, you give me pain]." He stressed the solemnity of the occurrence and repeated the need for respect. As soon as he returned to the line, however, the cameras reappeared.

We are not surprised that oral conversion narratives are all but absent in the work of the everyday mass. I never heard testimonials in the more-than-one-hundred masses I have attended. The rite of infant baptism in the context of the matter-of-fact way in which Catholicism permeates Spanish American life precludes the dramatization of conversion, except, of course, when one converts to evangelical Protestantism.[38]

The final discourse event in Baptist evangelical preaching is the altar call and the attendant public confession. A comparison with that event and the confession before the weekday mass at the *iglesia* in Nueva Esperanza discloses important differences not only in the respective confessions but also in the worshiping self.

In the confession before the weekday mass in Nueva Esperanza, the behavior of the older priest and of the worshipers implies that both approach the confession as part of the matter-of-fact strategy for getting things done. The priest issues no histrionic call for the lost not to wait for the final knock on their door; he simply taps on the panel to indicate he is ready for the next person in line. Likewise, the worshipers give no evidence in their response that this is a once-in-a-lifetime chance to redeem their condemned souls. In addition, we see once more the private, two-party nature of the ritual, even if here in Nueva Esperanza it occurs in full view.

Since Vatican II, participation in mass has been more participatory. The young priest is following Vatican II protocol when he asks the young girl to read and when he urges us to sit together as a family and to engage ourselves actively in the celebration. Extending *la mano de paz*, offering the hand of peace, is another example of Vatican II's changes and certainly brings about engagement. Even with the reforms, however, the worshiping self in Nueva Esperanza remains the individual self, in the company of others, to be sure, but secure in its solitude. People move about the *iglesia* during mass to attend to the priest, to one another, and to the saints in the context of a two-party, dyadic relationship. They predicate their acts on the core belief: "Es la fe que vale"; it is faith, the faith of each, each individual faith, that activates the dyadic tie.[39]

38. An intriguing, though distant, parallel with the Baptist conversion narrative was the spiritual autobiographies that nuns in New Spain were often asked to write by their confessors. These accounts sought to retell the spiritual conversion of each nun in the language of the hagiographic model of saints (Myers 1993).

39. In her discussion of the distinction between Catholic and Protestant worship, Miles (1985) offers an intriguing comparison between seeing and hearing. Seeing, she suggests, is the more active of the two. Hearing is more passive and conducive to dependency. Her distinction

The altar call, another metaphor for the metaphor-using Baptists, since they have no physical altar, sets the group stage for personal inspection. The outstretched arms of the preacher, the soft and tender singing of the choir, the silent praying of members of the congregation invite a personal decision that then becomes public confession. Penance is not assigned, since nothing that an individual may do secures grace, but perhaps walking the aisle is penance enough, the sacrifice of the sinner to the congregational self.

"Fellowship" is the key word in the Baptist church. Fellowship Hall is often the name for the Sunday School auditorium. The spirit of fellowship begins with Brother Womack's glad hand at the door as we enter the church and continues to his departing shake as we leave at the conclusion of the service. Fellowship perhaps even transcends stewardship, which means tithing and fund-raising, a perennial passion. In contrast to the pursuit of solitude by the worshiping self in the *iglesia* in Nueva Esperanza, the worshiping self of the Baptists in Mt. Hope performs in the spirit of fellowship lodged in a congregational structure.

Image

At the beginning of this section, I spoke of other significant contrasts: icon versus written word, sensing versus reading, intimacy versus distance. And you said, Wait. Don't go off the deep end just yet. But now, you agree, we are ready for the plunge. As Christians in both Nueva Esperanza and Mt. Hope bring together setting and performance, they create an image of Christ, so that they may be in-him. To help our comprehension of their accomplishments, let us line up the distinctive features of setting and performance:

PLACE AND BEING-IN-CHRIST

Nueva Esperanza *Iglesia*	Mt. Hope Church
Setting	*Setting*
Ornate	Plain
Temple	House, Auditorium
Performance	*Performance*
Accent on the act	Accent on the verbal

neatly parallels the distinction between Spanish American *fe* and Southern Baptist faith. "Es la fe que vale" expresses the feeling that it is my *fe*, my own unique *fe*, that engages the actions of a particular manifestation of Christ. "Putting your faith in Jesus Christ" means surrender.

Symbolic icon	Literal word
Ritual	Narrative
Individual	Group

Mystical experience is said to be the apprehension of undifferentiated unity (Tuzin 1984), and this appears to be what Christians aspire to in their effort to follow San Pablo "dentro del cuerpo de Cristo; to follow Paul into the body of Christ." However, as anthropologists, we need to point out that while being-in-the-world is a unitary phenomenon, it is not an undifferentiated one. There are the hyphens. And the hyphens reside between being and world. Being, in the Heideggerian sense, in itself is incomplete. It requires a world for its existence. The world, however, comes about through the process of be-ing. Likewise, Christian be-ing requires a Christworld for its fulfillment, and that Christworld comes about in the mass and in the Sunday service through the conjoining of setting and performance.

Although ordinarily image privileges seeing over the other senses, image here seeks to convey the sense of presence, the presence of the distinctly sacred, the presence of Christ. And in this presence, Christians are.

In Nueva Esperanza, among the Spanish American Catholics in the weekday mass, the image of Christ constructed is the corporeal Christ: Christ as we contact him with our eyes, Christ as we smell him in the candle smoke, and Christ as we taste him in our mouths, the Christ of Touch. In Mt. Hope, among the Southern Baptists in the Sunday service, the image produced is the invisible Christ: Christ as we sing Him, Christ as we read him, and Christ as Reverend Overton speaks him, the Christ of the Word.

Simplifying and completing our chart, we have:

PLACE AND BEING-IN-CHRIST

Nueva Esperanza *Iglesia*	Mt. Hope Church
Setting	*Setting*
Ornate Temple	Plain House
Performance	*Performance*
Act	Voice
Individual	Group
Image	*Image*
Christ of the Touch	Christ of the Word

In their living Christs, Christians are. In their unique achievements, they exemplify how we all, humans everywhere, dwell in our own creations, a true mystery. For Christians, in-Christ, dwelling in that mystery lets them challenge death.

Let us continue our search into their heroic challenge. Please remember that our aim, though pursued with all the rigor at our command, is not to explain away the challenge but to disclose it—to let it show itself as it is, to let it be—in all of its be-ing. To do so, we must go on a journey, the subject of the next chapter.

¡Oh muerte! ¿Qué se ha hecho tu aguijón?

—1 Corintos 15:55

5

THE JOURNEY (OURS AND CHRIST'S)

Kneeling in the *iglesia*, people in Nueva Esperanza produce an image of Christ that is a sensuous one of the Touch. Sitting in the pews at the First Baptist Church in Mt. Hope, the congregation brings about an image of Christ that is a verbal one of the Word. In pursuing this important distinction we journey across the regions and through the liturgical calendar.

In our trip through these regions, nowhere do we find the divergence between the two Christs more distinct than in the case of pilgrimages. Pilgrimage in Spanish America means travel, often long and difficult, to a holy shrine where Christ or the Virgin has appeared and where miracles have occurred and continue today to descend upon us. Conversely, we can go from Texas to Virginia, scarcely finding a single sacred spot. In the American South, pilgrimage may be a trip to Natchez, Mississippi, where you see the Old South rise before your very eyes or it may be a homecoming event with preaching and dinner on the grounds or it may be a song that takes you straight to Glory. Pilgrimage in Spanish America is a physical encounter, but in the American South, among the verbal Baptists, it is metaphor.

The distinction between the two forms of Christianity deepens when we tie our journey to the liturgical trajectory of Christ's own life. In Spanish America the birth of Christ is only one of several holy days that occur from October 31 through January 6. A consideration of those feast days takes us from All Saints Day through Christmas to the Day of the Three Kings, but in Mexico, we detour to the shrine of Our Lady of Guadalupe to ponder the occasion of December 12, arguably in Mexico as important as December 25. Why, I ask, do we find the insistence voiced among many that the Virgin of

Guadalupe is an Aztec goddess in disguise? Why this search into the pre-Columbian past for today's spirituality? Why don't we find in the American South a similar urge to look to Native Americans for authenticity? Could the reason be tied up in the inclusivity of a visual icon and the exclusivity of the sacred word? In any case, Christmas in Spanish America occurs as an important day among important days, while in the United States it crowns the festive year, which may mean that Southern Baptists, in spite of themselves, are co-opted in their perennial attempt to put "Christ back in Xmas."

As different as Christ's birth is in the two regions, his death brings the divergence between the two images to its final culmination. In Spanish America, *La Semana Santa*, "Holy Week," far exceeds Christmas as the most solemn occasion. Likewise, *Viernes Santo*, "Good Friday," the day Christ was crucified and died, continues to move us more deeply than Easter Sunday, the day of his Resurrection. In the South, however, Good Friday (except in idiosyncratic Louisiana) passes with scarcely a notice, whereas Easter Sunday, the day the rock was rolled away from tomb, dawns to the chorus, "He arose. Hallelujah, Christ arose!"

As this chapter ends with the Crucifixion and Resurrection, it leads the way to our final account of how these triumphal Christians put death in its place through each living Christ. Now, as we begin the journey of this chapter, let us listen once more to San Pablo saying, "*¡Oh muerte! ¿Qué se ha hecho tu aguijón?*," and hear Paul echo, "O death! Where is thy sting?"

Shrines and This Wearisome Land

In the landscape of places in Spanish America, shrines are among the most common and the most prominent structures throughout the region. Brought to the New World by Iberian Catholicism, the view that the sacred can take up residence in a physical domain (along a stream, on a hillside, in a pasture) has created holy locations to which people travel so as to be in the miraculous presence of Christ or the Virgin. While mass in the parish *iglesia* brings about the Real Presence of Christ, pilgrimage to a shrine brings the pilgrim in touch with miracles.

Shrines popular today often trace their origins to miraculous events that occurred in colonial times. The Virgin of Guadalupe (1531) and the Virgin of los Remedios (1540), both in Mexico, and the Virgin of Copacabana in Peru (1580) are among the many Marian shrines that claim to have originated in the sixteenth century. Examples of early Christ-centered shrines include the Lord of Chalma in Mexico (1539), the Lord of Miracles in Colombia (1550), and in Guatemala the Lord of Esquipulas, carved in 1594, who is said to have produced miracles by 1603. Other shrines have a somewhat more recent genealogy, such as the Virgin of San Juan de los Lagos in Mexico (1626), the Lord of Earthquakes in Peru (1650) and, even more recently, the Child of Atocha in Mexico (1829). Still other shrines are spin-offs of the major ones. The many "Black Christ" shrines in Honduras are, for the most part, derived from the one in Esquipulas, in neighboring Guatemala; the Lord of Miracles in Puerto Rico apparently came from the shrine in Colombia; and the Virgin of San Juan del Valle, near McAllen, Texas, was imported in the early 1950s from San Juan de los Lagos (Map 2).

Mary Lee Nolan (1991) estimates that close to a thousand of such widely recognized shrines dot the Latin American landscape. New shrines arise even today. In fact, the twentieth century has seen more shrines built than in the nineteenth; miracles still happen in Spanish America. Consequently, nearly every region has a holy place.

Throughout both Europe and Latin America, shrines devoted to the Virgin Mary outnumber those dedicated to the veneration of Christ or the saints. Contrary to popular belief, however, Christ-centered shrines are more numerous in Latin America than in Europe (Nolan 1991; Sallnow 1987). This frequency stems from the initial zeal, inspired by the Tridentine reforms (which we encountered in Chapter 2), to construct a purer Christianity in the New World than in the Old, one more focused on devotion to Christ.

Shrines are sites of contradictions and tensions (Sallnow 1987). One enduring tension is between the legitimizing authority and the venerating populace. The tension translates spatially into a contest between center and periphery. A classic example is the Virgin of the Angels in Cartago, Costa Rica. The founding legend recounts how in 1635 an Indian woman, called in Spanish an *indita* (literally, "little, female Indian"), a term that here conveys both affection and a trace of condescension, found an image of the Virgin on a rock near her home on the outskirts of the then colonial capital of Costa Rica, some distance away from the central plaza and the parish church. In contrast to the white, Spanish center, this area, as the residence of Indians and mixed racial types, became known as *La Puebla de los Pardos*, "the village of the brown ones." Upon hearing of the miracle, the priest attempted to install the Virgin in the parish church, but she kept reappearing where the woman found her. So, finally getting the message, the authorities erected a structure at the original rock. In so doing, the church recognized the spiritual source of the shrine and moved to incorporate it into the ecclesiastical sphere. Today, the Virgin, a tiny, dark figure called affectionately *La Negrita*, "the dear, little black one," reigns as the patroness of Costa Rica. She is housed in a splendiferous sanctuary, to which people on August 2 travel on foot from the present-day capital of San José to venerate the *indita*'s discovery. This repeats the earlier distinction between center and periphery, with San José now the center, the seat of the president and the bishop, and Cartago, the spiritual periphery. In a further permutation, the day after the pilgrimage, people in Cartago transport the image from its sanctuary to the parish church, where she resides for one month. Then, with some fanfare, she is restored to her national location. This movement seems to suggest that Cartago—the old capital in contrast to the new, the small town in opposition to the bustling city—acts to establish itself, at least for the one-month period, as the spiritual periphery.

Another site of tension in shrines lies between founding story and secular history. As the account of the Virgin of the Angels exemplifies, the stories of the initial appearance of the miraculous figure often follow the general Iberian pattern we met in Chapter 2: A person of modest means, a herdsman in Spain, a Native American in the New World, out in the wilds, away from civilization, finds an object, attempts to take it back to the center, only to find the object has a will of its own. In compliance with the object's desire, a shrine is built at the original location, and shortly miracles occur. In their set and recurrent manner, the stories convey, at least to us humanistic types, an attempt to explain and to sanctify a process already underway. People, for different reasons, journey to a site, and as their numbers increase, the story emerges to explain the particular properties of the shrine. Consequently, the dates given in the founding story seek to lodge the story at a miraculous time distant from the contemporary scene. For that reason, the dates, even when attributed to official documents in the archives, are not necessarily historically accurate.

Still another problematic issue is the contribution of pre-Columbian beliefs to the shrine's power. Not uncommonly, when faced with the spectacle of thousands of worshipers traveling from faraway homes to congregate around a shrine and to get as close as possible to the miraculous image, outsider interpreters attribute the appeal of the shrine to the retention of Native

American attitudes from preconquest times. As an example, let us take the color of the shrine figure. As in the case of the Virgin of the Angels in Costa Rica, Spanish American images of both the Virgin and Christ may be (but by no means always are) dark, even deep black. One explanation is that given the popularity of dark gods in the pre-Columbian pantheon, Native Americans found dark figures more understandable and appealing. A variant of the explanation tells how the early missionary priests, attempting to cross the bridge between the indigenous population and European Christianity, had the figures painted dark so as to appeal to the dark-skinned Indians (Kelsey and Osborne 1939; Borhegyi 1954). Yet if we look closely at the figures, we note that their facial features are European rather than Native American. In essence, the figures are Caucasians with dark skin. Furthermore, not only do we find dark shrine figures in areas adjacent to regions heavily populated by native Americans, as in the case of the Lord of Esquipulas in Guatemala, but we also encounter them in areas far from such populations, as in the case of the Lord of Miracles in Buga, Colombia, near the city of Cali. Still expanding our view, we encounter dark figures of Christ and the Virgin in Europe, such as the black Christ in Cracow, Poland, known as Queen Jadwiga's Crucifix, or that country's more famous Black Madonna. The dark Christ at Lucca, Italy, which dates to around the eleventh century, indicates that not only are dark figures found throughout Europe, but also they antedate the conquest of the New World (Nolan 1991; Richardson 1995b). In sum, the spatial and temporal evidence suggests that Europeans brought with them the pattern of dark shrine figures to the New World.

If Europeans brought this custom with them, two questions immediately arise: Why did the white Christians paint some of their icons dark? And why do observers often credit the dark color to centuries-old retention of Native American beliefs? An answer to the first question will be offered later. In responding to the second question, we must agree that in certain regions indigenous influence is clearly present. The meticulous work of M. J. Sallnow in the Peruvian Andes demonstrates that both the prehistoric Inca royalty and the post-Columbian Spanish authorities used control over sacred locations to establish hegemony over their subjects. Yet even here, where mountain spirits and Christian apparitions merged, it "is the contrasts rather than the continuities between the precontact and postcontact sacred landscapes that command attention and that betray the nature of Spanish domination" (1987, 98). Two factors seem to fuel the eagerness to find "idols behind the altar." One is the desire to credit indigenous culture with a staying power that undercuts and resists European domination. The other is an elusive tendency to say that if the religious phenomenon in Latin America appears strange and exotic in North American eyes, then that peculiar quality must stem from a Native American substrate. Here the goal appears, in its sly, yet pervasive manner, to dismiss Spanish American Catholicism, especially in its popular, everyday mode, as genuine Christianity. Later, in considering the veneration of the Virgin of Guadalupe, we will see the "sacred-as-indigenous" theme reemerge.

A final sphere of tension is between the sacred and the commercial. Perhaps there is no sight more horrifying to North American Protestants with the righteousness of the work-banned Sabbath stamped on their souls than the hawking of gaudy portraits, statues, crucifixes, and printed prayers to willing pilgrims on their way to miracles. While merchants everywhere love a big crowd and flock to exploit its potential for spending, the tie between the merchant and the pilgrim extends beyond a purely momentary opportunity to turn a quick peso. In Spanish America, in the same manner that the town market may have its busiest day on Sunday, when people from the countryside come to make their weekly purchases and to go to mass, shrines may become partners with regional markets. The location of Esquipulas, Guatemala, along routes that extend into neighboring Honduras and El Salvador made it a strategic location for a large commercial fair during the early nineteenth century (Map 6).

The fair and the shrine reinforced one another's drawing power, and by midcentury, when there were no wars to make the journey precarious, as many as 80,000 people assembled at Esquipulas at the beginning of each new year "to barter and pay homage to 'our Lord of Esquipulas'" (Stephens 1841, 168–69). Today, though far fewer in number because of the changes in transportation modes and routes, merchants continue to come to Esquipulas to sell dry goods along with objects associated with worship. The notion of a work-free and nonfestive holy time relates to the radical Protestant turn away from the sensuous. Pilgrimage, on the other hand, comes about only when the sacred becomes sensuous, when it establishes a where, when it dwells in a physical location to which the devotees can travel.

Movement is the heart of pilgrimage. The pilgrim journeys. William Christian (1972) reports that in northern Spain people say that when pilgrims travel to shrines *por devoción*, they go with no particular request; when they

MAP 6. The strategic location of Our Lord of Esquipulas in Central America

go *por promesa*, they go to complete a vow; and when they travel *por diversión*, they go for the pleasure of going. While no doubt pilgrims in Spanish America likewise journey for the other two reasons, the majority, I would suggest, go *por promesa*. In this instance, a person, faced with a child whom the doctors cannot cure or a damaged leg that will not heal or a practical matter, such as a husband who drinks too much, makes a vow that if the shrine figure lends assistance, then the individual will travel to the shrine in veneration. The child is cured, the damaged leg grows strong, and the husband turns away from the bottle, so in fulfillment of the vow, the person journeys to the shrine as a pilgrim in gratitude. The arrangement has that factual, two-party, face-to-face character we have encountered before. The shrine figure is addressed by its name, and the contract negotiated. And what happens if the child is not cured, the leg continues to fester, or the husband drinks more than before the vow? Then the individual is freed of any obligation. With regard to the other reasons for going on a pilgrimage, there is nothing in the instrumental nature of the contract that prevents the pilgrim from enjoying the camaraderie of the journey, the excitement of the arrival, and a feeling of purification and redemption upon returning home.

Throughout the year, pilgrims leave home to visit their favorite shrines. During the period immediately preceding the day that commemorates the originating miraculous event of a major shrine, thousands are on the road. As the shrine may be located away from major centers of population, the traveling spreads out over a day, a night, or several days. Today, pilgrims arrive in rented trucks or cars or more commonly on public buses, but the favorite mode of traveling remains walking. For example, pilgrims to the shrine of the Virgin of Talpa in western Mexico, near Guadalajara, frequently walk a route that lasts several days and traverses difficult terrain (Posey 1999). On other occasions, people will bus to a nearby location and then walk the remaining distance to a shrine. As they approach their goal, those who have vowed to do so descend to their knees and painfully negotiate the patio leading into the sanctuary, struggle up the stairs, and then proceed down the aisle to the altar over which the image presides.

Pilgrims travel in the company of other pilgrims. A man may announce his vow to others in his community, and several of his friends and acquaintances will volunteer to go with him (Reina 1966). In some areas, a devotional group, a neighborhood, or an entire barrio organizes itself and travels as a unit with banners and special insignia (Sallnow 1981, 1989). For many, if not most, however, the tie among pilgrims, rather than being determined before the trip, may emerge unspoken and spontaneously during the course of travel and may end, abruptly, with the completion of the journey.

Years ago, I made a pilgrimage to the Virgin of the Angels. I offer it to you, not as a paradigm, but as a journey an anthropologist took along his own road in the company of fellow sojourners.

On the eve of August 2, I joined those walking from San José to Cartago, a distance of some fifteen miles, the journey from the bustling, modern capital city, up across the continental divide, then down to the quieter, ancient capital of Spanish settlement. In preparation, I went to the cathedral, to a side altar devoted to the Virgin. As I had learned to do, I knelt and said, "Virgencita, ayúdame; Little Virgin, help me." Then, as if to balance that act, I bought a bottle of gin, which, at the time, I was drinking straight. Not the usual object a pilgrim carries, you might well remark, yet as it turned out, given the mixture of piety and frolic, of solemnity and profanity, the gin was not altogether out of place.

The night sky descended upon us in a heavy mist: middle-aged men by themselves; older women paired with a younger person, a daughter, a niece, or a friend; some families with their babies well wrapped against the chilly air; a few gringos, subdued and conversing softly in English; and a large component of teenage boys. The movement was a steady stream, with some pilgrims walking slowly, others more quickly. The teenagers wove in and out, stopping, shouting, then running ahead. They were alike in backpacks, transistor radios, and carnival hats. "*Puta;* whore," came off their lips in rhythmic frequency. Passing two gringos speaking English, one said enigmatically, "Fucking all right."

As the trip progressed, some stopped to rest along the banister of bridges, others to relieve themselves under the cover of nearby bushes, and still others to pause in front of the many roadside stands. The stands ranged from a single pot boiling on top of a homemade brazier, with the vendor, a woman, shouting out she had hot corn for sale, to small sheds with electric lights strung along the roofs, with several men inside selling cokes, coffee, tamales, and chunks of tough meat on charred sticks.

The night advanced through its own cycle. A weak moon now appeared through the lifting mist, and as the road climbed the divide, large mountains rose through the clouds, solid, black, majestic. Buses and trucks loaded with earlier pilgrims plied their way back to San José. Interspersed, motorcycles swung in and out, going in both directions. That no one was hit was itself a miracle. At the divide, the sky cleared, and the stars came out, bright and friendly. A small boy approached us, selling postcards with the Virgin's picture on them. "Ten *centavos míster*," he said to me in a mixture of English and Spanish. "*La Virgen* for ten *centavos*." The pilgrims were now moving through downtown Cartago, passing the house where I had rented a room for the summer, and on to the eastern outskirts, to the very spot where the *indita*, looking for firewood, had found the image.

The structure that housed the tiny Virgin had earned the title of "basilica," an honor bestowed only on major centers of Catholic worship. The edifice was the most recent temple to occupy the spot. Unlike its immediate predecessor, which the earthquake of 1905 destroyed, the building had moved away from the more angular, classic theme of pillars and pediment to a more rounded demeanor. Roofs, made of the earthquake-tolerant corrugated iron but ingeniously crafted to resemble tiles, formed domes that called to mind an eastern Mediterranean motif. Along one side, a stream, gushing from its mother spring, rippled past murals portraying the founding. Because of its association with the appearance of the Virgin to the Indian woman, the stream was said to have curative properties, and people filled a variety of containers with its healing power.

I followed the human stream across the patio and through the entrance. The heat of packed bodies struck my face. People were everywhere. Some were on their knees slowly moving in a rhythmic chain toward the altar. Others, having completed their journey, sat in clusters to share the last food brought along the way. Still others, exhausted from the trip, stretched out on the pews. The mood was quiet, dignified; no "*Puta*" here, no "Fucking all right." No priests were in evidence. This night, the basilica and its Virgin belonged to the people. I got to the front, knelt, and in the silent company of fellow pilgrims, crossed myself. "Ayúdame," I repeated.

Outside, people milled about, with late arrivals pushing around others waiting for transportation to return them to their daily lives. Reluctantly, but with a touch of relief, I joined those, too, and went back to the rented room where my bags were packed for the flight home to my family in Louisiana.

I offer my pilgrimage as only one among many. For accounts of Andean pilgrimages that pit one devotional group against another with competitive dancing and whip lashings and that, encouraged by drinking, constantly threaten to become a free-for-all battle, I refer you to those of Sallnow (1981) and Harald Skar (1985). In contrast, in his description of a pilgrimage to the Lord of Chalma, a shrine near Mexico City, John Hobgood (1971) presents an image of pilgrims traveling in groups but whose organization is much looser than those described by Sallnow and Skar.

These accounts of group pilgrimages notwithstanding, a principal component of many pilgrimages remains the upwelling of unspoken, spontaneous, intense, but short-term ties among individual pilgrims. This relationship harkens back to Chapter 1 and Duncan's terse assessment (1968): "No social self exists . . . save in the response of an other." Yet as Victor Turner insists, the response of pilgrims to each other brings about neither "a merging of consciousness, nor an emotional melding, but a mutual recognition of 'definite, determinate identities' . . . , each with its wiry, unique, and indefeasible outline. . . . Along the pilgrimage route, when each joins each, *all are one because each is one*" (Turner 1992, 34, emphasis added). Turner calls the special relationship that brings about such precious individuality "communitas." Communitas is the bond between the I that resides in me and the Thou that dwells in you. You recognize the bond immediately. You recall the instances of its occurring, those times when you and the person whom you were with shared a mystery. I, too, marvel at those occasions and the bright intensity of their happening. Later, as we reach the end of the journey of this text, this particular journey of you and me, we will consider the bond once more, for I am convinced that in its mystery, we, you and I, are each unique in the presence of one another. Furthermore, I am equally certain all that *is* in this text rests upon the "*are-ing*" of that I–Thou bond.[1]

The heart of pilgrimage is movement, but once the pilgrims have arrived at the shrine, they set about establishing a relationship with the shrine figure. The relationship emerges from a series of actions that include touching the figure, bequeathing objects, and securing artifacts for the return home. In so doing, the pilgrims create a sense of presence that infuses the material setting with their expectations. The complex of activities begins with gaining physical proximity to the shrine image.

To gain physical proximity, pilgrims employ the body and all of its senses: smell, sound, perhaps even taste, but especially sight and touch. These two, seeing and touching, if you recall our earlier discussion, work in apparent opposition. Seeing distances, but touching brings in close. At the shrine, the work of the two senses takes on a different nuance. As before, seeing distances in placing the image outside of and separate from the pilgrim's self, but now seeing with the pilgrim's eye of fond expectation positions the image immediately there. Almost on its own, the hand, then, reaches across the distance to the image, much in the same manner that I reach out to make sure you are here, on this page.

1. M. J. Sallnow, who draws attention to the predetermined quality of certain Andean pilgrimages near Cuzco, Peru, nonetheless gives voice to the communitas quality of pilgrimage. He describes his emotions as he joins a devotional group in preparation to travel to a mountainous shrine, Lord of the Snow Star, erected to venerate Christ: "I felt intensely exhilarated. . . . At last I was setting out for the fabled place, my welfare entrusted to the people into whose lives I had so rudely trespassed. From now on I was entirely at their disposal, and the thought of such dependence engendered a sense of oneness, of communion with them. . . . Was this feeling merely the self-indulgent sentiment of an anthropologist finally counting himself 'one of the people'? [But then, Manuel, master of the pilgrimage, turned to me,] 'Now,' he said emphatically, 'we're all brothers'" (1987, 179).

The image itself is often a visual feast. At the shrine of the Lord of Miracles in Buga, Colombia, the dark Christ hangs on his cross high above the gaze of the kneeling worshipers. From the rear of the massive basilica, the figure, which approximates life size, appears almost tiny and is nearly lost among the other figures on the *retablo*. Closer, the image emerges out of the confusion but remains sheltered behind a clear glass enclosure. At the conclusion of each of the many masses said during the day, pilgrims climb hidden stairs rising behind the left side of the *retablo* to enter a space immediately below the cross. Here they look upward to the dark figure splotched with red blood and nailed to a cross wreathed in gold. Three golden, spearlike rods, called *potencias*, radiate out from the thorn-crowned head. The head is slumped over, and the eyes are shut. The urge to touch, to bring the self and the image into intimate contact, for many seems irresistible. Unable to touch the icon itself because of the glass shield, many touch the glass then touch themselves and the babies in their arms and the children beside them. Inexplicably, the glass enclosure has an open slot at the foot of the cross. Some pilgrims put their hands through the opening and strain to extend their arm so their fingers reach the base of the cross. Eventually, and however reluctantly, the pilgrims leave the image to descend a second flight of stairs leading down on the right (Figure 26).

At Esquipulas, Guatemala, the pilgrims are more fortunate. Here, the Christ, who is likewise dark, also hangs high above the heads of the worshipers spread out on the floor of the massive structure. Grouped around the cross are three additional figures in brightly colored clothing. One kneels at the foot of the cross, and the other two stand on either side. The kneeling woman is Mary Magdalene; Mary, the Mother of Christ, and John, the Beloved Disciple, stand on the sides (Figure 27). A glass case also shields these figures, but it is open in the back. As in Buga, pilgrims climb hidden stairs that lead up, this time, to a space behind the figures. The opening in the glass, which puts them about waist level to the figure, allows them to touch or even kiss a leg of the crucified Christ. Encouraged by shrine personnel to maintain an orderly flow, pilgrims move past the figures constantly, and I have seen you give a start when, on the floor of the basilica listening to the mass, you catch out of the corner of your eye a fluttering around the scene. I suspect for the briefest of moments that the statues, aided by the candles' flickering glow, appear alive!

Fig. 26. The Lord of Miracles, Buga, Colombia, as depicted in market prints

FIG. 27. The Lord of Esquipulas, Esquipulas, Guatemala, as depicted in market prints

As part of establishing physical communication with the shrine image, touching suggests a transfer of power or grace from the image to the pilgrim. But touching and, especially, kissing are also acts of adoration and worship. Consequently, through these actions, the pilgrim is *bestowing* power or grace as much as receiving it. The bestowing quality comes to the fore during the act of bequeathing objects at the shrine.[2]

In accordance with an Iberian, if not a pan-European, tradition (Foster 1960; Nolan 1991), pilgrims frequently leave objects, or ex-voto offerings, that have the shape of the body part whose ailment had afflicted them. Thus, glass cabinets in Cartago, at the shrine of the Virgin of the Angels, are filled with tiny arms, legs, hearts, livers, and lungs. Having asked the Virgin to intercede on their behalf and having received the benefits of that intercession in the form of cures, grateful pilgrims purchase these silver and brass objects from nearby stands manned by private vendors or from the officially designated shrine store and deposit them at the shrine (Figure 28).

In addition to these metonymic objects that the now-cured bequeath, actual crutches, no longer needed, adorn the walls of many shrines. Other objects left may have closer ties to skills possessed by the pilgrims than the body parts restored to health. Wooden models of ships, airplanes, and cars—some elaborate, others quite simple, but all left with the same gratitude—crowd around overflowing cases. Written expressions, often accompanied with photographs, are perhaps the most frequent items the pilgrims deposit. The expressions may take the form of an expensive plaque with the writing embossed on it, but commonly the expressions are handwritten on tablet paper. Many begin with the formulaic "Doy gracias a la Virgen de Los Angeles [or Señor de los Milagros, etc.] por el favor concedido; I give thanks to the Virgin of the Angels [or Lord of Miracles, etc.] for the favor received." The note proceeds to describe the event that precipitated the request for divine assistance. These may well be unexpected occurrences, such as a bus going over a precipice or a robbery or a stabbing. Some of the most endearing objects that pilgrims leave in Mexico are metal plaques about one foot square

2. Two internationally recognized scholars on separate occasions assured me that in the two countries they knew best, Peru and Guatemala, people did not touch images, for to do so, at least in the opinion of one, would show disrespect. Neither statement, that people do not touch the images or that to do so would show disrespect, fits my observations. And in Spain, on sabbatical in the fall of 2001, while polishing the final draft of this book, I watched in Madrid, in the *iglesia* of San Antonio de Padua, a woman, like so many before, touch the shiny feet of a crucified Christ near a side altar, while an adjacent sign forbiddingly proclaimed, "*No tocar*; no touching." A few days later, I joined the pilgrims moving up the stairs above the altar at Santiago de Compostela to touch and even, in the case of some, to hug the icon of St. James, here, under the accepting eyes of a shrine officer. My consideration of bequeathing objects at sites of tragedies expands to become "The Gift of Presence" (Richardson 2001).

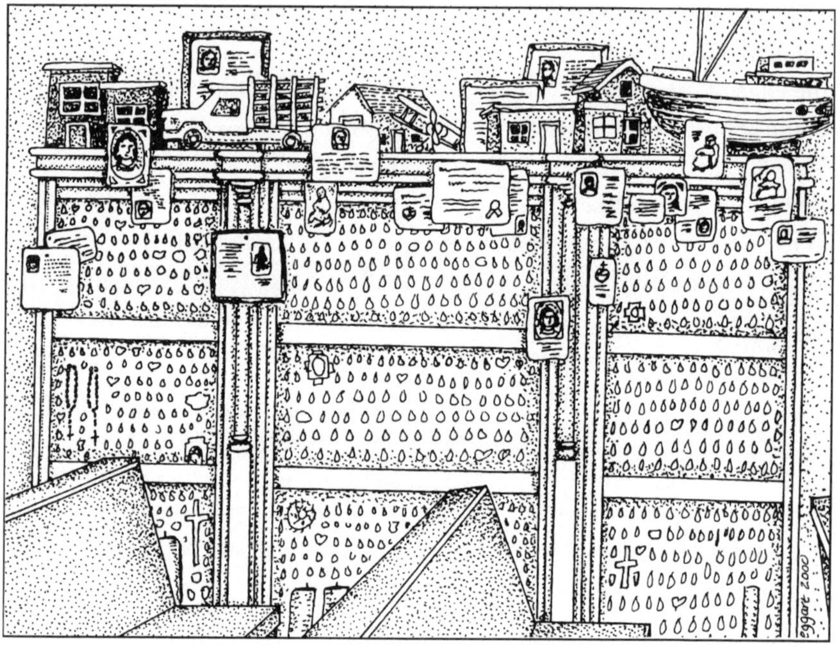

FIG. 28. Cabinets filled with ex-voto offerings, Cartago, Costa Rica

with the scenes that motivated the plea for help painted on them. Thus the walls of shrines, such as the one dedicated to the Christ Child of Atocha in Plateros or the one devoted to the Holy Cross in Parras, both in northern Mexico, are layered with paintings of doctors at an operation, a person on a sick bed, a swimmer fighting against a flood, figures successfully hiding from a border patrol helicopter, and other challenges besetting the faithful whose pleas the shrine figure has responded to with assistance. (For wonderful reproductions, see Durand and Massey 1995.)[3]

Bequeathing objects at shrines may well be a component of the general pattern of placing material items at the scene of unexpected occurrences. Some of the occurrences are tragedies that descend upon us without warning. In the spring of 1995, in Chapel Hill, North Carolina, where I was spending

3. Since first noticing the plaques in Mexico, I, like so many others, naturally assumed they originated in that country. Then we, you and I, saw similar plaques at the shrine devoted to Mary's sisters at Les-Saintes-Maries-de-la-Mer in the Camargue region of France. The oldest bears a date of 1591.

a sabbatical leave, a young student on his way to class fell dead, a victim of being in the sights of a M-1 rifle fired randomly by another student gone over the edge of sanity. That very night people began leaving objects at the spot of the killing, which had been a strip of anonymous sidewalk but now became known, but known for what? For over a week, as I passed by, the flowers, a Bible, a UNC lacrosse cap, a can of chewing tobacco posed their question: What does this signify? The street cleaners, in league with the rest of us, allowed the items to remain. A late snowfall covered the petals, the pages, the cap, the can, and the rest, and the next time I went by, they were gone.

The mind jumps to other, even larger tragedies, such as the bombing of the Alfred P. Murrah Building in Oklahoma City in April 1995. Long after the last bodies were taken from the rubble, people continued to place items on the chain-link fence that cordoned off the disaster. Among the items left—flowers, photographs, crosses, and autographed t-shirts of sport teams passing through—the most poignant were baby garments and dolls, recalling the occupants of the day-care center inside the building. Still another case, one closer to the example of the shrine, is the Vietnam Veterans Memorial in Washington, D.C. Even before its official inauguration, people began leaving flags, flowers, medals, and messages at "The Wall." On a day that I went to face the names inscribed on the black marble, I saw a wreath with this note: "20th Reunion, Class of 1965. Paul Fleming and Bob Sowlinski. We will not forget. South Hadley, Mass."

But filled with impatience, you exclaim, What connects the tragedies of insanity and war with shrines devoted to Christ? If I reply, I'm not sure, my uncertainty is certain to agitate you even more. Nonetheless, I'll risk the agitation for now and continue the examination of the pilgrims' actions.

Touching the shrine figure and leaving objects seem interrelated. Touching the image suggests securing some quality from the figure, and bequeathing objects implies giving a quality back. There is a reciprocity at work. Yet both actions tell us much about the bestowing quality of the human touch. Having bestowed qualities to the image by touching it, the person commemorates the event by leaving an object. There remains one more relationship with objects, and that is carrying them back home to adorn the family altar.

Similar to what happens when a person touches the shrine figure, objects that come in contact with the shrine image take on a quality they did not have before. For example, at the Lord of Miracles in Buga, a lady with a large package of items, by maneuvering it to the left and then to the right, managed to squeeze it through the slot in the glass shield so that it touched the base of the cross. Once in contact, the package possessed a quality it did not have before. Emile Durkheim (1947) recognized this occurrence as the contagiousness of the sacred. Whatever the basis of the contagion, we see it happening at the Vietnam Veterans Memorial. People not only leave objects, but they put paper against a name inscribed in the marble face and rub a pencil back and forth to produce the name on paper, which they carry home.[4]

Vendors offer a wide range of objects that pilgrims may purchase for their return trip. Typically, these are replicas of the shrine figure. These may range from large images, two feet or more, to tiny figures encased in plastic to ornament a key chain. Likewise, portraits, brightly painted in reds and yellows, go from wallet size to ones suitable for hanging on the wall above the family altar shelf. The duplication process may exaggerate well-known attributes of the shrine image. The reproductions of the Lord of Esquipulas, who is widely known in the vernacular as *El Cristo Negro*, "the Black Christ," are much blacker than the image above the altar. Consequently, the shrines that derive from Esquipulas often feature a coal-black Christ.

At Esquipulas pilgrims can also purchase small tablets of white clay, about two inches square, on which are embossed various designs, most frequently a single crucified figure with flowers around it. These are called *panitos del Señor*, or "little breads of the Lord." They are manufactured locally and sold widely throughout Guatemala and into neighboring Honduras and Mexico. Taken home, the *panito* may be eaten, especially by women who are pregnant. Clay-eating, or geophagy, is a worldwide practice, but here in Esquipulas, it acquires the symbolism associated with the Host and with the Body of Christ

4. Intriguingly, in a manner that suggests a fundamental similarity, the transportation for a time of a model of the Vietnam Veterans Memorial paralleled the movement of sacred images across the landscape. Labeled "The Moving Wall," this smaller replica of the Washington memorial was carried throughout the country by a group of Vietnam veterans who wanted others to have access to the power of the memorial. People responded to the replica much in the same manner as they interacted with the original. In Baton Rouge, when the Wall came in 1989, individuals left at the base floral arrangements, single roses, handwritten notes, photocopied poems, religious and military medals, and an empty beer can. They also took rubbings of the names (Kennedy 1991). One is tempted to note that the phenomenon of a replica receiving the power of that which it replicates appears antecedent to the much heralded proclamation by postmodernists that in this age in which we, you and I, live, the simulacrum has become the real reality. (For a full critique of the "genuine simulacrum," see Bruner 1994.)

as bread. Elsewhere in Central America and Mexico clay-eating may occur without any tie with pilgrimage. In Querétaro, Mexico, for example, in plastic bags in the market stall next to medicinal plants, you can buy small chunks of white clay ready to eat. At the pilgrimage shrine in San Juan del los Lagos, near the city of Guadalajara, Mexico, however, you encounter tablets of clay once again. Here, at a shrine devoted to the Virgin Mary, the tablets carry the Virgin's imprint. In the most intriguing manner, the bread metaphor of *pan* is dropped, and people call the tablets *tierritas de la Virgen*, or "the small earths of the Virgin." Thus, in Esquipulas, at a shrine devoted to Christ, the clay is "bread"; in San Juan de los Lagos, at a shrine venerating the Virgin, the clay is "earth" (Richardson and Davidson n.d.; Hunter, Horst, and Thomas 1989; Horst 1990).

Whatever the pilgrims buy, they prefer to have the items blessed. In doing so, the pilgrims, like the lady placing her package in contact with the Lord of Miracles at Buga, obtain qualities of the sacred. At Esquipulas, periodically, pilgrims form lines along one side of the basilica, and the resident priests of the Benedictine Order emerge to sprinkle holy water on the pilgrims and their purchases. The occasion is not without humor. The priests dispense the holy water by dipping small mops into plastic buckets and shaking them in the direction of the line. Every now and again, a priest, with a shy grin on his face, will thrust his mop deep into his bucket and swipe the loaded mop at the pilgrims, spraying holy water like rain.

Thus far, in telling you how pilgrims create a sense of presence at shrines through touching the image, bequeathing objects, and purchasing items to carry home, I have referred to acts of individuals—acts always, we must remember, in the company of other individuals doing similar things. We need now to consider how local residents in particular further activate presence by taking the shrine figure from its position above the altar and carrying it to other locations, spreading, as it were, its contagious qualities. Earlier, I mentioned that the people of Cartago, following the national day of pilgrimage, take the Virgin from the basilica in La Puebla and carry her to the parish church in the central part of the city. One summer I witnessed the adoration, and I offer this report (Richardson 1998b, 457–58):

> In Cartago, Costa Rica, I join the Virgin's people to carry
> Her from shrine to parish church. In 30 days, she goes back
> into Her palace of national renown, but today she's theirs.

Bells ring, sober men in somber suits march out
with Her on their shoulders. She is tiny, so tiny, just
a small, dark face peeping out from a jewel-laden cape.

She sways in heavenly grace to the band's drum and brass,
marching music, but measured and grave. Progress is
slow. Who wants to hurry? In the admiring throng are:

Two elderly *señoras*, black mantillas over bent, grey heads,
cotton stockings over ankles thick with varicose veins.

A *señorita* in a shirt so cut into Vs that it is
almost indecent. The tails hang over tight jeans.

One man in white shirt and suit but no shoes
walks beside another man with shoes but no suit.

A blind woman with an innocent smile led by her mother.
A completely bleached man, an albino, singing loud praise.

A boy cries, and his father bends to lift him up. With his other
arm, he leans down to hoist an even smaller guy to parental shelter.

A grandmother carries her granddaughter, while the daughter
shields all three with an umbrella held over their heads.

A man takes off his hat but holds it up to half cover his face,
torn between the hot sun and his duty to bare his head to the Virgin.

We arrive at the church door.
The devout follow the Virgin inside.
A policeman waves the rest on their way.

I peek inside, but leave to return to these notes
taken twenty-five years ago to recall the instant that I
(and you too?) walked alongside those who travel in faith.

Although the Virgin of the Angels makes a single round-trip journey from basilica to parish church and back, not uncommonly shrine figures travel a cycle. For example, every seven years, in what is called a *rogativo*, or "public veneration," the Lord of Miracles at Buga, Colombia, is taken from his glass shield and carried to various surrounding towns for short visits. Such processions are frequently the occasion for music, bells, and, a particularly distinctive feature, huge, exploding rockets. Even during times when national laws forbade such things, in Querétaro, Mexico, each June the Virgin of Pueblito, traveled from her small, rural hamlet to various barrios in the city. As the tiny Virgin, resplendent in her costume and regal in her countenance on the shoulders of her porters, approaches one of the barrio churches, bells peel vigorously, a brass band launches into a fast-paced tune, and large rockets zoom up into the sky and explode with sufficient force to cause the anthropologist, at least, to wince. At the entrance, the priest shouts, "¡Viva la Virgen del Pueblito!" And the crowd replies with great enthusiasm, "¡Viva! The priest shouts again, "¡Viva la Madre de Dios!" "¡Viva!" the crowd repeats. And once more, he shouts, "¡Viva La Pequeñita! Long live the small, dear one!" "Long live!" the crowd agrees. Inside, once she has been placed on a prepared platform in the tabernacle, he turns to crowd for the final time: "¡Mire nuestra Virgen! Behold our Virgin!" They roar their approval, and all burst into songs about the Virgin Mother of God.

As in the case of the Virgin of Pueblito, the music you hear is the work of a small ensemble of men playing trumpets, saxophones, clarinets, and drums. If you suddenly think, Jazz!, you can't be far wrong. In Cali, I witnessed the formation of a procession headed by the priest clutching the monstrance containing the Blessed Sacrament. Immediately behind stood a man holding a large umbrella to provide a canopy over both priest and monstrance. Positioning itself behind him was a band composed of a trumpet, a french horn, two clarinets, and three drums, one with cymbals on top. Once all were ready, a drummer beat the two sides of a small drum attached his chest and shouted to the participants, "¡Alabad a Dios Sacramentado! Praise God 'Sacramentalized'!" With that, the procession moved out of the *iglesia* to make its way through the nearby streets with the band producing a sound closer to Dixieland than anything you find in New Orleans today.[5]

Not long after hearing the Cali band sound the presence of the Blessed Sacrament, I witnessed the finale of a novena dedicated to the Virgin of Perpetual Succor in Buga. In the patio in front of the basilica, several men hoisted up a pole strung with explosives. With the image of the Virgin attending, the fireworks were ignited. As the flame sizzled up the pole, fiery wheels spun in counterpoint, and small rockets hurled brilliant light into the

5. This is not to suggest that the Cali band has imported Dixieland for religious processions. On the contrary, the Cali music suggests a religious origin of Dixieland, that Dixieland has its roots in the music of New Orleans' religious processions. Furthermore, the umbrella shielding the priest and the monstrance evokes the image of the use of umbrellas in New Orleans jazz funerals.

dark night. The end came with a crescendo and left a sign to glow atop the pole: "Madre de Dios Nos Da Paz; Mother of God Give Us Peace."

The raucous music and the exploding rockets seem so distant from the solitude of the individual kneeling before an image in the darkened interior of a quiet *iglesia*, not to mention the moment in a Southern Baptist church when the minister commands that "every head be bowed and every eye closed." Puzzled, you ask, Where is the sacred in all of this? Again I reply, The presence of the sacred in Spanish America is a physical reality. The heavily accented music and the bursting fireworks punctuate our shift from the ordinary of the everyday to the extraordinary of the sacred. The rockets literally blast us into heightened awareness. Silence, on the other hand, accomplishes the same goal by distinguishing the quietness of the sacred moment from the noisy chatter of our day-to-day lives. Thus, the silence of the interior of an *iglesia* and the ear-splitting explosion of rockets above our heads in the streets work together in their polar contrasts to establish aural boundaries that mark our transition from ordinary reality to the reality of worship (Tuzin 1984; Needham 1967; Brandes 1988). Furthermore, whatever their origin in Spanish American Catholic ritual, fireworks and other loud, nonrhythmic interruptions might well achieve their efficacy in the manner in which they so sharply depart from the rhythmic repetitiveness of liturgy. I suggest to you that the more liturgical the worship, the greater the blast. Conversely, the less liturgical the worship, the fewer the fireworks, except, in the case of evangelical preaching, the verbal kind.[6]

Thus far in our consideration of pilgrimage, we have examined how individual pilgrims create a sense of presence through touching, bequeathing, and securing objects infused with the sacred for the trip home. We have also reported how local residents further establish presence by carrying the shrine figure on a cycle of rounds during which music and fireworks mark the extraordinary nature of the occasion. Remaining to be tied in is my earlier thought that people leaving objects at the site of tragedies seems connected to these activities. To prepare the path to make that connection, let me take a detour to Honduras.

In the older, colonial regions of that Central American country, two communities with established ties of reciprocity take their respective patron saints

6. Please see Needham's note on Maurice Freeman's study of Chinese firecrackers (Needham 1967).

out in procession to visit each other. Riding on the shoulders of their townspeople, the two saints meet approximately half the distance between the two towns and exchange greetings. In some cases, the saints are said to be sweethearts, and if so, they may exchange kisses. Eventually, festivities concluded, the saints return to their respective *iglesias*. The festival of exchange is called *guancasco* (Chapman 1986).

The *guancasco* reciprocity is a reciprocity between communities conceptualized iconically as the interaction of patron saints. The reciprocity brings to the forefront the nature of shrine figures and the objects that are placed before them. The shrine figures and the objects achieve their presence by becoming social. They carry in their physical makeup relationships among people. And it is this relationship that allows us to see the connection between the actions of pilgrims and people leaving objects at places where death has unexpectedly struck or at locations such as the Vietnam Veterans Memorial, where death is inscribed in names.

First, I point out to you that the shrines at Esquipulas and at Buga, as well as many others throughout Spanish America, also have to do with tragedy. The God that hangs above those altars, the crucified Christ, is dead. His skin has turned black. He is dark with death. And the tomb awaits. Wait, wait, I hear you say. What about Mary? What about her shrines, the one in Costa Rica, for example? She is not dead. No, to be sure. But Mary suffers. She suffers the crucifixion of her son. The saints? The shrines to saints are also to those who suffered and died. One exception to my admittedly outrageous equation is shrines devoted to the Christ Child, to the Niño, such as the Niño de Atocha in Plateros. This exception takes on a new light if we remind ourselves that the Niño, Christ as a child, is alive. At Plateros and further north, in Chimayó, New Mexico, he walks about at night and so constantly needs new shoes. Christ on the cross, Christ as a man, is dying or is already dead. Can we see in the Niño the life of a child that must end when the child matures? Are the two icons bound together in some semiotic manner? Does one point to the other? But let me proceed.

In the face of tragedy, we offer gifts. As pilgrims, we are both giver and receiver of gifts. We bring objects to the shrine of tragedy; we take away objects that commemorate our offering. Our journey to the shrine, our viewing of it, our fulfilling the vow we made, our offering of objects, our touching of the shrine, all bestow power. Having bestowed power through our gifts—the gift of our journey, the gift of our objects—we now receive power. What power do we receive? The power to deny the event that would destroy us. The power to create meaning in the face of denial. The power to sustain the precious bond between you and me. The power to be in the world alongside one another. The power to be human. The power to put death in its place. The gift of the Neandertal.

Pilgrimages end, of course. The pilgrim returns home, exhausted, refreshed, full of wonder, to a world where illnesses strike, accidents happen, and husbands wander. We discover once more what we already knew but set aside during our journey, that the world of the everyday, the world of being-in-place in our conventional mode, so embraces us in its everydayness that we accept it as our primary reality. Meanwhile, death, being a thief in the night, leaves the place from where we put it and sneaks its way upstairs to enter our room of the ordinary and habitual. Listen. Can't you hear the stairs squeak?

In the South, there are no Southern Baptist holy places. Here in the land of religious fervor, the Bible Belt no less, the landscape is amazingly secular. If you travel from Texas to Virginia, you will not find one Southern Baptist shrine. Very occasionally, you will find locations, such as Belmont Abbey, North Carolina, in which a religious order has established a shrine based on a much more famous European one, in this case, Our Lady of Lourdes. Also, there are places, again widely scattered, where people report having seen visions, most commonly of the Virgin Mary. Some of these, such as Tickfaw, Louisiana, have roots in the local Catholic community; others, such as Conyers, Georgia, are apparently just there, without direct ties to local Catholic populations. None of these have the Southern Baptist stamp of approval; on the contrary, most Southern Baptists, believing that God reveals himself through the Scriptures, consider shrines as only one step removed from idolatry, if that.

To be sure, we do find places in the South that possess a shrinelike quality. One of these is Natchez, Mississippi. Self-consciously employing the word *pilgrimage*, the city seeks to entice people to travel to Natchez to marvel at the glories of the antebellum world. Ladies in hoop-skirted gowns welcome tourists, and not only Southern Baptists, into pre–Civil War Greek-Revival mansions and into the time "where the Old South still lives." So successful has been the effort that other historic towns throughout the South have established their own pilgrimages. Clearly oriented toward the tourist dollar, these pilgrimages nonetheless carry a connotation of the mythic South, the sacred South, the South of the Lost Cause. In recent years, with the rise to power of the former slaves of that South, the myth of the Lost Cause, of a South crucified and ennobled by a war it lost, has been increasingly difficult to sustain. Promoters, sensitive to such issues, have moved away from such explicit ties to the Old Confederacy and toward a "Parade of Homes" motif.[7]

And, of course, there is Graceland. Tours through this Memphis home of the King of Rock and Roll takes thousands of people daily from room to room in the mansion, out past the garage, around the grounds, and to the final stop, the Meditation Garden, where Elvis Presley lies buried among members of his family. The area is full of items (flowers, for the most part) that people have left or sent. There is no mistaking the continued fame, and the continuing ability to make money, of this singer from Tupelo, Mississippi. But for me and for all of those like me who remember where we were on January 1, 1953, a grave of much greater significance is the one on a hill in Montgomery, Alabama, the final resting place of Hank Williams.[8]

In the absence of, and in the disdain for, holy places, Southern Baptists do have a special service, the revival, that seeks to refresh the ordinary Sunday schedule. In the same manner that the pilgrimage experience has an out-of-place quality to it that contrasts with the in-place attributes of the weekday mass, so revivals seek to bring to the home church an extraordinary quality

7. And you tell me that on the Internet you find that the Spring Pilgrimage also includes "The Southern Road to Freedom," a musical tribute to the African American experience in Natchez. So they are covering all the bases.

8. Some, no doubt for good reasons, resist the idea that Hank is dead. David Allan Coe, better known as "The Mysterious Rhinestone Cowboy," sings how one cold night on the road, a man in '50s Cadillac gave him a ride. The driver was gaunt and hollow-eyed, but something kept coming back to Coe, like he knew the man. Just before they got to Nashville, the driver stopped and said this was as far as he could go. As Coe got out, he said, "Thanks for the ride, mister." And the driver replied, "Don't call me mister, mister. The whole world calls me Hank."

Another case of a loyal disbeliever is the narrator of a story titled "Hank Williams, You Wrote My Life," a title taken, incidentally, from a song by Moe Bandy, apparently also a fellow resister. The narrator, whose status-aspiring wife dumps him for a man more suitable to her station—and a "smart-talkin' nigger" at that—also takes to the road in a '50s Caddy, but he ends his story thus: "It's close to midnight now. I'm just south of the Mississippi line, heading north to Nashville. I got the back filled with Blue Ribbon and the front with J.D. I'm going to drive this thing until I find Hank or disappear myself, whichever comes first." The last I heard the narrator was still on the road. A Caddy filled with Blue Ribbon beer and Jack Daniels bourbon will take a man a long way. (See Richardson 1986a.)

of religious passion, which means, of course, the conversion of the lost and damned. In the past, churches in towns serving rural areas, such as the First Baptist in Mt. Hope, would schedule their revival after the crops were "laid by," after the last plowing and fertilizing, but before the harvest, which meant July, August, and early September. For the preaching, the church would search for a well-known evangelist but usually one who had his own church. To help with the singing, the evangelist might bring his own music director. Throughout the week, beginning on one Sunday and ending on the next, both in the morning and again at night, in gesture and in word, the evangelist would rail against the pleasures of this world and praise the joys of the next.

Today, revivals are less common. One author observes that two-week "revival meetings with preaching in the morning and evening of each day have generally given way to one-week preaching meetings with only evening services, and these, in turn, are giving way to half-week preaching meetings or week-end revivals." The hurry-up schedules of modern life, the distances from suburbia to the downtown churches, and the materialism of the day are cited as causes for the decline. Yet the same author insists that "even when the number of converts is small, many churches find revival preaching a vital source of spiritual renewal for the church members" (Cotey 1971, 1917). And in Baton Rouge, Louisiana, advertisements at least occasionally appear in the church news section of the paper urging the reader to "come hear this man. Hearing him could change your life." And the message of the visiting revivalist continues to be "you can be a good person, even a good Southern Baptist, and still not be saved. If you are not saved, you will live forever in hell. If you deny Christ, you doom yourself to torment."

The miracle that the evangelist seeks is the miracle of conversion. In the same manner that the regular pastor tells of his own conversion as a way of dramatizing his message, so too the evangelist offers his story. Since the evangelist may be famous, at least in Southern Baptist circles, the miracle of his conversion is even more miraculous. Reverend Rick Stanley came to Baton Rouge at the invitation of Parkview Baptist Church to preach, and as expected, his conversion was the centerpiece of his sermon. People were especially attentive because Reverend Stanley was Elvis Presley's stepbrother. He provided the congregation with images of his touring with Elvis as Elvis's personal aide. In time, drugs became a major part of his daily existence. When Elvis died, those in charge of Graceland handed him his belongings in a garbage bag and pointed him toward the door. He hit bottom hard. One day, he heard a surfer-turned-minister preach, and just as that person had turned his life around through the grace of Jesus Christ, so he too found the new path though rebirth in Christ. He finished his education, graduated from Southwestern Baptist Theological Seminary in Fort Worth, Texas, and became a messenger for the Lord. Everywhere he goes, people want to hear about Elvis, and he tells them that he is doing what Elvis always wanted to do, preach. "People don't know the spiritual side of Elvis. He always wanted God to answer, 'Why me?'" (*Advocate*, 17 May 1997).

Mass revivals, in contrast to the most modest but regular church-centered ones, are part of American history. As we found in Chapter 2, the Great Awakening of 1740–1742 and the Second Awakening in the early 1800s shaped American Christianity away from highly liturgical churches toward the more evangelical ones such as the Methodists and the Baptists. Famous evangelists are likewise a common feature in American, and Southern Baptist, "hagiography." There were Isaac Backus, John Wesley, and George Whitefield in earlier days; in more recent times, Charles Finney, a Presbyterian, who came down from the pill-box pulpit to preach without notes directly to his congregation; Dwight L. Moody, a Congregationalist, who moved evangelism from the confines of church buildings to the larger arenas of theaters and tents; and George W. Truett, a Southern Baptist, whose silver tongue and impassioned zeal made the First Baptist Church in Dallas, Texas, the largest Baptist congregation in the United States (see Leavell 1958). And now there is Billy Graham.

Or perhaps I should say, Now, there remains Billy Graham. Whatever you or I or his critics think of him, we have to admire his staying power. While others have fallen, victims of greed and sexual passion, Dr. Graham has kept to the course. In so doing, he has moved from just a notch above being a hillbilly preacher to becoming the spiritual advisor of presidents. Some might even, in a moment of unabashed enthusiasm, compare him to the pope. Without a doubt, he has become an icon, in the fashionable sense of the word. In Spanish America, we find in the many shrines that adorn the landscape, actual, physically real icons. In the American South—and here perhaps we can speak broadly of the United States in general—we find a man who, through speaking the Scriptures, has become a metaphorical icon. The one in Spanish America, after we have traveled some distance in the company of others, we can touch; the one in the United States, after we have turned on our television sets, we can listen to. In Spanish America, we see sacred shrines; in the South, we hear inspired words.

One additional pilgrimagelike occurrence needs our attention: the complex of homecomings, family reunions, all-day singing, and brush-arbor preaching commonly highlighted by "dinner on the grounds." Every summer, throughout the region, but particularly in the upland South, people not infrequently return home to the rural community where they were born and to the church where they were saved. On the Sunday after church services, under the friendly shade of a sprawling oak, the female members of the closely tied families lay out a feast of fried chicken, potato salad, and ice tea on planks laid over sawhorses and covered with tablecloths. Singing, before the meal and continuing afterward, may feature semiprofessional quartets invited for the occasion, or given the number of good voices in families of any size, the gathered crowd will harmonize a capella, and the haunting sounds of "Amazing grace, how sweet the sound, that saved a wretch like me" rise to mingle among the green leaves of the sheltering oak (Malone 1989). Some groups take hoes and weed cutters to the cemetery on the hill next to the church and scrape the ground clean. A few may still practice the custom of lining the graves with shell. Others, yielding to fashion, mow the grass allowed to grow over the graves and place plastic flowers by the headstones. Fences are repaired, and broken limbs of the evergreen cedars near the entrance are removed (Jeane 1989).

Brush-arbor preaching, probably a lineal descendant of the nineteenth-century camp meeting, is also a time for reunions, but here the families meet annually at a campground where they have erected shelters surrounding the arbor. In earlier days, the arbor was an open-air structure roofed with brush piled high; nowadays roofing material of one type or another has replaced the brush, but the structure commonly remains open on all sides. Preaching follows the style of a church revival but is more free flowing, with the congregation more ready to testify about "the day Jesus came into my life."

Why do I insist on calling this complex of events "pilgrimagelike," you ask with notable exasperation. Why not just call it pilgrimage and be done with it? Why not indeed? Carole Hill reports that one of her informants told her that here on the campground, "It is as if God is with me in a closer way than during the rest of the year" (1982, 40). She also relates a narrative of a boy who fell sick at the campground and was rushed to the doctor. As he lay near death, people on the grounds prayed that he be healed. He recovered completely, and each year now he repeats his story, and at his testimonial, others are converted. Why not call it a pilgrimage? In fact, Gwen Neville calls this complex exactly that term but with a modifier.

Neville (1987) describes Christianity in the South as the Christianity of North European Protestantism that arose in opposition to the established church of Roman, Mediterranean Christianity. In contrast to the compact, hierarchical society of classical heritage, particularly in the South among the plain folk, the basic social unit was the scattered, rural community, which we encountered in Chapter 2. Pilgrimage in the Roman, Mediterranean tradition is movement outward, away from the urban center, away from home, to a sacred place located in the peripheries. In contrast, in the South, pilgrimage is the exact opposite. It is movement inward, toward home, back to the crossroads church where we were saved and baptized, back to the location where the now-dispersed members of the family come together for singing, feasting, grave cleaning, and open-air preaching. Just as North European Christianity came about in opposition to Mediterranean Christianity, so too pilgrimage among Protestants arose in counterpoint to the Catholic form. Consequently, Protestant pilgrimage is pilgrimage turned on its head; it is inverted pilgrimage.

I agree with you that Neville's presentation of the complex of homecomings, reunions, singing, and preaching is especially insightful. She brilliantly underscores the difference between the Eucharist meal, in which individuals in series each accept the Body of Christ offered by the priest (a two-party exchange), and "dinner on the grounds," in which the gathered community shares the food that each adult woman has brought (a communal event). Whether we call it pilgrimagelike or inverted pilgrimage, it is important that we do justice to what is going on.

Both pilgrimage and inverted pilgrimage feature movements, physically and socially, from the everyday world to an extraordinary one. Yet pilgrims in Spanish America travel in the company of others who frequently are strangers, while travelers in an inverted pilgrimage travel in a group of kin. At the location, pilgrims in Spanish America encounter visually and tactually a sacred object that was there, at least as an artifact, before they arrived and with which they create a dyadic relationship. In contrast, in inverted pilgrimages, travelers come together as a group at a location where they bring about the extraordinary through communal voicing. There are no icons; the sacred is in the word, not in the touch. Pilgrimages in Spanish America, while they peak on a particular day fixed in a liturgical calendar, continue throughout the year. In the South, inverted pilgrimages are once-a-year events. Why go to the brush arbor in January when it is cold and nobody is there? In sum, (1) the sacred enjoys an external, physical presence in Spanish America, while in the South it resides in an internal, verbal place; and (2) the social relationship in the Spanish American pilgrimage is a dyadic, two-party exchange, while in the inverted pilgrimage of the South, the social relationship is congregational. Thus, pilgrimages in Spanish America fit into the dyadic Christworld of the touch, while the complex of reunions, singing, and preaching are part of the congregational Christworld of the word.

As part of the Christworld of the word, tellingly, the most common, principal use of pilgrimage among Southern Baptists is as a metaphor. At least for the remaining plain-folk component of the denomination, life itself is a pilgrimage with the journey headed toward Glory. Many songs recount how we are traveling the road to Beulah land, but my favorite is "I Am a Pilgrim." It is best sung in the clinched-voice, high-lonesome style of Bill Monroe's Blue Grass Quartet, with the bass coming in on "Good Lordy, and it's not."

One verse goes like this:

> I am a pilgrim and a stranger
> traveling through this wearisome land.
> I got home in that yonder city, Good Lord,
> and it is not (Good Lordy, and it's not) not made by hands.

El Niño de Dios and Santa Claus

In Spanish America, Christmas, *La Navidad*, the Birth (of Christ), might best be described as one of several feasts occurring toward the end of the old year and the beginning of the new. Starting in November, important dates throughout the region are *Todos los santos*, All Saints Day, on November 1, and *El Día de los Difuntos*, the Day of the Deceased, or All Souls Day, on November 2. In Mexico, two days tend to merge into a single *El Día de los Muertos*, the Day of the Dead, which begins on the evening of October 31 and continues through November 2. The occasion has become so popular with tourists that at the more celebrated places, the camcorders outnumber the candles. Knowledgeable observers draw a distinction between the participants' attitudes toward death and their attitudes toward the dead. In the first, in the dancing figures of papier-mâché skeletons or in the sweet taste of the candy skulls, death, Most Holy Death, *La Santísima Muerte*, is mocked; the Grim Reaper becomes domesticated into a joke. In the second, both at the cemetery, where flowers decorate the tombs, and at home, where an altar composed of food is set up for the departed, the beloved dead of the family are honored. Notwithstanding efforts at indigenization of the Day of the Dead, to root the activities in Aztec or even earlier Toltec practices, much of what goes on derives from European, popular Catholicism (Carmichael and Sayer 1991, Hernandez and Hernandez 1979). Be that as it may, in the feeding of the dead, we see once again the physical embodiment of the Spanish American sacred.

Immediately following All Souls Day is the feast on November 3 honoring San Martín de Porres. While not true of every *iglesia*, you recall the one at Nueva Esperanza has an altar to him along one of its walls. Many families in Nueva Esperanza and elsewhere keep his picture in their homes. He was born at the end of the sixteenth century in Lima, Peru, the son of a Spanish nobleman and a mulatto woman. During his lifetime as a Dominican friar, the poor and afflicted came to him in great numbers, and he healed them with his accumulated knowledge and by laying on his hands. It is said that he conversed with the rats in his cell and shared his meals with them, since they too were God's creatures. Shortly after his death in 1639, people began to receive help from him in their daily struggles. In recognition of his miracles, he was canonized as a saint in 1962. He is one of the very few Latin American saints and the only one of African descent.

In early December, on the 8th, the Feast of the Immaculate Conception is a major liturgical event. The belief that Mary herself was free of Original Sin and therefore was the perfect and divine instrument for the earthly birth of God, appeared among the Christian faithful during the Middle Ages. The Franciscan religious order in particular enthusiastically promoted this veneration of Mary, and in their efforts they received royal support from Isabel and Ferdinand, the Catholic monarchs of Spain. Due to opposition within the church, however, only in the nineteenth century, in 1854, did the Catholic hierarchy make it a part of church dogma. The common representation of the Immaculate Conception as a woman standing on a crescent moon with a sprinkling of stars about her comes from Revelation 12, in which there appears to the narrator of these last things a vision of a pregnant woman wrapped in the sun's rays as in a blanket and with the moon at her feet. On her head she wears a crown with twelve stars. At times, as in Figure 29, which is based on a Flemish painting popular in Seville, Spain, in the late sixteenth century, she is depicted as standing on top of the dragon that, in the text, threatens to devour her child as soon as it is born (Stratton 1994).

Quickly following the Immaculate Conception, on December 12, comes the Feast of the Virgin of Guadalupe. Given the religious importance of the

FIG. 29. The apocalyptic woman of Revelation as the Immaculate Conception. This is a Flemish painting, popular in Seville, Spain, in the late sixteenth century. From Stratton (1994, 60).

feast and the issues raised in its celebration, we must pause our journey through the liturgical calendar and consider this devotion to the Virgin in some detail.

We begin our deliberation by noting that while officially designated as the Empress of the Americas, the Virgin of Guadalupe is most closely identified with Mexico. Everywhere, and especially among Mexican immigrants to the United States, her presence announces *mexicanidad*, the essence of being *mexicano*. One might well venture the opinion that her feast rivals the people's participation in *La Navidad*, the birth of Christ. And it is true that millions travel to the new basilica we encountered in Chapter 3 in an effort to get as close to the Virgin as its modernist design permits.

Given her popularity, you can understand the uproar that greeted the allegations that Juan Diego, the Aztec whom the Virgin selected as her messenger back in 1531, may not have existed. In the summer of 1996, the newspapers were full of quotes attributed to Abbot Guillermo Schulemburg, the man in charge of running the basilica, that Juan Diego is best thought of as a symbol and not as a reality. Even more surprising, the abbot's remarks came in the face of Pope John Paul's act of beatifying Juan Diego in 1990. As beatification is the first step toward eventual canonization and sainthood, Abbot Schulemburg seemed to suggest that the pope was promoting sainthood for a nonexistent individual. If such was the case, then the pope's actions appeared to be as much political as religious.

The question of Juan Diego's flesh-and-blood reality and the politics of beatification relate to the larger question of the nature of the Virgin of Guadalupe and of Spanish American Catholicism. Earlier, when we were talking about pilgrimages, I mentioned the somewhat unholy eagerness of theorists and critics to find "idols behind altars." Nowhere do we find that eagerness more intense than with the patroness of Mexico.

A widely held belief among many people, both Catholic and Protestant and both layperson and scholar, is that the Virgin of Guadalupe is a syncretic blend of indigenous beliefs and Catholic concepts. She is said to be both Mary of Bethlehem and Tonantzin, the so-called mother goddess of the Aztec. Among scholars, and in particular among our anthropological colleagues, the conviction that the Virgin of Guadalupe (and, by extension, Catholicism in Spanish America) is a composite blend of indigenous and Iberian cultures carries great ideological freight. The conviction rests on the concept, developed in the United States between the world wars, in the heyday of Boasian anthropology, that particular cultural traditions have great longevity and staying power, even, or especially, among conquered people. It suggests that Native American cultures have a resilience that has allowed them over the centuries to resist and to outsmart Christian, European domination. Similarly, a theological interpretation, current in liberation circles, sees the Virgin of Guadalupe as an authentic symbol of *indigenismo*, of New World nativism, enduring in the face of Spanish cruelty and exploitation. She is the Indian who evangelizes the Spaniard, the woman who instructs the male-dominated church and the conquered who vanquishes the conqueror (as summarized in Poole 1995; see also Elizondo 1986 and Rodriguez 1994).[9]

Nearly all, both conservative anthropologists and radical theologians, concur that the Virgin is one symbol, perhaps the only one, that unites the Mexican people, that brings together the Indian and the white, the poor and the rich, the weak and the powerful into a national identity whose spirituality remains triumphant in the face of threats by the secular giant to the north. In sum, she is a startling presence, and who is to doubt her power? Certainly not you and I. Yet we must confront the overwhelming evidence that the claim she is a syncretic blend of Tonantzin and Mary with roots in pre-Columbian culture is, in fact, a recent creation driven by the compelling concerns of a modern Mexico. In addition, a consideration of evidence will provide an opportunity to emphasize a pervasive theme of this text: that our beliefs, even when lodged in the past, draw their strengths from the manner in which they address today's dilemmas. Furthermore, the consideration will reveal an unexpected power of the visual sacred to be inclusive, to reach out to diverse worshipers, while the verbal sacred, in pursuit of pristine holiness, hurries to draw boundaries that exclude the lost from the saved.

9. Boasian anthropology refers to the classic period in American anthropology in which the many brilliant students of Franz Boas, people such as Alfred Kroeber, Robert Lowie, Ruth Benedict, and Melville Herskovits, argued that culture, generally defined as a distinctive way of life, shaped the actions of individuals. They stressed culture as being deeply rooted in the past, with contemporary activities and beliefs branching upward from distant origins. Consequently, the explanation of what we do and value is to be sought in cultural traditions. Today, anthropologists, or at least many of them, including me and, I hope, you, see culture as the webs of significance that we ourselves have spun (Geertz 1973) or, perhaps even better, that we ourselves spin now, even, and especially, as we talk. Culture addresses issues of the right now, even if it does so in the language of the past. To give it a label, this view of culture is "constructivist" (Bruner 1994).

We begin our deliberation of the avowed Tonantzin-Mary syncretism by pointing out that no single mother goddess ruled Aztec cosmology. Rather, in accordance with Aztec duality, paired male and female figures permeated the cosmos. The female side included Cihuacoatl (Female Serpent), Yaocihuatl (Warrior Woman), and Coatlicue (She of the Skirt of Serpents). While these possessed positive attributes associated with fertility, they also had unpleasant, even monstrous, devouring aspects. Related to birth and the womb, they also evoked death and the grave (Burkhart 1993; Burland 1967; León-Portilla 1963, 1992).

Not only did the Aztec not have a single mother goddess, but the name "Tonantzin" best translates "our reverend mother." As such, it is honorific, not the proper name of any particular figure (Bierhorst 1985; Burkhart 1993). Furthermore, Tonantzin is a Nahuatl word, the language spoken by the Nahuas, the people who created the Aztec empire. Despite centuries of exposure to Spanish, Nahuatl speakers in contemporary Mexico number over 1,000,000, an impressive figure, but what of other Native Americans living in today's Mexico who do not speak Nahuatl? What about those who speak Yucateco, who reckon over 700,000 on the Yucatán Peninsula, or the more than 400,000 speakers of Zapoteco who live in the region of the state of Oaxaca, south of Mexico City, or the Mixtec, the Otomí, or the Chol? The list goes on (Lastra 1998). These people, if they know the word *Tonantzin*, learned it as a foreign word, as foreign a word to their native language as the word *María*, not to mention Mary.[10]

Tonantzin, we might opine, is a multifaceted, multivocalic figure whose attributes scarcely coincide with those of Mary, herself by no means a one-dimensional female. So, for Tonantzin to become Mary, people have to work at it. To work at it, they have to be terribly enthusiastic about the connection. Their enthusiasm comes straight and pure, not from an ancient tradition, but from recent preoccupations generated by contemporary societal conflicts. Indeed, the eagerness to establish the Tonantzin connection comes subsequent

10. In considering why among the numerous indigenous groups in Mexico, the Nahuas have persisted in occupying the central position in contemporary nation building, León-Portilla observes, "Although the Nahua narratives of divine intervention and triumph over impossible odds are only marginally connected to the origin myths of many Mexicans, such as the Maya, the Zapotec, and other non-Nahuatl-speaking peoples, the continued postcontact centralization of power in the area once controlled by the Nahuas has transformed the tale of the rise and fall of the Mexicas [the Aztec rulers] into the story of Mexico's collective past" (1992, xv).

to the development of the shrine to the Virgin of Guadalupe. In other words, the Virgin of Guadalupe was first the Christian Mary, and only later did she become the Nahuatl Tonantzin; rather than being a Native American goddess with Christian dressing, she was first Christian and then took on Aztec garments. The history of the shrine, drawn from Poole (1995), Burkhart (1993), Lockhart (1992), and Taylor (1985, 1987), makes this pattern clearer.

By the middle of the sixteenth century the Spaniards in their colony of New Spain had established a shrine at Tepeyac, the hill where the present shrine stands. The shrine was erected in veneration of the Nativity of the Blessed Virgin Mary and celebrated on September 8, the same date as the Guadalupe shrine in Spain. Contrary to the widely held opinion of today that the Spanish religious orders promoted syncretism as a strategy to make their evangelical efforts more palpable, the Franciscans, at least, vigorously opposed the shrine at Tepeyac because they feared the Indians might lapse into idolatry. The shrine became popular among the Spaniards, and during the feast, large crowds gathered in front. Upper-class women approached the shrine barefoot, and many walked the length of the chapel on their knees. Yet nothing in the accounts of the day suggests any large-scale Indian participation. Likewise, in contrast to the oft-repeated assertion that Tepeyac was a holy place before Hernando Cortés arrived, little evidence exists to indicate the hill had any special meaning to the indigenous population. In the centuries following the conquest, the devout among the native people reasoned that since the hill was special to Mary, it must have been holy in pre-Christian times; they adjusted their pre-Columbian past to fit with their present circumstances.

Some time prior to the seventeenth century, the painting of the Virgin that we now see in the basilica was placed in the shrine. Both the figure in Spain and the one in Mexico are dark. However, beyond skin color, little artistically connects the image of the Mexican Virgin with the one in Spain. Yet the painting follows a standard iconography of the time: the Virgin is with child, hands folded, head slightly bowed, eyes looking to her right, and a crescent moon beneath her feet, in brief, an image similar to the depictions of the Immaculate Conception (Figure 30). The association of the Nativity of the Virgin with the Immaculate Conception was common throughout the colonial period. The date of devotion eventually changed from September to December, but when that shift occurred is not known. The September date continued to be observed as late as 1797.

Fig. 30. The Virgin of Guadalupe

In 1648, a Spanish Creole, Miguel Sánchez, published an account in which he describes the miraculous appearance in 1531 of the Virgin to an Indian called Juan Diego. This is the earliest written account. A few months later another Creole, Luis Laso de la Vega, published an account in Nahuatl.

These two accounts are the bases for all subsequent versions. During the seventeenth and eighteenth centuries, the veneration of the Virgin of Guadalupe and the story of her miraculous appearance to Juan Diego became increasingly popular among the Creoles, who were European whites of Spanish descent born in the New World. As they grew in number and found their advancement blocked by favoritism to the European-born, they became increasingly estranged from their peninsular rulers. In the face of Old World arrogance, they began to see themselves as a chosen people, a new race in a new world, and as proof they pointed to the Virgin of Guadalupe. The Mother of God had elected to appear in their capital; she had blessed them with her presence. The triumphant narrative in Revelation 12, in which the dragon that threatened the Virgin's child is defeated, became their own story of predestined success. The popularity of the Virgin of Guadalupe among native people also increased, but for many of them, she remained a less central figure than the saints.

Although Father Miguel Hidalgo, "The Father of Mexican Independence," is said to have carried the emblem of the Virgin of Guadalupe in his battles against the Spaniards in 1810, William Taylor (1985, 1987) points out that Father Hidalgo planned his initial armed revolt to occur not on the feast of Guadalupe but on the date of another Virgin, the one of San Juan de los Lagos in western Mexico near the city of Guadalajara. He adds that the widespread attachment to the Virgin of Guadalupe may have emerged as a consequence of the mobilization in the wars for independence rather than as a motivating force for the revolt. Louise Burkhart (1993) goes even further to suggest that it was not until the Revolution of 1910, with its call for massive social restructuring and its promotion of *mexicanidad*, Mexican nativism, that the Virgin emerged as the embodiment of national identity that she now is.[11]

All right, you demand in a most exasperated tone, Tell me again what the point of this extended digression into the origins of the Virgin of Guadalupe

11. Both the Virgin of Guadalupe and the Virgin of San Juan de los Lagos are iconically tied to the Immaculate Conception. The emergence of the Guadalupe shrine as the national shrine and the acceptance of the apparition story as historically accurate reflect the continuation of Mexico City as the center of the Mexican state. Nonetheless, while the Virgin of Guadalupe enjoys national prominence, the Virgin of San Juan de los Lagos seems to have a regional popularity that extends northward to the Rio Grande and beyond. In town of San Juan, near McAllen, Texas, she takes up residence in a massive shrine and, as the Virgin of San Juan of the Valley, she becomes the object of devotion to people throughout the Texas region known as "The Valley."

is? Is it somehow to cast doubt on the Virgin's power? Again I repeat, Far from it. As you well know, people's faith rests upon foundations sufficiently firm to prevail against the feeble words of an anthropologist. Instead, let me repeat that the case of the Virgin of Guadalupe exemplifies the argument of this text, that our beliefs, even when lodged in the past, draw their strengths from the manner in which they address today's dilemmas. That being the case, let me also ask you a question: Why don't the Baptists in the American South lay claim that their Christ is partly Cherokee or Choctaw or Creek? But, you exclaim with even more exasperation, the Indians in the South never obtained the numbers present in Spanish America. That may well be, I reply in turn, but it's not a question of numbers. What about the Africans in the South? The percentage of African Americans in certain counties in the South exceeds any figure for Native Americans in Spanish America. Why don't Southern Baptists say their Christ is basically Yoruba or Dahomey or Ashanti, with a European overlay? The reason is clear. The ideological thrusts of the two regions travel in totally different directions. In Spanish America, at least among a certain segment of the population, there is a recent effort to draw strength from Native American peoples; in the American South, there is a long-term effort to deny strength to the African Americans.

Furthermore, the different ideological aspirations relate the differential manner in which the sacred comes to be in the two areas. In Spanish America the sacred appears in physical, sensuous form. Such a shaping of the sacred allows people to attribute diverse origins to a particular image. This is the power of the icon; it is inclusive. Native American and mestizo, orthodox and liberationist, altar boy and the pope see their own questions in the Virgin's eyes. In the American South, however, the sacred is verbal. For the sacred to be, people must speak to one another and, concomitantly, not speak to others or deny those others the right to speak. Thus, the power of the word is exclusive. Jesus himself said, "And ye shall be hated of all men for my name's sake: but he that endureth to the end shall be saved" (Matthew 10:22), and, more tellingly, "He that is not with me is against me" (Luke 11:23).

To end this brief exploration on how people take up the past of others for reasons distant to that past, let me quote Burkart's concluding words to her own consideration of this famous personage: "The story of a shimmering Virgin who appears to a humble Indian holds tremendous possibilities for present and future devotions; the people of Mexico continue to explore these possibilities" (1993, 221). With these words resounding before us in their own shimmering, let us return to our journey through the liturgical calendar.

As December 25 approaches, in continuation of a custom apparently begun by St. Francis of Assisi in the thirteenth century, manger scenes, called variously *pesebres*, *nacimientos*, and, my favorite, *belenes* ("Bethlehems") appear. These scenes recreate the event in Bethlehem when Joseph and his pregnant wife, turned away from all the inns, found shelter in a stable. People erect them at home, but the faithful may also create ones alongside the altar in their churches. In the past, talented members of the community carved the figures of José, María, and El Niño, as some still do in the small towns of northern New Mexico (Briggs 1980). Now, of course, people can buy paper cut-outs or plastic models from the local department store. In Guatemala, however, a special touch may be added by dressing Mary in *traje*, the highly embroidered dress of the Maya (Samson 1997). In addition to the manger scenes, families in some countries, such as Colombia, may put up an *arbol de la Navidad*, a tree of the nativity, or, if you prefer, a Christmas tree. But the tree bears absolutely no resemblance to the dense evergreen of North America. It is a small bush from which all the bark has been removed, and on it one might hang ornaments, such as angels, but never icicles!

In Antigua, Guatemala, each night during the nine days before December 25, processions reenact Joseph and Mary's trip to Bethlehem. Led by Mary on a burro with Joseph at the reins and singing *villancicos*, "carols," the crowd moves through the streets toward a previously designated house where it asks for shelter. At first, the family inside denies them admission, but upon hearing the couple are the parents of the Savior, the family invites the crowd in and offers refreshments. The next night it is another family's turn to act as host. The processions range in size, but the larger ones bring along a marimba to accompany the singing and send off rockets into the night sky (Alvarez Aragón 1982; Alvarez Arévalo 1980).

The night before Christmas day, *la Nochebuena*, "the Good Night," families frequently attend midnight mass, *la misa de gallo*, "the rooster mass." In the plaza, first launched shortly before midnight, giant rockets explode with cannonlike force continuously for a full thirty minutes (Samson 1997). *La Nochebuena* also is the night that El Niño himself brings presents to children. While Santa Claus has penetrated Spanish America to a much greater degree than has the Easter bunny, the North American man of good cheer with his eight tiny reindeer, led by Rudolph and his lanternlike red nose, still takes the back seat to El Niño. El Niño literally means "the boy child," but here, of course, it is the Christ Child. So when El Niño comes on *la Nochebuena*, we have the somewhat perplexing image of the Christ Child bringing gifts in honor of his own birth. But El Niño is not a helpless infant, newly born, a baby Jesus, as it were, but rather an individual. He is El Niño de Dios, "The Child of God," and as we have seen in Chapter 3 in connection with the shrine at Plateros, Mexico, he combines the charm of an infant with the intellectual and physical powers associated with adults. Given such a combination, he is surely capable of bringing gifts to his own birthday.

On the other side of Christmas, the cycle of feasts continues. December 28 is *el Día de los Inocentes*, "the Day of the Innocent Ones." As told in San Mateo, upon hearing that in Bethlehem there had been born the King of the Jews and he himself being the presiding king of the Jews, "Herod se enfureció muchísimo, y mandó mater a todos los niños varones de dos años abajo que se hallaran en Belén; Herod became furious and ordered killed all male children two years and younger that might be found in Bethlehem" (San Mateo 2:16). But an angel of the Lord had earlier appeared in Joseph's dreams and warned him of the danger, so Joseph fled with Mary and her child into Egypt, where they were safe from Herod's fury. Perhaps our remembrance on December 28 of the innocent children slain by a ruler enamored with his own power speaks to all of those occasions when parents find their children taken from them by those who speak so authoritatively of "duty," "patriotism," and, naturally, "sacrifice."

January 1 brings in the New Year, but on the heels of that celebration comes January 6, *el Día de los Reyes*, "the Day of the Three Kings." *El Día de los Reyes* "reigns" much more prominently in Spanish America than in North America. The image of three kings coming to bring gifts to an infant born in a barn strikes a chord in Spanish America that it doesn't north of the Rio Grande. North of the border, among the Southern Baptists, the three are better known as the Three Wisemen and appear only in manger scenes during the festivities occurring before December 25. In Spanish America, however, the three arrive as distinct persons: Melchor, old and with a flowing beard; Gaspar, young and blonde; and Baltasar, black with a heavy beard. In addition to bringing gifts to the Christ Child, in some locations, such as Puerto Rico, the three bring gifts to the children of the community. On January 6, 1998, the Argentinean minister of industry, commerce, and mines, no doubt in a whimsical moment, reported in the Buenos Aires newspaper *Los*

Andes, that he had asked the three kings to ensure a continual increase in the growth of his country's economy. There was no evidence of their reply (www.losandes.net).

In contrast to Spanish America, where the Nativity of Christ tends to be one feast among many, in the American South and, no doubt, throughout the United States, events such as Halloween and Thanksgiving lead up to and highlight December 25, the most festive time of the year.

Halloween, for most of the country comes on "All Hallows' Eve," the night before November 1, All Saints Day, but in Mt. Hope the city fathers will not hesitate to select another night if October 31 happens to be on Friday, because Fridays in the fall are dedicated to high school football. The date apart, even in Mt. Hope, and elsewhere in the South and the United States, Halloween has taken on a special perplexity of its own. Unlike the Day of the Dead, the main figure is not a skeleton but a female, a witch. She is depicted as thin, with an enormous hook nose, often with a wart on its end. She is dressed in black, crowned with a pointed hat, and placed astride a magical broom that flies her about. Pumpkins, usually an item of low demand, suddenly become sought after. Sculptured in the family kitchen, they turn into miniature glowing heads whose grinning, snag-toothed mouths greet passersby. To be sure, people tack skeletons to their doors, but more commonly, and increasingly so, they adorn their trees with small ghosts, which border on being cute, with big eyes and flowing bodies.

The ghosts appear in people's yards long before October 31, as each year Halloween starts earlier and gets bigger. Some say it now ranks next to Christmas in the number of parties thrown and the sums of money spent on apparel (Neville 1997). People exchange Halloween cards and wish each other "Happy Halloween," whatever that means. While kids still come to the door dressed in scary outfits, shout, "Trick or treat," and accumulate sacks of Halloween candy, grown-ups are taking over. In cities as different as Austin and Baton Rouge, adults parade on designated streets in full costume and party throughout the night.

Where's the religion in Halloween? you rightly wonder. Here in South Louisiana, as you well know, Catholics honor their dead by cleaning the cemeteries, whitewashing the above-ground tombs, and placing flowers at the headstones. Southern Baptists, though, in Louisiana or elsewhere, do not celebrate All Saints Day or All Souls Day. If you ask Reverend Overton at Mt. Hope FBC, he is sure to say, "It's against our religion." While individual members of various churches dress up or hand out trick-or-treats like anyone else, some churches sponsor a fall festival for children with games and prizes but no witches. Certain evangelical groups go even further and decry Halloween as the worship of Satan. During a recent Halloween, members of a nondenominational church in one of Baton Rouge's white-flight suburbs decided to make a stand against the diabolical practice. So they placed crosses in their yards and strung them with lights, so that at night people could see that instead of praising witches and ghosts, they glorified Jesus (*Advocate* 31 October 1997).

Beginning the day after Thanksgiving, the "Holiday Season," as Christmas is more commonly called in these politically sensitive days, is a celebration of consumption. It is a festival of capitalism, featuring "shop 'til you drop" consumerism, an American elaboration that has turned Christmas into a lavish extravaganza. Certainly, the pursuit of gifts to shower upon relatives, friends, office staff, and janitors greatly exceeds the more modest exchanges south of the border. Its fanatical quality has caused one critic to observe, "The circulation of gifts is an attempt to diffuse and circulate the guilt which many if not all feel in their inability to be generous, kind, loving and peaceable on a continuing basis throughout the year" (Cramer 1977, 21). Our fellow anthropologist, Claude Lévi-Strauss, feels called upon to make the professionally obligatory comparison between American gift exchange and potlatch, the ceremonial display and, at times, destruction of valued items in traditional Native American cultures along the northwest coast of the United States and Canada: "The exchange of gifts at Christmas, for a month each year, practised by all social classes, with a sort of sacred ardour, is nothing other than a gigantic *potlatch*, implicating millions of individuals, and the end of which many family budgets are faced with lasting disequilibrium" (1969, 96).

In addition to gifts, it is the season for music, and everywhere the stores resound with "Jingle Bells," even here in South Louisiana, where swamp buggies are much more common than sleighs. Radio personalities looking for laughs program their CDs to play the now well-known, and well-worn, Eartha Kitt's "Santa Baby," Spike Jones's "All I Want for Christmas Is My Two Front Teeth," and Jimmy Boyd's "I Saw Mommy Kissing Santa Claus." And you and I, and the dozen or more like us who can take just so much of the mellow Bing Crosby crooning dreams about a "White Christmas," find solace in Ernest Tubb, the Texas Troubadour, thumping the strings of his Jimmie Rodgers' guitar and singing in his raspy, honky-tonk voice about a Christmas that's done gone lonely.

As December 25 approaches, hometown ballet schools offer *The Nutcracker Suite*, and college choral groups attempt George Frideric Handel's *Messiah*. Churches struggle to break through the orgy of materialism with calls to put "Christ back into Xmas." Reverend Overton, who knows better but cannot resist the temptation, shouts at his congregation, "Xmas declares Christ, our Lord and Savior, is an X, an unknown. It is not Xmas. It is Christmas. Christmas. The day hope came to a wicked earth." In response, nearly every church has a special service during the days before Christmas. Drawing on Luke's narrative of glad tidings (Luke 2:8–14), these may be modest efforts featuring a manger scene of cut-out figures erected on the front lawn and, on the Sunday before December 25, the voices of the church choir. Often, however, the large First Churches and their suburban counterparts dedicate themselves to staging major productions. With orchestra and chorus drawn from local symphonies and university schools of music, the ministers of music put together elaborate pageants. Shepherds hear angels and travel across the stage to Bethlehem. Wise men enter with gifts, while Joseph stands proudly by Mary, who rocks the crib of baby Jesus. (Incidentally, as you quickly point out, none of the three wise men are black.) Live donkeys and sheep add touches of realism, some unwanted, to the nativity story. Among the most extravagant dramatizations is "The Jesus Story" performed by the Colonial Heights Baptist Church in Kingsport, Tennessee. Multimedia projections fill the great hall with luminous scrolls of Scripture in English, French, Spanish, and Korean as actors converge from all sides to form tableaux of biblical scenes (www.jesusstory.com 1997). Still other churches erect "living Christmas trees" with thousands of lights synchronized to the voices of the choir, the members of which are positioned throughout the tree.[12]

12. Although Reverend Overton has shamelessly played on the gullibility of his congregation when he equates the "X" in Xmas with "X the unknown" (in contrast to its being the Greek letter *chi* and, thus, a perfectly hallowed stand-in for Christ), his point about the distance between Christian worship and Christmas receives unexpected support from William Waits's cultural history of gift giving in the United States. Waits argues that religion has played little part in the emergence of modern-day Christmas. "The safest way to determine what is most important to people is to look at how they spend their time, money, and effort, and in the case of the modern Christmas celebration, they have spent it on secular matters. One must not confuse the rationale for the celebration (the celebration of the birthday of Jesus) with what is central to the celebration as indicated by the behavior of the celebrants" (1993, 3). Waits also points out that

Amongst all this splendor, the words from John 1:1–11, read by Reverend Overton from the pulpit at Mt. Hope, sound a somber note:

In the beginning was the Word, and the Word was with God,
and the Word was God. The same was in the beginning with God.
All things were made by him; and without him was not
any thing made that was made.
In him was life; and the life was the light of men.
And the light shineth in darkness; and the darkness comprehended it not.
There was a man sent from God, whose name was John.
The same came for a witness, to bear witness of the Light,
that all men through him, might believe.
He was not that Light, but was sent to bear witness of that Light.
That was the true Light, which lighteth every man that cometh into the world.
He was in the world, and the world was made by him, and the world knew him not.
He came unto his own, and his own received him not.

While some churches hold a candlelight service on Christmas Eve, December 25 itself, particularly if it falls on a weekday, usually finds the Baptist churches empty. It is as if the churches had exhausted themselves on all the pageantry beforehand. On the other side of December 25, the secular celebration continues on through January 1, but the services of the Baptists pretty much return to the regular Sunday service, with obligatory asides from the pulpits about college bowl games. At Mt. Hope, Reverend Overton remarks, "Brother Womack assures me that Alabama is going to make true believers out of Notre Dame at the Sugar Bowl."

Viernes Santo and Sunrise Sunday

La Semana Santa, "Holy Week," dominates the liturgical calendar in Spanish America. All other celebrations, including Christmas, lag behind at a consid-

---

in contrast to the Currier and Ives image of New England at Christmas, the Pilgrim fathers could find no biblical justification for the celebration and thus outlawed its celebration from 1656 to 1681. Even up to the Civil War, December 25 in New England was not a holiday, and children were required to attend school.

In years past, the county commissioners at Mt. Hope regularly used taxpayer money to construct an elaborate manger scene out in front of the courthouse. But eventually the resident atheist called in the American Civil Liberties Union and got a court order from a very reluctant district judge for the county to "cease and desist promoting private religion on public land." But erable distance. Furthermore, the week that begins with *Domingo de los Ramos*, "Palm Sunday," and ends with *Domingo de la Resurreción*, "Resurrection Sunday," reaches its apex on *Viernes Santo*, "Holy Friday," the day Christ died. Even today, notwithstanding the changes introduced by Vatican II and despite the influence of liberation theology, the death of Christ "triumphs," as it were, over his resurrection. Given that Protestant Christianity, and especially Southern Baptists, all but ignore Holy Friday in their eagerness to celebrate the Resurrection on Easter Sunday, the Spanish American preference strikes many as excessively morbid. Thus, it is up to us, you and me, to open the way toward a more ample interpretation of *La Semana Santa*.

Let's begin at the beginning; that is, let's go back to our first *Semana Santa*. You remember? Yes, of course you do. It was in 1963 in San Pedro, Colombia, and I wrote about it later (Richardson [1970] 1986b). But let's get back before the writing, if we can, back to the actual event. Remember? It is a bright, fresh Palm Sunday morning, suitable, you say, for a triumphal march. And before I can stop you, you repeat the account of San Marcos:

> En seguida le llevaron el burro a Jesús, le pusieron encima sus mantos, y lo montó. Muchos tendían sus mantos en el camino, mientras que otros lo tapizaban con ramas de plantas que cortaban de los campos. Los que iban delante y los que venían detrás iban gritando: "Hosanna; bendito sea el que viene en nombre del Señor."
>
> Immediately they took the burro to Jesus, they put their cloaks over it, and Jesus mounted it. Many spread out their cloaks along the road and other carpeted it with plants cut from the fields. Those who went in front and those that followed shouted, "Hosanna! Blessed be the one who comes in the name of the Lord." (San Marcos 11:7–9)

While you are holding forth, the procession tries to organize itself at the church steps. Father Restrepo, the parish priest, and Doña Jaél, the choir mistress, are debating a point of procedure. Doña Jaél jabs an authoritative finger at a small book in her hand, and Father Restrepo responds by looking off into the distance. The crowd of mainly small girls is occupied in waving about the palm branches. Some palms are only small twigs, but many extend several

---

pointing to the annual lighting of the Christmas tree on the White House lawn, the judge happily ruled that the brightly lit loblolly pine erected on the far corner of the square was essentially a secular emblem and therefore legally correct.

feet into the air, and their weight threatens to up-end their small bearers. Don Guido, the school principal, breaks off a conversation he is having with some of the mothers and tells me, with a giggle, that once they are blessed, the palms will ward off lightning. He likes it when I write down what he says, so he waits to make sure I have it in my notebook. Suddenly, Father Restrepo declares victory by rushing down the steps and motioning the procession to start. It heads toward the back of town to meet King Jesus. Three small boys in colorful robes lead the way, followed by a tiny "angel" in a white pinafore, and then the impatient Father Restrepo. Behind him come the twelve small "disciples" dressed in brilliant colors. Doña Jaél shepherds the boys around puddles left over from yesterday's rain. Two statues follow. They are nearly life-size, with porcelain faces and flowing garments. One is Mary Magdalene, and the other is John the Baptist. Fixed on platforms resting on the shoulders of the few men participating in the celebration, they sway above the crowd in magisterial fashion.[13]

The procession now reaches the point where they will accompany King Jesus back into the town's center, but the Lozano brothers are having trouble keeping the wooden figure, with moveable arms and legs, astride a live burro. "Only a minute more, Father," the oldest reassures the priest. "Hand me the hammer," he tells his younger brother. "I'll nail his legs to the pack saddle." The task completed, he steps aside to let Father Restrepo bless the statue with holy water. He grabs the lead rope and shouts to the men with the statues, "Let me get in front of you." He pulls the burro, which is not at all enthusiastic about its assigned role, to a space between the statues and the apostles. Father Restrepo assumes his position, and the march into Jerusalem is on its way.

As the procession passes their houses, people come to the doorways. The men remove their hats, and some of the watchers cross themselves. A few of the older marchers drop out, but the younger ones happily wave palm leaves at relatives and friends. The quick stride of Father Restrepo pulls the front half of the procession away from those behind the slow pace of the burro. To

13. The scriptural basis for palms is San Juan 12:12–13: "una inmensa multitud . . . sabiendo que Jesús iba a Jerusalén, cortaron ramas de las palmeras y salieron a encontrarlo gritando: 'Hosanna, bendito sea el que viene en el nombre del Señor, el Rey de Israel'; a great multitude . . . knowing that Jesus was going to Jerusalem, cut branches from palm groves and went out to meet him, shouting: 'Hosanna, blessed be the one who comes in the name of the Lord, the King of Israel.' "

hurry him along, a man from the crowd gets behind the burro and pushes while the older Lozano pulls on the lead rope. If anything, the burro slows down. "He needs gasoline," Lozano grins to his helper. A small boy rushes up. "Father Restrepo says hurry. He is almost at the highway." And at these words, the burro stops completely. Lozano pulls, the helper pushes, but the burro stands firm. "He needs more than gasoline," Lozano complains while pulling in exasperation. "A complete overhaul," the pusher agrees. "Let's make a switch. Go get your burro," Lozano tells the helper. "No, wait. Here comes Doña María." A woman steps out of the crowd, takes the lead rope from Lozano, and pulls. Recognizing his owner, the burro takes a few steps, as if to get started, and then proceeds to move steadily ahead.

The procession reaches the main highway that passes by San Pedro and turns to go along one side. The traffic slows, buses pull over, and passengers crowd the windows to watch. Suddenly, it's there. The instant that I said would not return. I was wrong. It has. It's there, before us. Out of the messy backdrop of buses and people emerges a clean, coherent portrait of the burro, the figure of Christ, and Doña María. Doña María, her dark brown face as stoic as her solid body, leans patiently forward. The burro's walk changes from a comical, stumbling gait to a calm, measured stride. Atop the burro, the thin, artificial figure of Christ and his doll-like face sit in cold contrast to the comforting warm of the woman and the animal. And the mind stretches out to embrace all the small-town processions carrying their Christs through the streets of the world.

The procession turns from the highway and heads for the plaza and the church. At the church steps, as the men take the figure of Christ into the church, Father Restrepo shouts,

> ¡Viva Cristo Rey! Long live Christ the King!
> ¡Viva! the crowd agrees.
> ¡Viva la fe católica! Long live the Catholic faith!
> ¡Viva!

And to both prod and reward, Father Restrepo concludes,

> ¡Viva la joventud estudiosa! Long live the studious youth!
> ¡Viva! people shout in accord.

So *la Semana Santa*, Holy Week, recapitulating the last days of Jesus, begins with a youthful, joyful, triumphal moment. As the week moves forward, through the smaller processions commemorating Jesus as the Good Shepherd and Jesus in the Garden, down on his knees asking that this cup might pass, it inexorably proceeds to *Jueves Santo*. Now music and work stop, and even the bells at mass are replaced by wooden rackets as the day commemorates the Last Supper, when Jesus first spoke the words "Take, eat, this is my body; take, drink, this is my blood." And then finally and inevitably the week leads to *Viernes Santo*.

Since I know I can't prevent you, go ahead and hold forth again. But hold forth *con dignidad*, with dignity.

> Pilato les volvió a preguntar: "¿Y qué haré con ese que llamáis 'rey de los judios'?" Ellos le gritaron otra vez: "Crucifícalo." Pilato les preguntaba: "¿Pero qué mal ha hecho? Pero ellos más recio le gritaban: "Crucifícalo."
>
> Pilate turned to them to ask, "And what shall I do with the one you call 'King of the Jews'?" They shouted again, "Crucify him." Pilate asked them, "What evil has he done?" But even more loudly, they cried, "Crucify him." (San Marcos 15:12–14)
>
> [Los soldados] lo vistieron de púrpura, y entretejiendo una corona des espinas, le ciñeron con ella la cabeza. En seguida comenzaron a saludarlo: "Viva el rey de los judios," y le golpearon la cabeza con un carrizo, y lo escupían, y poniéndose de rodillas le rendían homenaje.
>
> [The soldiers] dressed him in purple and weaving a crown from thorns, they clamped it around his head. At once, they began to salute him, "Long live the King of the Jews," and beat him around the head with a cane, and spit on him, and kneeling down, paid mock homage to him. (San Marcos 15:17–19)
>
> Así lo llevaron hasta arriba del Gólgota, que traducido significa: "Lugar de la Calavera." Le daban vino mirrado, per no lo tomó. Lo crucificaron, pues, y se repartieron sus vestiduras, echando suertes para ver qué le tocaba a cada uno. Era la hora tercia cuando lo crucificaron.
>
> And so they took him up Golgotha, which, translated, signifies "The Place of the Skull." They gave him wine mixed with myrrh, but he did not drink it. They crucified him, then, and divided his garments, casting lots to see which received what piece. It was on the third hour that they crucified him. (San Marcos 15:22–25)
>
> Al llegar la hora sexta, sobre toda la tierra vino una oscuridad que duró hasta la hora nona. A la hora nona gritó Jesús con fuerte voz . . . "Dios mío, Dios mío, ¿por qué me abandonaste?"

> On the arrival of the sixth hour, over the earth fell a darkness that lasted until the ninth hour. At the ninth hour, Jesus cried out in a loud voice . . . "My God, my God, why have you forsaken me." (San Marcos 15:33–34)

The forsaken moment comes into being in the streets of San Pedro on *Viernes Santo* in the *Vía Crucis*, the "Way of the Cross," or, more commonly, the "Stations of the Cross." Catholic churches everywhere, and certainly every *iglesia* in Spanish America, have plaques on their walls that portray the events on Christ's journey to Golgotha, the place of the *Calavera*, the place of the skull, the place of death. There are fourteen stations; they begin with Jesus being condemned to death, and they end with him being sealed in his grave.[14] In the *Vía Crucis*, the people of San Pedro reproduce the stations, or at least several of them, on the streets of their town. First, early Friday morning, city workers cut saplings from along the creek that flows nearby and line the route from church through the town and back again. Whenever they come to a Protestant home (and in 1963, there were only three or four families), they skip it. Small clusters of people position themselves at strategic corners to establish the stations. At the front of the church, four men lift the figure of the thorn-crowned King of the Jews up onto their shoulders. They walk a short distance to the first station in the San Pedro re-creation. They lower the figure to the ground, fix a cross over its shoulder, and add another figure behind the first. This is a Roman soldier, with a whip in his hand. When they raise the platform again to their shoulders, the scene is Jesus bent under the weight of his cross being lashed by the Roman soldier, whose face is grotesquely contorted as if it were he who was in pain.

As the procession moves toward the next station, the women, dressed in black, sing slowly and mournfully of *piedad*, *piedad*, *piedad*, "pity, pity, pity." The men walk behind them. You point out, as you are accustomed to do, that this number of men is the most you have seen at any San Pedro procession. At least half of the men are in suits, but among the others are those who are so poor as to be without shoes. At the station, the procession stops, the priest begins a prayer, the women gradually kneel, and then the men, at least most of them, follow. Those in suits first place a handkerchief on the ground to protect their finery. The priest finishes the prayer, the people rise, and a new

14. Ending the stations of the cross with the burial of Jesus caused some Vatican reformers, under growing "protestantization," to add a fifteenth station, featuring an empty tomb and an angel who says, "He has been raised, exactly as promised."

statue is added to the procession. She is Mary, the Mother of Jesus, dressed as the Queen of Heaven, with a jeweled crown and a black robe sprinkled with stars. The women sing once more of pity, and the procession goes forward.

At each station, additional figures take their places behind the others: Mary Magdalene; John, the Beloved Disciple; and Peter, the first pope (and patron of the town). At one stop, a young woman dressed in black holds stretched between her hands a large cloth with the face of the suffering Jesus imprinted upon it. She is Veronica, the lady whose heart broke at the sight of such agony and who wiped the face of our Lord in an attempt to comfort him. Search in vain, you biblical literalists, for this woman resides not in the Scriptures, but this Veronica, this *vera-icon*, this true icon, comes to be only at the moment of sorrow.

The procession now turns back toward the church. From where we anthropologists stand, it seems to move on two levels, the people below, the statues above. Paradoxically, the statues, the artificial portraits, assume an individuality greater than the mass of humans carrying them. From the effort below, they take on life, and led by their thorn-crowned king, they go striding down the street on the backs of their worshipers. And you ask, Who are the true bearers of the cross?

The morning of the *Vía Crucis* gives way to the afternoon of the Sermon of the Seven Words. Beginning at 3 P.M., when "darkness covered the earth," Father Restrepo takes the last words of Jesus spoken on the cross and elaborates on each into a two-hour harangue emanating from the loudspeaker on top of the church's tower and reverberating throughout the streets of the town. He begins with "Padre, perdónales, porque no saben lo que hacen; Father, forgive them because they know not what they are doing" (San Lucas 23:34) and moves on through the other final pleas, including the one you spoke earlier, from San Marcos 15:33–34: "Dios mío, Dios mío, ¿por qué me abandonaste?; My God, My God, why have you forsaken me?" But before the end of the Sermon, I break and run. The last words and final hours become more than I can take. The disembodied voice finds me no matter how I seek to hide from it. Even as I head out of town, I hear Father Restrepo pronounce the Seventh Word, "Gritando con voz fuerte, Jesús exclamó, 'Padre, encominedo mi espíritu en tus manos'; Crying out in a loud voice, Jesus exclaimed, 'Father, into your hands I commend my spirit'" (San Lucas 23:46).

You, of course, being the true anthropologist, remain, and you relate that after the sermon, Father Restrepo and local officials take Christ off his cross above the altar and place the figure in a small alcove, which now becomes the tomb of the Lord. Saturday night, at a mass called *El toque de Gloria*, "the sound of Glory," the figure is restored to its cross, where it hangs for another 364 days. By the time I return on Easter Sunday, the town is pretty much back to normal.

La Semana Santa begins with the joyful, youthful march into Jerusalem; it ascends to *Viernes Santo*, when in the morning, the way of the cross, the moment of forsakenness, is performed on the streets, and in the afternoon, the final sermon, the seven words, is offered from the pulpit. The week slides down through the Saturday night mass and back into an ordinary Sunday.

San Pedro is a small town and, in 1963, was quite poor; consequently, its Holy Week pales in comparison with those magnificent exhibitions farther south in the colonial city of Popayán or farther north in the equally old city of Tunja. In other parts of Spanish America, people are selected to replace the statues. In Costa Rica, for example, men carry on their shoulders a live Jesus bent under his cross being whipped by an equally live Roman soldier. Across the Atlantic, even more elaborate processions wind through the cities of southern Spain. There, the platforms, or *pasos*, frequently have scenes composed of several figures. To capture the moment that Judas, one of the Twelve, betrays Jesus with a kiss (Mark 14:45), one *paso* has the figure of Judas straining toward Jesus with pursed lips while the images of John, James, Peter, Andrew, and Thomas look on. There is also an olive tree and four huge gold-plated candelabras. Such a *paso* requires nearly fifty men to carry it through the streets past throngs of admirers. Once paraded through the streets, Judas is burned in effigy (Mitchell 1990).

Celebrating the Passion of Christ, as you may recall from Chapter 2, had its beginning back in the closing years of the sixteenth century, as a local adaptation to the Council of Trent's reaffirmation of the Real Presence of the Lord in the sacramental wafer. In the opinion of some (e.g., Payne 1984), through the seventeenth and eighteenth centuries, a "morbid" fascination with death became a central point to Spanish piety. "The people dressed and whipped themselves and wept so they looked like the images; and the images sweated blood and wept as if they were people" (Christian 1981b, 198). Today, both within and without academic fields, we encounter the assessment of *La Semana Santa* as "morbid" and the message of *Viernes Santo* as "fatalistic." While the following chapter addresses the issue more fully, we need to pause here and present another interpretation, one given to me in San Pedro in 1963 by a man whose nickname was Chucho, which in Colombia stands for "Jesús," or, in English, "Jesus," so he ought to know! Addressing my question of why Christ seemed to hang on his cross forever in such agony, Chucho insisted, "No, this is not fatalism. . . . It is realism. Christ died so that we too could learn how to suffer and how to die. To live is to die. It is part of the human tragedy. Through his actions, Christ teaches us this tragedy and how we must face death."

Not satisfied, I asked the question I had always asked, even back in the days when I was a Southern Baptist. When Jesus was on his way to the cross, would not it have been better if he had fought against his persecutors? Would not it have been more heroic to fight, even if he knew he was to lose?

> No. He wanted to set an example. He wanted to show us how to suffer patiently, how to accept death with tranquility. Today, humans do not suffer correctly nor formally. They do not patiently await the outcome. They fight against death. This is because they do not have the image of Christ in their minds. Because we are humans, we cannot die in the manner of Christ, who was God. But we must try. If God suffered patiently, then surely we must do likewise. We must try to conform to death. This is the reason why Holy Friday is more important than Resurrection Sunday. (Richardson [1970] 1986b, 78)

But still you ask, What about today? Chucho told you this in San Pedro back in the 1960s. What about the now? A perfectly good question, and one that I anticipated you would ask. So here is a sampling of newspaper accounts for the *Semana Santa* in 1996 (with one, *La Nación* in Argentina, from 1995).[15]

La Semana Santa in 1996 (which began on *Domingo de los Ramos*, March 31, and ended on *Domingo de la Resurreción*, April 7) in Mexico City received extensive coverage in the newspaper *La Reforma*. In its depiction, the week comes across as one of both secular vacations and religious ceremonies. Accordingly, its coverage is both light and pious. Its columns announce what its readers could do in "El DF en vacaciones" (DF, *Distrito Federal*, "Federal District," being the nickname for Mexico City), such as visiting the museums,

15. I am grateful to the most helpful librarians at the University of Texas's Nettie Lee Benson Library for allowing me access to their extensive newspaper collection.

taking in the race track, and dining out. With a certain sardonic twist, an editorial cartoon displays a vacationer in beach attire nailed to a cross with the sign *Inflación*, "Inflation," pinned above his head. The following day, under the headlines *Cristos Metropolitanos*, "Metropolitan Christs," it interviews a number of young men who are to play the role of Christ in various processions in nearby communities. It discovers that the "Christ" of Iztapalapa, overcome by the heat and emotion, has momentarily fainted. He recovers, however, to carry his cross in a procession that features five hundred actors, four thousand participants, and a multitude of worshipers, tourists, and vendors. Police, dressed as Roman soldiers in full regalia and many on horseback, accompany the march, while other actors, dressed in Holy Land attire, crowd around the cross (Figure 31).

Among the participants are *los nazarenos*, "the Nazarenes," who in this

FIG. 31. Christ on his way to Golgotha in Mexico City. Adapted from *La Reforma*, 6 April 1996.

case are not members of an organized brotherhood but rather individuals shouldering their own crosses in fulfillment of vows they have made, such as the young husband and father who promised that if his wife and new baby continue in good health, he will carry a cross for three years. After the *Vía Crucis* of Holy Friday, on Saturday, the day of Glory, several neighborhoods celebrate the burning of Judas. Usually, dolls dressed as the traitor to Christ are set afire or exploded, but recently people have started substituting politicians for Judas. A favorite doll for burning in 1996 was the former president Carlos Salinas de Gotari, once the darling of the international community, whose failed monetary policies and unsavory relatives caused him to flee the country in disgrace. Also, in an intriguing reversal of roles, men dressed as Judas, in red robes, a devil mask, and carrying whips, go from door to door threatening the occupants with whipping if gifts are not forthcoming. The gifts—sweets, nuts, beer, articles of clothing, even live chicks—are taken to the church to be distributed in the neighborhood. In a further twist, other young men step forward to challenge the Judas to whip them. And even if the Judas complies and the person whipped flinches with pain, he may taunt the Judas into more lashes. One girl, observing from afar, suggested, perhaps with a touch of scorn, that the men think what they are doing is *muy macho*, "playing the he-man" (Figure 32).

In Colombia, *El Tiempo*, in one of its more chatty sections, reports on the *corrida de Domingo de los Ramos*, the bull fight on Palm Sunday. The newspaper, however, gives serious coverage to the *Semana Santa* in the old city of Tunja. The paper highlights the four hundred years of *la Sociedad de los Nazarenos*, brought to Tunja from Seville, Spain, where the brotherhood originated as part of the popular enshrinement of the Passion of Christ in the aftermath of the Council of Trent. A photograph shows hooded men in flowing robes and bare feet carrying a *paso* upon which larger-than-life figures hammer nails through the hands of Christ supine on the cross (Figure 33). Below the photograph, a seventy-year-old *nazareno* recalls his fifty years of carrying the *paso* of the Virgin of Sorrows through the streets on Holy Friday.[16] An editorial suggests that by following the practices of Christ, we may understand better the urges within us and calm our passions and that if we

16. The hoods, with their resemblance to those of the Ku Klux Klan, can't help but appear sinister to an American viewer, but their purpose is to render each person anonymous so that he may not take false pride in his suffering (Mitchell 1990).

FIG. 32. The *Machos* challenge Judas. Adapted from *La Reforma*, 7 April 1996.

are successful in controlling our impulses, could not the guerrillas silence their guns?

El Mercurio in Santiago, Chile, offers its readers only a brief report of a *Vía Crucis* procession in one of the city's barrios. Although the archbishop of Santiago attends, the procession seems quite simple. A photograph depicts an older man carrying a plain cross followed by participants in street clothes with candles. No images or costumed figures are evident. *La Nación* of Buenos Aires, Argentina, has even less. A message from then-president Carlos Saúl Menem describes the occasion as one for the family to gather in happiness and peace. He makes no mention of Christ and concludes his words with "¡Que Dios bendiga la mesa familiar! Felices Pascuas; May God bless the family table! Happy Easter."

Peru, however, is a different story. *El Peruano*, in Lima, concentrates its coverage of the *Semana Santa* on the events happening in the Andean Department of Ayacucho and its regional capital, Ayacucho, famous for its colonial churches and the fervor of its faith. Devoting several issues to the region, the newspaper observes that while the area has suffered much in recent years from violence, it has not lost its mysticism. More than 15,000 tourists are

FIG. 33. *Los Nazarenos* walk the street of Tunja during *La Semana Santa*. Adapted from *El Tiempo*, 31 March 1996.

expected for *Viernes Santo* alone. Preceding *Viernes Santo*, in one barrio, the streets are "paved" with "rugs" of flowers and colored sawdust, and vendors set up stalls to prepare the best of Ayacucho cuisine. With the way made ready, *el Señor de Agonía*, the Lord of Agony, whose blood-stained countenance expresses an abiding pain, leaves the temple of the Magdalene. "With vestments bordered with threads of gold and silver, *El Cristo de Agonía* comes forth to placate the clamor of the faithful. '¡Oh Señor de la Agonía, [*El Peruano* records their plea] calma nuestras penas, guárdanos en tu corazón generoso. . . . ¡Oh Señor de Agonía, danos amor y paz'; O Lord of Agony, calm our pain, shelter us in your generous heart. . . . O Lord of Agony, give us love and peace."

On the actual *Viernes Santo*, the paper gives front-page coverage to the reenactment of the *Vía Crucis* in Lima but returns to Ayacucho (also known as Huamanga) in the following issue to report on its front page that the then-president of the country, Alberto Fujimori, had traveled to Ayacucho to participate in the final procession on *Viernes Santo*, that of the *Santo Sepulcro*, the placing of Christ in his tomb. It all but ignores the events of Resurrection Sunday.[17]

The day before *Viernes Santo* the paper editorializes under the heading *La Pasión de Cristo*, "The Passion of Christ," how the death of Christ fulfilled the prophecies of the Old Testament. It concludes by pointing to the parallels between the writing in Psalms (22:1) in which the Psalmist pleads that the Lord God not turn his face away and Jesus' agonizing cry from the cross, "My God, My God, Why hast thou forsaken me?" On *Viernes Santo*, its editorial titled "Passover and the Resurrection" describes how Christ, in the

17. While no doubt following the convictions of his faith, President Fujimori might well have had a political agenda in mind when he visited Ayacucho. The violence *El Peruano* alluded to was the devastation generated by the bloody clashes between the Shining Path (*Sendero Luminoso*) guerrilla movement and governmental forces. Beginning in 1980, the Shining Path "murdered political leaders, teachers, engineers, and ordinary peasants" throughout the Department of Ayacucho. In a "dirty" counteroffensive, the military "began to jail, torture, and kill people" (Mitchell 1991, 10–11). Eventually, the area was pacified, and President Fujimori's trip must have demonstrated, at least to his satisfaction, that the government had triumphed over the guerrillas. In light of these events, the people's prayers to *el Señor de Agonía* to give them peace carry a special poignancy. The subsequent years have not been kind to Fujimori. Although he won a third term in 2000, the national election was bitterly contested both in Peru and abroad. In November of that year, after tumultuous months of corruption scandals, President Fujimori, while on an alleged promotion trip to his parental homeland, sent word from Tokyo to Lima that he was resigning the presidency. At the time of this writing, he refuses to return to Peru, despite that country's attempts to extradite him.

Meanwhile, over in Argentina, former President Menem was indicted on a charge of illegally funneling weapons to Croatia and Ecuador during his ten years of power. Profit, rather than ideology, was the apparent motive of this "gun laundering." Paralleling Fujimori's success in stabilizing the countryside, Menem brought Argentina's runaway inflation under control, but following his departure from office, he likewise faced charges of rampant corruption.

words of Paul, replaced the animal sacrifice of the Jews by offering himself as the sacrificial lamb. It then proceeds with these telling words.

> Después de haber enseñado a los hombres cómo deberían vivir era preciso [que Cristo] enseñarles cómo morir. Lejo de evadirse del furor de sus enemigos, los espera y se les presenta; después de haber meditado sobre los ultrajes y tormentados que le aguardan, se somete al Padre; se dirige con paso firme a los soldados que le aguardan; presentado a los jueces responde con modestia y con firmeza; pendiente de la cruz, pide perdón para sus verdugos y promete la eterna felicidad a un criminal arrepentido.
>
> La muerte de Jesús fue el sello de su misión, la obra maestra de su enseñanza.
>
> After having taught men how they ought to live, it was necessary [that Christ] teach them how they ought to die. Far from avoiding the furor of his enemies, he anticipates them and presents himself to them; after having meditated upon the outrages and torments that lie ahead, he submits himself to the Father; without hesitation, he conducts himself to the soldiers awaiting him; taken before the judges he responds quietly and firmly; hanging from the cross, he asks that his executioners be forgiven and promises eternal happiness to a repentant criminal.
>
> The death of Jesus was the signature stamp of his mission, the master work of his teaching.

Don Chucho's words from 1963 that the message of Christ on the cross is to teach us how to die continue in the 1990s and remain with us today, in this new century.

"He Is Risen!" The signs outside Baptist churches all over the South announce the news on Easter Sunday. Here in Louisiana, in my neighborhood, the Southside Baptist assures us that "Celebrating Easter Is Better than Winning the Lottery."

In preparation for Easter Sunday, many churches may do absolutely nothing, thereby emphasizing by their very silence the coming glory of Easter. Others, however, cannot pass up the opportunity to prepare the way, as it were, for the day Christ rose from the dead. Some may go so far as to stage musical dramas. One of the more elaborate is *The Victor*, presented by the First Baptist Church in Durham, North Carolina.

Advertisements in the newspaper in the form of admission tickets—ADMIT

ONE, *The Victor*, Performance Time, 8 P.M., Saturday and Sunday—circulate the news. For the presentation on this Palm Sunday weekend, the space around the pulpit has been converted into a garden. On the left are two columns where Pilate will appear. To the right is the tomb. Behind the curtains hanging down from the choir area is the cross. The associate pastor comes to the front to greet us: "In the back of the pew in front of you, you will find a blue visitor card with a place to indicate how you heard about tonight's performance. By filling this out, you will help us to know how effective have been our various efforts to reach you." And sure enough, the form lists various media, with a space in front of each entry where you can check what influenced you: "Friend," "Newspaper," "Radio," "Poster," and even "Other."

The lights dim; the performance begins. People dressed in flowing robes, in actuality members of the choir, mill about and appear to chat. Off to one side, a narrator relates the events. The scene of Jesus praying in the garden takes shape. The pastor, a handsome young man with a rich head of hair, a neatly trimmed beard, and a pleasant tenor voice, plays Jesus. The choir sings of Jesus' plea that his burden pass. You, always the one to point out such things, notice that the choir is lip-syncing to piped music.

Jesus is brought before Pilate, whose deep voice rings true as he asks, "What has this man done?" Funny, you observe, how those with the bad-guy parts often do a better job. Roman soldiers take Jesus offstage and then return with him staggering under the weight of the cross with blood painted on his naked back. The lights go out, and when they come back on, the curtains over the choir area are pulled back to reveal Jesus tied to the cross, his head swaying back and forth. Eventually, he shouts, "Father, it is finished," not, you note, "My God, My God, Why hast thou forsaken me?" The stage goes dark, and we hear cries of alarm.

The scene passes on to Mary and a friend, and the friend sings how she wished the whole world could see through a mother's eyes. Mary, now joined with Mary Magdalene and the disciples, goes to the tomb, but they are amazed to find it empty. While they mill about, the narrator relates the events that occurred during the hundred days after the crucifixion. The drama comes to an end with Christ ascending through the clouds.

Following the applause, the associate pastor gives the invitation to lost sinners. "The space here," he gestures toward the steps coming down from the pulpit, "has become an altar, and while every head is bowed and every eye closed, I want you to pray these words, 'Father God, thank you for dying for me.' The wages of sin is death. God holds out a gift. Won't you humble yourself? 'Father God, this is your place. May you be exalted.'" He then continues at length, lest anyone think other than that the drama we have seen is for the sole purpose of praising the Lord.[18]

This time, I beat you to the draw and say out loud, "A little different from San Pedro, ain't it?"

Be that as it may, recently, some Baptist churches are beginning to give more attention to the Thursday before Easter. This Thursday, *Jueves Santo* in Spanish America, is called Maundy Thursday. The services are usually in the evening, after work. At the service in a Baptist church in my neighborhood, the pamphlet distributed at the door wanted us to understand the solemnity of the occasion, but it also wanted us to know that this service was "The Ordinance of the Lord's Supper"; that is, we should not, even if we were so inclined, confuse it with the sacrament of Holy Communion. The dim lighting further emphasized the attitude we were to take. Following a series of softly sung songs, including "The Old Rugged Cross"—"On a hill faraway stood an old rugged cross, the emblem of suffering and shame"—the pastor invited us to the front where, in his words, "the elements" were located. I noticed the high-church wording for the grape juice and crackers, but I was even more shocked to see to the left of the pulpit a large cross framed in purple lighting. I am confident that Brother Summerall, the pastor of the First Baptist in Palestine during the days of my childhood, turned over in his grave. Not deterred by my thoughts (which, of course, unlike you, he couldn't hear), the Baton Rouge pastor prayed that we might feel the pain "of you, God, of your broken body, bleeding for the sins of all creation." Members of the congregation filed down to the front, individually took the "elements," first the "body," then the "blood," and then went over to the plain cross where again, individually, they knelt and prayed. As they rose from their knees, several members left, and I followed. At the bottom of the pamphlet, words instructed, "Proceed out of the sanctuary during the chorus of the last hymn." and scolded, "Be silent! Remember Christ's grief for your sins. Remember the Cross."

18. May I be forgiven that at the sound of the associate pastor's request that we pray, "Father God, thank you for dying for me," the thought burst upon me, "Nope. You got it wrong, buddy. It was my mother who died for me."

Good Friday in Louisiana, where we believe in such things, is a holiday, and even the Baptists don't seem to mind. For the rest of the South, however, except perhaps for the Catholics in Maryland and Kentucky and those in Savannah, Georgia, Good Friday is an ordinary end-of-the-week day with the TGIF parties under way by 4 P.M. For the adoration of the cross, Catholics here in Baton Rouge frequently schedule a noonday service where individuals come forth to kiss a large crucifix held by an altar boy, who carefully wipes the cross after each kiss. This is followed at 3 P.M. by the stations of the cross. In the services that I have attended at the downtown cathedral, the two or so priests conducting the ritual go from station to station inside the church, while the parishioners, hardly ever more than thirty, remain in place and turn their bodies to follow the procession. At each station, we kneel, pray, and read from a booklet words appropriate for that station. Also at each station, an older woman reads what might have been the thoughts of Mary as she watched her son progress to his death and then resurrection. At a recent Good Friday, several advocacy groups joined together to walk the way of the cross from the cathedral to the state capitol and back. At each station, a representative from one or another of the groups reads a prayer, such as "Forgive us for allowing an impersonal economic system to exploit the most vulnerable in our communities" and "May the day come when the addiction to militarism be broken and may peace fill our hearts, our world, and our universe." I have no record of what the bishop thought.

Easter Sunday. The Day of the Resurrection. A day in America second in importance only to Christmas. A day, as are most special occasions in the United States, for consumerism, for displaying finery purchased during the weeks preceding. For many in the South, the day may begin with a sunrise service. The Moravians brought the service to North Carolina from their home in Herrnhut, Germany, where it was commonly held in the church's cemetery, located next to the church, on "God's Acre." The custom has spread among other Protestant churches throughout the region. Rural churches may still have the early morning service in the cemetery, but one favorite location for small-town churches is the high school football stadium, which has plenty of room for a community choir from cooperating churches. Too, in the South, there is something special about a high school football stadium, something that tugs at the heart strings, something that fits with songs of glory.

In Durham, North Carolina, just a bit north of the city limits, in an area that remains rural despite the spillover created by the famous Research Triangle of Chapel Hill, Raleigh, and Durham, a medium-sized Baptist church sits alongside Sharon Road. Given the nearness of the road, small wonder, you say, that the church is named The Rose of Sharon, and you go on to cite Solomon 2:1, "I am the rose of Sharon and the lily of the valleys" and pronounce in your know-it-all voice that the Rose of Sharon is Jesus. A flower that blooms in the desert when all others have died, I quickly add, not to be outdone.

The announcement in Saturday's paper said, "Sunrise Service at 7:15 A.M.," and assured us that at The Rose of Sharon "Everybody is Somebody." Mid-April in North Carolina can still be on the cool side, and I shiver in the chilly morning air. I see a small group behind the church, between it and the cemetery. They are chatting quietly to one another. This is not like going to a regular Sunday morning service, where the deacon stands at the door to greet you and to hand you a program. It's more like dropping in on someone else's family reunion. But I stay with it and ask a man about my age, in his sixties, if this is where the sunrise service is going to be. I'm not sure what he thinks about such a stupid question, but he offers his hand and his last name. I wander over to the cemetery. The plain headstones tell me that the oldest graves go back into the last century. A family group, the Scotts, have clear sand poured over their collective graves. Another group, the McClendons, have theirs covered with pea gravel. The rest are under mowed grass. There are two new graves.

I look back at the group, now about twenty or so. The pastor is running a bit late, but people are clearly at home with one another. In contrast, never have I felt such a fraud. The pastor now appears, a middle-aged man in a dark, double-breasted suit but with a light tie and a yellow handkerchief in his breast pocket. He moves through the crowd, shaking hands and greeting each by name.

A young man in blue jeans and laced boots begins the service. With the help of his amplified guitar, tied by an extension cord to an outlet inside the church, he leads us through several songs. The minister prays, and the young man steps forward. "I want to sing a song really special to me. It's from the perspective of Simon Peter. It's just after the Resurrection, and Peter and the other disciples are hiding out from the soldiers. Maybe some of you have heard it. It's called, 'He's Alive.'"

And he begins, his guitar soft and sad. He sings how Peter has lost hope and waits with the other disciples at a friend's house for the soldiers to come and drag them all away. But he hears a commotion at the gate. It's Mary. Through her tears, Mary tells them someone has stolen her son's body. The disciples rush to the grave, and, sure enough, they find it empty. And thinking how thieves must have made off with the body, Peter says,

> Where had they taken him was more than I could bear.
> John believes in miracles, but I just turn to go
> I saw them crucify him, and I saw him die.

And Peter recalls, "I denied that I knew him. I denied I knew his name."

Then the air around them is filled with sweet perfume. Jesus stands there, his arms outstretched. Peter falls at his knees. He begs forgiveness. Jesus leans over to lift Peter up.

Then the young man shifts from a soft strumming to thundering chords, as Peter realizes,

> He's alive! He's alive! He's alive!
> And I'm forgiven and heaven's gates are open wide.
> He's alive. He's alive. Oh, He's alive!

The preacher, like the rest of us, is a bit overwhelmed by the song, the soft narrative, the astonishing climax, and the sudden silence that follows. But he recovers rapidly.

"That's what it is all about. The Resurrection. Jesus paid the sin debt for you and me. Everyone here today is a sinner. From the little babies to the aged. We are all sinners. But there are two kinds of sinners. Those lost and doomed forever, and those found in Jesus.

"Jesus is a living savior. Make no doubt about it. Go to Confucius's tomb; you'll find he's still there. Go to Buddha's tomb; you'll find he's still there. But go to Jerusalem, and you won't find Jesus. He has triumphed over sin, death, hell, and the grave.

"A team of lawyers, some Christian and some not, met recently in England. They concluded there's more legal evidence for the Resurrection than for many other events we accept as fact.

"You know Michelangelo used to chide the artists of his day. 'Why do you fill your galleries with humiliation and punishment?' he asked. 'You always paint Christ on the cross. You need to paint the empty tomb. You need to paint the Glory and the Resurrection.'"

The pastor concludes with a prayer in which he asks, "If there is one here today who does not know Jesus, then would that person come to recognize Him as Lord and Savior? He is ready now with outstretched arms to receive them. May today be the day of their salvation experience."

He then invites all those who want to share in the Lord's Supper to come forward. He points to a table with a tray holding small glasses and a platter with tiny squares of bread. "We are not going to serve it, but we'll let those who want to participate to come by and serve themselves."

Everybody files by, myself included, more of a fraud than ever. After he has repeated the words of Jesus and we eat and drink the symbols, the pastor smiles expansively. "You are all invited now to come have breakfast with us. People have been up since four o'clock this morning, cooking eggs, sausage, grits, and biscuits. Everyone is welcome."

The older man, the one about my age, comes by and urges me to join them. I'm grateful for his kindness, which I can see now as no more than that, perhaps no more than that and a sense of duty to be kind and to be hospitable. But I'm not about to sit and eat. It's too scary. I am too full of fear for eating. I took the symbolic meal, but I can't take the real one. Instead, I go back to the graves. I wait until everyone has entered the church, and then I leave: "John believes in miracles, but I just turn to go."

Over at Mt. Hope, at the FBC, during the midday service, with Easter lilies decorating the tops of both piano and organ, Reverend Overton proclaims, "If Christ be not risen, then evil triumphs over good, falsehood over truth, hatred of man over the love of God." Earlier, the choir, as they have for many years past, offers a rousing rendition of "Low in the Grave, He Lay."

The lighter voices in the choir begin with "Low in the grave he lay, Jesus my savior / Waiting the coming day, Jesus my Lord." Now the piano crashes down, and the heavier voices come forth.

> Up from the grave, He arose,
> He arose.
> With a mighty triumph o'er His foes;
> He arose!
> He arose a victor from the dark domain
> And He lives forever with His saints to reign.

Now the finale, with the lighter voices reaching skyward and heavier ones close behind:

He arose! He arose!
He arose! He arose!
Hallelujah, Christ arose.

Before moving on to our last chapter, you offer a final thought about the two celebrations north and south. No Easter bunny hops down the bunny trail in Spanish America. The northern symbol of fertility and the capitalist mantra for another special sale going on in the mall has yet to jump the Rio Grande. Thus far, the good people of Mexico and lands south are safe from the hippity, hippity hop of this insidious rabbit.

O grave, where is thy victory?

1 Corinthians 15:55

6

BEING-IN-CHRIST IN THE PRESENCE OF DEATH

During the temporal sweep of the Pleistocene, a bipedal hominid became a two-legged human upon the twin discoveries of self and death. Since at least the time of the Neandertals, death has been the companion of the self. Perhaps it bears repeating that death as a biological process emerged along with life. The diversification of life and its development from single-cell, microscopic organisms to the multicellular giants, came about as death made space for innovations. Today, we know that through the process of apoptosis cells are programmed to die. The goal of life is new life, reproduction, not immortality. The death that we know, however, the death that we envision ahead of us, awaiting our arrival, that death is the consciousness of our finite self. Coming upon us from nowhere, that death mocks our efforts to be. In response, we fight to put death in its place.[1]

1. In such diverse animals as worms, insects, and vertebrates, "cells are programmed to commit suicide and require signals from other cells continuously in order to survive" (Steller 1995, 1446; see also Goldstein 1998). Since energy expended in one area cannot be expended in another, the life trajectory of organisms is a trade-off between reproduction and longevity, and in such a trade-off, reproduction always wins (Hill 1993). An extreme example occurs among the Australian redback spiders. During copulation, the tiny male positions himself between the jaws of the much larger female and is rewarded for his passion by being eaten. Such complicity in his own death contributes to his genetic fitness in that the cannibalized male fertilizes more eggs than the male whose sacrificial offering is rejected (Andrade 1996).

Reproduction wins out over longevity, even allowing for the fact that among humans women live long after their capacity to reproduce has ceased. In a closely reasoned argument, Hawkes et al. (1998) suggest that the evolution of a postmenopausal life span allowed grandmothers to earn more descendants through the provisioning of their granddaughters. The evolution of "grandmothering" in the hominid line permitted the expansion of hominids into previously un-

The world in which we create is a culture world, a world of symbols. The capacity to create this world of symbols developed as part and parcel of our evolutionary trajectory subsequent to bipedalism. The capacity is the key to our remarkable success as a species, up to this point in time. As we evolved, we thickened the culture dimension so that at present we live in a unique world composed of experiential nature and categorical culture. Unlike some of our colleagues who applaud with unbecoming adoration the (in)famous assertion of Derrida that there is nothing outside of the text because they love to argue that for humans culture is the only significant reality, we hold, with our five-fingered primate hand, that nature is still there. If nature is still there, then death awaits. It awaits in this text as a word, as a symbolic being, *La Muerte*, the Grim Reaper; it awaits outside the text, as a naturally occurring process, about which we can do nothing.[2]

Confronted with death, we have no choice but to create for it its place. To repeat the Jean-Paul Sartre-inspired paraphrase, "we are condemned to create." No more can we escape speaking than can we escape walking upright. Noam Chomsky, one of the foremost linguists of our day, argues that

---

occupied environmental zones and may have begun as early as the movement of the pre-*sapiens*, such as *Homo erectus*, out of Africa. Although Hawkes et al. do not so theorize, change in the *Homo erectus* tool kit, that is, the development of the hand ax, may have favored "grandmothering" by equipping senior women with tools that allowed them to secure and process foodstuffs previously unavailable to the grandchildren of the pebble-tool-using australopithecine females. Conjointly, the deepening social ties between the opposite ends of the life cycle would have favored the transmittal of hard-earned wisdom about life's troubled ways across the generations. In brief, not only does the grandmother hypothesis support the argument of reproduction over longevity, but it also demonstrates, once again, the intertwining of biology and culture in hominid evolution. (Parenthetically, I note that Hawkins has developed her theory in the face of criticism that human menopause is not adaptive but simply the consequences of the aging of the female reproductive system. See Gibbons 1998).

2. The fateful statement of Derrida is "Il n'y a pas de hors-texte," commonly translated as "There is nothing outside the text" (1976, 158). "Text," here, I take to mean not text in the conventional sense of a written document but the entire range of symbolic material that composes the reality in which we are. Furthermore, when Derrida insists that since there is nothing outside the text, we cannot gain access to the transcendental signified, I interpret him to say that since we exist in our symbolic reality, we cannot gain access to God. All we gain access to is more text, more words, more symbolic reality, that is, more talk about God, which leads to more talk about God, and so on, to constitute, as they say, a negative theology (Sell 1994). Nature, being nature, however, does not care what we say or think. Rains fall, rivers flow, and death comes, even though we shout, "How dare you! Stand back! Be gone!"

"language faculty appears to be a species property, common to the species and unique to it in its essentials" (1988, 39), which means we must speak. And when we speak, we create, for "language is far more than a mere system of communication" as in the case of animal calls (38). We use language "for the expression of thought, for establishing interpersonal relations . . . for play, and for a variety of human ends," such as putting death in its place (38). And when I say "we create" and "we speak," I am not just whistling Dixie. I am talking neither of the "royal we" nor of a generic human but specifically of you and me. For me to speak, you have to speak back. Speaking is as much a part of our being as is walking, but we acquire speaking together. As outlined in Chapter 1 and developed more fully in the Appendix, our ancestors walked across the boundary between hominid and human and into the world of the word together. This means that while speaking is something we *must* do, its acquisition by children is not a simple innate response or even a matter of behavioral reinforcement. Speaking a cross-cultural form of high-pitched, singsong "baby talk," known linguistically as "motherese" (which dads speak, too), parents provide "a rich and detailed source of information that instigates, before word learning, a process of species-specific mapping of information by the brain, a process that alters the infant's perceptual and perceptual-motor system to conform to a specific language" (Kuhl et al. 1997, 686). For me to speak English, you have to speak back. For me to create a Christ, you have to create back. For me to put death in its place, you must join me.[3]

Together, in the dialogue of this text, we have accomplished much. In Chapter 2 we watched the Europeans cross the Atlantic to establish the presence of the Christian Savior in the New World, and in Chapter 3 we saw that their success produced several images, including, at the close of the twentieth century, a Christ of liberation and a Christ of fundamentalism. In Chapter 4, we, you and I, knelt in the darkened *iglesia* and stood in the brightly-lit church to participate as observers while the Catholics of Spanish America and the Baptists of the American South created Christ images so that they, the worshipers, might be. We saw and felt how Christ in Spanish America became a Christ of the Touch, and we listened and heard how Christ among

3. Not to try your patience, but please note once more in this quote how the evolutionary interaction between culture and biology and the contemporary reciprocity between symbol and experience as laid out in Chapter 1 are implied in the statements on "species-specific mapping" and on the organization of the infant's perceptual-motor system "to conform to a specific language."

the Southern Baptists became a Christ of the Word. In Chapter 5 we saw the Christ of the Touch hang on his cross at the endpoint of a physical pilgrimage that took us across the Spanish American landscape; conversely, in the American South, we heard the Christ of the Word beckon us on a metaphorical trip to Beulah land, the place where we'll never grow old. Also in Chapter 5, we found the birth of Christ in Spanish America to be one day among several liturgically significant occasions, while in the American South and in the United States, December 25 rises above all other festive occasions like a loaded Christmas tree dazzling with ornaments. Finally, in Chapter 5, the distinction between the two Christs climaxes in the contrast between the celebration in Spanish America of *Viernes Santo*, the day Christ died, and the celebration in the American South of the Sunday morning worship on Easter, the day Christ arose from the tomb.

Now as we prepare ourselves to follow these New World people as they follow Christ, I must warn you of the twists and turns that lie ahead. I have this overwhelming feeling that the twists and turns are products of my seeking you. When I first started writing, I resisted the feeling, but as I placed one word after another, I became entranced, and thus beguiled, I committed myself to follow the path wherever it, or you, might lead. But now, as the path begins to unfold, ahead we hear the people shout, first with San Pablo, "Oh muerte! ¿Qué se ha hecho tu victoria?" (1 Corintos 15:55), and then repeat once more with Paul, "O grave, where is thy victory?"

Suffering and Glory Land Bound

In proclaiming victory over death, Christians in both regions use their respective Christ figures to put death in its place. How is this accomplished? In short, in Spanish America they achieve this goal through the lesson of suffering, and in the American South, the Baptists attain it through the message of salvation.

In pursuit of these strategies, however, both faiths confront fierce criticism that they promote images of Christ concerned with death rather than with life. Do the people of Spanish America, the critics charge, really need a Christ who teaches suffering? Don't they suffer enough in their daily living of poverty and despair? Likewise do the Baptists really need a Christ who directs their lives toward a future life in Glory? Don't they need a Christ who directs them toward the issues of injustice in this world rather than happiness in the next? In the pages ahead I explicate the two strategies, summarize the criticisms, and present my case that the critics who espouse them are, frankly, in error.

In anticipation, let me summarize my own position. My contention is that a Christ nailed to a cross with blood flowing down his face and a Christ strolling through the streets of gold in a heavenly city are, in fact, affirmations of our humanity. I make this claim from the theoretical position that our interpretations of people's actions must first be grounded in what they are doing now, at this moment.

This constructivist, humanistic position sees culture as "emergent, always alive, and in process" (Bruner 1994, 407). Exploration of the past, as surely Chapters 2 and 3 indicate, yields great insight in our comprehending what people do and say. But culture viewed as "emergent, always alive, and in process" means that in the actions unfolding around us even the past comes to be experientially in the present. In addressing religion, this position contends that worship has a transformative quality by which participants leave the world of the everyday to encounter, if for a brief moment, a heightened sense of being (Turner and Turner 1978). We can follow the participants' actions in our understanding only if we apprehend how ritual organizes contemporary experience into performances of joy and sadness, of ecstasy and despair, of unity and alienation, through the evocative, multivocalic power of symbols, both iconic and verbal. Consequently, even when the Baptists in their most fundamentalist mode are singing about how happy they'll be in a future life, the key to a humanistic interpretation of that singing is what they are doing now, the singing itself. The strength of their religion is not in what it promises in the distant future but in what, in so promising, it gives now. I hasten to add, as I see a frown appearing on your forehead, this is not a cynical disregard of their beliefs in an afterlife but a recognition of the power of those beliefs in addressing the present.

Yet in my anxiety to explain where I am and what I'm up to, I am ahead of myself and, I fear, ahead of you. Let us return to a careful examination of the twin strategies of putting death in its place, and let us begin first with the Christ of the Touch and the lesson of suffering.

Suffering, *sufrir*, is a fundamental aspect of the being-in-Christ world in Spanish America. There, Christ suffers on the cross so we too may learn from him how to suffer; in fact, it appears to me, as a student of San Pedro's Don

Chucho, that this is *the* lesson Christ teaches us in Spanish America: how to suffer. The gentle beating of the chest to the rhythm of "mi culpa, mi culpa, mi gran culpa" is a small, but expressive example of shaping the emotions to fit the model of Christ's sufferings. Fasting, though less important these days than previously, remains another example. Pilgrimage itself requires suffering. One is tempted to say the more physically difficult the pilgrimage, the more the lesson is learned. The most vivid testimony I have witnessed is older people—people my age—on their knees, crossing the plaza, climbing the stairs, and going down the aisle toward the sacrificial altar.

Suffering, however, is conjoined with faith. Faith, *la fe*. How many times have we heard people say to us in explaining miracles, "Es la fe que vale; it is faith that matters"? Both Spanish American Catholics and Southern Baptists speak freely of faith. Among the Southern Baptists, at least as I have heard them, faith means surrender, giving your heart over to Jesus in the belief that your soul, destined for hell, will be saved. *La fe*, however, among Spanish American Catholics, is action. Your action. Your own personal action. It is your faith, a thinglike possession you have and that you put into play, that brings about wonders.

A perfect example of Spanish American faith was one I found in New Mexico, at the shrine to the crucified Christ in Chimayó, a traditional site of pilgrimage for Hispanics throughout the region. In a side room of the shrine there is a small hole in the floor full of dirt that purports to heal if applied, for example, to an aching joint. A priest, newly arrived from Spain, explained that since God is all-powerful, if he chooses to cure through the dirt, he may. People, on the other hand, much more commonly replied to questions about the dirt's healing power, "Es la fe que vale."

Focused by faith, suffering celebrates Christ's human aspect. In the battles at the beginning of Christianity, the issue of Christ's nature presumably was settled with the Nicene Creed, which proclaimed Christ was both fully human and fully divine. The Southern Baptists do not recite the creed, because, as they say, they are not a creedal religion. Human creeds run counter to the divine authority of the Bible, to the Church as a band of baptized believers, and to the notion of personal profession of faith. Yet Baptists believe that Christ lived among us for thirty-three years and suffered the agony of the Crucifixion. Even, however, as they sing "The Old Rugged Cross," they look beyond the cross to the heavenly city. The Spanish American Catholics stand in full agreement about life beyond the resurrection and recite the time-honored words: "Creo en un solo Señor, Jesucristo [quien] resucitó al tercer día, según las Escrituas, y subió al cielo, y está sentado a la derecha del Padre; I believe in one Lord, Jesus Christ [who] arose on the third day, according to the Scriptures, and ascended to the sky, and sits at the right hand of the Father." Yet they look not to the heavenly city with streets paved with pure gold but at Christ being whipped, crowned with thorns, and nailed to the cross. He hangs there on the cross, his side, where the soldier stabbed a spear, still oozing. Materially, as an icon, Christ resides in the visual world of humans. This means that Christ "is a Jesus who bleeds . . . a Jesus made of flesh-and-blood like us. The blood on his face, side, hands, and feet are the signs of his humanity; not the abstract 'humanity' of the philosophers and theologians [nor the verbal humanity of the Baptists, you insert], but the flesh-and-blood humanity of those who dare to kiss his wounds" (Goizueta 1995, 67). Being human, Christ teaches us the human lesson: how to die.

Throughout Spanish America, a common name for human is *cristiano*, "Christian." "*Cristianos* . . . are subject to certain known rules of morality. Specifically they are governed by all the constraints and prescriptions that anthropologists would subsume under the rubric of 'culture'" (Brandes 1988, 135). Even more, *cristianos* possess *cultura*, which is "culture" pushed to a higher level in which people exhibit those behavioral qualities that characterize the very best of humanity. Creatures without *cultura* are animals, prototypically dogs, but any other animal, domestic or wild. While no anthropologist would argue there are humans without culture, *cristianos* insist some humans live as if they had no *cultura*. They act like animals, violent, promiscuous, without constraint. Frequently, such people live in the wilds, away from the grid pattern of urban settlement, the locus of civilized life. In the minds of many of those who claim to be *cristianos*, such people are *indios*, "Indians," another name for savage.

Cristiano, then, is a synonym for *cultura* and civilization; it stands in opposition to life outside the urban grid, a life that resembles the unrestrained ways of animals. Furthermore, the path to becoming a *cristiano* is through the sacraments, beginning with the baptism of the newborn baby. Since, at least until quite recently, nearly every person in Spanish American communities receives the blessing of baptism as a matter of course, becoming a *cristiano* and growing up with *cultura* merge into a single process. In sum, *cristiano* bids to join one fundamental feature of Spanish American heritage, the concept of an urbane, civilized life bounded by the rationality of the grid pattern, with another, the call to follow the teachings of Christ.

In following the teachings of Christ we learn how to die, as he himself died, this God who was fully human. In his suffering he died "con paciencia, con resignación, con tranquilidad; patiently, with resignation, with tranquility." To die in the manner of Christ is to die in a human manner of a *cristiano*, one who has learned to live a life of balance, of restraint, of control. To die in the manner of Christ, we too must learn *how* to suffer. Otherwise, we die like a dog, without reason, without acceptance, without patience, without *cultura* (Brandes 1984, 1988; Richardson, Bode, and Pardo 1971).[4]

Upon hearing that Christ died "con paciencia, con resignación, con tranquilidad," critics rush to condemn: The suffering Christ is one "who has been thoroughly defeated and humiliated" (Batstone 1991, 17). Liberation theologians such as David Batstone and Jon Sobrino long to establish the Kingdom of God on earth, and for them the "means to that end is love—not love as mere suffering, as in the crucifixion, but as effective action made possible by the resurrection" (Dodson 1988, 239). The scorn directed toward the suffering Christ goes back at least to John Mackay's well-known *The Other Spanish Christ* (1932). Mackay suggested, tongue in cheek, that Christ on his way from Calvary to Spain was imprisoned and that another Christ, the Christ of Tangiers, of Africa, took his place. On arriving in the New World with the conquistadors, on the last of the holy crusades, this other

4. What about those who do not receive the sacraments, you ask? Among those who do not but who yet live within the urban grid are Jews. Since they do not receive the sacraments, they are not *cristianos*, and not being *cristianos*, they are without *cultura*. Being without *cultura*, they are, in the harsh, prejudiced voices of *cristianos*, *perros judios*, "Jewish dogs" (Brandes 1984). The Vatican, led by Pope John Paul II, who has worked to rectify the silence of the Church during the Holocaust, condemns such language and the brutality the words convey. Apart from Jews, what about Protestants? Are Protestants *cristianos* or *perros protestantes*? You remember the priest in San Pedro, Colombia, back in the early 1960s? He was fond of getting on the loudspeaker strategically fixed on the church's steeple and haranguing the people to come to mass. "If you don't," he shouted, "you'll turn into Communists or Protestants." With the increase in Protestantism, particularly the evangelical variety, the tables in some communities are being turned. In those Andean villages where Protestants have gained the upper hand, the pre-Protestant era "is represented as a dark world where victimized Indians, shrouded in illiteracy and ignorance, were driven by their masters [including the local priest] to shoulder . . . unending ritual obligations that condemned them to a life of brutish drunkenness, servility, and poverty" (Thurner 1993, 45). Today, Protestants proudly proclaim it is they who have *cultura*; it is they who are *cristianos*.

Spanish Christ became still third, the Creole Christ. This Creole Christ has only two dramatic roles, either as a babe in his mother's arms or as the suffering victim. The Creole Christ is "a Christ who was born and died, but who never lived" (Mackay 1932, 110). Since Mackay's assessment, other voices have continued in the same vein. An anthropologist considering Mexico declares that the Virgin of "Guadalupe stands for life, for hope, for health; Christ on the cross [stands] for despair and death" (Wolf 1958, 37). Still another finds that the peasants in central Panama stress the death of Christ, not his resurrection; consequently, "their religion offers little in the way of redemption" (Gudeman 1976, 713). Architectural historians argue that the "greatest monuments of Colonial structure are lacerated blood-stained statues of Christ. The oppressed Indian identified himself with the suffering Christ [and] often gave him Indian features" (Kubler and Soria 1959, 164). Basing his argument in part on what he sees as the "goddess cult" in the religions of Native Americans, another historian concludes, Christ in Spanish America developed into a "sorrowful mother-suffering . . . archetype [and] came to be the favoured role model of the masses, reduced to a fatalistic acceptance of earthly privation and powerlessness" (Pike 1992, 433).

As this sampling shows, the critics, as diverse as liberationists, anthropologists, and historians, concur that the lesson the suffering Christ teaches is a fatalistic one. Since I accept the evidence that the lesson of suffering that the Spanish American Christ teaches us is a lesson on *how* to suffer and that lesson directs our efforts on *how* to die and since I propose that from a constructivist, humanistic perspective such knowledge affirms our humanity, I suggest the critics have got it wrong. To correct their misguidance requires further clarification of the issue of putting death in its place through suffering.

We begin the clarification by noting the tendency on the part of the critics to derive their fatalistic message from the unhappy lot of Native Americans. If, however, we actually look at the religion of indigenous communities, for example, among the Maya in Mexico and Guatemala, as provided by John Watanabe's masterful summary (1990), we see that neither the Crucifixion nor the Resurrection are central concerns. Postconquest religion in indigenous villages more commonly revolved around the saints, and consequently, the figure of Christ was frequently recast into Santo Cristo, St. Christ (Lockhart 1992). As a saint, Santo Cristo not uncommonly displayed a loving kindness associated with mothers. Among the Tzeltal Maya, people addressed Christ as "flowery bosom, our flower giver of birth" (Maurer Avalos 1993,

230). If there is a people to blame for the presence of a suffering Christ in the New World, as Mackay noted, it is more likely the Spaniards. That being the case, we must retrace the journey of the Iberian Christ to the New World and return to Spain.

In returning to Spain, we encounter the so-called morbid strain in Spanish religiosity (Payne 1984, 56–59). The "morbid strain" waxes in the southern part of the country, especially in the province of Andalusia. In the Andalusian city of Seville, for example, "The Christ of the Good Death" is a figure of "tragic vehemence," whose mouth opens "in agony and the eyes seem to burst, resulting in an expression of unbearable torture" (Kubler and Soria 1959, 151–52). "On Good Friday," an older resident recalled to folklorist Candace Slater during her research in Granada, an Andalusian city to the east of Seville, "husbands and wives slept apart. Whole families wore black. . . . 'Hush, now,' mothers would tell their children if they talked or giggled. 'Don't you know Our Lord is dying on the cross?' "(1990, 169).[5]

What are we to make of this celebration of death? Timothy Mitchell, a folklorist like Slater and a student of Andalusia, agrees that Andalusians are fatalistic, but they are fatalistic passionately. Their songs are filled with rage, with dependency, and with rage at being dependent. One goes:

Qué desgraciadito soy mala estrella a mí me guía por dondequiera que voy.	What a wretched one am I, an evil star guides me wherever I go.
El hombre va por la vía como la piedra en el aire esperando la caía.	Man goes through the life like a stone in the air, waiting to fall.
Qué bonito está el camino de olivios y de palmeras pero que triste es mi sino sembrao de sudó y pena.	How petty the road is with olive and palm trees but how sad is my fate sown with sweat and pain.

(1990, 13)

5. According to some observers, the Portuguese Christ differs considerably from his Spanish brother: "The Spanish Christ . . . never comes down from the cross but hangs there bleeding. The Portuguese Christ plays in the fields with the people, has his lunch with them, and only at certain times has to be on duty and hang himself on the cross again" (Trend 1957, 191; see also Joyce Riegelhaupt's similar views discussed in Schneider and Lindenbaum 1987).

How like the South! you exclaim. W-w-what? I stutter in amazement. Sure, you say, you who are never without doubt. The Lost Cause. Born to lose. Short life of trouble. Whiskey-bent and hell-bound. And isn't one of your favorite songs "Highway of Sorrow"? And before I can stop you, you cut loose, high and lonesome:

> Down a highway of sorrow,
> I'm traveling all alone.
> I've lost all my true friends;
> I've lost a happy home.
> I'm headin' for destruction;
> I'm on the wrong track.
> Down a highway of sorrow,
> There's no turning back.[6]

Let's get back to Mitchell, I insist, not wanting to get distracted. Mitchell starts from a location not far from our consideration of self and death and place and out-of-place. We humans, he maintains, seek to be our own autonomous selves. Death, everywhere, threatens our goal. Death throws us into an autonomy crisis. The crisis generates such strong emotions that we take the emotional state as the foundation of our being. The pervasive tone of crisis constitutes our grasp on reality. Consequently, we seek to perpetuate, even to augment, the upheaval. In the Andalusian case, the path takes the route of dying, dying again and again, with Christ during *Semana Santa*. Filling the streets of Seville during Holy Week, the giant *pasos* hoisted onto the shoulders of crowds of straining men constitute a street liturgy that dramatizes a scriptural reference almost beyond recognition. For "every inch of scriptural foundation, Andalusian street liturgy will take a mile" (1990, 146). Furthermore, in contrast to the "sheer amount of culture . . . devoted to . . . the Passion and Death of Christ, the theme of the Risen Christ (*Cristo Resucitado*) has elicited little culture and less interest" in the region (165).

So where does the story of the Passion of Christ end? Mitchell asks. And immediately he answers his own question: It doesn't end. It continues on in the suffering of Mary. The Passion of Mary, though theologically subordinate to that of Christ, parallels his Passion with her own image as *Mater Do-*

6. One of Bill Monroe's Blue Grass Boys, Pete Pyle, wrote this song, which Bill recorded in 1951.

lorosa. The Passion of Christ ends with his death, but the Passion of Mary goes on forever. "The plot line of the Passion according to Andalusia can be summarized as suffering, death, burial, and suffering without end." Nevertheless, Mitchell hastens to add, it is a mistake to think that the Andalusian street liturgy is indifferent to redemption. "The whole penitential ideology underlying Passional culture is dedicated to the removal of sin through suffering—because it is suffering that removes sin, not Resurrection" (178).

What is the relevance of Mitchell's study to our attempt to explicate being-in-Christ in Spanish America? As he says, the Andalusians did not invent the idea of redemption through suffering; they simply have developed it beyond other aspects of Christ's message. Certainly, I am not implying that we see today's celebration in Andalusia as the historical cause of the Spanish American one. At the same time, the Spanish case does undercut the easy attribution of the suffering Christ in Spanish America as stemming from the lot of Native Americans. We best view the Andalusian example as an analogous, parallel development of the lesson of suffering. That resemblance beckons us to continue our interrogation of suffering. What further clarifications might we encounter?

"Suffer, then, suffer, and resign yourself to suffering so that you may believe," Miguel de Unamuno urges (1974a, 132). Here, Unamuno, in his typical paradoxical manner, addresses us by talking to another, one Nicodemus. Nicodemus, you recall, was the Pharisee who came to Jesus in the middle of the night so that none of his scholarly colleagues might see him and make fun of him. There, alone with Jesus, he asked how these things could be, how a man could be reborn when he was old. In his abrupt reply, Jesus said, "Marvel not that I said unto thee, Ye must be born again" (John 3:7). And he went on to deliver the famous words "For God so loved the world, that he gave his only begotten Son, that whosoever believeth in him should not perish, but have everlasting life" (John 3:16). John is silent on how Nicodemus reacted to this outrageous claim of love. But in the silence, we feel the agony of Nicodemus, the agony, Unamuno says, the agony of Christianity, the struggle within each of life and death, the struggle of the Crucifixion and Resurrection. In solidarity with Nicodemus, we hear Unamuno instruct us, "Set yourself to thinking of that immense doctrine of a God who descends in the Son to incarnate pain and suffer it, and thus make it divine; think on it, and ask for sorrows so that you may become divine" (133). Suffer as did Christ in his agony, suffer and make the agony divine. We see little more of Nicodemus until he reappears after the Crucifixion to help prepare the body for burial. Again he says nothing, but as he joins with others to lay the body in the grave, we know in his silence that Nicodemus the Pharisee weeps.[7]

Let us turn to Albert Schweitzer and consider his presentation of suffering in the First Epistle of Peter. As Schweitzer notes (1931, 141–42), 1 Peter is filled with injunctions on how to suffer: "For what glory is it, if, when ye be buffeted for your faults, ye shall take it patiently? but if, when ye do well, and suffer for it, ye take it patiently, this is acceptable with God. For even hereunto were ye called: because Christ also suffered for us, leaving us an example, that ye should follow his steps" (1 Peter 2:20–21). "Forasmuch then as Christ hath suffered for us in the flesh, arm yourselves likewise with the same mind: for he that hath suffered in the flesh hath ceased from sin" (1 Peter 4:1). "But rejoice, inasmuch as ye are partakers of Christ's sufferings" (1 Peter 4:13). And finally, "But let none of you suffer as a murderer, or as a thief, or as an evil doer, or as a busybody in other men's matters. Yet if any man suffer as a Christian, let him not be ashamed; but let him glorify God on this behalf" (1 Peter 4:15–16).

Can't you hear the voice of Don Chucho in Chapter 5, talking to us from San Pedro: "Cristo murió para enseñarnos como sufrir; Christ died in order to teach us how to suffer." To live is to die. It is part of the human tragedy. Through his actions, Christ teaches us this tragedy and how we must face death, "con paciencia, con resignación, con tranquilidad." And if the words of a cigar maker from a small town in Colombia don't carry enough weight, we might recall the example of Philip II, the King of Spain.

Philip was king of Spain in the sixteenth century during the country's Golden Age, when the Spanish empire ruled nearly half of the entire world. Death came upon Philip in the most gruesome manner, as for fifty-three days, covered in sores, he lay on his bed dying. Because the slightest touch brought agony, he could not be turned, so he became encased in his own filth. But as his body literally rotted away, Philip died the good death. Know-

7. Unamuno's call for us to ask for suffering so that we may make it divine echoes the words of the philosopher Max Scheler. According to Scheler's understanding, "At its core, the Christian attitude toward suffering is based on a belief that only the person who is blessed and depends upon God can tolerate pain and suffering correctly, can love and, where necessary, seek suffering out" (1992, 112). Similarly, in words attributed to her, Simone Weill observes that the greatness of Christianity inheres in the fact not that it provides supernatural relief from suffering but that it provides a supernatural use for it (Wiman 2001).

ing that the "redemptive value of suffering—especially patient suffering—had no better model than Christ himself," Philip ordered crucifixes to be placed throughout his room, so that whichever way he looked, he might see Christ dying on the cross (Eire 1995, 317). Filled with the sight of his Lord and finding transcendence in that image, Philip died the good death. He died in the manner of Christ, "con paciencia, con resignación, con tranquilidad."

If we return to Schweitzer and follow him as he goes from 1 Peter to Paul's epistles, we discover an even closer tie among suffering, dying, and Christ. Paul equates suffering with dying; suffering means dying with Christ. Here are some of the many citations that Schweitzer gives (1931, 143) from Paul's letters: "I die daily [in Christ]" (1 Corinthians 15:31); "Know ye not, that so many of us as were baptized into Jesus Christ were baptized into his death?" (Romans 6:3); "Now if we be dead with Christ" (Romans 6:8); "And if Christ be in you, the body is dead" (Romans 8:10); "Always bearing about in the body the dying of the Lord Jesus" (2 Corinthians 4:10); "For we which live are always delivered unto death for Jesus' sake" (2 Corinthians 4:11); and "I am crucified with Christ" (Galatians 2:20).

At this moment, you can take no more. You burst into Spanish, quoting San Pablo: "Si no resucitó Cristo, vana es vuestra fe." And you continue. "Vana es nuestra fe. ¿Oyes? Vana. Si nuestra esperanza en Cristo se reduce a lo de esta vida, seremos los más desdichados de todos los hombres. Pero es un hecho que Cristo resucitó . . . [Y con la resurrection] el último enemigo, la muerte, será aniquilado; If Christ did not rise from the dead, vain is thy faith. Vain is our faith. Do you hear? Vain. If our hope in Christ is only in this life, we will be the most wretched people on earth. [Wretched! you fairly shout the word. Wretched, you repeat.] But the fact is that Christ rose from the dead . . . [And with the resurrection] the final enemy, death, will be destroyed" (1 Corintos 15:17–20, 26).

But I, along with Unamuno, can't resist reminding you that Paul never saw Christ as a man of flesh and blood. Unlike Veronica, who wiped the blood from his eyes, or Simon, who carried his cross, or the God-forsaken soldier who stabbed him in the side, or even Nicodemus, who grieved before the dead body, Paul never saw the carnal, mortal Christ, and so "this first Christian mystic dreamed . . . of a final triumph" (1972, 262). On the road to Damascus, Paul was struck blind; then while blind so he could not see the Lord, he heard a voice. In this connection, Richard Palmer tells us that Paul, like the Protestant Luther, was fond of saying "salvation comes through the ears" (1969, 18). For Paul, indeed for all of us, the Resurrection is a verbal event. Suffering, though, as Sartre reminds us, "has *being*." This is true especially when instead of speaking of suffering, we see it in the faces of others, in portraits, in statues, in tragic masks, and, one might add, in the fixed agony on the cross. Suffering "is there in the midst of the world, impenetrable and dense, like this tree or stone; it endures; . . . it is what it is" (Sartre 1956, 91).

Suffer, then, suffer that you may believe. Suffering, faced honestly, makes resurrection a possibility. Likewise, the suffering has its lesson precisely because of the Resurrection. Contrary to Mitchell, the story of the Passion of Christ does have an end. And even as we on the streets of San Pedro, Colombia, and Seville, Spain, follow Christ to his death and learn once more the lesson of suffering, we await the Resurrection.[8]

Yet we must be careful. If we put too much emphasis on the Resurrection, we miss the Spanish American and Spanish message of the Crucifixion, if not of Christianity. If we keep our eyes fixed on the icons that depict the last hours of Jesus, the whipping at the column, the mocking of his kingship, the carrying of the cross, the stumbling and falling under its weight, the Crucifixion itself, and then the burial, we encounter the exaltation of despair and the power that derives therein.

When we are in-Christ, the weak, the tortured, the despised, the crucified, and the dead, normally objects of scorn, become icons of solidarity. This symbolic reversal, so compelling in all religions, is Christianity's strong suit. When the critics dismiss the bloody figures on Spanish American crosses as the emasculation of strength, they misread the reversal. It is the exaltation of the emasculation that gives the bloody figures their power. It is the exaltation of the weak that draws us together in this moment of extraordinary intensity. And it is the exaltation of despair that turns suffering into the touchstone of our lives.[9]

8. I am indebted to Valerie Richardson for these words about suffering and honesty.

9. Victor Turner led the way, as he did on many other occasions, to the clarification of symbolic reversals. In their departure from the everyday, particularly intense modes of being are symbolically "likened to death, to being in the womb, to invisibility, to darkness, to bisexuality, to the wilderness, and to an eclipse of the sun or moon" (1969, 95). Later, in words that warned against an overly dispassionate (i.e., structuralist) analysis of these reversals, he said when "symbols are rigidified into logical operators and subordinated to implicit syntax-like rules [we become] blind to the creative or innovative potential of symbols as factors in human action" (1982, 23). To remain open to the power of these symbols and not misread or dismiss them, we must

Yes, you say, but then there is Vatican II. What happens to suffering in the reforms that talk so much about the Resurrection? You have a point, I agree, so let's address those reforms and see where they take us.

What is striking about the new directions laid down in the 1960s and 1970s is the shift in the manner in which people are encouraged to be in-Christ and the image of Christ that arises from that effort. We see in that shift an interacting change among material setting, performance, and image.

In the material setting, new religious structures in Spanish America resemble cavernous, indoor stadiums, such as the new Villa of the Virgin of Guadalupe. Few have saints in residence. When we went back to San Pedro in '92 and entered the remodeled and largely plain *iglesia*, I asked my friend Seneca, "Where are the saints?" With a certain smile on his face, he replied, "They have been retired." The new crucifixes de-emphasize the suffering of Christ. The modern figures are nearly bloodless, and the stark agony of earlier facial portrayals has gone (Figure 34).

All this brings to mind the great English cathedrals and abbeys stripped of their icons and color by the Puritanical Roundheads during the English Civil War of the seventeenth century. The difference, of course, is that the denuding of the English structures came about through violence. The present stripping comes from within the Church establishment, the members of which seem hell-bent on turning themselves into high-church Anglicans.

Related to transformation of the setting, the present church, as we heard from the young priest in Nueva Esperanza, longs to be more interactive and more communal. While the consecration of the host remains paramount, the mass, especially in the United States, seems drifting toward a focus on communion. Even in Spanish America, we encounter an urge to shift away from the lesson of suffering. When, upon our return, I mentioned to the San Pedro priest—a priest as young and as interactive as the one in Nueva Esperanza—how in '62 Don Chucho explained how we should suffer in the manner of Christ, he, in words as sanctimonious as any spoken by the Southern Baptists, set the record straight: "Today, we teach the agony of Christ, the Christ of the Crucifixion, but also we teach the triumph of Christ, the Christ of the Resurrection. Today, we teach the whole Christian experience." Later that night, when certain, odd, disturbing feelings persisted in intruding on my

---

follow the manner in which people, in concrete, historical settings, use symbols to address the experiential crevasses in their lives.

Fig. 34. Crucifixion without suffering, in the cathedral in Mérida, Mexico

sleep, I sought to brush them away. If Protestantism is on the rise in Colombia and elsewhere and if La Iglesia Pentecostés, out by the highway in San Pedro and in Nueva Esperanza, rings with spirit-filled tongues, why should I care? It's all same to me, isn't it? (Richardson 1998a).

The movement of feast days to the closest Sunday, such as with Corpus Christi and the Day of the Three Kings, or Epiphany, further hints at a growing "Protestantization" of Catholicism, by which I mean a reduced emphasis on the visual (i.e., fewer icons), an increased emphasis on congregationalism, and a shift from the Crucifixion to the Resurrection. The eagerness of some to add a fifteenth station to the *Vía Crucis* adds frosting to the Protestant lookalike cake. Previously, the *Vía Crucis*, the way of the cross, moved through the stations to station thirteen, a dead Christ in a grieving Mary's arms, and ended with station fourteen, Christ's body in his tomb. The addition (by some) of station fifteen, however, gives us, in one wording at least, the angels in John 20 berating Mary Magdalene for searching the tomb for Christ. She should know that he has risen. The responsorial reading is "Dying you destroyed our death. Rising you restored our life. Lord Jesus, come in glory" (http://ivory.lm.com/~kclark/xvtext.html 1998; see also Cabestrero 1994).

In her chapter on devotion in *Modern Catholicism* (1991), Margaret Hebblethwaite summarizes the changes in Catholic worship. In words particularly relevant to North America, she begins:

> Before Vatican II, the devotional practices of Catholics were easier to pin down than they became after the Council. There was a recognizable culture expressed in prayers specific to Catholics and in many devotions performed in Church. Examples of these would be the lighting of candles before statues of the saints, the stations of the cross, visits to the Blessed Sacrament. . . . Benediction was a regular—often weekly—devotion of great popular appeal: reverence and love were fostered in a rite that enriched the senses of smell—with clouds of incense; of hearing—with sweet singing; and of sight—with the awe-inspiring presence of a consecrated host, exposed in a golden spiky monstrance.

Vatican II, she continues, brought a critical reappraisal of many of these customary practices. Such was the reappraisal that "Questions crept in as to whether the Lord had rather instituted the Eucharist for us to share in a common meal, than for us to kneel down and worship and then replace in the tabernacle. . . . Devotion at mass changed from gazing with love in silence on one's knees . . . to more standing, singing, participating and responding. In the same mood of urged participation, weekly communicating has become the almost universal norm, bringing to completion a trend towards frequent Communion."

In the "shared spirituality," where there is "less silence" and more "group dynamics," she concludes that popular "religious art and holy pictures went through a transformation. Images became less identifiably Catholic: sacred hearts and crowned virgins were on the decrease; golden sunsets, billowing waves, snow-clad mountain peaks and leafy glades took their place" (240–41). All who rejoice in the innovations of Vatican II, please read the sadness between the lines.[10]

The Christ of the Touch is the Christ of immanence. Immanence? Yes, immanence, meaning "dwelling within the universe." The Christ of the Word, to the contrary, is the Christ of transcendence, meaning "going beyond, rising above." Before we rise with Christ in the South, we must kneel in solitude once more before the bloodied figure above the altar in Spanish

10. For another dose of what used to be, consider the before and after photographs of St. Donatus Church of Brooten, Minnesota, that McDannell provides in her *Material Christianity* (1995, 172–73). In the early 1950s, a large St. Donatus occupied the central niche in a tableau that would be comfortable in a Baroque church in Mexico. On either side two other figures stared out across the massive altar, and they in turn were flanked by two angels. By the end of the 1950s, in response to criticisms by Catholic liturgical specialists, the sanctuary was gutted, the tableau cast aside in favor of an enigmatic wall plaque, and the altar changed into a spiny-legged table. With the exception of the small crucifix, the setting would welcome almost any Protestant congregation.

Here are two additional observations about the shift toward a more congregational style of worship and a greater focus on the Resurrection. "The Council of Trent . . . stressed the representation of the sacrifice on the Cross. But Vatican II now spoke more readily of the paschal mystery of Christ's death and resurrection" (Thurian and Wainwright 1983, 106). And Suzanne Campbell-Jones notes that at mass in a modern English convent, the priest and the nuns have a meal, then they celebrate mass, and afterward they have a group discussion. "Whereas before communion involved a relationship between each nun and the awesome God, now communion also [expresses] inter-relationships within the community" (1980, 98). As the priest moves from a position of sole authority to being more a member of the group, at least temporarily, he "loses power . . . and the Mass reverts to a communion meal—a commemorative rite rather than a sacrifice" (104).

Finally, you recall the bookstore at the famous shrine in Lourdes, France, during the brief visit in late spring of 1998, offered a booklet in several languages on the "The Lourdes Way of the Cross." In its introduction to meditations for the different stations of the cross, the English language version flatly states that "Jesus did not take up the Cross to teach us how to die but how to live." It assures us that the meditations contained within will "help us to rediscover the Good News of the Gospel." Not surprising, it proudly included a fifteenth station to move us from the traditional end at the fourteenth station, with Jesus being laid in the tomb, to the moment when we realize that the stone has been rolled away and "Jesus is Risen." Even you were impressed with the sharp contrast with Spanish America's continuing message on how to suffer and the close parallel with the Baptist, congregational message of the "Good News" of the risen Christ.

America and review the lesson on how to suffer and to die. As we considered earlier, in Spanish America *cristiano* is a widely accepted synonym for human. A human, in turn, is a person with *cultura*. Those having *cultura* live within the grid of urbanity, while those without *cultura* live in the wildness of nature. Likewise, those with *cultura* practice the sacraments, while those without *cultura* die like dogs. Thus, as followers of Christ, we are *cristianos*, people with *cultura*, and we face death as he faced it, fully human, with patience, with resignation, and with tranquility. Small wonder, then, that the day Christ suffered and died, *Viernes Santo*, when he was most human, becomes the focus of our passion. If we learn how to suffer, we do not necessarily suffer less, but we make the agony divine. In transforming the agony through parading it in the streets of Andalusia, we seek the strong suit of Christianity, the exaltation of the weak. And in exalting the weak, we affirm our humanity. The reformation of Vatican II, in "teaching the whole message," removes the icons, turns the altar into a table, makes the Eucharist less a sacrifice and more a communion meal, and points less toward the Crucifixion and more toward the Resurrection. In so doing it risks losing the visual and immanence, to be replaced by the verbal and transcendence. Small wonder, then, that we find sadness in Margaret Hebblethwaite's lines.[11]

The risen Christ is a resurrected Christ, a victorious Christ, one who has conquered death. Yet in our eagerness to hear the Southern Baptists celebrate victory over death, we must not overlook the place of suffering in their worship. Before we attend to Baptist suffering, however, we must say one last word about icons and their absence in the Southern Baptist church.

The risen Christ of the Southern Baptists is a Christ not of this world and, being such, challenges any visual portraiture. The very touch of the brush upon canvas runs counter to the ethereal nature of transcendence. This is not to say artists have not accepted the challenge. Famous responses, to mention two, include "The Resurrection" by Piero Della Francesca, in which Christ stands triumphant over his tomb, and "The Ascension" by Rembrandt van Rijn, in which Christ, with arms outstretched and head tossed back, stands amidst a heavenly radiance. These works, however, are those of the masters. The art of the type found on the señora's table in front of the *iglesia*

11. I am indebted, as so often, to one of my students, Julie Walsh, for drawing my attention to the division between immanence and transcendence.

in Nueva Esperanza is not equal to the task. And even among the works of the masters, Peter Paul Rubens's "Descent from The Cross," in which the dead Lord is lowered from the cross, carries a conviction that Charles-Antoine Coypel's "The Resurrection," with its image of the expectant Jesus soaring upward through the clouds, cannot sustain in viewers such as you and me. The word, however, lodged in the biblical narrative, augmented by the doctrine of inerrancy, and preached each Sunday from the pulpit creates images of the risen Savior that bid to transcend the painter's brush.

The one icon that Southern Baptists have, other than the Holy Book itself, is the baptistery. Situated above the choir, at the natural focus point of the eyes, the baptistery becomes the symbolic empty tomb, filled with water, in which one, again "symbolically," dies and rises again, reborn in Christ. Naturally, the water is just tap water, ordinary H_2O; there is nothing holy about it. The entire occasion, as Reverend Overton makes clear, is doubly symbolic, for not only is the baptistery a "symbolic" tomb, but the immersion itself is "symbolic." It carries no sacramental power, or, as Reverend Overton is prone to say, "it's not magic." Only a personal confession of faith, alone and in itself, brings about, through the grace of Jesus Christ, salvation.

The price of salvation is not cheap. The price is suffering, Southern Baptist style. All Christians believe we were born in sin and, without Christ, will die in sin, wretched creatures that we are. So it is appropriate that we suffer, and in the South, we suffer. We suffer the sin of slavery, the defeat of Reconstruction, the hatred of Jim Crow segregation, and the perennial plague of "New Souths." Also in the South, we suffer plentifully and loudly and with all the sentimentality we can muster:

> Passing by a lonesome graveyard
> Everything I love is gone
> Weeping as they laid my darling
> 'Neath a cold, gray tomb of stone.
> (Williams 1983, 200)

Years ago, if you remember, we heard a story about suffering that got to me. It got to me so much it made me mad. We had been making our rounds of Southern Baptist churches in Baton Rouge, a different one each Sunday, and this Sunday we happened into one where the preacher was a guest minister, a missionary from Lebanon. An older man, gray-haired, pleasant, but though he spoke softly (for a Baptist preacher), you knew that he knew life's many turns.

"God calls us all," he began, "but some he calls to be his disciples. To be a disciple, you have to love God so much that any other love is like hate. God doesn't want us to hate, but as a disciple our love for him grows to the point it makes other loves look unlovely. God wanted me to go back to Lebanon. My baby boy didn't want me to go. He cried so loud and so long, a neighbor came over to see if he was all right. God wanted me as his disciple in Lebanon. And God does not want his disciples to have possessions. I bought this house in Pineville [a small town in the middle of the state and the home of Louisiana Baptist College]. I loved that house. I fixed it up. I painted it. I wanted it for my retirement. But I hadn't talked to God about it. And God asked for it. God spoke to me as clearly as I am speaking to you. God asked for that house. At first, I balked. I didn't want to give up my house. But I knew I would. Because it was God's to begin with. So I went back to Lebanon.

"I'm here now to visit my daughter and my grandchild. My grandchild was born with cerebral palsy." Here for the first time, the smooth telling halted. We waited for him to go on. He started, but his voice broke, and then almost in a whisper, he said, "He is three years old, and he can't walk or talk." As if telling us gave him strength, he recovered.

"I asked the Lord, 'Do you have the right? I've been a Christian since I was twelve. I've been preaching since I was fifteen. Do you have the right?'" But answering his own question, he told us, "Yes, you know he does. God has the right, and he never makes mistakes."

There were more than a few people holding back tears. Several ladies in the choir ducked their heads and brushed at their eyes. Me? I wanted to cry, too. I felt awful. I wanted to cry, too, but I got mad.

God has the right? Just what gives him the right? Who is this God that decides little three-year-olds can't walk or talk? Or—thinking of a scene from long ago—that won't let Lazarus, cradled in Abraham's bosom, take water to cool the parched tongue of the rich man burning in hell?

Then you told me, Miles, you're an anthropologist. Act like one. Listen.

Listening, we hear that suffering, spoken here, echoes the trials of Job: "Naked came I out of my mother's womb, and naked shall I return thither; the Lord gave and the Lord hath taken away. Blessed be the name of the Lord" (Job 1:21). Suffering, here, seems to be an affirmation of faith. The more we suffer, the more God loves us. Suffering is not joining in fellowship with Christ on the cross, but suffering is joining with the risen Savior as he ascends to Heaven. It is the path to Glory. Suffering is the public affirmation of Jesus Christ as the resurrected Lord, which separates us from the lost, the non-Christians, the Jews and, for many, the Catholics, and now the Mormons. Suffering comes from the Baptist self-conscious attack on the world, from their insistence on the literal interpretation of the Bible, from the desire to seek total immersion at baptism, and from all the fundamentalist-inspired barriers they so gladly erect between themselves and others, including, most certainly, the regional one, being southern.[12]

Suffering in Spanish America beneath the figure of a crucified Christ is the lesson of solitude. We suffer, almost alone, paired solely with Christ. Suffering, among the Southern Baptists in an auditorium empty of icons but filled with people, is the joy of union, union with each other. Baptist suffering is congregational and verbal. It's the Glory Land way: "Fill your hopes on things eternal. Hold to God's unchanging hand."

Baptist suffering, then, centers on their proclamation of the Christ of the Word, the risen Christ, the Christ of transcendence. Through their embattled engagement with the world, Baptists attempt to convert suffering into the joy of the Resurrection. This joy rests upon, or surges up from, the conversion experience.

After our consideration of the conversion experience in Chapter 4, I believe you will agree that being born again is the central experience in Southern Baptist religious life and its telling, the central theme of Baptist discourse. We can imagine Brother Tommy sticking his finger in Don Miguel's face and shouting, "'Verily, verily, I say unto thee, Except a man be born again, he cannot see the kingdom of God.' John 3:3." To be Glory Land–bound is to be born again.

"As I was mowing alone in the field, August 24th, 1741, all my past life was opened plainly before me, and I saw clearly that it had been filled up with sin." To refresh our hearing of the conversion story, here are selections from

12. The Southern Baptist Convention held its 1998 meeting at Salt Lake City, the international headquarters of the Church of Jesus Christ of Latter-Day Saints, specifically to bring the message of salvation to the Mormons. While the delegates elected Paige Patterson, one of the principal architects of the conservative takeover of the convention, evangelists were out in the streets under the rubric of "Crossover Salt Lake City." The Baptist press, while commenting that not every one of the 1,200 conversions occurring during the event were Mormon, did not hesitate to quote preachers who quoted converted Mormons, saying that the Holy Spirit had led them to see the errors of the Mormon doctrine (http://www.namb.net/press 1998).

the testimony of Isaac Backus we first heard in Chapter 2. "Divine justice appeared clear in my condemnation, and I saw that God had a right to do with me as he would. My soul yielded all into his hands, fell at his feet, and was silent and calm before Him. The word of God and the promise of His grace appeared firmer than a rock, and I was astonished at my previous unbelief. My heavy burden was done, tormenting fears were fled, and my joy was unspeakable" (Grenz 1983, 65). The unspeakable joy, which Baptists are always speaking about, rises with the Resurrection. If the lesson of the Crucifixion in Spanish America dwells in the language of how to suffer, the lesson of the Resurrection in the American South, among the Baptists, finds its home in the language of rebirth.

In narrating their new birth, the Southern Baptists are voicing a familiar tale. Children who grow up in the local church walk the aisle to make a public confession of their sins as nonchalantly as any parishioner kneeling hurriedly in the confessional booth in the *iglesia* in Nueva Esperanza. At the same time, the narrative of conversion, as opposed to the event itself (or, as one might unkindly put it, the "*un*event"), may well be a "ritual that integrates unacknowledged purposes into a socially construable project—namely, being an Evangelical Christian [i.e., in our case, Southern Baptist]—and thus makes those purposes understandable" (Stromberg 1993, 30). In relating an individual experience to others, even as a retrospective account, the "conversion narrative is . . . a story about the concerns of a present self moving toward a particular vision of its future" (Cucchiari 1988, 429) and, in the telling, joins its vision with that of the denomination. The conversion narrative is a performative bridge between the individual's experience and the congregation's being. As central as they are to individual lives, conversion narratives are equally central to the congregation's life. They are told to be heard and to be heard in the context of congregational worship. Thus, in its telling, as a bridge, the conversion narrative lets both the individual and the congregation come to be, for those who can walk the aisle.

As we have heard so frequently, the narrative of rebirth often stresses the life of sin before the light came. In the same manner, the preaching and singing of the Glory Land way stresses the evils of this world and the blissful life with Jesus. Some misread the emphasis on this world of trouble to say it actually reflects the downtrodden life of many poor white people victimized by the elite and condemned to lives of racism and bigotry. A sympathetic scholar of the southern scene writes, "Reflecting the strong impress of Calvinism, southern religion portrays this life as a vale of tears, wherein suffering is the common lot. This is a terrible commentary on the debilitating poverty and other social and spiritual problems in southern history. Death in this society was a comfort, a release from endless toil and suffering of one sort or another, and not altogether to be feared" (Wilson 1995, 107). The link between the narrative and the actual life may not be that tight. The conversion narrative and preaching the coming of the Glorious Resurrection are, after all, in the genre of religious language. And the strength of religious language lies in its ability to take conventional understanding and turn it on its head. In the narrative and the preaching, we experience the same symbolic inversion we encounter in the lesson of the crucified Christ. Just as the people, kneeling before the agony of the crucified Christ, make the suffering of Christ into the way of the *cristiano*, a way of restraint, patience, and resignation, so those who tell of their awful life before rebirth and the awful condition of the present world are in fact affirming their chosen state now. That they may be affirming their chosen state surrounded by the many sorrows that dog the South is a matter of no little consequence; yet in our constructivist, performative approach, we come closer to understanding the power of the conversion narrative when we hear it less like a representation of the world out there and more of an evocation of what we are about now, which, in the end, is putting death in its place.[13]

In the previous section, we recognized how, under the impetus of Vatican II, worship among Catholics, especially among American Catholics and even more among "Bible Belt Catholics" (Anderson and Friend 1995), betrays a movement toward a less iconic and a more congregational style, with a

13. I am treading a thin line, and I need your help to keep me from falling off. In referring to the contrasts drawn in the narrative between the previous life of sin the converted lived and the spiritual joy of the present and in the preaching between the benighted state of the world today and the world of glory, I know, after all we have been through, you understand that I am not dismissing those words as inconsequential. On the contrary, I am taking those words very seriously, as religious language. Likewise, I am not dismissing the harsh conditions of southern life among the plain folk, especially in the formative years of the Southern Baptists. Again, on the contrary, I find more than a little cultural resistance in the rhetoric of salvation. In brief, the resistance verse goes, "If capitalism has created such a world that poor suffer and the rich prosper, then to hell with it, I'm bound for Glory." Finally, the role of the conversion narrative runs throughout African American worship. Starting life anew appeals to us all and to start the life anew free of racism holds great promise—a promise that Martin Luther King Jr., a Baptist, urged us to keep and one we are still working on.

greater voicing of the message of the Resurrection: in a word, a "Protestantization." Is there a corresponding trend among the Southern Baptists but in the opposite direction, a "Catholicization"? In an even shorter word, no.

That *is* a bit short, you complain. What about the Maundy Thursday observances and the opening processional in gowns we saw? Don't they indicate a shift to a more high-church style?

All right, let's review the recent changes among the Southern Baptists. First of all, the "shift," as you put it, to a more liturgical style does appear among churches of the moderate wing, churches more likely to promote an ecumenical voice. However, these are the very churches that lost the battle for the control of the Southern Baptist Convention. Churches affiliated with the conservative majority also have promoted changes. There are, as we encountered in Chapter 3, the megachurches, with something for everyone. Apart from these special cases, others with more modest agendas have sought strategies for increasing their membership. Crosses, once an anathema, appear embedded in the designs of recently built churches. "Auditorium," as the term to designate where the word is preached, has all but succumbed to "sanctuary," but "sanctuary" itself may be giving way to "worship center." And these "worship centers" may hang brightly lettered banners from the walls and place screens near the pulpit upon which are projected words from songs featuring a contemporary sound. The congregation may opt for jeans and slacks, and the preacher, if in fact he wears a coat, sports one of many colors. Furthermore, the preaching itself may be interactive, with the preacher posing a question and asking for the audience response. Yet in all this upbeat, almost frenzied worship, the message remains, as in Chapter 3, fundamental and inerrant. To repeat: hell is hot, heaven is sweet, and Jesus saves. And Catholics, not to mention Jews and Mormons, are fair game for the message of Zion. To hear a former Catholic speak the conversion narrative and affirm the passage to Glory must rank in today's Baptist scheme of things with the testimony of the most hardened atheist as a certain sign of their chosen status as the children of God.[14]

14. In our comparison of the Christ of Spanish America with the Christ of the Southern Baptists of the American South, I keep getting the feeling we are paralleling the distinctions between classicism and romanticism that persistently recur in Western culture. Classicism, with its inevitable image of a sun-drenched landscape of pediments and columns, stresses external objectivity and internal constraint. Romanticism, with an equally inevitable evocation of brooding forests and penetrating sunrays, emphasizes internal subjectivity and external outbursts. The Christ of Spanish America, through the performance of sacramental forms, teaches the lesson of

And What of Mary?

In our journey, we have spoken much about the presence of Christ in New World narratives and in the worship performances of Catholics in Spanish America and Baptists in the American South. Surely, when talking about Christianity, one must talk about Christ. Yet there is this other figure. How does she fit into the lesson of the Crucifixion and the message of salvation? I can legitimately restrict, don't you agree, any considerations to such a complex question to a few observations, which follow.

Any time spent in Spanish America, or for that matter with Catholicism in general, soon brings to the foreground how the image of Mary parallels that of Christ. In their lives, both had parents: Anne and Joachim for Mary; Mary and Joseph for Christ. Both Mary and Christ were born of humans, but with the Immaculate Conception, Mary was conceived without sin, while, of course, Christ was born of a virgin. The birthdays of both appear in the liturgical calendar, the nativity of Mary on September 8, that of Christ, December 25.

The families of both figures are said to have included siblings. Mary's siblings were Mary Jacobus and Mary Salome, while Jesus, according to Paul, had James as a brother (Galatians 1:19), and indeed, Mark lists James, Joses, Judah, and Simon as the Lord's brothers and refers to his anonymous sisters (6:3). Intriguingly, just as James converted Spain, Mary Jacobus (also called Mary, the wife of Cleophas and the mother of James the Less and Joseph) and Mary Salome (the wife of Zebedee and mother of James and John) carried Christianity across the Mediterranean to southern France, where they landed at a place now known as Les-Saintes-Maries-de-la-Mer and where their relics are preserved (*Enciclopedia* 53, 1925; Pope [1913] 1966; Mazel 1935; Sautman

---

suffering, which is a lesson on being human, on having *cultura*, on having *paciencia*, on having *tranquilidad*, on possessing restraint. The rich, visual imagery of icons that shaped the emotions they portray conveys qualities that, ideally at least, take one past the raw, naked emotions of animals. In contrast, for both romanticism and evangelism, emotion is the touchstone. What matters for both is heart-felt experience, which transcends form; both the poet and the preacher speak best when they speak from within. The most heartfelt of all experiences is death. The romantic writers found a favorite subject in the beautiful death, the moment when death becomes sublime (Kennedy 1987), and evangelical preachers, in their most evangelical moments, find their favorite testimony in the joy of going to live with Jesus. The pursuit of ecstasy, not restraint, is a common ideal in both romanticism and born-again Christianity.

1990) and where in 1998 I had the privilege of joining the pilgrims as they carried the relics to the Mediterranean shore and back.[15]

Another parallel between the image of Christ and the one of Mary is the display of their hearts. While the liturgical devotions of Catholics to the Sacred Heart of Jesus far exceeds those to Mary, nonetheless, the Immaculate Heart of Mary has her devotees, who celebrate this feast on the Saturday after the Friday devoted to the Sacred Heart (Figure 35). An aspect of popular Catholicism demonstrates the parallel vividly. The ever-astute vendors at pilgrimage sites now sell trick portraitures of Christ in which the image changes according to the angle viewed. At one angle, Christ on the cross has his eyes shut, but at a different angle, his eyes open; or in another portrait, Christ peers out as in real life, but with a change in the angle, his face turns into the imprint on the Shroud of Turin. In the case of the Sacred Heart, at one angle, you see Jesus pointing to his heart, but at another, the figure becomes Mary revealing her own immaculate heart.

Still another resemblance between the two figures is the one mentioned earlier in our discussion of dark images venerated at important shrines. Among the Spanish American examples of dark Christs are the Lords of Esquipulas and Buga, and among European cases there are the figures at Lucca, Italy, and at Cracow, Poland. Dark Virgins may be even more numerous. They include the one at Cartago, Costa Rica (fondly called *La Negrita*, "little dark one") and the one at Guadalupe, Mexico City (*La Morenita*, "little brown one") among those in the New World, and in Europe there are the famous Black Madonna in Poland and several in France and Spain. While the darkness may well carry different significance for Mary from what it means for Christ, dark images of both are more likely to be associated with major pilgrimage centers than are white ones. Hence the color is not likely to be simply incidental (see Nolan and Nolan 1989 for a thorough review).

Another striking pairing of the two figures is what occurs to both after

15. In addition to the two images of the Marys, the church at Les-Saintes-Maries-de-la-Mer also shelters the image of Sarah, a small, doll-like figure with a dark face, who resides in the grotto under the altar. She is said to be the patroness of gypsies, and the festival at Les-Saintes-Maries-de-la-Mer (which is usually in late May, a week before Pentecost) has become an occasion for a major gathering of European gypsies. Traveling in their RVs, gypsies pour into town, and on the day before the display of the relics of the two Marys, they escort Sarah on her own journey to sea and back. While the gypsies are in town, the streets resound with guitars and quavering voices of flamenco singers.

FIG. 35. The Immaculate Heart of Mary

death. Christ, of course, ascends into heaven, but as the official proclamation recognized in 1950, Mary also arises from her tomb. As Christ is the new Adam, so Mary is the new Eve (Langlinais 1967). Needless to say, Christ ascends on his own, as it were, while Mary is bodily assumed. Yet in religious art, both are depicted as ethereally ascending the terrestrial plain.[16]

16. Indeed, in depicting Mary, "ethereal presence" seems to be the goal of popular iconography. While traditional icons of Christ may twist his face to depict agony, with notable exceptions the face of Mary appears quite placid, and while Christ hangs all but naked on the cross, Mary's femaleness is hidden under a gown of white. For a mother figure, she is amazingly flat-chested.

A final parallel is the suffering of each. Similar to the manner in which Christ's suffering evokes disputes about its meaning, so, too, Mary's grief over the death of her son is a much-debated topic. The often-heated exchanges center on the significance of *marianismo*, or "Mary-ism." *Marianismo* is contrasted both in the literature and in the street (and home) with *machismo*, or "he-manliness." While Spanish American men make the world of the street their domain and stress the masculine virtues of honor and sexuality, Spanish American women, the argument commonly goes, are relegated to, if not sequestered in, the patios of the courtyard house and the domestic life of the family. Unable to make their own way and dependent on whatever their husbands may see fit to provide, they find in the suffering of Mary a spiritual strength that permits them to endure and, indeed, to gain a symbolic power of their own. Some anthropologists, such as Tracy Bachrach Ehlers (1996), cite the economic vulnerability of women in poorer communities as the primary cause of women accepting, however reluctantly, the *marianismo* model. Others, such as C. H. Browner (1986) and Joann Martin (1990), while admitting the role of economics, accentuate how women consciously adopt *marianismo* to strengthen ties with their children and to claim a political power born of their capacity to suffer for others. Still other researchers are skeptical of the whole complex. Marina Arrom (1985), in her historical study of women in Mexico City, finds *marianismo* to be not a Latin American cultural pattern inherited from the past but a Victorian import of the mid-nineteenth century designed to remove women from the work force under the guise of sacred motherhood.

Perhaps the most substantial rethinking of *marianismo* is that proposed by Debra Sabia (1995). Her observation of and involvement in local Bible study groups (Christian base communities) in El Salvador and Nicaragua lead her to see *marianismo* not as a passive ideology of putting up with one's lot but as an active, feminized theology born out of the liberation movement. Such a theology sees Mary as a courageous, self-assured woman "whose speech and

---

The parallels between Jesus and Mary reach their ultimate with Mary as co-redeemer. According to a *Newsweek* article, present-day promoters of Mary both within and without the Catholic Church, conservatives, feminists, and New Age spiritualists are flooding the Vatican with petitions calling for her elevation to "Co-Redemptrix, Mediatrix of all Graces and Advocate for the People of God" (Woodward 1997; see also Kinsley 1989). The desire for such an exalted position for Mary recalls medieval paintings in which she, as the Bride of Christ and the Queen of Heaven, sat on her own throne next to Christ's (Miles 1985).

life denounces sin and all things opposed to God's enterprise." Connected to this re-seeing of Mary is "a perspective of Jesus as both a loving brother and *sister*. Like God, Jesus is both man and woman" (1995, 29, emphasis added).

May we follow Sabia's hint that the two, Christ and Mary, are the same, that is, that they are complementary images of a same being? The recurrent, pervasive parallelism between the two certainly suggests such a complementariness. And on that basis, dare we, as anthropologists, go even further and propose that Christ and Mary as complementary images of a single being are grounded in the complementariness of you and me?

Such a proposal has not, by any means, been unspoken. Let us hear what others say and then consider where such a proposal leads us.

Erich Fromm ([1930] 1963), in one of his earlier, more critical, and more psychoanalytical interpretations of Christianity, describes how Christians merge their identities with that of the crucified Christ. Filled with reproach for our hatred of parental authority figures, we displace the self-loathing on Christ. Consequently, in penance for our anger, it is we who suffer and die upon the cross. More to the point here, Fromm stresses the complementary role of Mary. In our search for redemption, we become the Christ child in her maternal lap and nurse at her breasts. This shining act of love (characteristic of mammals, I must point out) moves us toward a relationship of forgiveness that transcends, or at least compensates for, the one based on our self-imposed crucifixion.

A more recent, and more ambitious, psychoanalytical interpretation is that offered by Michael Carroll (1986). Carroll begins by noting that in orthodox Catholic doctrine Mary not only gave birth to Jesus without sexual intercourse but also she remained a virgin, with her hymen intact, throughout her life. This separates her from Near Eastern goddesses who were often sexually promiscuous. The exaltation of Mary's virginity reaches its greatest intensity in those countries that also pride themselves on elaborate displays of Christ's Passion during Holy Week, namely Spain and southern Italy. The exaltation of virginity and the dramatization of the Crucifixion arise from the same source, namely sons' strongly repressed desire to copulate with their mothers. The stress on virginity denies the desire and the dramatization of the Crucifixion inflicts self-punishment upon the sons for their subconscious lust.

What about the daughters? you burst out. Devotion to Mary is as much a female preoccupation as it is a male's, perhaps more so. True, but Carroll will not be caught lacking on that score. Just as Mary was impregnated by God the Father, so a daughter's identification with her mother, and through her mother with Mary, permits her to experience vicarious sex with her own father and to have his baby.

Spiraling his way along the pages, Carroll gives the argument one more twist. The desire of sons to have sex with their mothers and the wish of the daughters to have babies by their fathers attain greatest ardor in families where the father is an ineffective parent. For one reason or another, but commonly associated with economic factors, the father in a father-ineffective family is conspicuous in his absence and sporadic in his parenting. Thus the de facto power of running the family and caring for the children's material and psychic needs falls upon the mother. Yet when the father appears, being macho, he demands both mother and children submit to his authority. He displaces the mother's authority and becomes a rival for her affection, a powerful rival that tolerates no competition. The children can do little except build up resentment, which they wisely suppress. Eventually, they develop strategies appropriate for their gender on how men deal with women and women with men. And the tragedy reproduces itself.

Not surprising, Carroll finds "the father-ineffective family especially common in" southern Italy and Spain (1986, 50). Thus, it all forms a neat package: fervent devotion to a virgin mother, self-inflicted punishment in a Christ-like manner, strongly repressed lust by both sons and daughters, and father-ineffective families. Too neat, you add.

And I have to agree. Despite the contribution of Freudian psychoanalysis in accounting for the compulsive, ambivalent characteristic of worship and worship's bewildering mixture of assertive independence and groveling dependence, both interpretations, of Fromm and of Carroll, appear too functional and overly mechanical, if not more than a little circular. In addition, both continue to view Christ and Mary as separate personages, albeit arising from a single source.

More to the point in our pursuit of Sabia's hint that Christ and Mary are complementary images of a single being grounded in the complementariness of you and me is the work of Caroline Walker Bynum. Bynum notes in her amazing book *Jesus as Mother* (1982) that from the eleventh century on, European Christianity strove to portray the humanity of Christ, and to do so, it called upon female imagery as the most effective and powerful metaphor to accomplish that portrayal. "Nursing at the breasts of Christ" was a common verbal statement designed to convey a more intimate and a more dependent relation with God. She observes that concentration "on the eucharist and on Christ's suffering in the Passion, which increases in the thirteenth- and fourteenth-century devotion," rather than arising from a morbid fascination with death, expressed "an identification with the fact that Christ is what we are" (Bynum 1982, 130). And the what we are is you and I, male and female, and don't argue about who is what. An intimate, dependent relationship with God, one in which the wounds of Christ bleed milk as if from a mother's breasts—as Bynum reports the medieval male image of the divine in a later, equally fascinating volume, *Holy Feast and Holy Fast* (1987)—is a relationship best depicted in child-mother (mammalian) language.

Perhaps the fullest development of the idea that Christ and Mary are complementary images of a single being, best represented as Christ-Mary, just as you and I are best described as you-I, flowers in the work of feminists. Our brief encounter with Sabia's article has alerted us to the potentiality of that work. For a fuller engagement, we turn to the longer study of Jeanette Rodriguez, herself a complex figure. As a self-confessed light-skinned person of Ecuadorian descent, she has become very much part of the Latina reworking of the symbolic potential of the Mexican Virgin of Guadalupe, *La Morenita*, that Louise Burkhart alluded to earlier in Chapter 5. To her investigation of the presence of the Virgin of Guadalupe among Mexican American women, Rodriguez brings her training as a Catholic theologian and as an anthropologist. Her work leads her to "challenge the perception that Guadalupe is the model of submissive, passive Mexican womanhood. Rather she is a role model of strength, enduring presence, and new possibilities" (1994, 160). Yet Rodriguez wants to go even further, further perhaps than what the women she interviewed told her. As a feminist and a theologian, she wants to disclose how the image of the Virgin of Guadalupe is meant not to replace a male figure but to enhance the personhood of God. She argues that the symbol of Our Lady expresses the creative energy that is God. Our Lady is God's love. Then, Rodriguez adds a crucial elaboration. She understands God's love, she says, in relational terms. The way to experiencing love "is within the dynamic of a relationship . . . for God to give God's whole self to us, means that we live in some kind of relationship" (150). To live in an intimate relationship with God, to know his love, to partake of his creative energy, we best approach God as feminine.

Rodriguez's suggestion that we experience God's love in relational terms reminds me of the expression we have heard so frequently and used here, "es la fe que vale." It is faith, my own particular faith, that establishes my tie with God. Her suggestion also resonates with the Heideggerian position we visited in Chapter 1, namely that being-in-the-world is a with-world; for us to be you and me, we require the presence of one another. I cannot know love until you offer it to me.

Wait, you hold up your hand. When you say you cannot know love until I offer it to you, aren't you saying in effect that you cannot know love until I offer *myself* to you? That's asking a lot. Too much, in fact. Do you really think that is what Rodriguez has in mind? Aren't you moving away from what she says? Yes, but it's down a path we want to take shortly, in the last section of this final chapter. We'll see what develops there. Now, what about Mary among the Southern Baptists? What do you have to say about that?

Not a lot to be sure. But more than one might imagine. What is the official position of the Southern Baptist Convention? There is, of course, no "official" position. Southern Baptists, as we have heard them say more than once, are not a creedal people. Each person's reading of the Bible guides his or her thinking and worship. Naturally, some readings are more common, more acceptable, and even, dare we suggest, more "Baptist" than others. Be that as it may, as the Bible doesn't have much to say about Mary, so the Southern Baptists likewise limit their description of her to the virgin who gave birth to Jesus. She appears in the nativity scenes during Christmas and in the readings of the Gospels, especially Luke, during the Christmas pageants but then generally fades away to reappear briefly during the preaching of the Crucifixion and Resurrection. There is, as you well know, no talk about her being bodily taken up to heaven. So we might conclude, since the Bible says little about Mary, the Baptists say little. Nonetheless, the matter is not that simple.

First of all, why have the Baptists turned their backs on Mary? Why did the "iconoclasm associated with the Protestant reforms . . . [destroy] images of Mary with special venom" (Miles 1985, 12)? Why did the radical groups, such as the Baptists, come to have such disdain for the whole complex of rituals and stories that had evolved about Mary?

A cultural historian, one who stresses the continuity of culture across generations, might be tempted to evoke distinct southern and northern European cultural traditions to explain not only the devaluation of Mary but the Reformation itself. Marija Gimbutas, in a series of massively illustrated books, marshaled an impressive array of archaeological evidence for the existence of a European mother goddess cult that extended from the Paleolithic through the Neolithic into the emergence of civilization. The goddess, she argued, was "parthenogenetic, creating life out of herself," so the "Christian Virgin Mary is a demoted version of this original deity" (1991, 233). Gimbutas, for all of her derring-do archaeology, did not venture into making a southern and northern European division of the mother goddess, but the implication that we draw from her work is that the northern European, radical Protestant Virgin Mary is an even more demoted version of the mother goddess.

Another logical place to look for the reason the radical Protestants grew to discount Mary is a devaluation of women in general. After all, today's Southern Baptists argue that God's plan is for women to "graciously submit to their husbands." Indeed, the stereotype of the submissive woman in Spain and Spanish America would seem to fit right in the Baptist heritage; yet one group venerates Mary and the other ignores her. Also, as is the case in Spanish America, in the American South, women, especially mothers, are subjects of adoration. Just think of the number of country songs about "Mamma." Yet again, one group elevates Mary as the Queen of Heaven, while the other speaks of her only as the virgin that gave birth to Jesus.

While the causes of the radical Protestant, i.e., Baptist, turning away from Mary remain complex, if not obscure, I trust by now you see that their turning away composes part of their larger performance that I have sought to clarify. Margaret Miles, in her insightful consideration of visual and verbal understanding in Western Christianity, argues that the difference between the Catholic and Protestant reforms of the sixteenth century "was not primarily theological but perceptual" (Miles 1985, 125)—a difference emerging from the differential stress on sight and sound in the construction of worship. Following her lead, I would say that the restricted role of Mary among the Baptists stems less from historical causes and more from the Baptist performance of worship based on text instead of icon, on speaking as opposed to seeing, on a congregational bond rather than a dyadic one, and on the construction of an ascending Christ of the Word in counter-distinction to a suffering Christ of the Touch.

All well and good, I hear you say, but what about the idea that Jesus and Mary are complementary images grounded in the complementariness of you and me? If that idea can be applied to the Catholics in Spanish America, what happens to it when it is applied to the Southern Baptists? To express the issue in more general terms, if our images of sacred figures spring from the experience of being human, that is, of being you and me, and if that holds true for the Catholics, why doesn't it hold true for the Baptists?

I believe that it does. Despite the de-emphasis of Mary, the feminine side of us and of them will not be denied a place in Baptist worship. It is too strong. As a basic component of being human, femininity everywhere flowers, even among Southern Baptists.

Here is my argument. Among the Baptists, the Apostle Paul is far more important than Mary. Paul is the one whose faith came through the ears: He did not see God; he heard him, like a good Baptist. Furthermore, his encounter on the road to Damascus is the archetypical conversion experience. His transformation from Saul the persecutor to Paul the evangelist becomes the model for all subsequent conversions and their narrations. Given Paul's prominence, more critical than Peter's, the rock upon which Christ will built his church (Matthew 16:18), more central than John the Baptist's, the voice crying out in the wilderness to make straight the way (Luke 3:4–5), we have two males figures in the Baptist horizon: Paul and Jesus. Paul assumes the masculine side, so Jesus is freed to develop his femininity. While Paul instructs the church, "Let your women keep silence" (1 Corinthians 14:34), Jesus says, "Suffer little children to come unto me" (Luke 18:16).

I have argued that Christ and Mary are complementary images of a single being grounded in the complementariness of you and me. Given this fact, among the Southern Baptists, without Mary, Christ in opposition to Paul takes on feminine attributes. Quite apart from the psychoanalytical drama of oedipal lust and the consequences of father-ineffective families (of which there were, and are, plenty in the South, and indeed I could offer my own as an example), our very humanity, surging forth from our mammalian, nurturing, breast-feeding constitution and articulated into symbolic form, brings about selves crisscrossed with the duality of male and female.[17]

Jesus healed the sick, cured the blind, and fed the five thousand. These acts he accomplished not through the application of superior knowledge,

17. For an additional example of femininity in patriarchal religion, consider Susan Sered's comparison (1991) among Rachel in Judaism, Fatima in Islam, and Mary in Christianity. While they are surrounded by different myths and occupy distinct theological statuses, all three ameliorate suffering and offer understanding. Thus, they inhabit the same structural slot. God cannot deny anything they ask, but none threaten the patriarchal status quo.

through masculine domination, but through the application of a spiritual superiority, through his feminine presence. He was supposedly a carpenter, or at least a carpenter's son, yet we never hear how he gripped the hammer or plied the saw. We never hear of him boasting, as did his predecessor, Gilgamesh, of the city he had built with his hands. The only purely masculine act Jesus did during his thirty-three years was to drive the moneychangers out of the temple.[18]

As a boy in East Texas, I thrilled to hear the preacher read that Jesus "cast out all of them that sold and bought in the temple, and overthrew the tables of the moneychangers" (Matthew 21:12). For some reason, drawing on a painting I must have seen in Sunday School, I imagined him with a whip, whirling it around his head to crack it in the faces of frightened moneylenders, the bankers of their day. Today, I love to think the painting was the one by El Greco, but, of course, no Baptist church would adorn its walls with art that contained the voluptuous, bare-breasted women in El Greco's depiction. More likely it was one by Gustave Doré, a popular illustrator of biblical themes in the mid-to-late nineteenth century, with all figures decently clothed (McDannell 1995). Back then, in my confused adolescent mind, a battleground of desire and remorse, I desperately wanted Jesus to be masculine, to be more manly, to be like my cowboy heroes that rode the range of the silver screen. Instead, not only did he turn the other cheek, but he loved me. Like a mother. He loved me so much he died for me. Not dying for me in a battle we fought, shoulder to shoulder, but dying for me through surrender. Much like a woman. A lot like a woman. It's like what we used to say about Gene Autry.

Gene Autry! What could he possibly have to do with Jesus?

Well, not to speak ill of the dead, but Gene Autry wasn't a real cowboy. Not like Buck Jones, Wild Bill Elliot, or Charles Starrett, better known as "The Durango Kid." So? Well, he wasn't a real cowboy. He had to squat to pee.

18. To call Gilgamesh a predecessor of Christ will strike many as odd. Perhaps only an anthropologist would be prone to see a connection between the Mesopotamian hero of 2000 B.C., who was restless and full of lust and left no woman a virgin for her lover, and Christ, who, seemingly, was devoid of sexual passion. But they both were Near Eastern figures, both were a mixture of the divine and the human, and both struggled with the problem of death. Even odder is the argument that Gilgamesh's failure offers us a closer model of being human than Christ's success (Richardson 1972, 1991).

Listen to that! How outrageous! And I thought you had got beyond being a redneck.

Well, as they say, you can take the red out of the neck, but not the neck out of the red. Whatever that means. In any case, shall we continue?

Against redneck sexism and general belligerence, against the ideology of southern *machismo* and the mythic figure of the self-sufficient man who is ready to kick, bite, and gouge all who stand in his way, the feminine features of Jesus appear in enigmatic relief. What feminine features? The feminine features of love: "Love your enemies, do good to them which hate you. Bless them that curse you, and pray for them which despitefully use you. And unto him that smiteth thee on the one cheek offer also the other. . . . Love ye your enemies, and do good . . . and ye shall be the children of the Highest" (Luke 6:27–29, and 35).

Why is love feminine? What makes love female? Abstractly considered, perhaps such love is not gender-bound, and, in fact, I know it is not. But in the South, among the plain folk and their upscale, 4 × 4 cousins, however, it looks awfully feminine, especially to those old-time, one-time shit-kickers who recall Faron Young's signature song popular in the late '50s: "Live fast, love hard, die young, and leave a beautiful memory."

If that is so, if in the South love is feminine, what then is the appeal of the feminine Jesus to the male-dominated Southern Baptists? Or, as Heyrman put it in Chapter 2, "the association of evangelical loyalties with unmanly dependence"? That's the question. That's the puzzle. What is the pull of turning the other cheek among men so eager to make a last stand for lost causes? What is the attraction of loving one another to men who, in the heat of the battle for civil rights, stood in front of schoolhouse doors and shouted, along with Governor George Wallace of Alabama, "Segregation today, segregation tomorrow, segregation forever!"?

Dickson Bruce, in our review of the frontier experience and the formation of plain-folk religion in Chapter 2, persuaded us to consider the civilizing message of that religion. He contended that by condemning gambling, drinking, swearing, and fighting, what today you would call "good ole, redneck fun," and by urging the individual to surrender to the conversion experience, which implied a capitulation to group conformity, the camp meeting, for all of its jerking and barking, sought to transform the antisocial element into more cooperative and docile Christians, a point with which Eugene Genovese, a noted interpreter of the South, agrees (Genovese 1992).

Despite the unenviable Southern Baptist record in support of slavery and, later, segregation, we may think the feminine Christ has modulated these dark passions. As evidence, we can point to the statement passed by the Southern Baptist Convention in 1995 apologizing for the Southern Baptist acquiescence to the southern slave system. And shortly before his death, Governor Wallace became more civil, if not civilized (*Newsweek* 25 August 1997).

Yet there is more at work. For one thing, there is "The Head of Christ," a portrait so popular during the pre–World War II years and immediately after that every Protestant church in America and many homes had one somewhere. Even today, after a period of rough treatment by the "Jesus freaks" of the 1960s and 1970s, it has come back to symbolize enduring faith (Morgan 1966b). The painting is a young man's face in profile. Soft, flowing hair falls to the man's shoulders and equally soft brown eyes look gently out of a face covered by a neatly trimmed beard. A radiance emerges from the face and fills the portrait with a distinct glow. The radiance apart, "The Head of Christ, is, for all the world, that of movie star, and conforms to the standards of popular commercial portrait photography" (Morgan 1996a, 31), which is not surprising given that the painter, Warner Sallman, was a commercial artist, albeit a genuinely pious one.

Its artistic credentials apart, "The Head" is clearly an attempt to illustrate the biblical figure verbally present in the New Testament. Referred to by scholars as an icon, it is, nonetheless, a metaphorical one and not a "true" icon, that is, it has, as far as I know, never cried, bled, or protected illegal immigrants from the border patrol. Rather, it has the same ontological status of the grape juice and crackers present in the Southern Baptists' Lord's Supper; it is "only symbolic." Consequently, though visual, "The Head of Christ" is very much part of the Christ of the Word. In this truly Protestant, Baptist painting of Jesus, we catch a glimpse of Mary, and in that glimpse, we see the conflict generated by the longing for a "motherly God" and a desire for a "he-man God" (Morgan 1996a, 60). In this single picture, then, reside the complementary images of a single being grounded in the complementariness of you and me.

If we accept that "The Head of Christ," in particular, and the Christ of the Word of the Southern Baptists, in general, is a feminized Jesus, how may we explain or comprehend the appeal of that femininity to a denomination that advises women to "graciously submit to their husbands"? As I said, that would seem to be the Paul side of Christ. Yet, at this point, I can go no further. As I confess my failure to comprehend love and the Southern Baptists, I note that the Christian love of which the Baptists so fondly speak is not flesh-and-blood love. It is not mammalian love, it is not the love of the breast and the lip, but it is a spiritual love. An ethereal love. A love that dwells in heaven, in the ascending figure of Jesus. A love that is incarnate not in the flesh but in the word, a sound ascending. And the sound ascending is "I surrender all."

In answering the question What about Mary?, I have ventured, with your encouragement, to argue that the feminine side of us—a side that each, male or female, possesses—permeates our creative efforts to portray an understanding of our dwelling together here on this planet. In Catholicism and perhaps especially Spanish American Catholicism we see the portraiture of the feminine side most pronounced, even if we remain uncertain what that femininity signifies, passive acceptance or passionate engagement. Among the Southern Baptists, the portraiture, less clearly drawn, nonetheless resides in the figure of a gentle, nurturing Jesus, even if love, a word so dominant in Southern Baptist discourse, ascends beyond our grasp.

From the lesson on suffering to the message of salvation, as different as the two may be, we detect the common issue of death, an issue we now directly face.

Putting Death in its Place: The Social Construction of a Unique Event

Some years ago, back when I was much younger, I stumbled across the justifiably famous book by Peter Berger and Thomas Luckmann *The Social Construction of Reality* (1966) and Berger's own wonderful *Invitation to Sociology* (1963). The argument in both books that our everyday life is a constant negotiation hiding under the guise of the "taken-for-granted" and that the locus of that negotiation is social—"social" being something not automatically shared but something up for grabs—liberated me from the conventional anthropological notion that culture, as an impersonal design for living inherited from the past, causes us to do the things we do. From my earlier encounters with Ernest Becker and Miguel de Unamuno, I had rejoiced in their insistence on the centrality of human experience, on what Unamuno called in several instances the world of *el hombre de carne y hueso*, "the world of the man of flesh and bone." Now with the concept of social construction I could move toward bringing together the centrality of action with the way in which that action becomes social. From that point, with erratic reading that bounced back and forth from existential phenomenology to the fossil record (with recent venturings into deconstructionism), I arrived at the position of this book, the Heideggerian being-in-the-world, which is that we humans, you and I, as a continuing project of the evolutionary process, are genetically compelled to create and that we live, we two, in our creations. Such a life, as we both are well aware, is not without its tragic consequences, yet it is also a life that is ours; it is our possession, yours and mine, together.

The creativity in which we live begins within the experiential space between your body and mine, the intersubjective experience between your gesturing presence and my own reply. In our gesturing to one another, we shape that experience using the same genetically endowed facility that the carpenter used in building the shed in your backyard, the same facility that the Pleistocene knapper used in shaping stone into hand ax, flake, and blade, and the same facility I use in writing these sounds on the pages before your reading eyes. We objectify the flow of intersubjective experience into objects whose being transcends the quick immediacy of the moment: the carpenter's shed, the knapper's tools, the writer's words. Once objectified, the experience becomes symbols that communicate back to us what we have done. Here, we encounter our discussion of the Neandertal burial and self. The burial objectified the experience of death and communicated back to the living Neandertals that a fellow human had died. The burial as a burial signified to the Neandertals. They awoke to death and found themselves.

As we applied Derrida's argument to the Neandertal discovery, what the Neandertals discovered was the presence of absence, which, in the language of deconstructionism, we might say is another word for symbol, the very "core" of our being. Now, in furthering the presentation of the social construction of death, let us continue to follow his argument in a more recent book, *The Gift of Death* (1995).

Only in deconstructionist speech, you sardonically intrude, could death become a gift. To be sure, I reply, but let's listen. The discovery of death was a discovery of a gift that is outside of the economy, a gift that is priceless. The priceless gift of death is the gift of our singularity, our intrinsically irreplaceable quality, or, in other words, our own unique selves: in my case, my Miles; in your case, your you. In accepting death's gift, the self "separates itself in recalling itself to itself, and so it becomes individualized, interiorized, becomes its very invisibility. . . . The psyche as life, as breath of life, as *pneuma*, only appears out of this concerned anticipation of dying." Furthermore, "this awakening that keeps vigil over death, this conscience that looks death in the face is another name for freedom"; that is, we, in the face of death, are now responsible (1995, 15).

The focus of our responsibility is the death of the other. "I am responsible for the death of the other to the extent of including myself in that death. . . . I am responsible for the other's death inasmuch as the other is mortal. It is the other's death that is the foremost death" (46).

Being responsible, I can offer my death for another. Yet I cannot die the other person's death. Each of us dies his own death; the gift is uniquely ours alone. Dying "can never be taken, borrowed, transferred, delivered, promised, or transmitted" (44). Consequently, death becomes a truly human act: each person dies, I, you, male, female, rich, poor, white, black, those who dine in the halls of the mighty, and those who scrounge a meal from the dumpster down the street. No one can die my death. Not even you. Only I can die my death. It is mine alone. Yet in the social construction of death we, drawing upon our Neandertal, human capacity to objectify experience, turn this intensely private experience into a social act. Death becomes part of our everyday vocabulary, a subject that ranks with taxes in conversations about our fate.

Furthermore, though, as Derrida says, the gift of death is priceless in the social construction of this intensely unique, singular experience, in certain economies, death in fact may become a commodity, with a market value. In the capitalistic United States, the commodification of death generates an industry that even now has gone nationwide, with annual receipts over $9.2 billion (U.S. Bureau of the Census 1997). No one can die my death, but as a commodity and coupled with the good, old American passion for turning a buck, my death may bring a fair price and more.

The social construction of death, then, awakens us to death, and in our awakening, we seek to transform the singular experience into a public, commonly acknowledged act, which is to say, in the vocabulary of this book, to put death in its place. In the Christian social construction of death, as I have asserted more than once, Christians create Christ so as to put death in its place. Here, in complete opposition to Derrida, a Christian of any persuasion, Catholic, Baptist, or Pentecostal, would insist that what separates Christ's death from any other is that He, in fact, died our death. To the explication of how, in the Christian construction, Christ died our death, we now turn.

In Chapter 1, to circle back for our last turnings, we first brought up the manner of how we live our lives, how we-are-in-the-world. Ordinarily, we-are-in-the-world in such an engaged manner that objects are located in the acts we use them for: The hammer is already in the act of hitting the nail even as the carpenter lifts it from the belt tied to his waist. In this mode, the world has an aroundness to it, and our spatiality extends outward to blur the distinction between us and the artifacts we employ. We can, however, place the hammer outside its acts and view it as an object among objects. In this disengaged viewing, there appears substantial distance between our scrutinizing self and the object that becomes the focus of our attention. In one mode, the world is in our grasp, ready-to-hand; in the other, the world is an object, viewed present-at-hand. We went on to suggest that the engaged mode is that of the engrossed participant and the disengaged one is that of the observing scientist. However, as soon as we made that distinction, we hastened to say that as anthropologists, we want to engage the world of the people with whom we work in such a manner so as not to turn that world into a neutral object but to see it from the perspective of their doing. We strive not to denude the being-in-the-world of participants from whom we seek understanding but to disclose the bases upon which they construct it. In our search, we bring ourselves face-to-face in the Heideggerian text with the need to assess the bases as being inauthentic or authentic.

Wait! Wait! you exclaim, the words hurling forth between us. How can an anthropologist, of all people, assess the bases of people's lives as being inauthentic? Trying to calm your rightful indignation, I reply, While Heidegger and Heideggerians insist they use these terms in a philosophical, nonjudgmental sense, I agree that the bias in the two words is inescapable. It is easy to see that we, you and I, always act authentically, while they, to the contrary, they, the great unwashed, live inauthentically. We may substitute, as intimated in Chapter 1, "conventional" and "poetic" for "inauthentic" and "authentic." Yet, even here, bias, always lurking in its lair of words, threatens. So imperfectly, let us proceed.

We begin by observing that we all, even the most tortured romantic forever wailing against the dullness of humanity, live inauthentically and conventionally. Likewise, we all, even the most placid, going-with-the-flow, laid-back fellows, experience the *Augenblick*, the moment of vision, when each person, each object, stands forth in total clarity. So whatever bias the words carry, it is not a distinction between people.

In the inauthentic, conventional mode of being-in-the-world we are the who we have been; the past, in all its routinized, already ready-made decisions, covers us in its warm, stifling security. In the authentic, poetic mode we are the who that sees the not-yet; the seemingly endless possibilities of being beckon. In the one, we exist in the present; in the other, we anticipate in the future. In one, we close the world down and shut ourselves in; in the other, we open the world up and walk out the door. And with our first step out the door, we awake to the potentiality of death, which is usually enough to send us scurrying back inside, slamming the door, and throwing the bolt, the dead bolt.

Which is primary: the stifling present of the inauthentic or the frightening beyond of the authentic? This is a critical, if not *the* critical, question in our understanding of who we humans are. And the answer: While we all are born into a world not of our making and while we live that world in the present, with the past all around us, the authentic, poetic mode is primary.

John Richardson, no relation to me and certainly not to you, clarifies the issue, "In anxiety we are not-at-home in the world in which we happen to have been, and hence lose our tendency to grasp ourselves solely in terms of that world" (1986, 136). In anxiety "we flee *in the face of* the 'not-at-home'; that is, we flee in the face of the uncanniness" that constitutes us (137). Everydayness, in its conventionality, is a modification of the poetic, not vice-versa. And to clinch the matter, Richardson quotes Heidegger himself, italics and all, "*From an existential-ontological point of view, the 'not-at-home' must be conceived as the more primordial phenomenon*" (153). The inauthentic, then, you query, is the in-place and the authentic out-of-place?

In response, let me recall our contrasts from Chapter 1. On the one side, the in-place is the reassuring, comforting mode, and the out-of-place, the anxious, disturbing mode.

In-Place	*Out-of-Place*
Being home	Being away
Being with	Being alone
Participant	Observer

But when we look again, at the other side, the in-place is the stifling, confining mode, whereas the out-of-place is the animating, liberating side.

In-Place	*Out-of-Place*
The world of the familiar	The world of the strange
Stifling, ordinary	Stimulating, exotic
To disappear	To stand out

Likewise, the inauthentic, conventional mode and the authentic, poetic mode appear in similar dialectic tension. Yet the antagonism between the first two modes moves toward a subtler interplay whereby the authentic, being the primary mode, reveals the inauthentic. The authentic discloses the conventional in its conventionality and thereby unveils it as a creation whose put-together basis has been disguised and even divorced from its creators.

At this point, to clarify how creation may become divorced from its creator we need to inject a note on the twin processes of reification and alienation. Reification is a commonly occurring process that extends our objectification of experience to its fullest measure. In objectification, we transform experience into symbols; in reification, we turn symbols into things. Around academia, we commonly say, "The university requires assistant professors to publish or perish." In this speech, the university, a general category, becomes a thing, and a thing that acts, that requires its youngest faculty to produce scholarly articles or lose their jobs. This use of figures of speech is so much a part of our lives we take it for granted and treat it as no more than a convenient shorthand. Yet the practice contains within it the truly mysterious transformation whereby we take a figure of speech, a symbol, and turn it into a coercive force, an agent that compels us to act. We become victims of our own metaphors. This is especially true of alienation. Alienation separates us from our words so that we forget we are the words' speakers. Alienation, Berger and Luckmann remind us, is "the paradox that [we are] capable of producing a world [we then experience] as something other than a human product" (1966, 61). What we produced now produces us.

"What we produced now produces us" sounds much like the conventional, Boasian notion of culture, from which you say you have been liberated. Yes, precisely. The reification of culture into an impersonal cause turns what we humans do into the determinant of the doing. We must remember, however, that while reification is a fallacy in anthropology and in social science, it is part and parcel of everyday life, particularly as we live it in the inauthentic, conventional mode.

And the ready-to-hand and the present-at-hand? you who are nothing if not persistent ask. The ready-to-hand resembles the inauthentic, conventional mode in its unity between the carpenter and his hammer, between being and the world, but the inauthentic adds to being-in-the-world its dogged effort to conceal itself under the cover of inevitability. The present-at-hand, by its vision, shows the hammer as a hammer and brings it out of the action of the carpenter's nailing, but in so doing it rips apart the unity between subject and object that being-in-the-world manifests. As John Richardson (1986) leads us to understand, the explicitness of the present-at-hand destroys, whereas the explicitness of the authentic, poetic mode reveals. And what it reveals is that we, you and I, are primarily possible.

As primarily possible, as bipedal primates with culture, we are nature's uncanny creatures. But specifically because of our uncanniness, we flee the not-at-home, the out-of-place, the nowhere of death, and with a great sense of relief we take up residence in the everydayness of the everyday world, first making sure the door is closed and the bolt thrown.

Closing down means putting death in its place, and to do so we employ well-worn expressions for well-worn routines. The principal routine we employ is to call upon the "they." In calling upon the "they," we place ourselves in the service of the third person plural, which is as far removed from the first person singular as speakers of English can get. The existential distance between "I say" and "they say" is vast. To rephrase "I" as the "they" is to go from a single, solitary being, bolt upright in capitals, to an anonymous group in small letters. So if the I wants to hide, the they is a good place.

Here, I must point out that "we" may also hide. "We" points to us, right here, rather than to them over there. But "we," for all of its first person character, may depersonalize. Whom are we speaking about when we say "we"? We southerners? We anthropologists? We humans? For that reason, when I say, "we," I say, "you and I." And when I say, "you and I," I mean you who even now read these words and I who present them to you.

The they is the principal actor in the discourse of the everyday. In my conventional talk, even when I say, "I," I am talking less about the I who dwells within and much more about the me who resides outside, my public self, the they-self. This being the case, when the subject turns to death, the they-self remarks, "I know it is sad, but he lived a good life, and as they say, we all have to go sometime." In talking in this manner, I unburden the task of facing death—the task that makes us so fully individual and so uniquely human—and place it out there. I turn death over to the they-self. And the they-self, being the reified self that floats free of any specific person, willingly and eagerly accepts my gift.

In Christianity, who accepts the gift of death? Who is the principal actor in Christian discourse? When the priest in Nueva Esperanza lifts up the wafer and says, "Tomad y comed porque esto es mi cuerpo; Take and eat because this is my body," in whose voice is he speaking? When the congregation at Mt. Hope sings, "In his arms He'll take and shield thee. Thou wilt find a solace there," who is the He? The answer, of course, both for us and for Christians is Christ. In Christian discourse, the discourse of the mass in the *iglesia* at Nueva Esperanza and of the Sunday service at the FBC in Mt. Hope, Christ is the principal actor, the they-self.

Christ is the they-self of Christian discourse, and as such, he is the reified self that floats free of any specific Christian. Consequently, as the object of reification, he becomes the repository of all that Christians bring as they flee from the face of death. And they carry much to lay upon him. To see how much of just what, let us go back to Timothy Mitchell's discussion of autonomy and the autonomy crisis.

You recall that Mitchell, in his effort to explain the passions the Andalusians in southern Spain pour forth during the Passion of Christ, began with the general assumption that we humans everywhere seek autonomy, to be our own selves. Death, likewise everywhere, threatens our goal of being. Death throws us into an autonomy crisis. In the face of death, we can no longer claim an enduring self. We become filled with rage, with dependency, and with rage at being dependent. In the Andalusian case, the path the rage takes us is dying, dying again and again, with Christ during *Semana Santa*.

Mitchell's argument echoes the earlier words of Ernest Becker. You remember what Becker said in Chapter 1? That we, possessors of symbolic selves, are creatures with names and a history. At the same time, we are worms and food for worms. To repeat Becker's own words, "Man is literally split in two: he has an awareness of his own splendid uniqueness in that he sticks out of nature with a towering majesty, and yet he goes back into the ground a few feet in order blindly and dumbly to rot and disappear forever" (1973, 26). In response to our fate "blindly and dumbly to rot," we, you and I, create a "codified hero system, which means that society everywhere is a living myth of the significance of human life, a defiant creation of meaning" (7).

At the center of the defiance is our compulsive, *causa-sui* project to create ourselves, or, as Becker says, to be our own cause. To be our own cause is the ultimate in the denial of our mammalian nature. Thanks to two of the anatomical features that make us what we are, upright stature and a large brain, we come into the world with great difficulty. Getting the big head through a birth canal narrowed by upright posture takes its toll. Compared to our close relatives, the gorilla and the chimp, as newborns we are more completely dependent upon others, particularly our mothers. Yet being human, we soon develop the notion that we are in fact the center of the universe. We are awash with omnipotence. Glowing with power, we make our demands known, only to discover, soon for some, later for others, that we are, at the pleasure of others. The final downfall from our throne of infantile authoritarianism comes with the awareness of death. Death reveals the *causa-sui* project as a miserable failure. Yet stubbornly being human, we never take no for an answer, especially not the no of death. And cowboys, who never die, ride across the prologue to our rescue. Consequently, we juggle, ineptly for the most part, our assertive desire to be independent with our longing for safety in the comforting embrace of others.

For Mitchell death creates an autonomy crisis, and for Becker, it shows the failure of the *causa-sui* project. Clearly the two concepts, autonomy crisis and *causa-sui* project, intertwine and, in so doing, mutually support their respective validity. While Mitchell, however, turns to the Andalusian display of the crisis during *Semana Santa*, Becker deepens his analysis of the failure of the *causa-sui* project to reveal a fundamental flaw in our human character.

Becker, in developing the *causa-sui* project, has recast the Freudian play of infantile sexuality into the drama of existence. It is not longing to have sex with mother or father that generates guilt; it is existence itself. In human existence, we strive to stand out, to create, to aspire to heroic ideals, but no sooner do we succeed than the great fear of being alone, of being exposed, of being totally abandoned pervades us. And we scurry to shelter.

Why are we such cowards? Becker asks. Because of our capacity to symbolize, we awake to life as a mystery. Our very existence seems incomprehensible. How can we be? An aspiring god with a body, and a body that bleeds, smells, and even shits. Truly to open ourselves to our very evolution, to the paradoxical impossibility of being a two-legged primate who speaks, and beyond, to the evolution of life, so hardy yet so frail, so pervasive and yet so precious, and still further, to the evolution of the universe and to its forever expanding immensity, is to open ourselves to something close to madness. "Full humanness means full fear and trembling" (1973, 59).

Full of fear and trembling at the sight of our awakened mystery, we nonetheless toy with existence. We flirt with madness. We test ourselves, but dishonestly, Becker says, so we always win.

> We enter symbiotic relationships in order to get the security we need, in order to get relief from our anxiety, our aloneness and helplessness; but these relationships also bind us, they enslave us even further because they support the lie we have fashioned. So we strain against them in order to be more free. . . . We seek stress, we push our own limits, but we do it with our *screen against despair* and not with despair itself. . . . It is fateful and ironic how the lie we need in order to live dooms us to a life that is never really ours. (56)

Now as we examine Becker's analysis, you can see that in contrasting the lie we live to protect us from the truth that we flee in the face of, he draws a distinction not unlike that between the interplay of the inauthentic, conventional, on the one hand, and the authentic, poetic, on the other. In both we find a similar to-and-fro-ing. We found this to-and-fro-ing also in the exchange of the in-place with the out-of-place. In all three, lie and truth, inauthentic and authentic, and in-place and out-of-place, we feel the tension of being-in-the-world. The tension of being-in-the-world is no less than a dialogue of be-ing. Keeping in mind that "be-ing" here is not a static noun but a gerund and is best hyphenated, we may summarize the to-and-fro-ing thus:

The Dialogic of Be-ing

Independence	Dependence
Self	Other
Symbol	Body
Creativity	Dissipation
Giver	Taker

Which side is courage? you immediately ask. And without stopping for my response, you demand, Which is fear? And burrowing straight to the center, you virtually shout, Where is Mother? What? I shout back, flustered. Where is Mother? Didn't Becker call her the witch of darkness? Yes, but . . . No buts. She is on the right, isn't she? The ultimate Other, the Body, into which the Self dissipates, the Taker away of Creativity, the Great Absorber.

Turning red in the face from your onslaught, I manage to plead, Listen to Becker once more, the Becker of *Escape from Evil* (1975), the work barely completed before his death at the age of fifty.

In *Escape from Evil*, Becker clarifies the twin themes of heroism and expiation. I strive to be my own cause, defiantly to create meaning in the face of my ultimate fate, death. In my quest, I threaten the gods themselves. Agog with the strength of my endeavors, I come to believe that the power of being lies within me and me alone. As I pursue these truly herculean efforts, I awake to the fear of my vulnerability. The more I stand out, the more vulnerable I become. Foolish me. Exposed, naked, I cannot continue my defiance. I arrive at the point I must renounce my usurpation.

And to succeed in renouncing my revolt against the gods, I enlist your help. Through subterfuge, through coercion, through throwing myself at your feet, I entice you to join me so that we together can expiate the guilt of be-ing. Join me, please, and let us repeat together, "Mi culpa, mi culpa, mi gran culpa"; "Oh, Lord, Our God, we come before you burdened with sin." With you by my side, we may succeed in turning the defiant creation of meaning into a dramatization of dependency. What irony! We, the occupiers of the planet with Martian sands beckoning, we convert heroism into expiation.

So Christ is on the right side, you leap ahead to put words in my mouth. Christ is on the right side, not only on the right side of the Father, but on the right side, the dependency side, of the dialogue of be-ing. The side with Mother. The side of the they-self. The side of inauthenticity.

You, persistent as ever, continue, sarcasm held high, So Christ is a victim of people's inauthenticity. Christ died for our inauthenticity. Blessed be the Name, the Name of Jesus!

Sacrifice. Sacrifice, I repeat, trying to regain control of this text. Sacrifice. Is not sacrifice the principal theme of Christ's life? Both the Christ of the Touch and the Christ of the Word are Christs who offer their lives for us. The mass itself, even with the Vatican II shift toward a Protestant-like memorial, remains a sacrifice. The altar, even as it moves toward becoming a table for a communion meal, continues to be the site where the priest prepares the lamb to be offered up (Kilmartin 1981).

In studying sacrifice, anthropologists (for example, Bourdillon and Fortes 1980) have noted in their consideration of such worldwide practices that a peculiar bond comes to be between the sacrificial offering and the giver of the sacrifice. If the offering is alive, the giver gives through killing. In the act of killing, the giver also dies, at least in part and in some measure. On another level, in the act of killing, the giver releases the power of death. "Death is in some sense an anomaly, a disruption, a breach of right order. And as such it may be a source of power" (Beattie 1980, 34).

The connection between the giver and the sacrificial offering, I suggest, is the connection between Christians and Christ, the connection that resides in the hyphens of being-in-Christ. To be the Christians they desire so fervently to be, Christians need Christ. Whom they *create.*

Being-in-Christ goes beyond the argument of Christians identifying with a pre-existing figure. It is not that Christ first is and then Christians are. It is not a matter of a pre-existing Christ to which Christians come. In the presentist, constructivist position of this text, the self is not antecedent to our actions; rather through our actions, yours and mine, the self of each comes to be. Likewise, through their actions in the Mass and in the Sunday service, in the contextual setting of the sensuous *iglesia* and of the auditorium church, in the icon frozen in agony and in the text spoken vehemently, the Christ in which Christians are comes to be. "Ven, Señor, a salvarnos; Come, Lord, to save us."

In our performance of the weekday mass and the Sunday service, we act in deed and word, directly or more distantly, the drama of Christ's life. In our actions his drama becomes our creation. The art of Christ is our art. Yet through the process of reification, we transform our creation into the they-self. We alienate ourselves from our product and respond to Christ as if he has a life of his own, and then we crucify him.

No wonder the Baptists are always praising Christ for his sacrifice and praying, along with the associate pastor of the First Baptist Church in Durham, North Carolina, "Father God, thank you for dying for me." Since it is the Baptists who create Christ so that he may die for them, it follows that they are always thanking him for his sacrifice, for dying on their behalf.[19] Consequently, it is true, is it not, that Christ dies anew each time we gather in his name. He is the actual sacrifice, the really Real Presence we construct so that we may put death in its place.

Putting on your philosopher's hat, you observe, Your position that at each

19. And I repeat, in case the pastor didn't hear me the first time, "You got it wrong, buddy. It was my mother who died for me."

Mass and during each Sunday service Christ dies anew is clearly and highly nominalistic. Nominalism, you continue, denies the existence of universals. Each event is separate unto itself. During the Reformation, Protestants charged that the Catholic' doctrine of the Real Presence meant the Catholic theologians taught that the Crucifixion was actually duplicated at each mass, and consequently Christ literally died each time the priest consecrated the host.

Yes, I respond. Yes what? you respond back. Yes, the Protestants did in fact accuse the priests at each mass of slaying Christ anew. But in fact the Catholic position was and is that at mass Christ "is not offered . . . in a sense which entails suffering, as if he were again wounded, again suffered and died, for he rose from the dead in an impassible and glorious body and dies no more" (Clark 1960, 317).

The point, you insist, is not what the Catholics say, but what you say. As an anthropologist, as a scientist of some kind, how can you possibly deny the existence of universals? We humans today are all *Homo sapiens*, are we not? Yes. Well, isn't that statement a testimony to the existence of universals? To be sure, I concede, but, I continue, we first are you and I. We first are specific individuals, and from that very specificity we construct *Homo sapiens*. To repeat, as flesh-and-blood, bipedal primates, we do not dwell first and foremost in abstractions.

All right, you say, and in the tone of your saying, I know something else is on its way. All right, what about Landmarkism? What about it? Landmarkism, at least as you described it in Chapter 3, contends that Christian churches are composed of only those who undergo full immersion at the hands of a particular Baptist-ordained minister in the company of a specific Baptist congregation. This suggests the Landmarkers hold there is no universal Church. On the contrary, I reply, Landmarkers assert that since the days of the Jerusalem church, there have always been Baptists. Furthermore, while baptism in the presence of a particular Baptist congregation is the only way to become a church member, Landmarkers insist that all who have accepted Christ as their personal savior constitute the invisible kingdom of Christianity.

All right, you try one more shot. If Christ dies anew with each mass and ascends with each Sunday service, if Christ is the art of our creation, then what about the past? Doesn't the material in Chapters 2 and 3 have an impact on our creation? Of course, it does. The position of this text, however, is that the past, like culture, is not a cause but a conversation.

Turning red yourself, you say, That's it? That's all you have to say about all the events that have happened before us, all the heartaches, all the triumphs, all the despair, all the bliss: All that is just talk? Trying to sound reasonable and soothing, I reply, Talk is what we do best. We constantly talk, and talk about our past, especially here in the South. We engage the past through talk. Furthermore, the talk we speak, while not a cause in any physical sense of the word, certainly structures our being. Talk may open up new horizons, or it may close down around us and become, in those famous words of Friedrich Nietzsche, a "prison-house."

And the prison-house we ourselves build? you ask with brave incredulity. Every brick, every bar, I reply. And we do this willingly? you sneer with righteous disbelief. You got it. Since the Pleistocene. Since at least the Middle Paleolithic. Since the Neandertals awoke to death. Since, in Burke's words, we became "inventors of the negative." Since we, again in Burke's words, became free, *necessarily* free, "to be [our] own tyrant, inexorably imposing upon [ourselves] the peculiar combination of insights associated with [our] peculiar combination of experience" (1966, 52). Since, to evoke Becker once more, we fashioned unfreedom as a bribe for self-perpetuation (1975). Consequently, and to paraphrase Berger (1963), every culture is a conspiracy, and its principal conspiracy is to deny conspiracy.

"To meditate on [the fact that our reality is our symbols] until [we see] its full implications is much like peering over the edge of things into an ultimate abyss" (Burke 1966, 5). The ultimate abyss. The *Augenblick*. The moment of vision, when all that we are becomes clear to us. Is that what Backus saw while mowing hay? Or Brother Tommy out in the fields? Or me over by the pigpen? If so, they, the two of them, found in the conversion narrative a bridge to transport them to the bosom of Jesus. Me? I took another route.

As I traveled that route, more than once I came to the edge of things. Even now, after years on that road, considering the likelihood that I dwell in a self-constructed conspiracy whose very conspiracy is to deny its conspiratorial nature, the edge beckons, and I am tempted. As I step toward the ultimate abyss, the well from which my mother never returned, I want to proclaim along with Robert Lowie, one of the famous Boasians, in his most un-Boasian moment, that human life is "that planless hodge-podge, that thing of shreds and patches" (1920, 441) or to conclude with Macbeth that it is "full of sound and fury, signifying nothing." But bless your heart, as you have done before, you grab my hand and pull me back.[20]

Having rescued me, you feel free to put me on the rack: When you say, "prison-house," "unfreedom," "toying with existence," are you not saying Christianity is a prison-house into which people gladly enter, and Christ is the jailer? Is the conspiracy constructed here one of enslavement? No. It is not. The conspiracy, the ultimate conspiracy, here and elsewhere, is the affirmation of being human. All that conspiracy, you complain, makes my head spin. And how can a conspiracy be an affirmation? Stay with me, I plead. Stay with me for one more turn.

Christians create Christ to put death in its place. And its place is in the they-self. This means that in Christ death dwells.

What is the color of death? I ask. How can death have a color when it is the nothing? you fuss. Color has substance; death is nothing. No, I counter back. Viewed biologically, death is a naturally occurring process. Get off my back, you wave your hand in disgust. Death is a naturally occurring process, I persist, which we humans turn into nothing. Yet nothing is the abyss. To fill the abyss, to give it substance, or at least to bridge it, we color death. And Christians color it black. So that's why, you exclaim, the light dawning once more, many icons of Christ, particularly powerful ones such as the Lord of Miracles and the Lord of Esquipulas are black! Precisely. What they are dark with is death. Death dwells in Christ and turns the they-self dark—dark with power, the power released by death. Black Christs, while putting death in its place, open the door to death. Opening the door before our eyes, as we kneel before them and seek to touch their power, they permit us to see death.

The gift of Christ is the gift of death. The abyss. The *Augenblick*. The moment of vision.

The vision of death brings awareness of self, and the self, once awake, knows death. Our death, your death, my death, not the deaths of others, not the dead who are already buried. Let the dead bury the dead. But our death.

20. By the very next sentence, Lowie, like me, recovered and concluded that the anthropologist "will not grovel before [culture] in fatalistic acquiescence but dream of a rational scheme to supplant the chaotic jumble" (1920, 441). I'm not into groveling either, but I dream less of a rational scheme, at least as I understand Lowie, and more of a poetic disclosure.

My death. Your death. The death that cuts off each of us from the other. The death that bursts between us. That ruptures forever our relationship. That turns this page blank.

The anthropologist's account, if we can but stay true to it, is not to turn the page blank or color it with despair. It is to affirm our humanity. After all, black as darkness is associated with rain, fertility, potentiality, and "unfathomable knowledge" (Beidelman 1987, 546). Black as death points to decomposition, which in turns points to fermentation and life and to the resurrection (Pandolfo 1989; Richardson 1995b)! Following the path of Christ among the Catholics in Spanish America is to be a *cristiano*, to be human, and to learn how to suffer so that the suffering does not destroy one's humanity. Singing the Glory Land way among the Baptists of the American South is to sing in unison, in the joy of shared salvation, in the fellowship of a new birth, together. Both, in their distinct manners, affirm the discipleship of being human.

In Spanish America and in the American South, the death of Christ signifies absence. This absence stands in opposition to the presence of people worshiping. Absence is the death of Christ; presence is the people in the act of worship. And in the act of their worship, they affirm.

The power of death that is released is the power of our presence. We affirm our solidarity in the face of absence. We, together, repeat with Paul, "O, death where is thy sting? O, grave where is thy victory?

Wait, you intrude, however reluctantly. Since you brought Paul into our conversation, he also said, did he not, that "If in this life only we have hope in Christ, we are of all men most miserable" (1 Corinthians 15:19). Yes, he did, but here in this anthropological text our hope in Christ is our hope in each other. And we may say with Jesus, "Abide in me, and I in you" (John 15:4). I, writing, come to be through your reading. As I write and as you read, as we travel from the first pages of our journey until now, we abide.

Traveling the pages of this book parallels the traveling of pilgrimage. In pilgrimage, the everyday tie between you and me becomes communitas, the bond between the I that resides in me and the Thou that dwells in you. When we first talked of this bond, you recognized it immediately, but now as we approach the end of this journey, this journey of you and me, we return to its mystery.

Thou My Hope

The phrasing "I and Thou" came from the writings of Martin Buber, indeed, from one of his books so titled, *I and Thou* ([1958] 1987). Maurice Friedman, in his introduction to *Between Man and Man* (1965), in which Buber offers a fuller, if less poetic statement than in *I and Thou*, insists that Buber depicts God as Lord of the Voice. As such, God speaks to us not apart from the world but through it. Consequently, even though others may call him a mystic (e.g., Pfuetze 1954), "Buber is best understood not as a theologian . . . but as a philosophical anthropologist," who sets himself the task of investigating the problem of being human (Friedman 1965, xviii). The problem is that we are creatures of the "between." All that happens between us—and there is so much, so much that is joy, so much that is sad—cannot be reduced to the behavioral sum of two individuals or attributed to separate psychological realities of each.

The "between" is at once both established and bridged through dialogue. Buber insists there are two primary words that, when spoken, bring about an existence. These are I-It and I-Thou. As with Heidegger's being-in-the-world, each is a single entity, joined in their individuality by a hyphen. The I-It existence corresponds to the world of the everyday. Although the stress on the It implies an objectivity and neutrality indicative of nature, the I-It world is made up of people. In the I-It world people become those over there who are speaking: he, she, they. And that's who you would become as part of the I-It mode of being. Furthermore, the I-It world is a world with a past, perhaps with too much past; in any case, our actions within this world are anchored and rarely spontaneous. Being anchored in the past gives the I-It world a stability and a predictability that permits us to proceed to address the tasks at hand.

In contrast, the I-Thou is a present world. Indeed, I am in the present in the presence of Thou. Thou bring me out of the past and its well-trodden walkways. I do not find Thou by coercive expectation; Thou meet me freely. Yet I step forward to greet you. It is I who say, "Thou." The relationship of I to Thou, in contrast to the one between I and you as It, is a chosen one. I choose to speak "Thou" and to be, in Thy presence. And considering the nature of our relationship, such an act of commitment on my part, I must agree with Buber, is "bound to resemble suffering" (1987, 11).

We might be prone to see the I-It and the I-Thou as the worldviews of two separate individuals, say, the scientist and the mystic. But Buber, much to his credit, insists the I-It and the I-Thou are not two types of people but "two poles of humanity" (65). We each have the capacity to be an It and a Thou.

The It of the I-It, to repeat, is not an object without meaning. As a demonstration, let us consider the tools of the Paleolithic that we first encountered in Chapter 1. Those tools, "Acheulean hand ax, Mousterian flake, and Solutrean blade" (if not the hammered pebble of *Australopithecus*) are conveyers of signification, statements, technological but also poetic, made between people then, in that distant world, yet testimonies that speak to us now of human existence, of struggle and achievement. In this manner, when we see the hand ax, flake, and blade, we relate to them thusly and quite correctly, but I long for the I who sees them as Thou.

To speak of I-It and I-Thou in English inevitably focuses on the It and the Thou. English, in its poverty, does not have a second "I." It does, however, have a "Me," the objective outcome of our public interaction. I am fully aware how I change when I go from I-It to I-Thou, even if I cannot linguistically mark the change in the same manner that you can, as you move from you to thou. The I of I-It is the Me of this one who is speaking. I of It is the Me of detachment, but I of Thou is I of solidarity. I of It is the Me of individuality, but I of Thou is I of personhood.

Whenever I see you as Thou, I feel a kinship with the *alumbrados* of Spain, the heretics burned because they saw Mary in every woman and Jesus in every man, or, to put it more accurately, *más alumbrado*, every woman a Mary and every man a Jesus, or, even more accurately, *aún más alumbrado*, every woman a Jesus and every man a Mary.

Buber was a believer. He worked his way toward an eternal Thou. In doing so, he observes that those who call God "Thou," and we have heard such many times in both the *iglesia* and church, often as not speak of God the It. To speak of God the It is to understand the relation to God as one of dependence upon the It and absorption into the It. To speak thusly, he insists, is to empty us of our reality. "A subject deprived of its object is deprived of its reality" (90). God the It is Christ the they-self. To speak of God the It and Christ as the they-self may well make the intolerable bearable, or even edifying, but in so doing, it removes from us our joint burden of being human, the Sisyphean gift.[21]

In contrast to Buber's criticism of what I have called conventional Christianity, that is, those who turn Christ into a they-self, he praises those of us who are godless but who nonetheless seek each other out. In support of our quest, he writes, "The relation with man is the real simile of the relation with God; in it true address receives true response" (103).

Isn't he saying, you query, that those who are claim to be godless have, in their dedication to one another, found God? And in so doing, affirm the existence of God? And therefore are not truly godless?

He may well be saying thus, I reply as patiently as I can. The argument, however, that I put before you in this book turns his simile relation on its head. It is not that humans are a simile for God, but God, in the language that we use, is a simile for humanity.

So why do we need the language of God if it is not God we are talking to? If being-in-the-world is a with-world, then why, as Allen Thiher (1984) asks, do we have such difficulty in articulating our love for each other? If being-in-the-world is being-alongside-you, why do I need the God-language to talk to you?

Why indeed? The question haunts us with its paradox. Since the brilliant days of Emile Durkheim, when he interpreted God as society, humanistic investigators have sought to understand theistic claims as mistakes but not illusions. Why indeed? Our primate relatives apparently have fewer difficulties in directing their affections, though when we become tempted to think their lives are one of utopian directness and simplicity, we must remember the mayhem that erupts and the infanticide that occurs in primate society. So it is back to language, to symbols, and to Derrida: "Differance produces what it forbids, makes possible the very thing that it makes impossible" (1976, 143).

I need God-language to talk to you because you create the very thing that you deny. To be the I that I claim I am depends on your response. Yet I know more than anything that you are going to die on me. I am dependent on you, yet you turn your face to the wall. Small wonder I use God-language. The

21. This gift theologian S. W. Stykes identifies as that "ultimately mysterious moral situation of [humanity], caught between responsibility and compassion" (1980, 81).

conventional language of Christianity is the language of dependency. In speaking this language, we "misrecognize" ourselves in Christ.[22]

Buber, even as he speaks in such lovely tones of the Thou, remains a realist, that is, he knows what words do. Indeed, it "is the . . . melancholy of our fate that every *Thou* in our world must become an *It*" (16). Here, I am reminded of you.

Whenever I talk of loneliness, you brush my words aside. Loneliness is no big deal, you say. Bolstered by a reading of Jessica Benjamin's *The Bonds of Love* (1988), you insist it is nothing more than a temporary glitch, a moment in passing. Love, however, as you continue supported by her text, is intersubjective, not intrapsychic. It resides in our mutual confirmation of one another. So true, I agree, but no sooner do we move toward the I-Thou and get a notion of its mystery, then you disappear behind the shell of conventionalized discourse. Whenever you thus flee from the Thou I seek and hide within your shell, I think of Miguel de Unamuno and his essay on solitude.

Unamuno, in *Soledad* (1974b), tells us that he has often considered what a terrible fate it would be if we suddenly found ourselves condemned to live the life of a crustacean, to be encased in a carapace and forced to use the feelers of a crab or a crawfish to touch the outside world. But in fact, he concludes, that is how we humans are, crustaceans with the skeleton on the outside and the flesh within. We have secreted shells around our spirits. Furthermore, our calls and shouts to each other, far from breaking our shells, harden them and make them grow. We are not like baby chicks that, as they sense the world outside, break open the eggshells that imprison them. On the contrary, we treasure our prisons. Should I take up a hammer and pound your

22. As you no doubt recognize, the term *misrecognize* comes from Jacques Lacan, who puts language and the subconscious together in fascinating ways. The unconscious is that part of discourse that is not at the disposal of the speaker in establishing the speaker's continuity. Because of the unconscious, the ego misrecognizes itself (Lacan 1977). Without implying a thorough reading of this doctrine of misrecognition, I suggest that the focus on the ego might best be shifted to you and me. In our talking about Christ—or, better, in our talking Christ, directly, without the "about"—we misrecognize one another. Like Derrida, Lacan applauds the absence of a center, but with a erogenous twist: "Lacan describes language in terms of Desire, for to enunciate a word presupposes the absence of the object. Language, therefore, in Lacan's terms is a constant process of filling the void caused by absence" (Tesser 1991, 595). In sum, as a word, death creates absence. Flooded with desire, which we rush to fill with other words and, in so doing, misrecognize our passion for the passion of Christ.

shell with the goal of setting you free, you would not rejoice at my act of liberation. Instead, as you felt the first cold air of freedom, you would whine and whimper how unkind I was, how unsympathetic, and retreat to the farthest corner of your beloved carapace. Unamuno, being Unamuno, would urge me not to turn aside from my task. Pound, he would say, Don't hesitate, pound, and pound again.

But even Unamuno, and perhaps especially the Unamuno who never stopped pounding in his effort to set us free, treasured solitude. In the *Augenblick* of solitude, at the moment of vision, which comes with silence, the carapace thins. It weakens. It becomes a membrane that permits a spiritual exchange and even allows, perhaps, interior flesh to touch interior flesh.

How gruesome, you exclaim, with a shudder. And at the very thought of delicate flesh touching delicate flesh, you cringe. How painful!

Don't turn away. Not now. Especially not now. Don't retreat behind the you shell. Thou for whom I search. Thou who make possible all that I may be. Thou who precede me. Thou-I. My loneliness needs you. Don't hide. Don't withdraw into the corners of your being. Come. Let us be, together. Let us be, together, now.

Yes, there is a triumphant Christ, celestial and glorious; the Christ of the transfiguration, he of the ascension, he who sits at the right hand of the Father; but he is for when we have triumphed, when we have been transfigured, when we have ascended. But here in this world . . . here there is the other Christ, the livid one, the one of welts, the one blood-drained and pale.

—Miguel de Unamuno, *Mi Religión y Otros Ensayos Breves*

And when I'm gone and at my grave you stand
Just say God's called home your Ramblin' Man.

—Hank Williams, "Ramblin' Man"

EPILOGUE

In the fall of 1954, still some time before you and I met, I went home to my father's funeral. I went without any thoughts of grief. He had been such a hard man, silent, angry, distant. Then he got old, and all his hardness turned into a bent, frail figure whose hands constantly shook. And that, rather than evoking sympathy in me, awoke only scorn.[1]

So I stood dry-eyed during the funeral at First Baptist in Palestine and stayed like that all the way to the cemetery. At the cemetery, we collected under the tent set up over the grave for the final words. Then they tricked me. They sang.

My father had a great love for gospel music. In Palestine during the 1930s and 1940s and even into the 1950s, they held "singing conventions." Once a month, on a Sunday afternoon, quartets from around the county gathered at the courthouse and filled the courtroom with counterpoint harmony. The male tenor would take the lead, followed by the female alto, a second tenor,

1. Reading my scornful response to my father's Parkinson's disease confirms what you well know, that I can be, without ever trying, an asshole. Yet here is something else to put on the scale of my life. In the mid '90s, in the company of two fellow searchers, I traveled up from Honduras in search of shrines devoted to the "Black Christ." South of Veracruz, Mexico, at the Black Christ shrine of Otatitlán, people directed us to the priest's residence, a small two- or three-room house. We found him lying on a small cot. I caught my breath. He was pale, his sleeping clothes dangled from his thin frame, and as he struggled to get up, his hands shook. He gave us the information about the location of several Black Christ shrines. My buddies left, but I hung back. Bent over, even standing, he stood hardly up to my shoulders. He waited, and then I said what I knew I would say when I first saw him, "Padre, déme su benedición, por favor." With his hands quaking the shape of the cross before me and his voice cracking, he blessed me. So add 'em up. Add 'em up, damn it!

and then the bass. It was just the kind of music the choir at the First Baptist shunned, with all their respectability showing. My father complained, "I keep asking the choir why don't they sing gospel? And they say they would, but they don't have the music. So I bought song books for them, but still, it is one reason after another why they won't." I'm not sure if he understood the reason for their upscale put-down. Probably so. Nonetheless, especially after his wife's suicide, he became one of the church's most loyal members.

Now, at his grave, they, as a quartet, sang one of his favorites, "Jesus, Hold My Hand." Damn them to hell! They had no right. No right, do you hear me! No right.

Yet as my hardened heart broke and as I approach the age my father was when he died, in a gesture as close to reconciliation as I can get, I'll sing you the chorus.

> Jesus, hold my hand (my hand).
> I need thee every hour (every hour).
> Through this pilgrim land (this land),
> Protect me by thy power (saving power).
> Hear my feeble plea, oh Lord, look down on me,
> When I kneel in prayer, I hope to meet thee there.
> Blessed Jesus, hold my hand (hold my hand).

Now that we have traveled this long distance from the prologue, from our first encounter, from the first words spoken on these pages, may I ask you this question? Who is being sacrificed when Jesus goes to the cross? You remember the Spanish for death? *La muerte*. In Spanish, death has a gender, and it is feminine. The death that hangs on the cross is feminine. The sacrificed is female. The one who died for our sake is female. That's what my mother did, those years ago. She did it for our sake, she said.

But what about *la verdad*? you protest. Isn't it also female? Yes, truth and death are both female. So then, I ask, Is it you? You who abide with me in the space between these words, is it you who hang there?

What a strange question! you turn to me in wonder. Yes, but I know I'm right to ask it. The wonderment in your eyes grows wide as you approach the image of you on the cross. You beseech me for an answer. But I have none.

I believe, however, the answer resides in the story of Sisyphus, recounted by Camus (1942). The gods have condemned Sisyphus to push a boulder up a mountain. We don't know their reason. Some say it is because he was an outlaw; others say it is because he told the truth about the gods. In any case, it is a big boulder and a tall mountain. Sisyphus, however, is strong. With his shoulder straining against the rough stone and his legs churning, he gets the boulder to the top. No sooner does he succeed then the boulder rolls back down. And Sisyphus descends to start the task once more. What despair! To be condemned to perform labor that has no meaning. And you think the gods, as they watch from afar, must be pleased. But Sisyphus is strong. As he descends, he plans the route for the return up the mountain. He is man who knows his work. Each push back to the top comes from that knowledge. Each step arrives with its own purpose. And the gods begin to have their doubts. Could it be that their punishment has been vanquished?

Let us accept the gift of Sisyphus and tackle the rock together. The gift requires we know that once we reach the top, the rock will roll back down. But in that knowledge, together, we unite our strength, and in our love, neither the gods nor the rock will prevail.

APPENDIX

I begin this attempt to present the issues of competing classifications of the primate order and alternative interpretations of hominid evolution by professing that I am a four-field anthropologist. Being a four-field anthropologist means that while you have a specialty in one of the four fields of biological, archaeological, linguistic, or cultural anthropology, you pursue the goal of gaining a comprehensive view of the species. Consequently, while keeping abreast of your own particular field, in my case, cultural anthropology, you persist in the effort to stay informed of developments in the other three fields. No one ever said being a four-field anthropologist was an easy or a sure thing, but if you are an anthropologist, why be anything else? It helps if you approach the task with some unifying notion, however implicit, about what it is to be human. In my case, as laid out in Chapter 1, the notion is that we humans are active creatures with the unique destiny to create symbolic worlds in which we then are. Consequently, I seek to bring the experiential, flesh-and-blood, creature side and the categorical, symbol-producing, transcendental side together through emphasizing our constructivist, activist being-in-the-world.

CLASSIFICATION

Classification of life forms aspires to group forms most clearly similar and separate them from those less similar. Inevitably, the classification is hierarchical. We more closely resemble apes than monkeys, monkeys more than prosimians, primates more than rodents, mammals more than reptiles, vertebrates more than invertebrates, multicellular forms more than single-cell ones, and, within the single-cell groups, amoebas more than bacteria. We ascend the classification until we reach the ultimate divide, life versus not-life. But even there we continue between matter and not-matter. The classification is a human device, not one that grows on trees, and so it is subject, like other human endeavors, to revision and debate. The classification that I have employed, which is the product of the synthesizing work of the paleontologist George G. Simpson, done in the 1950s and 1960s, focuses on the interplay among form, adaptation, and environment. It has the advantage of showing how we resemble the apes by placing ourselves, the chimpanzee, the gorilla, the orangutan, and the gibbon into one category, *Hominoidea*, and then how we differ from them by putting them in the group *Pongidae* and us in the category *Hominidae*. (The gibbon, the most unique ape, may be placed in a family of its own, *Hylobatidae*.) The pongid adaptation exploits the arboreal niche by using all four limbs, in varying ways, to be sure. The hominid adaptation exploits the terrestrial niche by using the legs. The classification is straightforward and inclusive; that is, any member of the group *Hominoidea* that walks upright is a member of the family *Hominidae*, or a hominid.

Recently, classifying has moved from its focus on the interplay among form, adaption, and environment toward one based on molecular evidence. On the basis of how our DNA resembles that of the great apes, various scholars have proposed to maintain the *Hominoidea* category as one that encompasses us and the apes but to include at the next level, *Pongidae*, only the orangutan, while *Hominidae* includes us, the chimpanzee, and the gorilla. The *Hominidae* is divided again to constitute *Homininae*, us, and *Gorillinae*, the chimp and the gorilla. The advantage of this division stresses how much of our genetic inheritance we share especially with the chimp and, to a lesser degree, with the gorilla. Yet for all of its molecular insight, the classification has its faults. For one thing, the relationship between DNA and morphology (and behavior) is not a straightforward connection. Different morphologies may be produced by the same genes and the same morphology produced by different genes (Marks and Lyles 1994). For another, the method says nothing about the interplay of form, adaptation, and the environment. And it is the interplay of those three components that addresses the divergent uniqueness of the pongids, on the one hand, and us hominids, on the other. (Please see Lewin 1998 for a succinct discussion of the issues.)

PHYLOGENY

Given the tendency today to separate the various fossil hominids into divergent phylogenies, it might be instructive to recall the situation in the 1950s. Ralph Beals and Harry Hoijer (1953), in a basic textbook of the time (and the one I had when I took "intro to anthro" in 1954 and one I still treasure), give these fossil types: for the australopithecines, they list three genera, *Australopithecus*, *Paranthropus*, and *Plesianthropus*; for the *erectus* forms, they recognize two precursors, *Gigantanthropus blacki* and *Meganthropus paleojavanicus*, and for the *erectus* proper, *Pithecanthropus erectus*, *Sinanthropus pekinensis*, and *Africanthropus njarasensis*. But it is in the genus *Homo* that the greatest proliferation occurs: *Homo modjokertensis*, *Homo soloensis*, *Homo wadjakensis*, *Homo rhodesienses*, *Homo heidelbergensis*, *Homo neanderthalensis*, and finally, *Homo sapiens*. (To Beals's and Hoijer's credit they place the hoax *Eoanthropus dawsoni*, the Piltdown man, to one side, "pending further examination.")

The abundance of types made it difficult to trace the course of hominid evolution. The prevailing opinion not uncommonly declared the many forms not to be directly ancestral to humans. Instead of evolving, they reached dead ends and became extinct. The results of this reasoning left the evolutionary line to *sapiens* largely unoccupied. Upon recognizing this paradox, critics referred to the "hollow" phylogeny as one of "ancestraless man."

In response to the proliferation of types, with all becoming extinct and leaving anatomically modern *sapiens* on top of a hollow evolutionary tree, scholars began to synthesize and group. Among the synthesizers was W. E. Le Gros Clark. In his influential *Fossil Evidence of Human Evolution* (1955, 1964), he attacked the problem of extreme "splitting" through urging classifiers to stop focusing on isolated traits and to look for a "total morphological pattern." When we do so, Le Gros Clark noted, we see an early hominid pattern of upright stature and small brain, with the subsequent increase in brain size. Under the impact of the writing by such people as Le Gros Clark, all the *erectus* forms became grouped under the taxon *Homo erectus*; the australopithecines, under a single genus, *Australopithecus*, with only two species, one smaller, *africanus*, and one larger, *robustus*; and more recent types divided into archaic *sapiens*, including *Homo sapiens neanderthalensis* and modern *sapiens*, that is, *Homo sapiens sapiens*. The evolutionary tree was filled in with a fairly straight growth from *Australopithecus* to *Homo erectus* to *Homo sapiens*, archaic and modern.

Recent, exciting discoveries and the application of cladistics to the fossil record combine to produce a very bushy tree of hominid evolution. Genera and species abound, with many becoming extinct, leaving only us, *Homo sapiens sapiens*. One renowned scholar in his review of the panorama of human evolution observed wryly, if not sadly, that a "new era of splitting is upon us" (Tuttle 1987, 1973). Since that comment, recognition of species in the fossil record is itself said to be recognition of arbitrary units. This is especially true if, as some have maintained, "there is not a consistent relationship between morphological distance and species formation" (Foley 1991, 414); that is, dissimilarities in fossil forms do not necessarily indicate the presence of different species. Nonetheless, splitting has continued its frenetic pace. Figure 36 presents a representative example of a prevailing view of human phylogeny.

Although published in 1996, the scenario depicted in Figure 36 is already incomplete. Discoveries and assessments going on at the time require the insertion at around 4.4 million years of *Ardipitheus ramidus* (White, Suwa, and Asfaw 1994, 1995) and somewhat later, at around 4 million years, *Australopithecus anamensis* (Leakey et al. 1995). While both *A. ramidus* and *A. anamensis* were bipedal, evidence suggests they also foraged in trees; that is, they were bipedal climbers (Culotta 1995). Still a more recent discovery places a new

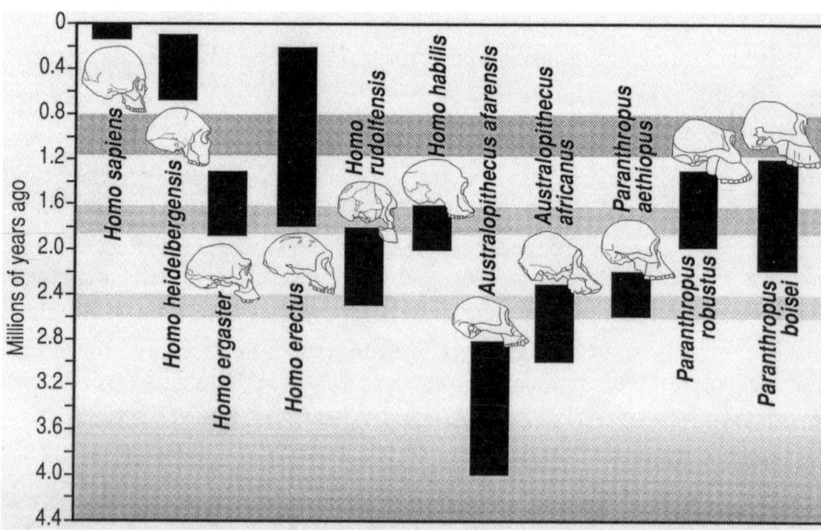

FIG. 36. A contemporary view of human phylogeny. Redrawn from Larick and Ciochon (1996).

species of *Australopithecus*, *A. garhi*, more directly ancestral to the genus *Homo* than *A. africanus* (Culotta 1999a; Heinzelin et al. 1999; Asfaw et al. 1999). Finally (at least finally for the moment), a team headed by Meave G. Leakey (Louis Leakey's daughter-in-law) reports a hominid contemporaneous with *A. afarensis* that has a flat face and small molars, supposedly more modern features, yet with a brain size of a chimpanzee. The mixture of primitive and modern features forces them, they argue, to create a new genus and species. Voila *Kenyanthropus platyops* (Leakey et al. 2001; Lieberman 2001)! In all of these reports lurks a hidden irony, maybe even a moral. In the early 1960s, Leakey himself proclaimed that then-recent finds at Olduvai Gorge in east Africa constituted the earliest evidence of the genus *Homo* and that these individuals were the makers of the Oldowan pebble tools found nearby. Consequently, the new finds were assigned to a new species, *habilis*, or handy man. Just a few years earlier, the same Leakey had announced with equal conviction that a find made by his wife, Mary Leakey—a find that was clearly a member of the robust lineage of the australopithecines—was the maker of those same tools. Now, *Homo habilis* gained the honor of being the first human, with Leakey, of course, its discoverer. Currently, with the disclosure in the fossil record of *erectus*-like individuals the same age as *habilis*, some have concluded that "*Homo habilis* is morphologically too primitive to be an ancestor of *Homo erectus*" (Larick and Ciochon 1996, 542). Thus, what was once heralded as the first human is now judged to be a dead-end lineage.

One could say, along with John Fleagle (1995), that the 1950s splitting was the result of a lack of understanding of the range of variation within a single taxon and that the splitting going on today comes from a more rigorous application of taxonomic principles. No doubt, but as the example of *Homo habilis* illustrates, a certain amount of "name determinism" seems to be at work. If the hominid is classed as *Homo* (however arbitrary the decision to so classify), then it must have been *Homo* who made the tools and not members of the genus *Australopithecus*. As we will soon observe, if a hominid is "unlucky" enough be called a Neandertal, then its symbol-making capacity is obviously no match for the anatomically modern fellows.

Related to splitting is the nondiscriminating evocation of extinction. Having brought about, as it were, a separate hominid lineage through the bestowing of a new species designation, the splitter might be asked the fate of that particular lineage or, more commonly, the outcome of the lineage created by a competing splitter, and the off-handed reply frequently is "It became extinct." Little explanation is offered as to the process that led to the so-called extinction. The oft-asserted belief that competition between lineages, such as one between the australopithecines and the early members of the genus *Homo*, led to the elimination of the less "advanced" forms, in this case, the australopithecines, finds little support in a comprehensive review of the role of extinction in evolution (Raup 1995). In essence, extinction becomes a sort of *deus ex machina* argument in reverse, that is, as my friend Scott Smiley observes, a *hades ex machina*.

Perhaps the principal culprit, if that is the word, in the contemporary battle of the lineages is cladistics (Foley 1991; Smith 1997). Cladistics is a procedure that purports to separate traits that are derived from those that are primitive, or, in other words, to identify "the evolutionary novelties that separate the species from their common ancestor" (Lewin 1998, 100). Associated with cladistics is the idea that change within a particular lineage comes about only through speciation. The combination yields the prevailing picture of a lineage splitting into sister branches, those branches splitting again into sister lines and so on. Naturally, the only way to account for the later existence of a sole surviving lineage is to have the unfortunate sister lineage become extinct or, perhaps to put a more positive spin on the process, to say that the surviving lineage has "replaced" the ill-starred sister. In case of *sapiens*, for example, the precursor lineage, presumably a form resembling *Homo erectus*, split into archaic and modern *sapiens*, with modern *sapiens* replacing the archaic sister.

Cladistics and "replacement" both have their critics (Clark and Willermet 1997). Shortly after the emergence of cladistics as a popular method for establishing phylogenetic relationships, one of the most prominent evolutionary theorists, Ernst Mayr (1981), criticized the method as focusing exclusively on genealogy and ignoring adaptation. In the case of humans and chimpanzees, for example, because of differential adaptations our evolutionary history is strikingly different from the chimp sister lineage. A decade later, Robert Martin (1992) echoed the same criticism when he re-emphasized the widely familiar knowledge that evolutionary rates, as measured by the appearance of morphological adaptations, differ for different lineages. Similarly, John Moore (1994), concerned about the application of cladistics to assessing linguistic and cultural affiliation, points out that the branches resulting from cladistic analysis do not necessarily reflect real populations but rather indicate gene frequencies. If the genes in one lineage become the object of adaptive pressures, then they may well change at a greater rate than genes in a so-called sister lineage. Even more recently, David Fox et al. (1999) point out that cladistics as such has a built-in flaw: it cannot distinguish between parallel sister lineages and an ancestor-descendant one; consequently, it cannot select among competing phylogenetic possibilities. Likewise, Melanie McCollum, in her review of the robust australopithecines, states that recent "cladistic analyses have not resolved the phylogenetic history of these early hominids. Efforts to increase cladistic resolution by defining traits at greater level of anatomical detail have instead introduced substantial phyletic error" (1999, 301). Instead, she calls for a morphogenetic perspective that takes certain features as more primary than others in shaping, say, the face. In so doing she concludes that the robust face is largely the result of exceptionally large molars, which, in turn, require a large jaw and associated masticatory musculature. Parenthetically, I cannot resist noting that McCollum's "morphogenetic perspective" sounds a lot like Le Gros Clark's "total morphological pattern."

But perhaps the most outspoken critic of cladistics is C. Loring Brace. In conversation, Brace, in a characteristic mode, refers to cladistics as "the great leap backward." In print, he refers to it as "medieval thinking" (1988, 1989, 1997). Cladistics is "medieval thinking," specifically, "Neoplatonic," because it works on the assumption that a species is a fixed type and can only change through speciation. It ignores variation within a species in favor of variation between species. G. A. Clark (1989), in his comment on Brace's observations, agrees that the cladistic procedure fails to recognize the change of one species to another through time, or "phyletic evolution," and instead, it prefers to view change as speciation, or "phylogenetic evolution." Both types of changes may well occur, Clark agrees (just as Simpson had posited in his original formulations [1944]), but he argues that members of a polytypic, wide-ranging species with a broad range of environmental tolerances, such as was the case of the australopithecines, would more likely *not* become reproductively isolated from one another, as speciation would require, and would, instead, move through time, changing in response to selective pressures and differential gene flow, as an interbreeding population.

With the objections to cladistics reviewed, we now consider replacement. As related to the hominid record, replacement has a long, if not distinguished, history dating back to colorful accounts of the disappearance of the bestial Neandertal at the hands of the noble Cro-Magnon offered early in this century. It gained respectability in the 1980s when molecular analysis of mitochondrial DNA of existing human populations indicated that contemporary African populations exhibit the greatest degree of mitochondrial variation and thus are presumably older than and ancestral to non-African populations. Therefore, the speciation event that produced anatomically modern humans happened in Africa, and assuming that mutations of mitochondrial DNA occur at a constant rate, the event took place anywhere from 100,000 to 200,000 years ago. As it moved out of Africa, this anatomically modern human replaced all existing archaic *sapiens* and any lingering *erectus* types!

Although in one or another form the replacement hypothesis has enjoyed widespread popularity within and without the scholarly community, it has been subjected to severe criticism, both at the molecular level (Templeton 1993, Melnick and Hoelzer 1993) and at the more general morphological level. With regard to the latter, Alan Templeton, for example, points out that the replacement argument assumes that the replacement of one physical feature in a fossil series by another means that an entire population (the existing "species") has been replaced by another (a new "species"). On the contrary, the replacement of one feature by another does not require the eradication of an entire population but may be accounted for on the basis of gene exchange among interbreeding populations or by natural selection selecting for or against a particular feature. "Morphological replacement should not be equated with population replacement," Templeton insists, and he concludes that "research indicates that all humans constitute a single evolutionary lineage" with differences among populations being largely the result of the differential exchange of genes (Templeton 1996, 1363; see also Wolpoff 1994).

Templeton's two points, that morphological replacement does not equal population replacement and that humans constitute a single evolutionary lineage, are the central feature of the encompassing model formulated in direct opposition to the replacement argument, the multiregional hypothesis. In one of their most comprehensive statements, the architects of the multiregional model first establish the existence of regional continuity from *erectus* forms in Europe and the Near East, Africa, East Asia, and Australasia. They then argue that gene flow (promoted perhaps by the widespread human strategy of selecting mates outside the local group, that is, exogamy, Wolpoff 1999a) and actual migration connected these regional lines of continuity so that the *sapiens* form emerged throughout the human population. In this manner, they argue not for the emergence of anatomically modern humans as a species but rather for the appearance in different regions of different features characteristic of us. In other words, the various features indicative of *sapiens sapiens* originated at different times and places, but the constant flow of genes and movement of people maintained us as an interbreeding, albeit polytypic, population (Frayer et al. 1993; see also Wolpoff's monumental text, *Paleoanthropology* [1999b], and Clark's tour-de-force argument [1992], repeated in Clark and Willermet 1997). Recent assessment of the molecular evidence supports this comprehensive account of human evolution (Ayala et al. 1995).

HUMANIZATION

Even the most ardent splitter must agree that two themes predominate the record of hominid evolution. To wit, bipedality preceded the expansion of the brain and cultural "thickening" accompanied subsequent hominid development, in other words, the humanization process.

We may gain a critical perspective of the humanization process by placing it within the context of mammalian adaptive radiation. Upon their emergence as a distinct life form, featuring, among other attributes, live birth and nursing, plus all the accompanying social components, such as male-female-infant interdependency, mammals diversified to occupy different environment zones: bats the air, whales the sea, horses the plains, and primates the trees. Within each, further diversification permitted a finer tuning in the interplay among form, adaptation, and environment. Among the primates, this finer tuning resulted in the ancestral lineage of apes and humans, the *Hominoidea*, and still further and still finer tuning to the sibling array of orangutan, gorilla, chimpanzee, and human: the *Pongidae* and the *Hominidae*.

By placing the humanization process within the adaptive radiation of mammals, I am clearly not suggesting that we humans are an entity to which the entire record of life points. The lesson of the dinosaurs teaches us otherwise. These magnificent creatures came to an end not because mammals outcompeted them but, as is generally accepted, because of the effects of an asteroid crashing into earth (Russell and Dodson 1997). Thus, at any time during the humanization process, even or especially now, our record on this earth can come to a screeching halt. In other words, we are not preordained in the record of life. Yet this very fact, that our genesis was not inevitable, makes what we have done even more remarkable. In viewing our record, from African savannah to lunar plain, who cannot marvel at what we humans have accomplished? And is it not true that Mars awaits us?

The humanization process takes with it this terminology: a hominid is any bipedal member of the *Hominoidea* and any hominid with culture is human. "Human," then, is a broader term than anatomically modern *Homo sapiens sapiens*, that is, you and me today. Rather than pose a categorical question, who is human and what is not, the humanization process focuses on becoming human, a process that began at least with the pre-*sapiens*, if not with the australopithecines.

To say that "human" is any hominid with culture highlights the adaptation component in the evolutionary interplay of form, adaptation, and environment. Indeed, since it links together form and environment, adaptation, specifically in the sense of behavior, may be the crucial component in the evolutionary process in general. In the case of humans it is a unique kind of adaptation, symbolic adaptation.

The multiregional model stresses the role of gene flow in the "across the board" transformation of pre-*sapiens* into archaic *sapiens* and archaic *sapiens* into modern forms. Gene flow occurs through population movement and particularly through interbreeding. Parenthetically, with regard to interbreeding, at some time in human evolution, the avoidance of mother-son, father-daughter, and sister-brother mating got transformed into the incest taboo. The emergence of this universally recognized norm that prohibits mating among these pairs and its frequent extension to include other kin, thereby promoting mating outside the local group, or exogamy, have surely contributed to the "across the board" evolution of human populations, notwithstanding cases of the taboo's violation.

As this parenthetical statement implies, to the multiregional stress on gene flow, we may add phyletic evolution. In the human case, phyletic evolution is the adaptation to culture; it is selective pressure, operating throughout the emerging human population, for enhancing the facility to communicate with symbols.

As introduced in Chapter 1 and further developed in Chapter 4, my approach to human tools views them as symbolic communication. Human tools partake of the same objectification process that turns our intersubjective experience into words. This objectification process allows us to create a world distinct from the continuous flow of experience. Once created, the world shapes our experience, even as it is refreshed by new happenings. Initially inspired by my mentor in cultural geography, Fred Kniffen, and later augmented with insights gained from Peter Berger and Clifford Geertz, my attempt at clarifying this communicative operation dates back practically to the beginnings of my academic career (Richardson 1974a, 1974b).

Recently, several authors have sought to draw a tighter connection between hominid toolmaking and language. They seek to relate the logical operations necessary to produce an Acheulean hand ax, a Mousterian point, or a Solutrean blade to the operations required in language production. Glynn Isaac, for example, proposes that the increasing orderliness discernible in the manufacturing of stone tools indicated an increased orderliness in hominid cognition (summarized in Lewin 1998, 462). For example, Bruce Knauft (1991) argues, especially in footnote 8 of his text, that despite the current splitting of the hominid trajectory into various separate destinies, a clear pattern of the emergence of symbolic communication can be ascertained beginning with *Homo erectus*. Sue Taylor Parker (1985) offers a comprehensive overview of the tie between the production of tools and of language. Although she directs her attention more toward the facility of language to transmit information, she also observes that to be an effective transmitter of information, language must create a reality and entice people to enter it; and the production of tools, and more generally material culture, contributes substantially to the creation of that reality. In his "New Models and Metaphors for the Neandertal Debate," Paul Graves (1991) parallels the points I make here: Toolmaking is a social activity, and human social activity is based on our ability to take the role of the other and to reflect back upon the social exchange and thereby objectify that exchange—that is, to think. Human toolmaking and human thinking are concordant. Given the tool inventory of the Neandertals and their record of successful existence over the millennia, it is reasonable to assume they thought.

Chapter 1 outlined the humanization process as one in which the enlargement of the brain in hominid evolution was in response to selection for communicative behavior based on symbols. In arguing so, it drew on the insights of others, such as Sherwood Washburn, whom I quoted as saying, "Our species only survives in culture, and in a profound sense, we are the product of the new selection pressures that came with culture" (1962, 28). To Washburn's statement, we may add the argument of fellow biological anthropologist, Ralph L. Holloway Jr., who, in a truly comprehensive statement that perhaps has not received the recognition it deserves, stated, "Tool-making and language are concordant. Selection favored the cognitive structures dependent on brain organization and social structure which resulted both in language and tool-making" (1969, 404). Likewise in cultural anthropology, the work of Clifford Geertz has moved us away from the "stratigraphic notion" of the cultural strata sitting unconformably on top of a biological one. In an article written in the same decade as those of Washburn and Holloway, Geertz insisted that the record of hominid evolution demonstrates "that culture, rather than being added on to a finished or virtually finished animal, was ingredient, and centrally ingredient, in the production of that animal itself" (1965, 110).

Despite these carefully advanced arguments, the prevailing opinion, voiced within anthropology and out, remains that we humans today are basically apes with a daub of culture. G. A. Clark, who otherwise has made the most sensible analysis of the transition between archaic and modern *sapiens* (Clark and Lindly 1989; Clark 1992), recently asserted that sex roles in humans have little to do with "intentional, quasi-rational choice, moral values, or other epiphenomena" but are a product of natural and sexual selection at work during the last five million years of human evolution. "Seen from this perspective, humans are only animals . . . and culture is a thin veneer" (1998, 1047).

In light of this widespread misconception, the recent work of a biological anthropologist, Terrance Deacon, is a delight. In *The Symbolic Species: The Co-Evolution of the Language and Brain* (1997), Deacon, whose specialty is the hominid brain, has written what surely will be recognized as one of the most outstanding decipherments of hominid evolution. It is a big book, physically as well as conceptually, with over five hundred pages of carefully documented arguments. It is particularly impressive in its combined, page after page, diagram after diagram, examination of the workings of the brain with an equally close appraisal of the properties of language. Let me give a taste of this uncommonly rich book: "The remarkable expansion of the brain that took place in human evolution . . . was not the cause of symbolic language but a consequence" (340). "It is simply not possible to understand human anatomy, human neurobiology, or human psychology without recognizing they have been shaped by . . . symbolic reference" (410). "Language is a social phenomenon. To consider it in purely formal, psychological, or neurobiological terms is to strip away its reason for being" (115). "Symbolic reference . . . cannot be an intrinsic quality. . . . The source of symbolic reference is not in the brain at all" (447). "There never was a creature who was half-ape, half-human, who was a bit duller than most people but slightly more savvy than most chimps, and who communicated with a half-language" (377).

In essence, Deacon's argument is that we humans are the outcome of the adaptation of hominid biology to symbolic communication. Thus, far from being a "thin veneer," communicating with symbols is central to our existence. Or to repeat the formulation I offered in Chapter 1, as a product of millions of years of selective pressure, for us humans to be, we have to have a world to be in, which we, you and I, create. If we are, we are being-in-the-world.

For a thorough scrutiny of the book with a focus on the brain side of the co-evolutionary process, I ask you to consider Holloway's review (1998). Here let me briefly present the language side. By language, Deacon means communication with symbols, a broader arena than grammar and even speech. Yet it is not the same as nonhuman vocalization and nonverbal gesturing, which are indexical. In indexical communication, form (a sound or a gesture) is concretely tied to its referent. In symbolic communication, the physical connection between form and referent is replaced with links to other symbols. The logic of the relations among symbols takes precedence over any individual tie between a particular symbol and its referent. Symbolic communication is categorical and goes from category to category or slot to slot. Furthermore, this categorical logic requires that some slots are negative. Indicating the negative is a near impossibility with indexical communication but is a quality inherent in symbolic communication. Here, I hope you see the connection that I see between Deacon's presentation of symbolic communication and Derrida's concept of "differance," reviewed in Chapter 1, and its oppositional logic of absence and presence.

To confirm the importance of symbol communication in our makeup, Deacon coins the term *Homo symbolicus*. *Homo symbolicus* is an inclusive category encompassing all "symbolizing hominids," which "are linked via a common pool of symbolic information, one that is inaccessible to other species" (341), and one that, I might add, separates and isolates us from other species as firmly and completely as any organic barrier. Deacon's term "symbolizing hominids" is equivalent to my term *human* and consequently reaches back beyond archaic *sapiens*, practically beyond pre-*sapiens*, to the diffused zone between the australopithecines and later hominids.

If we take a truly evolutionary view of the development of symbolic communication, Deacon insists, we will see it as a particular specialization by a divergent branch of the *Hominoidea.* In this manner, development of symbolic communication corresponds to the developments mentioned earlier in connection with the adaptive radiation of mammals. It is not an end rung in a stepladder sequence but bears the same relation to us humans as echolocation bears to bats. This is the reason we do not find half-languages among our nearest animal siblings. The development of symbolic communication occurs subsequent to the ape-hominid split.

The emergence of symbolic communication was not due to some rare, "hopeful monster" mutation, nor was it the result of a speciation event so commonly evoked to account for anatomically modern *sapiens* and the cultural explosion occurring in Upper Paleolithic Europe. Its origin is not directly tied to speech as we know it. The shift of sound production from "visceral control" to control by the brain, or "cortical control," and the descent of the larynx in the throat to form the voice box were not antecedent to symbolic communication but were subsequent adaptions to it. Indeed, the "origins of the first symbolic communication have nothing intrinsically to do with language per se" (412).

In a masterful weaving of current sociobiological interpretations of reproductive success, Deacon lodges the beginnings of symbolic communication in the australopithecine attempt to solve the problem of how to avoid "getting stuck with an incompetent, unreliable, or unfaithful mate" (383), something we post-australopithecines are still working on! Given the advantages of cooperation by males in hunting and the advantages of male provisioning of females and offspring, how did the australopithecines ensure, as best they could, that males did unite to hunt, that individual males, returning from the hunt, provisioned the mother of their offspring and not the offspring of some philandering ne'er-do-well, and that particular females, once they had placed their lots and those of their offspring in the hands of particular males, could rely on that male provisioning them, not some beguiling coquette down by the water hole? To be sure, the information transmitted by mating displays of other animals addresses these issues of choice, yet the indexical character of these displays limits their capacity to enhance solidarity and alleviate tension. They cannot address "what might be" or "what could be" and, especially, "what ought to be." The shift from indexical communication to symbolic communication moves the social exchange from the fluidity of the moment to the greater clarity of categories that become the identity, the personhood, of those occupying the categories: mother, son, father, daughter. With the shift to symbolic communication, social interaction becomes symbolic interaction.

Yet the mating displays carry with them the power of actual, physical, sweaty presence, of face-to-face, body-to-body engagement. One aspect of human communication that combines both the physical power of the body and the ideational power of the symbol is ritual. Thus, the earliest form of symbolic communication was not some monosyllabic "Me Tarzan, you Jane" exchange but rather the compelling, participatory drama of ritual. Drawing upon the widespread recognition that the logic of ritual frequently asserts what *is* by demonstrating what *is not*, that what is peace is not war, Deacon suggests that the australopithecines discovered solidarity and peace could be achieved through rituals that acted out conflict and war. War and peace are negations of each other. To achieve peace through ritual, to create solidarity and dissipate tension, requires the display of what peace is not, thus a drama of war and chaos.

In ritual, we repeat again and again with our sensory-rich, primate bodies the categorical negation of what we seek. The redundancy of our actions creates reliable associations among the symbolic forms and consequently addresses the dual problem of symbols difficult to believe and symbols difficult to grasp. Through the ritualization of conflict we create solidarity and trust. To be sure, as you well know, ritualization, to the extent that it becomes purely "symbolic" and loses its experiential dimension, may fail, as in the case of my "salvation." Yet, as Deacon discloses, ritual permits us to convey to one another the most ineffable symbolic notions, such as love, trust, and in the australopithecine case, as with us, what it is to be human.

Reviewing Deacon's wonderful book and considering how the origin of symbolic communication may be sought in the ritual of negation brings us directly to the issue of the Neandertal discovery of the not-there, the presence of death.

NEANDERTAL BURIALS

The amount of material coming out about the Neandertal threatens to swamp even the most dedicated enthusiast. In 1998, a leading world journal, *Current Anthropology*, devoted an entire issue to "The Neanderthal Problem," with discussion continuing in the subsequent issues. As of the fall of 1999, there are some sixteen books in print with "Neandert(h)al" in the title. In this outpouring of material, we can distinguish two diametrically opposed assessments of the human status of this bipedal hominid: they were human; they were not human. Let us call the first "Assessment H" and the second, "Assessment NH." For convenience, we will date the appearance of Assessment H with the publication of C. Loring Brace's "The Fate of the 'Classic' Neanderthals: A Consideration of Hominid Catastrophism," which appeared in *Current Anthropology* in 1964. In this article, Brace successfully moved the prevailing opinion away from the earlier position that the Neandertals were a distinct and inferior species to the position that they were fully sapient. Here are the attributes that compose Assessment H.

Assessment H

1. Formal classification as *Homo sapiens neanderthalensis*.
2. Genetic exchange possible between Neandertal and anatomically modern forms.
3. No sharp division between Middle Paleolithic and Upper Paleolithic archaeological stages.
4. Mousterian artifacts associated with Neandertals constitute evidence of symbolic communication. Therefore, Neandertals spoke and knew death.
5. Consequently, speech.
6. Burials.

Again as a manner of convenience, we may date Assessment NH with the appearance of Robert H. Gargett's "Grave Shortcomings: The Evidence for Neanderthal Burial," which appeared in the same journal, *Current Anthropology*, in 1989, twenty-five years after Brace's article.

Assessment NH

1. Formal classification as *Homo neanderthalensis* (a return to the earlier nomenclature).
2. No genetic exchange between Neandertals and anatomically modern forms.
3. Sharp boundary between Middle Paleolithic and Upper Paleolithic.
4. Mousterian artifacts not evidence of symbolic communication.
5. Consequently, no speech.
6. No burials.

We may note also that scholars in the Assessment H camp generally support the "across the board" multiregional model of hominid evolution, at least from the australopithecines on, while those professing Assessment NH support the replacement model (Clark 1992). As is the case with any argument, some support a mixture of the two assessments. Paul Graves (1991), for example, sees the Neandertals as a localized but distinct form of the *sapiens* species who were absorbed, through interbreeding, into our gene pool. For the central position it plays in my presentation, I will focus on the debate about the burials.

Let me repeat my argument for the significance of the Neandertal burials. Through our capacity for symbolic action, we humans voice, in word, artifact, and behavior, a distinction between self and not-self, between presence and absence, between where and nowhere, between "You are" and "You are not." Tools such as the Acheulean hand ax strongly suggest that the humanization process of which that capacity is an integral part was under way at least by pre-*sapiens* times, if not earlier, but the Neandertal burials are our first direct evidence of that capacity. That being said, we must bear in mind that the Neandertal burials in the Middle Paleolithic or the later burials in the Upper Paleolithic containing anatomically modern forms are *not* final products. The humanization process is a process, ongoing through the Middle Paleolithic, proceeding past the Upper Paleolithic, and continuing today. Not even the most ardent anthropocentric, a label I gladly claim, can imagine that we today, at the beginning of a new millennium, have reached the conclusion of that process. The conclusion will be attained only when we have conquered our own invention, when we once and for all have put death in its place, that is, when we humans vanish.

If we assume, then, an acceptance of the interpretation of the burials as awareness of self and death, the question becomes: Were the burials in fact burials or artifacts of the excavation process? To speak frankly, did the excavators of the Neandertal sites know what they were doing, or did they confuse random associations of human bone and artifacts with patterns of signification?

Please note I refer to the burials as "patterns of signification" rather than "intentional burials." To speak of intentionality moves us too close to guessing what was in the Neandertals' hearts when they buried a fellow member. Who knows what is in anyone's heart? My heart is as opaque to you as yours is to me. What you do know is my words. Consequently, when we review the evidence, we are not looking for intentionality, but we are looking for signs, that is, symbols that not only communicate to us but also communicated to the Neandertals as they reflected upon their acts. Burials are acts of reflection rather than acts of intention. With that point clarified, let us stop reflecting and jump into the fray.

Some seventy Neandertal sites dot the map from Gibraltar in the west to Teshik Tash to the east (Map 7). The habitation of these sites ranges from 150,000 to 35,000 years ago, and they contain an estimated 275 individuals (Klein 1996). Among those who accept the evidence for burials, the number of burials range from an earlier forty-nine (Rowlett and Schneider 1974) to a later thirty-six (Harrold 1980) to a more recent fifty-nine (Smirnoff 1989). I know you will agree that as fun as it would be to descend fully into the fray, we can only focus on a dig here, a dodge there, a flashy maneuver to outflank opponents, or a straight-out, in-your-face confrontation. First, some specific cases.

The site at a cave near Monte Circeo, Italy, was first exposed in 1930. Workers brought a skull to an anthropologist and later showed him where

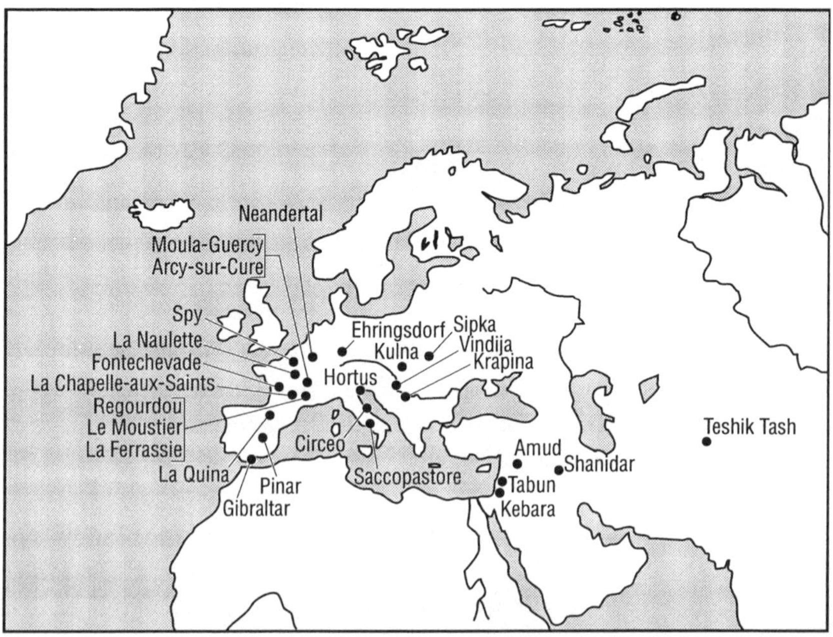

Map 7. The location of major Neandertal sites

they found it, in a side chamber within a ring of stones. The hole in the bottom of the skull where the neck articulates, the foramen magnum, had been enlarged. It eventually entered into the list as a burial with the attendant explanation that the hole was the act of cannibals seeking the soft brain to devour. Recently, Mary Stiner (1991) reexamined the cave. She found a higher percentage of Mousterian artifacts in the lower levels than in the upper ones. In the upper strata she found an array of hyena bones with a large percentage being juveniles, which suggested the hyenas were denning in the cave, a suggestion bolstered by the large number of gnawed ungulate bones scattered about. The distinction between the levels indicated that the hominids occupied the cave earlier than the hyenas. Although the evidence for gnawing was not conclusive, she argued that hyenas dragged the skull into their den and enlarged the foramen magnum in their attempt to get to the brain. Her conclusion gained support in the manner in which the Neandertal skull differed from other human skulls more clearly modified by cannibalistic efforts (White and Toth 1991). Phillip Chase, in his comment on Stiner's reexamination, concedes that perhaps Monte Circeo is not a burial but maintains that other Middle Paleolithic sites clearly indicate Neandertal burials. He adds that burials may signal a strong attachment to the deceased and a desire to protect the body against scavengers without the burial being "embedded in any symbolic context" (1991, 124), a curious observation to which we will return later.

To balance, as it were, Stiner's meticulous examination, we turn to an equally close examination of burials in the Levant. The Middle Paleolithic in the Levant includes both anatomically modern humans at Qafzeh and Skhul and archaic humans at Tabun, Amud, and Kebara. In their review, Anna Belfer-Cohen and Erella Hover (1992) find nothing to distinguish between the graves of anatomically modern humans at Qafzeh and Skhul and those of the archaic humans at Tabun, Amud, and Kebara. Furthermore, and more tellingly, they compare the Middle Paleolithic burials with those associated with the much later Natufian period. All of the Natufian burials are readily accepted as such. Yet the authors find little to separate Natufian from Middle Paleolithic burials. For example, only 10 percent of the Natufian burials contain any type of grave goods. They conclude that only the tendency to see archaic *sapiens* as less than human accounts for the rejection of burials at Tabun, Amud, and Kebara.

Evidence of the burial at Kebara seems exceptionally strong (Bar-Yosef et al. 1992). Referred to as KMH 2, the remains suggest an adult male about twenty-five to thirty-five years old. The remains are in an excellent state of preservation and include most of the skeleton, with the exception of the head, which had been removed after the initial interment. The sides of the burial pit are clearly distinct, with sediments inside the pit a yellow brown in contrast to the blackish soil outside the pit. There are no carnivore marks on the bones. The pit contains numerous lithics, but these were probably part of the refilling of the pit once the head was removed. Significantly, the hyoid bone was still in place between the jaw bones. The hyoid is a small U-shaped bone that is positioned immediately above the larynx and forms part of the vocal apparatus. The hyoid of KHM 2 is indistinguishable from the hyoid of anatomically modern humans.

In addition to the Kebara adult male, recent excavation at nearby Amud has disclosed an Neandertal infant burial. Evidence of burial centers on the fully articulated remains, the location in the corner of the cave, and the presence of a red-deer maxilla resting on the pelvis of the infant. The red-deer maxilla is reminiscent of the deer antlers associated with a Qafzeh remains and a pig mandible with a Skhul skeleton. Qafzeh and Skhul are frequently designated as anatomically modern and are accepted as burials with the antlers and mandible said to be grave goods. If such is the case, then the maxilla found in situ with the Neandertal infant should likewise be so interpreted. Interestingly, even though they make a strong argument for burial, the authors prefer the designation of Neandertal as *Homo neanderthalensis* (Rak, Kimbel, and Hovers 1994).

Among those who accept the evidence for burial, we find those who, paradoxically, conclude the burials were not symbolic acts, that is, acts shaped by symbols. Chase and Dibble (1987) interpret the Neandertal burials as such but conclude the burials express the Neandertals' emotional attachment to the recently deceased and a desire to protect the valued loved one from predators. More recently, they insist that Neandertals, whom they class as archaic *Homo sapiens*, were capable of symbolic behavior, yet possessing it and using it are two different things. So the Neandertals failed to use this behavior when they buried their dead (Dibble and Chase 1993). Mellars, in a massive, impressive review of the Neandertal legacy in western Europe, asserts that the burden of proof rests with those who argue that Neandertals had cognitive abilities less than anatomically modern humans. Yet while he accepts several European Neandertal burials, he adds that the artifactual material found in the graves is more likely the results of the Neandertals accidentally scooping in the artifacts from the cave floor when they interred the body. He concludes, "At the very least we must assume that the act of deliberate burial implies the existence of some kind of strong social or emotional bonds within Neanderthal societies, which dictated that the remains of relatives or other close kin should be carefully protected and perhaps preserved in some way after death. But to suggest that the burial must be seen as necessarily symbolic seems difficult to sustain" (Mellars 1996, 381). His assessment of the lack of symbolic behavior seems to fly in the face of his earlier assertion about the burden of proof. Concurring with Chase and Dibble and perhaps with Mellars in their review, B. A. Schumann and P. B. Petit conclude, enigmatically, that "there is no evidence of [Neandertal] burial in a social sense" (1999, 165).

William Noble and Iain Davidson (1996) are among those who reject outright the existence of burials. Their conclusion develops out of their reluctance to accept any worked stone prior to the Upper Paleolithic as "minded-behavior." Acheulean hand axes and Mousterian flakes, no less than Oldowan pebble tools, were probably the residues of what remained after the knapper chipped off usable material. In other words, the symmetry of the hand ax is an accidental leftover. Despite their careful bringing to bear the insights of Mead, Berger and Luckmann, and L. S. Vygotsky upon the emergence of a reflexive self as a particularly human feature, they dismiss in a page and a half the evidence that Neandertal behavior was self-reflexive. Instead they point to the human occupation of Australia as the first direct indication of such behavior.

Before ending our consideration of the human status of the Neandertal, we need to consider the significance of cut marks discernible on some Neandertal skeleton remains. Cut marks come from defleshing the bone. With a tool in its grasp, the hand cuts through the flesh and into the fresh bone. Some interpret the cut marks in the Neandertal bones found at the site in Kaprina, Croatia, as acts of the living preparing the dead for secondary burial (Gibbons 1997). Others, however, while generally accepting that Neandertals did bury their dead, interpret the Kaprina material as cannibalism (Villa 1993, but see Trinkaus 1985). This interpretation, boosted by the resurrection of the credibility of cannibalism from its earlier assignment to myth, has been applied to the Vindija site also in Croatia (Gibbons 1997) and more recently to the Moula-Guercy remains in France (Culotta 1999b; Defleur et al. 1999). Unfortunately, if the Neandertals butchered one another, that act alone joins them with modern *sapiens*. So burial or cannibalism, while important to determine for other reasons, both testify in different ways to Neandertal's human status.

In the continuing story of the Neandertal, two recent events point, typically, in different directions. Molecular analysis of the mitochondrial DNA (mtDNA) of the remains of a Neandertal infant in the Caucasus region of eastern Europe shows greater affinity with similar DNA analysis of the Neandertal remains in Germany (the original Neandertal skeleton from the Neander Valley) than does either one with the mtDNA of modern human populations. The molecular evidence from two different Neandertal individuals from different regions of Europe mutually reinforces the credibility of the molecular analysis and argues for an early separation of the Neandertal lineage from the lineage of modern humans and its subsequent replacement by that same lineage (Ovchinnikov et al. 2000). While the evidence supports the hypothesis that the Neandertals made no contribution to the mtDNA of modern humans, it does not rule out a contribution of Neandertal nuclear DNA to the modern gene pool; that is, interbreeding remains a possibility (Höss 2000).

The genetic inference comes subsequent to a discovery of an early Upper Paleolithic burial of a four-year-old individual in Portugal. Dating at 24,000–25,000 years ago places the burial subsequent to transition from Middle Paleolithic to Upper Paleolithic, yet the mosaic of skeletal features indicates the individual combines the skull of modern humans with the stature of an archaic one. The remains clearly indicate population mixing between early modern and late archaic, that is, Neandertal, humans, and therefore "it is inappropriate to apply a species distinction with strict implications of reproductive isolation to the Neanderthals versus early modern humans" (Duarte et al. 1999, 7608).

SUMMARY

We, you and I, are part of a humanization process that began subsequent to the emergence of bipedality. How subsequent is unclear; perhaps the process was even concordant with the selection for upright stature. We may certainly consider the tools associated with pre-*sapiens* as indicating the appearance of culture. Neandertal behavior, however, is our first direct evidence of the capacity to communicate symbolically. The acceptance of Neandertal burials as symbolic acts constitutes part of the paradigm associated with the multiregional model, labeled here Assessment H. The interpretation of the Neandertal burials as "yes, but" or their outright rejection forms an item in the paradigm that makes up the replacement model, called here Assessment NH.

We may conclude that if we accept the definition of human as a bipedal primate with culture, then those who place the Neandertals within Assessment NH find themselves apparently quite willing to argue for the existence of a bipedal primate *without* culture. We might ask: If form, adaptation, and environment interrelate, then what is the adaptation of this cultureless bipedal? If they argue that the Neandertals had some culture or that they could only imitate anatomically modern *sapiens*, is that not the same argument voiced years ago at the turn of century? That Neandertals are the half-wit cousins of modern *sapiens*? To the contrary, let's listen to Wolpoff (1998).

In a recent assessment, Wolpoff refers to the hypoglossal canal, a hole in the bottom of the skull through which nerves pass to move the tongue, the size of which in the Neandertal compares to that found in modern humans. (For the ins and outs of this, see Holden 1998.) He also points to Neandertal remains associated with the beginning of the Upper Paleolithic, long thought to be the exclusive invention of modern *sapiens*. He writes, "Perhaps we should . . . consider [in contrast to the counterargument] a more parsimonious explanation for why Neandertals seem so human-like in brain size and anatomy, the speech-related details of the hypoglossal canal, hyoid bone anatomy, burial behavior, hunting prowess, and the invention of a true Upper Paleolithic industry in Europe. If it looks like a duck and quacks like a duck . . ." (Wolpoff 1998, 1991).

In 1993, Kathleen Gibson and Tim Ingold compiled a comprehensive review of the interrelations among tools, language, and cognition that features contributions on gesturing, nonhuman primate tool skills, neurological linkages, developmental parallels, and the archaeological record. Ingold set the tone for this volume that juxtaposes the technical and the social with the observation that the "human hand is a restless organ" (1993, 35).

Inspired by Ingold's apt characterization, I cannot resist ending this appendix with my own paean of praise (Richardson 1994, 190–91) for it.

The Hand

"Where is the mind?
In the hand or the brain?"
"In the brain, of course,"
students always reply.

"Look how the hand
reaches out. How it grasps.
Look at the way
it touches. How it caresses.

Look at the hand,
holding a hammer,
threading a needle,
cuddling a baby.

Look at the hand,
as it feels,
as it writes,
even as it speaks.
Look at the hand
and tell me,
Where's the mind?"

The human hand is the ancient, mammalian claw
that scurried out of the clutch of the Cretaceous
before the claw's grasp specialized into the hoof
of the horse, the flipper of a whale, or the wing
of a bat. We encounter nature and one another with
the eye, the ear, the mouth, the skin, and the hand.
With the hand, we extend out and bring near;
with the hand, we lift up and pull down;
and with the hand, we tear apart and join together.
With the hand, we hate; and with the hand, we love.
Blessed are we who have the hand.

Of all the world's creatures, we are uniquely alone in our luck,
the luck of the hand, the deal of the five-fingered stranger,
for in the beginning, even before the Word, along with the foot,
there was the hand. From African savannah to lunar dust, from
pebble tool to computer chip, all hail the hand. Touch me now
before I go. And when I'm gone, say goodbye with
the hand.

REFERENCES

Allen, Judson Boyce. 1958. Preaching, Southern Baptist. In *Encyclopedia of Southern Baptists*. Vol. 2. Nashville: Broadman Press.

Alvarez Aragón, Rosa María. 1982. El ciclo de navidad en la ciudad de Antigua, Guatemala. In *Historia y antropología de Guatemala*, edited by Jorge Luján Muñoz. Guatemala City: Facultad de humanidades, Universidad de San Carlos.

Alvarez Arévalo, Miguel. 1980. Etnografía de la fiesta de navidad de Guatemala. *Antropología e Historia de Guatemala* 2 (2):105–39.

Ammerman, Nancy T. 1991. North American Protestant fundamentalism. In *Fundamentalism observed*, edited by Martin E. Marty and R. Scott Appleby. Chicago: University of Chicago Press.

Anderson, Jon W., and William B. Friend, eds. 1995. *The culture of Bible Belt Catholics*. New York: Paulist Press.

Andrade, Maydianne C. B. 1996. Sexual selection for male sacrifice in the Australian redback spider. *Science* 271:70–71.

Andrews, Peter, and Chris Stringer. 1989. *Human evolution: An illustrated guide*. Cambridge: Cambridge University Press.

Ankerson, Dudley. 1984. *Agrarian warlord: Saturnino Cedillo and the Mexican revolution in San Luis Potosí*. DeKalb: Northern Illinois University Press.

Annis, Sheldon. 1987. *God and production in a Guatemalan Town*. Austin: University of Texas Press.

Archdale, John. 1836. A new description of that fertile and pleasant province of Carolina . . . (1707). In *Historical collections of South Carolina*, edited by B. R. Carroll. Vol. 2. New York: Harper and Brothers.

Arrom, Marina. 1985. *The women of Mexico City*. Stanford: Stanford University Press.

Asfaw, Berhane, et al. 1999. *Australopithecus garhi*: A new species of early hominid from Ethiopia. *Science* 284:629–35.

Attwater, Donald, ed. 1958. *Catholic dictionary*. 3rd ed. New York: Macmillian.

Axtell, James. 1985. *The invasion within: The contest of cultures in colonial North America*. New York: Oxford University Press.

Ayala, Francisco J., Ananías Escalante, Colm O'Huigin, and Jan Klein. 1995. Molecular genetics of speciation and human origins. In *Tempo and mode in evolution: Genetics and paleontology 50 years after Simpson*, edited by Walter M. Fitch and Francisco J. Ayala. Washington, D.C.: National Academy of Sciences,

Bailey, David C. 1974. *Viva Cristo Rey! The cristero rebellion and the church-state conflict in Mexico*. Austin: University of Texas Press.

Barkow, Jerome H. 1978. Social norms, the self, and sociobiology: Building upon the ideas of A. I. Hallowell. *Current Anthropology* 19:99–118.

Barnadas, Josep M. 1984. The Catholic Church in colonial Spanish America. In *Colonial Latin America*. Vol. 1 of *The Cambridge history of Latin America*, edited by Leslie Bethel. Cambridge: Cambridge University Press.

Barnette, J. N. 1958. Sunday school. In *Encyclopedia of Southern Baptists*. Vol. 2. Nashville: Broadman Press.

Barr, James. 1966. *Old and new in interpretation: A study of the two Testaments*. New York: Harper & Row.

Bar-Yosef, O., et al. 1992. The excavations in Kebara Cave, Mt. Carmel. *Current Anthropology* 33 (5):497–550.

Bataillon, Marcel. 1966. *Erasmo y España: Estudios sobre la historia espiritual del siglo XVI*. Segunda edición español. Mexico: Fondo de Cultura Económica.

Batstone, David. 1991. *From conquest to struggle: Jesus of Nazareth in Latin America*. Albany: State University of New York Press.

Bauer, Arnold. 1989. Rural society. In *Latin America: Economy and society, 1870–1930*, edited by Leslie Bethel. Cambridge: Cambridge University Press.

Bauman, Richard. 1977. *Verbal art as performance*. Rowley, Mass.: Newbury House.

Beals, Ralph L., and Harry Hoijer. 1953. *An introduction to anthropology*. New York: Macmillan.

Beattie, J. H. M. 1980. On understanding sacrifice. In *Sacrifice*, edited by M. F. C. Bourdillon and Meyer Fortes. New York: Academic Press.

Beck, Benjamin D. 1980. *Animal tool behavior*. New York: Garland STPM Press.

Becker, Ernest. 1973. *The denial of death*. New York: Free Press.

———. 1975. *Escape from evil*. New York: Free Press.

Beidelman, T. G. 1987. Sacrifice and sacred rule in Africa. *American Ethnologist* 14 (3):542–51.

Belfer-Cohen, Anna and Erella Hover. 1992. In the eye of the beholder: Mousterian and Natufian burials in the Levant. *Current Anthropology* 33 (4):463–71.

Benedict, Ruth. 1934. *Patterns of culture*. Boston: Houghton Mifflin.

Benjamin, Jessica. 1988. *The bonds of love: Psychoanalysis, feminism, and the problem of domination*. New York: Pantheon Books.

Berger, Peter L., 1963. *Invitation to sociology: A humanistic perspective*. Garden City, N.J.: Anchor Books.

Berger, Peter L., and Thomas Luckmann. 1966. *The social construction of reality: A treatise in the sociology of knowledge*. New York: Doubleday & Co.

Berryman, Philip. 1987. *Liberation theology: Essential facts about the revolutionary movement in Latin America and beyond*. Philadelphia: Temple University Press.

Bierhorst, John. 1985. *A Nahuatl-English dictionary and concordance of the CANTARES MEXICANOS with an analytic transcription and grammatical notes*. Stanford: Stanford University Press.

Blattner, William D. 1994. Heidegger's debt to Jaspers's concept of the limit situation. In *Heidegger and Jaspers*, edited by Alan M. Olson. Philadelphia: Temple University Press.

Bloch, Maurice, and Jonathan Parry, eds. 1982. *Death and the regeneration of life*. Cambridge: Cambridge University Press.

Blum, Edwin A. 1980. The apostles' view of the Scripture. In *Inerrancy*, edited by Norman L. Geisler. Grand Rapids, Mich.: Zondervan.

Blumer, Herbert. 1969. *Symbolic interactionism: Perspective and method*. Englewood Cliffs, N.J.: Prentice-Hall.

Boles, John B. 1976. *Religion in antebellum Kentucky*. Lexington: University of Kentucky Press.

Bolton, Herbert Eugene. 1933. The epic of the greater America. *American Historical Review* 38:448–74.

Bonino, José Míguez. 1984. Who is Jesus Christ in Latin America today? In *Faces of Jesus: Latin American christologies*, edited by José Míguez Bonino. Maryknoll, N.Y.: Orbis Books.

Bonner, John Tyler. 1988. *The evolution of complexity by means of natural selection*. Princeton: Princeton University Press.

Borchert, Catherine M., and Adrienne L. Zihlman. 1990. The ontogeny and phylogeny of symbolizing. In *The life of symbols*, edited by Mary LeCron Foster and Lucy Jayne Botscharow. Boulder: Westview Press.

Borhegyi, S. F. de. 1954. The cult of our Lord of Esquipulas in Middle America and New Mexico. *El Palacio* 61:387–401.

Botscharow, L. 1989. Sites as texts: An exploration of Mousterian traces. In *The meanings of things*, edited by I. Hodder. New York: Routledge, Chapman, and Hall.

———. 1990. Paleolithic semiotics: Behavioral analogs to speech in Acheulean sites. In *The life of symbols*, edited by Mary LeCron Foster and Lucy Jayne Botscharow. Boulder: Westview Press.

Bourdillon, M. F. C., and Meyer Fortes, eds. 1980. *Sacrifice*. New York: Academic Press.

Boyarin, Jonathan, ed. 1993. *The ethnography of reading*. Berkeley: University of California Press.

Boylan, Anne M. 1988. *Sunday school: The formation of an American institution, 1700–1880*. New Haven: Yale University Press.

Brace, C. Loring. 1964. The fate of the "classic" Neanderthals: A consideration of hominid catastrophism. *Current Anthropology* 5:3–43.

———. 1988. Punctuationism, cladistics, and the legacy of medieval Neoplatonism. *Human Evolution* 3:121–38.

———. 1989. Medieval thinking and the paradigms of paleoanthropology. *American Anthropologist* 91:442–46.

———. 1991. *The stages of human evolution*. 4th ed. Englewood Cliffs, N.J.: Prentice-Hall.

———. 1997. Modern human origins: Narrow focus or broad spectrum? In *Conceptual issues in modern human origins research*, edited by G. A. Clark and C. M. Willerment. New York: Aldine de Gruyter.

Brandes, Stanley. 1984. Animal metaphors and social control in Tzintzuntzan. *Ethnology* 23 (3):207–16.

———. 1988. *Power and persuasion: Fiestas and social control in rural Mexico*. Philadelphia: University of Pennsylvania Press.

Brenner, Anita. [1943] 1971. *The wind that swept Mexico: The history of the Mexican Revolution, 1910–1942*. Photographs assembled by George R. Leighton. Austin: University of Texas Press.

Briggs, Charles L. 1980. *The wood carvers of Córdova, New Mexico: Social dimensions of an artistic "revival."* Knoxville: University of Tennessee Press.

Brown, Peter. 1981. *The cult of the saints: Its rise and function in Latin Christianity*. Chicago: University of Chicago Press.

Browner, C. H. 1986. Gender roles and social change: A Mexican case study. *Ethnology* 25 (2):89–106.

Bruce, Dickson D., Jr. 1974. *And they all sang hallelujah: Plain-folk camp-meeting religion, 1800–1845*. Knoxville: University of Tennessee Press.

Bruner, Edward M. 1994. Abraham Lincoln as authentic reproduction: A critique of postmodernism. *American Anthropologist* 96 (2):397–415.

Buber, Martin. [1958] 1987. *I and thou*. New York: Scribner's.

———. 1965. *Between man and man*. New York: Macmillan.

Burke, Kenneth. 1966. *Language as symbolic action*. Berkeley: University of California Press.

Burkhart, Louise M. 1993. The cult of the Virgin of Guadalupe in Mexico. In *South and Meso-American Native Spirituality*, edited by Gary H. Gossen in collaboration with Miguel León-Portilla. New York: Crossroad.

Burland, C. A. 1967. *The gods of Mexico*. New York: G. P. Putnam's Sons.

Bushnell, David, and Neill Macaulay. 1994. *The emergence of Latin America in the nineteenth century*. 2nd ed. Oxford: Oxford University Press.

Buttimer, Anne. 1976. Grasping the dynamism of lifeworld. *Annals of the Association of American Geographers* 66:277–92.

Bynum, Caroline Walker. 1982. *Jesus as mother: Studies in the spirituality of the high middle ages*. Berkeley: University of California Press.

———. 1987. *Holy feast and holy fast: The religious significance of food to medieval women*. Berkeley: University of California Press.

Byrne, W., and Andrew Whiten, eds. 1988. *Machiavellian intelligence: Social expertise and the evolution of intellect in monkeys, apes, and humans*. Oxford: Oxford University Press.

Cabestrero, Padre Teófilo. 1994. Viacrucis: The way of the cross. *El Momento Católico*. Chicago: Claretian Publications.

Cadwallader, Douglas. 1994. The Istrouma Baptist church: How one congregation adapted to the demographic change and the effects of that change. Master's thesis, Louisiana State University.

Calvez, Jean-Ives, S. J. 1990. Medelln and Puebla in the perspective of the world church. In *Born of the poor: The Latin American church since Medelln*, edited by Edward L. Cleary, O.P. Notre Dame: University of Notre Dame Press.

Campbell-Jones, Suzanne. 1980. Ritual in performance and interpretation: The mass in a convent setting. In *Sacrifice*, edited by M. F. C. Bourdillon and Meyer Fortes. London: Academic Press.

Camus, Albert. 1942. *Le mythe de Sisyphe*. Paris: Gallimard.

Carmichael, Elizabeth, and Chloë Sayer. 1991. *The skeleton at the feast: The day of the dead in Mexico*. Austin: University of Texas Press.

Carroll, Michael P. 1986. *The cult of the Virgin Mary: Psychological origins*. Princeton: Princeton University Press.

———. 1989. *Catholic cults and devotions*. Montreal: McGill-Queen's University Press.

Casalis, Georges. 1984. Jesus—neither abject lord nor heavenly monarch. In *Faces of Jesus: Latin American christologies*, edited by Jos Míguez Bonino. Maryknoll, N.Y.: Orbis Books.

Cátedra, María. 1992. *This world, other worlds: Sickness, suicide, death, and the afterlife among the Vaqueiros de Alzada of Spain*. Chicago: University of Chicago Press.

Chacón de Umaña, Luz Alba. 1967. *Don Diego de Haya Fernández*. San José: Editorial Costa Rica.

Chafe, Walter. 1982. Integration and involvement in speaking, writing, and oral literature. In *Spoken and written language: Exploring orality and literacy*, edited by Deborah Tannen. Norwood, N.J.: Ablex Publishing Corporation.

Chafe, Walter, and Deborah Tannen. 1987. The relation between written and spoken language. *Annual Review of Anthropology* 16:383–407.

Chapman, Anne. 1986. *Los hijos del cópal y la candela*. Vol. 2. Mexico: Universidad Nacional Autónoma de México.

Chapman, James Horton. 1958. Religion education. In *Encyclopedia of Southern Baptists*. Vol 2. Nashville: Broadman Press.

Chase, Philip G. 1991. Comments on "The faunal remains from Grotta Guattari: A taphonomic perspective." *Current Anthropology* 32 (2):124–25.

Chase, Philip G., and Harold Dibble. 1987. Middle paleolithic symbolism: A review of current evidence and interpretations. *Journal of Anthropological Archaeology* 6:263–96.

Chevalier, François. 1977. *L'Amérique latine de l'indépendance a nos jours*. Paris: Presses Universitaires de France.

Chomsky, Noam. 1988. *Language and problems of knowledge: The Managua lectures*. Cambridge, Mass.: MIT Press.

Christian, William A., Jr. 1972. *Person and God in a Spanish valley*. New York: Seminar Press.

———. 1981a. *Apparitions in late medieval and renaissance Spain*. Princeton: Princeton University Press.

———. 1981b. *Local religion in sixteenth-century Spain*. Princeton: Princeton University Press.

Christ-Janer, Albert, and Mary Mix Foley, eds. *Modern church architecture: A guide to the form and spirit of 20th century religious buildings*. New York: McGraw-Hill.

Clark, Francis, S.J. 1960. *Eucharistic sacrifice and the reformation*. London: Newman Press.

Clark, G. A. 1989. Paradigms and paradoxes in paleoanthropology: A response to C. Loring Brace. *American Anthropologist* 91:446–50.

———. 1992. Continuity or replacement? Putting modern human origins in an evolutionary context. In *The middle paleolithic: Adaptation, behavior, and variability*, edited by Harold L. Dibble and Paul Mellars. University Museum Symposium Series, Vol. 4. Philadelphia: University Museum.

———. 1998. Human monogamy. *Science* 282:1047.

Clark, G. A., and C. M. Willermet, eds. 1997. *Conceptual issues in modern human origins research*. New York: Aldine de Gruyter.

Clark, G. A., and J. M. Lindly. 1989. Modern human origins in the Levant and western Asia: The fossil and archaeological evidence. *American Anthropologist* 91 (4):962–85.

Cleary, Edward L., O.P. 1985. *Crisis and change: The church in Latin America today*. Maryknoll, N.Y.: Orbis Books.

Cohn, Deborah N. 1999. *History and memory of the two Souths: Recent southern and Spanish American fiction*. Nashville: Vanderbilt University Press.

Colson, Howard P. 1958. Inspiration of the Scriptures. In *Encyclopedia of Southern Baptists*. Vol. 1. Nashville: Broadman Press.

Conroy, G. C., et al. 1998. Endocranial capacity in an early hominid cranium from Sterkfontein, South Africa. *Science* 280:1730–31.

Cook, Noble David, and W. George Lovell. 1991. *"Secret judgments of gods": Old world disease in colonial Spanish America*. Norman: University of Oklahoma Press.

Cotey, Haddon Eugene. 1971. Preaching, Southern Baptist. In *Encyclopedia of Southern Baptists*. Vol. 3. Nashville: Broadman Press.

Cox, Harvey G. 1984. *Religion in the secular city: Toward a postmodern theology*. New York: Simon and Schuster.

Cramer, John. 1977. Christmas: An American paradox. *Humboldt Journal of Social Relations* 5 (1):2–26.

Cresswell, Tim. 1996. *In place / out of place: Geography, ideology, and transgression*. Minneapolis: University of Minnesota Press.

Cucchiari, Salvatore. 1988. "Adapted for heaven": Conversion and culture in western Sicily. *American Ethnologist* 15 (3):417–41.

Culotta, Elizabeth. 1995. New hominid crowds the field. *Science* 269:918.

———. 1999a. A new human ancestor? *Science* 282:572–73.

———. 1999b. Neanderthals were cannibals, bones show. *Science* 286:18–19.

Dale, William Pratt. 1958. Alabama Baptist Convention. In *Encyclopedia of Southern Baptists*. Vol. 1. Nashville: Broadman Press.

Davies, Horton. 1961. *Worship and theology in England: From Wesley to Maurice, 1690–1850*. Princeton: Princeton University Press.

———. 1975. *Worship and theology in England: From Andrews to Baxter and Fox, 1603–1690*. Princeton: Princeton University Press.

Deacon, Terrance. 1997. *The symbolic species: The co-evolution of language and the brain*. New York: W. W. Norton.

Defleur, Alban, et al. 1999. Neanderthal cannibalism at Moula-Guercy, Ardêche, France. *Science* 286:128–31.

Degler, Carl N. 1977. *Place over time: The continuity of southern distinctiveness*. Baton Rouge: Louisiana State University Press.

Denevan, William M., ed. 1992. *The native population of the Americas in 1492*. 2nd ed. Madison: University of Wisconsin Press.

Derrida, Jacques. 1976. *Of grammatology*. Baltimore: Johns Hopkins University Press.

———. 1978. *Writing and difference*. Chicago: University of Chicago Press.

———. 1995. *The gift of death*. Chicago: University of Chicago Press.

De Waal, Frans B. M. 1993. Intentional deception in primates. *Evolutionary Anthropology* 1 (3):86–92.

Dibble, Harold L., and Philip G. Chase. 1993. On Mousterian and Natufian burials in the Levant. *Current Anthropology* 34:170–76.

Dillenberger, John. 1988. *The visual arts and Christianity in America*. New York: Crossroad.

Dobzhansky, Theodosius. 1965. Religion, death, and evolutionary adaptation. In *Context and meaning in cultural anthropology*, edited by Melford Spiro. New York: Free Press.

Dodson, Michael. 1988. The church and the political struggle. *Latin American Research Review* 23 (1):230–43.

Donghi, Tulio Hapern. 1987. Economy and society. In *Spanish America after independence, c. 1820–c. 1870*, edited by Leslie Bethell. Cambridge: Cambridge University Press.

Dorgan, Howard. 1987. *Giving glory to God in Appalachia*. Knoxville: University of Tennessee Press.

Duarte, Cidália, et al. 1999. The early upper paleolithic human skeleton from the Abrigo do Lagar Velho (Portugal) and modern human emergence in Iberia. *Proceedings of the National Academy of Sciences* 96:7604–7609.

Dunbar, Robin. 1998. The social brain hypothesis. *Evolutionary Anthropology* 6 (5):178–90.

Duncan, Hugh. 1968. *Symbols in society*. New York: Oxford University Press.

Durand, Jorge, and Douglas S. Massey. 1995. *Miracles on the border: Retablos of Mexican migrants to the United States*. Tucson: University of Arizona Press.

Durkheim, Emile. 1947. *The elementary forms of religious life*. Glencoe, Ill.: Free Press.

Eggan, Fred. 1954. Social anthropology and the method of controlled comparison. *American Anthropologist* 56:743–63.

L'eglise–Forteresse des Saintes-Maries-de-la-Mer. n .d.

Ehlers, Tracy Bachrach. 1996. Debunking *marianismo*: Economic vulnerability and survival strategies among Guatemalan wives. *Ethnology* 30 (1):1–16.

Eighmy, John Lee. 1972. *Churches in cultural captivity*. Knoxville: University of Tennessee Press.

Eire, Carlos M. N. 1995. *From Madrid to purgatory: The art and craft of dying in sixteenth-century Spain*. Cambridge: Cambridge University Press.

Elizondo, Virgil. 1986. Popular religion in support of identity. In *Popular religion*, edited by Norbert Greinacher and Norbett Mette. Edinburgh: T. & T. Clark.

Elliot, J. H. 1963. *Imperial Spain: 1469–1716*. London: Edward Arnold.

———. 1987. The Spanish conquest. In *Colonial Latin America*, edited by Leslie Bethell. Cambridge: Cambridge University Press.

Enciclopedia universal ilustrada. 1925a. Tomo 9. Barcelona: Hijos de J. Espasa.

———. 1925b. Tomo 26. Barcelona: Hijos de J. Espasa.

———. 1925c. Tomo 53. Barcelona: Hijos de J. Espasa.

Encyclopedia of Southern Baptists. 1958, 1971, 1982. Vols. 1–4. Nashville: Broadman Press.

Eslinger, Ellen. 1999. *Citizens of zion: The social origins of camp meeting revivalism*. Knoxville: University of Tennessee Press.

Falk, Dean. 1998. Hominid brain evolution: Looks can be deceiving. *Science* 280:1714.

Farías, Victor. 1989. *Heidegger and nazism*. Philadelphia: Temple University Press.

First Baptist Church. 1987. *The dream lives on*. Raleigh: First Baptist Church.

Fischman, Joshua. 1993. New clues about the making of the mind. *Science* 262 (3):1517.

Fitts, Leroy. 1985. *A history of black Baptists*. Nashville: Broadman Press.

Fleagle, John G. 1995. Too many species? *Evolutionary Anthropology* 4 (2):37–38.

Flores, Angel. 1961. *An anthology of Spanish poetry*. Garden City, N.Y.: Anchor Books.

Flynt, J. Wayne. 1988. Southern Protestantism and reform, 1890–1920. In *Varieties of southern religious experience*, edited by Samuel S. Hill Jr. Baton Rouge: Louisiana State University Press.

Foley, R. 1991. How many species of hominids should there be? *Journal of Human Evolution* 20:413–29.

Forbes, Wesley L., ed. 1991. *The Baptist hymnal*. Nashville: Convention Press.

Foster, George M. 1960. *Culture and conquest: America's Spanish heritage*. Chicago: Quadrangle Books.

Fox, David, et al. 1999. Reconstructing phylogeny with and without temporal data. *Science* 284:1816–19.

Fraser, Valerie. 1990. *The architecture of conquest: Building in the viceroyalty of Peru, 1535–1635*. Cambridge: Cambridge University Press.

Frayer, David W., et al. 1993. Theories of modern human origin: The paleontological test. *American Anthropologist* 95 (1):14–50.

Fremantle, Anne, ed. 1963. *The papal encyclicals in their historical context*. New York: New American Library.

Friedman, Maurice. 1965. Introduction. In *Between man and man*, by Martin Buber. New York: Macmillan.

Fromm, Erich. [1930] 1963. *The dogma of Christ and other essays on religion, psychology, and culture*. New York: Holt, Rinehart, and Winston.

Gargett, Robert H. 1989. Grave shortcomings: The evidence of Neandertal burial. *Current Anthropology* 30 (2):157–90.

Geertz, Clifford. 1965. The impact of the concept of culture on the concept of man. In *New views of the nature of man*, edited by John R. Platt. Chicago: University of Chicago Press. (Reprinted in Geertz 1973.)

———. 1973. *The interpretation of cultures*. New York: Basic Books.

———. 1983. *Local knowledge*. New York: Basic Books.

Genovese, Eugene D. 1992. Town and village in the consolidation of southern slave society. In vol. 1 of *Civilization in crisis: Anthropological perspectives*, edited by Christine Ward Gailey. Gainesville: University Press of Florida.

Genovese, Eugene D., and Elizabeth Fox-Genovese. 1988. The religious ideals of southern slave society. In *The evolution of southern culture*, edited by Numan V. Bartely. Athens: University of Georgia Press.

Gergen, Kenneth J. 1991. *The saturated self: Dilemmas of identity in contemporary life*. New York: Basic Books.

Gibbons, Ann. 1994. Rewriting—and redating—prehistory. *Science* 263:1087–88.

———. 1997. Archaeologists rediscover cannibals. *Science* 277:635–37.

———. 1998. A blow to the "grandmother theory." *Science* 280:516.

Gibson, Kathleen R., and Tim Ingold. 1993. *Tools, language, and cognition in human evolution*. Cambridge: Cambridge University Press.

Gimbutas, Marija. 1991. *The civilization of the goddess*, edited by Joan Marler. San Francisco: HarperSanFrancisco.

Glade, William. 1989. Economy, 1870–1914. In *Latin America economy and society*,

1870–1930, edited by Leslie Bethell. Cambridge: Cambridge University Press.

Goffman, Erving. 1959. *The presentation of self in everyday life*. Garden City, N.Y.: Anchor Books.

Goizueta, Roberto S. 1995. *Caminemos con Jesús: Toward a Hispanic/Latino theology of accompaniment*. Maryknoll, N.Y.: Orbis Books.

Goldberger, Paul. 1995. The gospel of church architecture, revised. *New York Times*, April 20.

Goldfield, David R. 1982. *Cotton fields and skyscrapers: Southern city and region, 1607–1980*. Baton Rouge: Louisiana State University Press.

———. 1997. *Religion, race, and cities: Interpreting the urban South*. Baton Rouge: Louisiana State University Press.

Goldstein, Pierre. 1998. Cell death in us and others. *Science* 281:1283.

Góngora, Mario. 1975. *Studies in the colonial history of Spanish America*. Cambridge: Cambridge University Press.

Gottdiener, M. 1995. *Postmodern semiotics: Material culture and the forms of postmodern life*. Oxford: Blackwell.

Graves, Paul. 1991. New models and metaphors for the Neandertal debate. *Current Anthropology* 32 (5):513–41.

Greenleaf, Richard E. 1962. *Zumárraga and the Mexican inquisition, 1536–1543*. Washington, D.C.: Academy of American Franciscan History.

———, ed. 1977. *The Roman Catholic church in colonial Latin America*. Tempe, Ariz.: Center for Latin American Studies.

Gregory, Wayne. 1992. "Getting saved": Harmonizing the sacred and the secular in oral testimonies. Paper presented at the Ethnography of Communication Conference, Portland, Oregon, April 13–15.

Grenz, Stanley. 1983. *Isaac Backus—Puritan and Baptist*. Macon, Ga.: Mercer University Press.

Grieshaber, Erwin P. 1979. Hacienda-Indian community relations and Indian acculturation: A historiographical essay. *Latin American Research Review* 14 (3):107–28.

Gudeman, Stephen. 1976. Saints, symbols, and ceremonies. *American Ethnologist* 3 (4):709–29.

Gudmundson, Lovell. 1986. *Costa Rica before coffee: Society and economy on the eve of the export boom*. Baton Rouge: Louisiana State University Press.

Hale, Charles A. 1989. Political and social ideas. In *Latin America economy and society, 1870–1930*, edited by Leslie Bethell. Cambridge: Cambridge University Press.

Hallowell, I. 1960. Self, society, and culture in phylogenetic perspective. In *The evolution of man*, edited by Sol Tax. Chicago: University of Chicago Press.

Hanke, Lewis U. 1959. *Aristotle and the American Indian: A study of race prejudice in the modern world*. London: Hollis and Cater.

———, ed. 1964. *Do the Americas have a common history? A critique of the Bolton theory*. New York: Alfred A. Knopf.

Harding, Susan. 1987. Convicted by the Holy Spirit: The rhetoric of fundamental Baptist conversion. *American Ethnologist* 14:167–81.

Hardon, John A. 1980. *Modern Catholic dictionary*. Garden City, N.Y.: Doubleday.

Harris, J. William. 1998. *Plain folk and gentry in a slave society: White liberty and black slaves in Augusta's hinterlands*. Baton Rouge: Louisiana State University Press.

Harrold, F. B. 1980. A comparative analysis of Eurasian paleolithic burials. *World Archaeology* 12 (2):195–210.

Harvey, David. 1990. *The condition of postmodernity: An inquiry into the origins of cultural change*. Oxford: Blackwell.

Hastings, Adrian, ed. 1991. *Modern Catholicism: Vatican II and after*. New York: Oxford University Press.

Hatch, Nathan O. 1989. *The democratization of American Christianity*. New Haven: Yale University Press.

Hawkes, K., et al. 1998. Grandmothering, menopause, and the evolution of human life histories. *Proceedings of the National Academy of Sciences* 95:1336–39.

Hebblethwaite, Margaret. 1991. Devotion. In *Modern Catholicism: Vatican II and after*, edited by Adrian Hastings. New York: Oxford University Press.

Heidegger, Martin. 1962. *Being and time*. Translated by John Macquarrie and Edward Robinson. New York: Harper & Row.

Heinzelin, Jean de, et al. 1999. Environment and behavior of 2.5-million-year-old Bouri hominids. *Science* 284:625–29.

Heriot, M. Jean. 1994. *Blessed assurance: Beliefs, actions, and the experience of salvation in a Carolina Baptist church*. Knoxville: University of Tennessee Press.

Hernandez, Joanne Farb, and Samuel R. Hernandez. 1979. *The day of the dead: Tradition and change in contemporary Mexico*. Santa Clara, Calif.: Triton Museum.

Heyrman, Christine Leigh. 1997. *Southern cross: The beginnings of the Bible Belt*. New York: Alfred A. Knopf.

Hill, Carole. 1982. The meaning of the religious campmeeting experience in the American South. *Anthropology and Humanism Quarterly* 7 (2–3):39–44.

Hill, Kim. 1993. Life history theory and evolutionary anthropology. *Evolutionary Anthropology* 2 (3):78–88.

Hill, Samuel S., Jr. 1972a. Epilogue. *Churches in cultural captivity: A study of the social attitudes of Southern Baptists*, by John Lee Eighmy. Knoxville: University of Tennessee Press.

———. 1972b. Introduction. In *Religion and the solid South*, edited by Samuel S. Hill Jr. et al. Nashville: Abingdon.

———. 1972c. The South's two cultures. In *Religion and the solid South*, edited by Samuel S. Hill Jr. et al. Nashville: Abingdon.

———. 1980. *The South and the North in American religion*. Athens: University of Georgia Press.

Hilliard, Sam B. 1987. A robust new nation, 1783–1820. In *North America: The historical geography of a changing continent*, edited by Robert D. Mitchell and Paul A. Groves. Totowa, N.J.: Rowman & Littlefield.

———. 1990. Plantations and the molding of the southern landscape. In *The making of the American landscape*, edited by Michael P. Conzen. Boston: Unwin Hyman.

Hobgood, John J. 1971. The sanctuary of Chalma. *Verhandlungen des 37 internationalen Amerikanistenkongresses*. Band III. München: Klaus Renner.

Holden, Constance. 1998. How much like us were the Neandertals? *Science* 282:1456.

Holloway, Ralph L., Jr. 1969. Culture: A *human* domain. *Current Anthropology* 10:395–412.

———. 1998. Language's source: A particularly human confluence of hard wiring and soft. *American Scientist* 86:184–86.

Horst, Oscar H. 1990. Arcilla geofágica en América. *Mesoamérica* 19:169–76.

Höss, Matthias. 2000. Neanderthal population genetics. *Nature* 404:453–54.

Houston, James M. 1978. The concept of "place" and "land" in the Judaeo-Christian tradition. In *Humanistic geography*, edited by David Ley and Marwyn S. Samuels. Chicago: Maaroufa Press.

Humphrey, N. K. 1976. The social function of intellect. In *Growing points in ethology*, edited by P. P. G. Bateson and R. A. Hinde. Cambridge: Cambridge University Press.

Humphreys, S. C., and Helen King, eds. 1981. *Mortality and immortality: The anthropology and archaeology of death*. New York: Academic Press.

Hunter, John M., Oscar H. Horst, and Robert N. Thomas. 1989. Religious geophagy as a cottage industry: The holy clay tablet of Esquipulas, Guatemala. *National Geographic Research* 5 (3):281–95.

Huxley, Thomas H. 1902. *Man's place in nature*. New York: H. L. Fowle.

International Commission on English in the Liturgy. 1991. *The rites of the Catholic church*. Vol. 2. Collegeville, Minn.: Liturgical Press.

Jeane, D. Gregory. 1989. Cemeteries. In *Encyclopedia of southern culture*, edited by Charles Reagan Wilson and William Ferris. Chapel Hill: University of North Carolina Press.

Jennings, Francis. 1975. *The invasion of America: Indians, colonialism, and the cant of conquest*. Chapel Hill: University of North Carolina Press.

Jordan, Terry G. 1986. Evolution of American backwoods pioneer culture. In *Mississippi's piney woods: A human perspective*, edited by Noel Polk. Jackson: University Press of Mississippi.

Jordan, Terry G., and Matti Kaups. 1989. *The American backwoods frontier: An ethnic and ecological interpretation*. Baltimore: Johns Hopkins University Press.

Kamen, Henry. 1985. *Inquisition and society in Spain in the sixteenth and seventeenth centuries*. London: Weidenfeld and Nicolson.

Kaplan, Lawrence, ed. 1992. *Fundamentalism in comparative perspective*. Amherst: University of Massachusetts Press.

Kehoe, Alice B. 1979. The sacred heart: A case for stimulus diffusion. *American Ethnologist* 6:763–71.

Kelsey, V., and L. de J. Osborne. 1939. *Four keys to Guatemala*. New York: Funk and Wagnalls.

Kennedy, J. Gerald. 1987. *Poe, death, and the life of writing*. New Haven: Yale University Press.

Kennedy, Kathleen E. 1991. Reflecting darkly: Face to face with the Vietnam Veterans Memorial. Master's thesis, Louisiana State University.

Kennedy, Roger G. 1989. *Greek revival America*. New York: Stewart, Tabori, and Chang.

Kilmartin, Edward J., S.J. 1981. *Church, eucharist, and priesthood*. New York: Paulist Press.

Kinsley, David R. 1989. *The goddesses' mirror: Visions of the divine from east and west*. Albany: State University of New York Press.

Klauser, Theodor. 1979. *A short history of the western liturgy*. 2nd ed. London: Oxford University Press.

Klein, Richard G. 1996. Middle paleolithic people. *Science* 272:822–23.

Knauft, Bruce. 1991. Violence and sociality in human evolution. *Current Anthropology* 32 (4):391–428.

———. 1996. *Genealogies for the present in cultural anthropology*. New York: Routledge.

Knight, Walker L. 1993. Race relations: Changing patterns and practices. In *Southern Baptists observed: Multiple perspectives on a changing denomination*, edited by Nancy T. Ammerman. Knoxville: University of Tennessee Press.

Krantz, Grower. 1980. Sapienization and speech. *Current Anthropology* 21 (6):773–92.

Kroeber, Alfred L. 1952. *The nature of culture*. Chicago: University of Chicago Press.

———. 1957. *Style and civilization*. Ithaca: Cornell University Press.

Kubler, George. 1948. *Mexican architecture of the sixteenth century*. New Haven: Yale University Press.

Kubler, George, and Martin Soria. 1959. *Art and architecture in Spain and Portugal and the American dominions*. Baltimore: Penguin.

Kuhl, Patricia, et al. 1997. Cross-language analysis of phonetic units in language addressed to infants. *Science* 277:684–86.

Kummer, Hans, et al. 1997. The social intelligence hypothesis. In *Humans by nature: Between biology and the social sciences*, edited by Peter Weingart et al. Mahwah, N.J.: Lawrence Erlbaum Associates.

Lacan, Jacques. 1977. *Escrits: A selection*. London: Tavistock.

Lange, Yvonne. 1978. Santo Niño de Atocha: A Mexican cult transplanted to Spain. *Palacio* 84 (4):2–7.

Langlinais, J. W. 1967. Assumption of Mary. In *New Catholic encyclopedia*. Vol. 1. New York: McGraw-Hill.

Larick, Roy, and Russell L. Ciochon. 1996. The African emergence and early Asian dispersal of the genus *Homo*. *American Scientist* 84:538–51.

Larkin, F. 1967. Sacred Heart, iconography of. In *New Catholic encyclopedia*. Vol. 12. New York: McGraw-Hill.

Lastra, Yolanda. 1998. *Las lenguas amenazadas en México*. In *Convergencia e individualidad: Las lenguas Mayas entre hispanización e indigenismo*, edited by Andreas Koechert and Thomas Stolz. Handover: Verlag für Ethnologie.

Leakey, Meave G., et al. 1995. New four-million-year-old hominid species from Kanapoi and Allia Bay, Kenya. *Nature* 376:565–71.

Leakey, Meave G., et al. 2001. New hominid genus from Eastern Africa shows diverse middle Pliocene lineages. *Nature* 410:433–40.

Leavell, Roland Q. 1958. Evangelism. In *Encyclopedia of Southern Baptists*. Vol. 1. Nashville: Broadman Press.

Le Gros Clark, W. E. [1955] 1964. *The fossil evidence for human evolution*. Chicago: University of Chicago Press.

Leonard, Bill J. 1990. *God's last and only hope: The fragmentation of the Southern Baptist Convention*. Grand Rapids, Mich.: William B. Eerdmans.

León-Portilla, Miguel. 1963. *Aztec thought and culture: A study of the ancient Nahuatl mind*. Norman: University of Oklahoma.

———. 1992. *The Aztec image of self and society: An introduction to Nahua culture*. Edited with introduction by J. Jorge Klor de Alva. Salt Lake City: University of Utah Press.

Levine, Daniel H. 1990. The impact and lasting influence of Medellín and Puebla. In *Born of the poor: The Latin American church since Medellín*, edited by Edward L. Cleary, O.P. Notre Dame: University of Notre Dame Press.

———., ed. 1986. *Religion and political conflict in Latin America*. Chapel Hill: University of North Carolina.

Levinson, Stephen C. 1996. Language and space. *Annual Review of Anthropology* 25:353–82.

Lévi-Strauss, Claude. 1969. *The elementary structures of kinship*. Rev. ed. Boston: Beacon Press.

Lewin, Roger. 1998. *Principles of human evolution: A core textbook*. Malden, Mass.: Blackwell.

Ley, David, and Marwyn S. Samuels. 1978. Introduction: Contexts of modern humanism in geography. In *Humanistic Geography*, edited by David Ley and Marwyn S. Samuels. Chicago: Maaroufa Press.

Lieberman, Daniel E. 2001. Another face in our family tree. *Nature* 410:419–20.

Lockhart, James. 1992. *The Nahuas after the conquest: A social and cultural history of the Indians of central Mexico, sixteenth through eighteenth centuries*. Stanford: Stanford University Press.

Lockhart, James, and Stuart B. Schwartz. 1983. *Early Latin America: A history of colonial Spanish America and Brazil*. Cambridge: Cambridge University Press.

Lowie, Robert H. 1920. *Primitive society*. New York: Boni and Liveright.

Lumpkin, William L. 1959. *Baptist confessions of faith*. Chicago: Judson Press.

Lynch, John. 1989. The Catholic church. In *Latin American economy and society, 1870–1930*, edited by Leslie Bethell. Cambridge: Cambridge University Press.

Mackay, John A. 1932. *The other Spanish Christ: A study in the spiritual history of Spain and South America*. New York: Macmillan.

Mâle, Émile. 1983. *Chartres*. New York: Harper & Row.

Malone, Bill C. 1985. *Country music U.S.A.* Austin: University of Texas Press.

———. 1989. All-day singings. In *Encyclopedia of southern culture*, edited by Charles Reagan Wilson and William Ferris. Chapel Hill: University of North Carolina Press.

Marks, Jonathan, and R. Bent Lyles. 1994. Rethinking genes. *Evolutionary Anthropology* 3 (4):139–46.

Marsden, George M. 1980. *Fundamentalism and American culture: The shaping of twentieth-century evangelicalism, 1870–1925.* New York: Oxford University Press.

———. 1982. Everyone's one's own interpreter? The Bible, science, and authority in mid-nineteenth-century America. In *The Bible in America: Essays in cultural history*, edited by Nathan O. Hatch and Mark A. Noll. New York: Oxford University Press.

Martin, Joann. 1990. Motherhood and power: The production of women's culture of politics in a Mexican community. *American Ethnologist* 17 (3):470–90.

Martin, Robert. 1992. Classification and evolutionary relationships. In *Cambridge encyclopedia of human evolution*, edited by Steve Jones, Robert Martin, and David Pilbeam. Cambridge: Cambridge University Press.

Marty, Martin E. 1991. *Modern American religion, Vol. 2: The noise of conflict, 1919–1941.* Chicago: University of Chicago Press.

———. 1992. Fundamentals of fundamentalism. In *Fundamentalism in comparative perspective*, edited by Lawrence Kaplan. Amherst: University of Massachusetts Press.

Maston, T. B. 1958. Race relations. In *Encyclopedia of Southern Baptists.* Vol. 2. Nashville: Broadman Press.

Maurer Avalos, Eugenio. 1993. The Tzeltal Maya–Christian synthesis. In *South and Meso-American native spirituality*, edited by Gary H. Gossen. New York: Crossroad.

May, Lynn E., Jr. 1958. Crises, Southern Baptist. In *Encyclopedia of Southern Baptists.* Vol. 1. Nashville: Broadman Press.

Mayr, Ernst. 1981. Biological classification: Toward a synthesis of opposing methodologies. *Science* 214:508–16.

Mazel, A. 1935. *Les saintes-Maries-de-la-mer et la Camargue.* Vaucluse: Bonne Presse du Midi.

McBeth, Leon. 1968. *The First Baptist church of Dallas: Centennial history.* Grand Rapids, Mich.: Zondervan.

McClellan, Albert. 1982. Southern Baptist convention. In *Encyclopedia of Southern Baptists.* Vol. 4. Nashville: Broadman Press.

McCollum, Melanie A. 1999. The robust australopithecine face: A morphogenetic perspective. *Science* 284:301–305.

McDannell, Colleen. 1995. *Material Christianity: Religion and popular culture in America.* New Haven: Yale University Press.

McGlothlen, Gayle L. 1958. Worship service, Baptist. In *Encyclopedia of Southern Baptists.* Vol. 2. Nashville: Broadman Press.

McGrew, W. C. 1992. *Chimpanzee material culture: Implications for human evolution.* New York: Cambridge University Press.

McWhiney, Grady. 1986. Antebellum piney woods culture: Continuity over time and place. In *Mississippi's piney woods: A human perspective*, edited by Noel Polk. Jackson: University Press of Mississippi.

Mead, George Herbert. 1972. *The philosophy of the act*. Chicago: University of Chicago Press.

Meinig, D. W. 1986. *The shaping of America: Atlantic America, 1492–1800*. New Haven: Yale University Press.

———. 1993. *The shaping of America: Continental America, 1800–1867*. New Haven: Yale University Press.

Mellars, Paul. 1996. *The Neanderthal legacy: An archaeological perspective of western Europe*. Princeton: Princeton University Press.

Melnick, Don J., and Guy A. Hoelzer. 1993. What is mtDNA good for in the study of primate evolution? *Evolutionary Anthropology* 2 (1):2–10.

Merrill, James H. 1989. Some thoughts on colonial historians and American Indians. *William and Mary Quarterly* 46:94–119.

Metcalf, Peter, and Richard Huntington. 1991. *Celebrations of death: The anthropology of mortuary ritual.* 2nd ed. Cambridge: Cambridge University Press.

Miles, Margaret R. 1985. *Image as insight: Visual understanding in western Christianity and secular culture*. Boston: Beacon Press.

Miller, Daniel. 1998. Introduction. In *Material culture: Why some things matter*, edited by Daniel Miller. Chicago: University of Chicago Press.

Mitchell, Nathan, O.S.B. 1982. *Cult and controversy: The worship of the eucharist outside of mass*. New York: Pueblo.

Mitchell, Robert D. 1987. The colonial origins of Anglo-America. In *North America: The historical geography of a changing continent*, edited by Robert D. Mitchell and Paul A. Groves. Totowa, N.J.: Rowman & Littlefield.

Mitchell, Robert D., and Milton B. Newton Jr. 1988. The Appalachian frontier: Views from the East and from the Southwest. *Historical Geography Research Series*, no. 21.

Mitchell, Timothy. 1990. *Passional culture: Emotion, religion, and society in southern Spain*. Philadelphia: University of Pennsylvania Press.

Mitchell, William P. 1991. *Peasants on the edge: Crop, cult, and crisis in the Andes*. Austin: University of Texas Press.

Mithen, Steven. 1994. From domain specific to generalized intelligence: A cognitive interpretation of the middle / upper paleolithic transition. In *The ancient mind: Elements of cognitive archaeology*, edited by Colin Renfrew and Ezra B. W. Zubrow. Cambridge: Cambridge University Press.

Moell, C. J. 1967. Sacred Heart, devotion to. In *New Catholic encyclopedia*. Vol. 12. New York: McGraw-Hill.

Moore, John H. 1994. Putting anthropology back together again: The ethnogenetic critique of cladistic theory. *American Anthropologist* 96 (4):925–48.

Morgan, David. 1996a. Warner Sallman and the visual culture of American Protestantism. In *Icons of American Protestantism: The art of Warner Sallman*, edited by David Morgan. New Haven: Yale University Press.

———, ed. 1996b. *Icons of American Protestantism: The art of Warner Sallman.* New Haven: Yale University Press.

Morell, Virginia. 1994. Did early humans reach Siberia 500,000 years ago? *Science* 263:611–12.

———. 1997. Fossilized hatchling heats up the bird-dinosaur debate. *Science* 276:1501.

Morris, J. U. 1967. Sacred Heart, iconography of. In *New Catholic encyclopedia.* Vol. 12. New York: McGraw-Hill.

Morse, Richard M. 1987. Urban development. In *Colonial Latin America*, edited by Leslie Bethel.Cambridge: Cambridge University Press.

———. 1989. *New World soundings: Culture and ideology in the Americas.* Baltimore: Johns Hopkins University Press.

Moser, Stephanie. 1992. The visual language of archaeology. *Antiquity* 66 (253):831–44.

Mullins, E. Y. 1958. Baptists and the Bible. In *Encyclopedia of Southern Baptists.* Vol. 1. Nashville: Broadman Press.

Murdock, George P. 1949. *Social structure.* New York: Macmillan.

Murray, Robert, S. J. 1991. Revelation *(Dei Verbum).* In *Modern Catholicism: Vatican II and after*, edited by Adrian Hastings. New York: Oxford University Press.

Myers, Kathleen A. 1993. A glimpse of family life in colonial Mexico: A nun's account. *Latin American Research Review* 28 (2):63–83.

Needham, Rodney. 1967. Percussion and transition. *Man* 2 (4):206–614.

Nelson, Susan Rosales. 1986. Bolivia: Continuity and conflict in religious discourse. In *Religion and political conflict in Latin America*, edited by Daniel H. Levine. Chapel Hill: University of North Carolina Press.

Neville, Gwen Kennedy. 1987. *Kinship and pilgrimage: Rituals of reunion in American Protestant culture.* New York: Oxford University Press.

Neville, Lee. 1997. Grownup holiday. *U.S. News & World Report* 123 (17):14.

Newton, Milton B., Jr. 1974. Cultural preadatation and the upland South. In *Man and cultural heritage*, edited by H. J. Walker and W. G. Haag. *Geoscience and man*, Vol. 5. Baton Rouge: Geoscience Publications.

Noble, William, and Iain Davidson. 1996. *Human evolution, language, and mind:*

A psychological and archaeological inquiry. Cambridge: Cambridge University Press.

Nolan, Mary Lee. 1991. The European roots of Latin American pilgrimage. In *Pilgrimage in Latin America*, edited by N. Ross Crumrine and Alan Morinis. New York: Greenwood Press.

Nolan, Mary Lee, and Sidney Nolan. 1989. *Christian pilgrimage in modern Western Europe*. Chapel Hill: University of North Carolina Press.

O'Brien, Eileen M. 1981. The projectile capabilities of an Acheulean handaxe from Olorgesailie. *Current Anthropology* 22 (1):76–79.

O'Shea, W. J. 1967a. Christ the King, feast of. *New Catholic encyclopedia*. Vol. 3. New York: McGraw-Hill.

———. 1967b. Corpus Christi. *New Catholic encyclopedia*. Vol. 4. New York: McGraw-Hill.

Ovchinnikov, Igor V., et al. 2000. Molecular analysis of Neanderthal DNA from the northern Caucasus. *Nature* 404:490–93.

Packer, James I. 1980. The adequacy of human language. In *Inerrancy*, edited by Norman L. Geisler. Grand Rapids, Mich.: Zondervan.

Palmer, Richard E. 1969. *Hermeneutics*. Evanston: Northwestern University Press.

Pandolfo, S. 1989. Detours of life: Space and bodies in a Moroccan village. *American Ethnologist* 16 (1):3–23.

Panourgiá, N. 1995. *Fragments of death, fables of identity: An Athenian anthropography*. Madison: University of Wisconsin Press.

Parker, Sue Taylor. 1985. A Social-technological model for evolution of language. *Current Anthropology* 26 (5):617–40.

Parman, Susan. 1990. *Orduighean*: A dominant symbol in the Free Church of the Scottish Highlands. *American Anthropologist* 92 (2):295–305.

Patterson, W. Morgan. 1969. *Baptist successionism: A critical view*. Valley Forge, Pa.: Judson Press.

Pavelka, Mary S. McDonald. 1991. Sociability in old female Japanese monkeys: Human versus nonhuman primate aging. *American Anthropologist* 93 (3):588–99.

Payne, Stanley G. 1984. *Spanish Catholicism: An historical overview*. Madison: University of Wisconsin Press.

Peacock, James L., and Ruel W. Tyson Jr. 1989. *Pilgrims of paradox: Calvinism and experience among the Primitive Baptists of the Blue Ridge*. Washington, D.C.: Smithsonian Institution Press.

Pérez Firmat, Gustavo, ed. 1990. *Do the Americas have a common literature?* Durham: Duke University Press.

Pfuetze, Paul E. 1954. *The social self.* New York: Bookman Associates.

Pike, Fredrick. 1992. Latin America. In *The Oxford illustrated history of Christianity*, edited by John McManners. Oxford: Oxford University Press.

Poblette, Renato, S.J. 1980. From Medellín to Puebla: Notes for reflection. In *Churches and politics in Latin America*, edited by Daniel H. Levine. Beverly Hills: Sage Publication.

Poole, Stafford, C.M. 1995. *Our Lady of Guadalupe: The origins of the sources of a Mexican national symbol, 1531–1797*. Tucson: University of Arizona Press.

Pope, Hugh. [1913] 1966. Mary of Cleophas. In *The Catholic encyclopedia*. Electronic version, New Advent. (www.knight.org).

Posey, Miranda. 1999. Reciprocity and penitence: The pilgrimage to Talpa de Allende. Manuscript.

Purdy, A. C. 1962. Paul the Apostle. In *The interpreter's dictionary of the Bible*. Vol. 3. Nashville: Abingdon Press.

Purefoy, George W. 1858. *History of the Sandy Creek Baptist association*. New York: Sheldon & Co.

Pyron, Darden A. 1989. Plantation myth. In *Encyclopedia of southern culture*, edited by Charles Reagan Wilson and William Ferris. Chapel Hill: University of North Carolina Press.

Raglan, Lord. 1956. *The hero: A study in tradition, myth, and drama*. New York: Vintage Books.

Rak, Y., W. H. Kimbel, and E. Hovers. 1994. A Neandertal infant from Amud Cave, Israel. *Journal of Human Evolution* 26:313–24.

Raup, David. 1995. The role of extinction in evolution. In *Tempo and mode in evolution: Genetics and paleontology 50 years after Simpson*, edited by Walter M. Fitch and Francisco J. Ayala. Washington, D.C.: National Academy Press.

Redford, Courts. 1958. Negroes, Southern Baptists' relations to. In *Encyclopedia of Southern Baptists*. Vol. 2. Nashville: Broadman Press.

Reina, Ruben. 1966. *Law of the saints*. Indianapolis: Bobbs-Merrill.

Ricard, Robert. 1966. *The spiritual conquest of Mexico*. Berkeley: University of California Press.

Richardson, John. 1986. *Existential epistemology: A heideggerian critique of the cartesian project*. Oxford: Clarendon Press.

Richardson, Miles. 1972. Gilgamesh and Christ: Two contradictory models of man in search of a better world. In *Aspects of cultural change*, edited by Joseph B. Aceves. Southern Anthropological Society Proceedings, No. 6. Athens: University of Georgia Press.

———. 1974a. The Spanish American (Colombian) settlement pattern as a societal expression and as a behavioral cause. In *Man and cultural heritage*, edited by H. J. Walker and William. G. Haag. *Geoscience and man*, Vol. 5. Baton Rouge: Geoscience Publications.

———. 1975. Anthropologist—The myth teller. *American Ethnologist* 2:517–34.

———. 1978. La plaza como lugar social: El papel del lugar en el encuentro humano, *Vínculos: Revista de Antropología del Museo Nacional de Costa Rica* 4:1–20.

———. 1982. Being-in-the-market versus being-in-the-plaza. *American Ethnologist* 9:421–36.

———. 1986a. Hank Williams, you wrote my life. *Sidewinder* 3 (1):5–17.

———. [1970] 1986b. *San Pedro, Colombia: Small town in a developing society*. Prospect Heights, Ill.: Waveland Press.

———. 1987. A social (ideational-behavioral) interpretation of material culture and its application to archaeology. In *Mirror and metaphor: Material and social constructions of reality*, edited by Daniel W. Ingersoll, Jr., and Gordon Bronitsky. Lanham, Md.: University Press of America.

———. 1991. Point of view in anthropological discourse: The ethnographer as Gilgamesh. In *Anthropological poetics*, edited by Ivan Brady. Savage, Md.: Rowman & Littlefield.

———. 1994. Unamuno and the flesh-and-blood, celebratory critique of the postmodern play of signification. In *Personal meaning and cultural commitment: Critical reactions to postmodernism*, edited by Daniel W. Ingersoll Jr. Special issue of the *Journal of the Steward Anthropological Society* 22 (2):177–94.

———. 1995a. Speaking and hearing (in contrast to touching and seeing) the sacred. In *Religion in the contemporary South: Diversity, community, and identity*, edited by O. Kendall White Jr. and Daryl White. Southern Anthropological Society Proceedings, No. 28. Athens: University of Georgia Press.

———. 1995b. Clarifying the dark in black Christs: The play of icon, narrative, and experience in the construction of presence. In *Yearbook of the conference of Latin Americanist geographers*, edited by David J. Robinson. Vol. 21. Austin: University of Texas Press.

———. 1998a. The poetics of a resurrection: Re-seeing thirty years of change in a Colombian community and in the anthropological enterprise. *American Anthropologist* 100 (1):11–21.

———. 1998b. Poetics in the field and on the page. *Qualitative Inquiry* 4 (4):451–62.

———. 2001. The gift of presence: The act of leaving artifacts at shrines, memorials, and other tragedies. In *The textures of place: Exploring humanist geographies*, edited by Paul C. Adams, Steven Hoelscher, and Karen E. Till. Minneapolis: University of Minnesota Press.

———. 2002. The speech of *habitus* in the New World: Divergence and convergence in landscape practices of administrative towns in Spanish America and the American South. In *Cultural and physical expositions: Geographic studies in the southern United States and Latin America*, edited by Michael K. Steinberg and Paul F. Hudson. *Geoscience and man.* Vol. 36. Baton Rouge: Geoscience Publications, Louisiana State University Department of Geography and Anthropology.

Richardson, Miles, ed. 1974b. *The human mirror: Material and spatial configurations of man*. Baton Rouge: Louisiana State University Press.

Richardson, Miles, and Robert Dunton. 1989. Culture in its places: A humanistic presentation. In *The relevance of culture*, edited by Morris Freilich. New York: Bergin & Garvey.

Richardson, Miles, and William Davidson. n. d. The earth as the Lord's bread. Manuscript. Department of Geography and Anthropology, Louisiana State University, Baton Rouge.

Richardson, Miles, Barbara Bode, and Marta Eugenia Pardo. 1971. The image of Christ in Spanish America as a model for suffering. *Journal of Inter-American Studies* 13:246–58.

Richmond, Brian G., and David S. Strait. 2000. Evidence that humans evolved from a knuckle-walking ancestor. *Nature* 404:382–85.

Rockmore, Tom, and Joseph Margolis, eds. 1992. *The Heidegger case on philosophy and politics*. Philadelphia: Temple University Press.

Rodriguez, Jeanette. 1994. *Our Lady of Guadalupe: Faith and empowerment among Mexican-American women*. Austin: University of Texas.

Romero, Oscar. 1982. *Romero: Martyr for liberation*. London: Catholic Institute for International Relations.

Rosaldo, R. 1989. *Culture and truth: The remaking of social analysis*. Boston: Beacon Press.

Rosenberg, Ellen M. 1989. *The Southern Baptists: A subculture in transition*. Knoxville: University of Tennessee Press.

Rowlett, Ralph M., and Mary Jane Schneider. 1974. The material expression of Neanderthal child care. In *The human mirror: Material and spatial configurations of culture*, edited by Miles Richardson. Baton Rouge: Louisiana State University Press.

Rubin, Miri. 1990. *Corpus Christi: The eucharist in late medieval culture*. Cambridge: Cambridge University Press.

Russell, Dale A., and Peter Dodson. 1997. The extinction of the dinosaurs: A dialogue between a catastrophist and a gradualist. In *The complete dinosaur*, edited by James O. Farlow and M. K. Brett-Surman. Bloomington: Indiana University Press.

Sabia, Debra. 1995. *Marianismo*: Expressions of faith and liberation. *Southeastern Latinamericanist* 39 (1):25–40.

Safford, Frank. 1987. Politics, ideology, and society. In *Spanish America after independence, c. 1820–c. 1870*, edited by Leslie Bethell. Cambridge: Cambridge University Press.

Sallnow, M. J. 1981. Communitas reconsidered: The sociology of Andean pilgrimage. *Man* 16:163–82.

———. 1987. *Pilgrims of the Andes: Regional cults in Cusco*. Washington, D.C.: Smithsonian Institution Press.

———. 1989. A trinity of Christs: Cultic processes in Andean Catholicism. *American Ethnologist* 9 (4):730–49.

Samson, C. Mathews, Jr. 1995. Protestant religious presence in Mexico: Origins and impact of recent constitutional changes. Paper presented at the 42nd meeting of the South Eastern Council on Latin American Studies. Chapel Hill: University of North Carolina Press.

———. 1997. Personal Communication.

Sartre, Jean-Paul. 1956. *Being and nothingness*. New York: Philosophical Library.

———. 1971. *Existentialism and humanism*. London: Methuen, 1948. Reprint, Brooklyn, N.Y.: Haskell House.

Saussure, Ferdinand de. 1986. *Course in general linguistics*. La Salle, Ill.: Open Court.

Sautman, Francesca. 1990. Saint Anne in folk tradition: Late medieval France. In *Interpreting cultural symbols: Saint Anne in late medieval society*, edited by Kathleen Ashley and Pamela Scheingorn. Athens: University of Georgia Press.

Scheler, Max. 1961. *Man's place in nature*. Boston: Beacon Press.

———. 1992. The meaning of suffering. *Max Scheler on feeling, knowing, and valuing*. Chicago: University of Chicago Press.

Schneider, Jane, and Shirley Lindenbaum. 1987. Frontier of Christian evangelism: Essays in honor of Joyce Riegelhaupt. *American Ethnologist* 14 (1):1–8.

Schumann, B. A., and P. B. Petit. 1999. Time, temporal envelopes, and the middle to upper paleolithic transition. In *The biological basis of human behavior: A critical review*, edited by Robert W. Sussman. 2nd ed. Upper Saddle River, N.J.: Prentice-Hall.

Schweitzer, Albert. 1931. *The mysticism of Paul the Apostle*. New York: Henry Holt.

Scobie, James R. 1989. The growth of cities. In *Latin America: Economy and society*,

1870–1930, edited by Leslie Bethell. Cambridge: Cambridge University Press.

Scott, Anne Firor. 1972. Women, religion, and social change in the South, 1830–1930. In *Religion and the solid South*, edited by Samuel S. Hill Jr. et al. Nashville: Abingdon.

Searle, G. W. 1973. *The Counter-Reformation*. Totowa, N. J.: Rowman & Littlefield.

Sell, Michael A. 1994. *Mystical languages of unsaying*. Chicago: University of Chicago Press.

Semaw, S., et al. 1997. 2.5-million-year-old stone tools from Gona, Ethiopia. *Nature* 385:333–36.

Serbin, Ken. 1993. Latin America's Catholic church: Religious rivalries and the north-south divide. *North-South Issues* 2 (1):1–6.

Sered, Susan. 1991. Rachel, Mary, and Fatima. *Cultural Anthropology* 6 (2):131–46.

Sherzer, Joel. 1987. A discourse-centered approach to language and culture. *American Anthropologist* 89 (2):295–309.

Shurden, Walter B. 1972. *Not a silent people: Controversies that have shaped the Southern Baptists*. Nashville: Broadman Press.

Shurden, Walter B., ed. 1993. *The struggle for the soul of the SBC*. Macon, Ga.: Mercer University Press.

Simpson, George G. 1944. *Tempo and mode in evolution*. New York: Columbia University Press.

Sims, Walter, ed. 1956. *Baptist hymnal*. Nashville: Convention Press.

Skar, Harald O. 1985. Communitas and schismogenesis: The Andean pilgrimage reconsidered. *Ethnos* 50 (1–2):88–102.

Slater, Candace. 1990. *City steeple, city streets: Saints' tales from Granada and a changing Spain*. Berkeley: University of California Press.

Smirnoff, Y. 1989. Intentional human burials: Middle paleolithic (late glaciation) beginnings. *Journal of World Prehistory* 3:199–233.

Smith, Fred H. 1997. Neandertals. In *History of physical anthropology*, edited by Frank Spencer. Vol. 2, M–Z. New York: Garland.

Smith, Sidney. 1982. Black Southern Baptists. In *Encyclopedia of Southern Baptists*. Vol. 4. Nashville: Broadman Press.

Smith, T. C. 1958. Baptism. In *Encyclopedia of Southern Baptists*. Vol. 1. Nashville: Broadman Press.

Smuts, Barbara S. 1985. *Sex and friendship in baboons*. New York: Aldine.

Solecki, Ralph S. 1971. *Shanidar: The first flower people*. New York: Knopf.

———. 1989. On the evidence for Neandertal burial. *Current Anthropology* 30 (3):324.

Spencer, Frank. 1984. The Neandertals and their evolutionary significance: A brief historical survey. In *The origins of modern humans: A world survey of the fossil evidence*, edited by Fred Smith and Frank Spencer. New York: Alan R. Liss.

Stanton, Phoebe G. 1968. *The gothic revival and American church architecture: An episode in taste, 1840–1856*. Baltimore: Johns Hopkins University Press.

Steller, Hermann. 1995. Mechanisms and genes of cellular suicide. *Science* 267:1445–49.

Stephens, J. L. 1841. *Incidents of travel in Central America, Chiapas, and Yucatán*. Vol. 1. New York: Harper & Brothers.

Stewart-Gambino, Hannah. 1992. Introduction: New game, new rules. In *Conflict and competition: The Latin American church in a changing environment*, edited by Edward L. Cleary and Hannah Stewart-Gambino. Boulder: Lynne Rienner.

Stilgoe, John R. 1982. *Common landscape of America, 1580 to 1845*. New Haven: Yale University Press.

Stiner, Mary. 1991. The faunal remains from Grotta Guattari: A taphonomic perspective. *Current Anthropology* 32 (2):103–17.

Stoll, David. 1990. *Is Latin America turning Protestant? The politics of evangelical growth*. Berkeley: University of California Press.

Storer, J. W. 1958. Southern Baptist Convention. In *Encyclopedia of Southern Baptists*. Vol. 2. Nashville: Broadman Press.

Stratton, Suzane L. 1994. *The immaculate conception in Spanish art*. Cambridge: Cambridge University Press.

Strauss, Ansel, ed. 1964. *George Herbert Mead on social psychology*. Chicago: University of Chicago Press.

Stromberg, Peter G. 1990. Ideological language in the transformation of identity. *American Anthropologist* 92 (1):42–56.

———. 1993. *Language and self-transformation: A study of the Christian conversion narrative*. Cambridge: Cambridge University Press.

Stroupe, Henry S. 1983. Shubal Stearns: Sandy Creek's Separate Baptist leader. Special Collections, University of North Carolina at Chapel Hill. Chapel Hill: University of North Carolina Press.

Susman, Randall L. 1994. Fossil evidence for early hominid tool use. *Science* 265:1570–73.

———. 1998. Hand function and tool behavior in early hominids. *Journal of Human Evolution* 35:23–46.

Sweet, William Warren. 1931. *Religion on the American frontier: The Baptists, 1783–1830.* New York: Henry Holt.

Stykes, S. W. 1980. Sacrifice in the New Testament and Christian theology. In *Sacrifice*, edited by M. F. C. Bourdillon and Meyer Fortes. London: Academic Press.

Tannen, Deborah. 1989. *Talking voices: Repetition, dialogue, and imagery in conversational discourse.* New York: Cambridge University Press.

———. 1995. Waiting for the mouse: Constructed dialogue in conversation. In *The dialogic emergence of culture*, edited by Dennis Tedlock and Bruce Mannheim. Chicago: University of Chicago Press.

Taves, Ann. 1986. *The household of faith: Roman Catholic devotions in mid-nineteenth-century America.* Notre Dame: University of Notre Dame Press.

Taylor, Wilburn S. 1958. Norris, John Franklin. In *Encyclopedia of Southern Baptists.* Vol. 2. Nashville: Broadman Press.

Taylor, William. 1985. Between global process and local knowledge: An inquiry into early Latin American social history. In *Reliving the past: The worlds of social history*, edited by Olivier Zunz. Chapel Hill: University of North Carolina Press.

———. 1987. The Virgin of Guadalupe in New Spain: An inquiry into the social history of Marian devotion. *American Ethnologist* 14 (1):9–33.

Templeton, Alan R. 1993. The "Eve" hypothesis: A genetic critique and reanalysis. *American Anthropologist* 95 (1):51–72.

———. 1996. Gene lineages and human evolution. *Science* 272:1363.

Tesser, Carmen Chaves. 1991. Post-structural theory mirrored in Helena Parente Cunha's *Woman between mirrors. Hispania* 74 (3):594–97.

Textes Liturgiques. 1980. *Liturgie de la Messe.* Paris: Tardy.

Thiher, Allen. 1984. *Words in reflection: Modern language theory and postmodern fiction.* Chicago: University of Chicago Press.

Thompson, Edgar T. 1972. God and the southern plantation system. In *Religion and the solid South*, edited by Samuel S. Hill Jr. et al. Nashville: Abingdon.

Thompson, James J., Jr. 1982. *Tried as by fire: Southern Baptists and the religious controversies of the 1920s.* Macon, Ga.: Mercer University Press.

Thurian, Max, and Geoffrey Wainwright. 1983. *Baptism and eucharist: Ecumenical convergence in celebration.* Geneva: World Council of Churches.

Thurner, Mark. 1993. Peasant politics and Andean haciendas in the transition to capitalism: An ethnographic history. *Latin American Research Review* 28 (3):41–82.

Tilley, C. 1994. *A phenomenology of landscape: Places, paths, and monuments.* Providence, R.I.: Berg.

Trend, J. B. 1957. *Portugal.* London: Ernest Been.

Trinkaus, E. 1985. Cannibalism and burial at Kaprina. *Journal of Human Evolution* 14:203–16.

Tuan, Yi-Fu. 1976. Humanistic geography. *Annals of the Association of American Geographers* 66:266–76.

———. 1977. *Space and place: The perspective of experience.* Minneapolis: University of Minnesota Press.

———. 1982. *Segmented worlds and the self.* Minneapolis: University of Minnesota Press.

Turner, Harold. 1979. *From temple to meeting house: The phenomenology and theology of places of worship.* The Hague: Mouton.

Turner, Helen Lee. 1993. Myths: Stories of this world and the world to come. In *Southern Baptists observed: Multiple perspectives on a changing denomination,* edited by Nancy Tatom Ammerman. Knoxville: University of Tennessee Press.

Turner, Victor W. 1969. *The ritual process: Structure and anti-structure.* Chicago: University of Chicago Press.

———. 1982. *From ritual to theater.* New York: Performing Arts Journal Publications.

———. 1985. *On the edge of the bush.* Tucson: University of Arizona Press.

———. 1992. *Blazing the trail: Way marks in the exploration of symbols.* Tucson: University of Arizona Press.

Turner, Victor W., and Edith Turner. 1978. *Image and pilgrimage in Christian culture: Anthropological perspectives.* New York: Columbia University Press.

Turner, Victor W., and Edward M. Bruner, eds. 1986. *The anthropology of experience.* Urbana: University of Illinois Press.

Tuttle, Russell H. 1987. Review of *Major topics in primate and human evolution,* edited by Bernard Wood et al. *American Anthropologist* 89:972–73.

Tuzin, Donald. 1984. Voices: The auditory experience of numinous objects. *Current Anthropology* 25 (5):579–96.

Twain, Mark [Samuel L. Clemens]. [1883] 1968. *Life on the Mississippi.* New York: Dodd, Mead.

Unamuno, Miguel de. 1972. *The tragic sense of life in men and nations.* Princeton: Princeton University Press.

———. 1973a. *Del sentimiento trágico de la vida.* Buenos Aires: Editorial Losada.

———. 1973b. *Mi religión y otros ensayos breves.* Madrid: Espasa-Calpe.

———. 1974a. *The agony of Christianity and essays on faith.* Princeton: Princeton University Press.

———. 1974b. *Soledad.* Madrid: Espasa-Calpe.

U. S. Bureau of the Census. 1997. *Statistical abstracts of the United States: 1997*. Washington, D.C.: Government Printing Office.

U. S. Department of Commerce. 1943. Reports on agriculture. *Sixteenth census of the United States, 1940*. Washington, D. C.: Government Printing Office.

———. 1961. Louisiana. *United States census of agriculture, 1959*. Washington, D. C.: Government Printing Office.

Villa, Paola. 1993. Cannibalism in prehistoric Europe. *Evolutionary Anthropology* 1 (3):93–104.

Waits, William B. 1993. *The modern Christmas in America: A cultural history of gift giving*. New York: New York University Press.

Wamble, Hugh. 1964. Landmarkism: Doctrinaire ecclesiology among Baptists. *Church History* 33:429–47.

Washburn, Sherwood. 1962. The study of race. *American Anthropologist* 65:521–31.

Watanabe, John M. 1990. From saints to shibboleths: Image, structure, and identity in Maya religious syncretism. *American Ethnologist* 17 (1):131–50.

Webb, Robert K., and Leslie H. Peek. 1989. Southeastern Baptist theological seminary (North Carolina). *Academe: Bulletin of the AAUP* 75 (3):35–45.

Weber, Timothy P. 1982. The two-edged sword: The fundamentalist use of the Bible. In *The Bible in America: Essays in cultural history*, edited by Nathan O. Hatch and Mark A. Noll. New York: Oxford University Press.

Weismann, Elizabeth Wilder. 1950. *Mexico in sculpture, 1521–1821*. Cambridge, Mass.: Harvard University Press.

Weismann, Elizabeth Wilder, and Judith Hancock Sandoval. 1985. *Art and time in Mexico: From the conquest to the revolution*. New York: Harper & Row.

Wethey, Harold E. 1949. *Colonial architecture and sculpture in Peru*. Cambridge, Mass.: Harvard University Press.

White, Leslie. 1949. *The science of culture*. New York: Farrar, Straus.

White, Tim D., and Nicholas Toth. 1991. The question of ritual cannibalism at Grotta Guattari. *Current Anthropology* 32 (2):118–24.

White, Tim D., Gen Suwa, and Berhane Asfaw. 1994. *Australopithecus ramidus*, a new species of early hominid from Aramis, Ethiopia. *Nature* 371:306–12.

———. 1995. Corrigendum. *Nature* 375:88.

Wiebe, Robert H. 1975. *The segmented society: An introduction to the meaning of America*. New York: Oxford University Press.

Wilkie, James W. 1966. The meaning of the *Cristero* religious war against the Mexican revolution. *A Journal of Church and State* 8 (2):214–33.

Williams, Hank. 1983. *The complete works of Hank Williams*. Nashville: Acuff-Rose.

Williams, Peter. 1988. Religious architecture and landscape. In *Encyclopedia of American religious experience*. Vol. 3. New York: Charles Scribner's Sons.

———. 1997. *Houses of God: Region, religion, and architecture in the United States*. Urbana: University of Illinois Press.

Wilson, Charles Reagan. 1989. Jim Crow. In *Encyclopedia of southern culture*, edited by Charles Reagan Wilson and William Ferris. Chapel Hill: University of North Carolina Press.

———. 1995. *Judgment and grace in Dixie: Southern faiths from Faulkner to Elvis*. Athens: University of Georgia Press.

Wiman, Christian. 2001. Fugitive Pieces. *Poetry* 179 (2):90–102.

Wolf, Eric. 1958. The Virgin of Guadalupe: A Mexican national symbol. *Journal of American Folklore* 71:34–39.

———. 1982. *Europe and the people without history*. Berkeley: University of California Press.

Wolpoff, Milford H. 1994. How does evolution work? *Evolutionary Anthropology* 3 (1):4–5.

———. 1998. Neandertals: Not so fast. *Science* 282:1991.

———. 1999a. *Paleoanthropology*. 2nd ed. Boston: McGraw-Hill.

———. 1999b. The systematics of *Homo*. *Science* 284:1774–75.

Woodward, C. Vann. 1974. *The strange career of Jim Crow*. 3rd rev. ed. New York: Oxford University Press.

Woodward, Kenneth L. 1997. Hail Mary. *Newsweek* 130 (25 August):49–55.

Wrenn, Tony P. 1984. *Wilmington, North Carolina: An architectural and historical portrait*. Charlottesville: University of Virginia Press.

Wynn, Thomas. 1989. *The evolution of spatial competence*. Urbana: University of Illinois Press.

Yamei, Hou, et al. 2000. Mid-Pleistocene Acheulean-like stone technology of the Bose Basin, south China. *Science* 287:1622–26.

INDEX

Page numbers in italics refer to illustrations.